"I Never Wanted To Be Vice-President of Anything!"*

* Nelson Rockefeller, quoted by Nick Thimmesch, in *The Condition of Republicanism* (New York: Norton, 1968), p. 107.

"I Never Wanted To Be Vice-President of Anything!"

An Investigative Biography of

NELSON ROCKEFELLER

Michael Kramer & Sam Roberts

Basic Books, Inc., Publishers

NEW YORK

Library of Congress Cataloging in Publication Data

Kramer, Michael S.
  "I never wanted to be vice-president of anything!"

  Includes bibliographical references and index.
  1. Rockefeller, Nelson Aldrich, 1908–
I. Roberts, Sam, 1947– joint author. II. Title.
E748.R673K72   973.925'092'4   [B]   75-36380
  ISBN 0-465-03194-3

7-26-7⟨

For our families

"Only three men in America understand the use of power. I do. John Connally does. And, I guess Nelson does." *

* Richard Nixon, quoted by William Safire, in *Before the Fall: An Inside View of the Pre-Watergate White House* (Garden City, N.Y.: Doubleday, 1975), p. 498.

PREFACE

THIS book explores the public and private lives of Nelson Rockefeller. We know, as a congressional committee concluded following its cursory investigation into his life and works, that Nelson Rockefeller is a very rich man. We know, too, that he is powerful—as the very rich usually are. We knew all of this before, as did everyone else even slightly acquainted with the famous, continually profiled Rockefeller family.

What we did not know were two quite basic things: first, *why* has Nelson Rockefeller aggressively pursued the presidency for almost all of his 40 years in public life when his family has spent 75 years and millions of dollars obscuring its role in the realpolitik of American government? And second, *how* has Nelson Rockefeller utilized the vast, often hidden, resources of Rockefeller wealth and influence to achieve his political triumphs —all but the one he wants most?

Our task has not been an easy one. Even his most severe critics were unspecific or could rarely substantiate their information. The public papers said little. Relatives and friends discreetly declined to provide more than a polite peek; family firms, such as the International Basic Economy Corporation, predictably rebuffed inquiries concerning their political clout. We expected all of this, so we were not surprised when trusted associates sought to preserve the secrets of our subject's successes and failures behind a barrier of evasion and loyal silence.

We conducted dozens of interviews, examined thousands of pages of public documents and confidential files, and eagerly accumulated those stories and anecdotes that, finally, have provided the pieces of the crazy quilt from which our portrait of Nelson Rockefeller emerges. "Everyone," wrote Machiavelli, "sees what you seem to be, few experience what you are." So it is with the Prince of Pocantico who, in private interviews with us cramped into the backseat of his bullet-proof limousine, proved Machiavelli's adage by revealing himself at once sincere, self-confident, cocky, pragmatic, patronizing, patriotic, loyal, naïve, repetitious, insensitive, and insulated.

It is through stories and anecdotes—sometimes incredible tales of Rockefeller's determination to get what he wants—that a real understanding of his personality and power emerges. Nevertheless, he remains an enigma. No accounting of his vast fortune reveals his web of influence; no recitation of his public and private statements suggests the driving ambition behind his career of more than 40 years. He remains a mystery, full of fascinating contradictions and complex motivations, a man who in every sense has never settled for second best—a man who utters a deeply felt, personal truth when he declares, as he did in 1967: "I never wanted to be vice-president of anything."

Many sources—precinct politicians, functionaries in the family offices, members of the financial community, and countless government employees—insisted on anonymity. We acknowledge their help and admire their courage in risking the wrath of Rockefeller. On numerous occasions we received invaluable aid from Robert Douglass, Hugh Morrow, Joseph Ernst, Theodore White, Richard Reeves, Joseph Martin, Jon Margolis, Ed Hershey, and Annmarie Walsh. We thank Michael O'Neill, Editor of the *Daily News*, and Clay Felker, Editor of *New York Magazine*, for their patience and their support. And we are especially grateful to Paul Neuthaler of Basic Books, without whose encouragement, advice, and persistence this book could not have been written.

CONTENTS

PREFACE   ix

PROLOGUE: The Man Who Would Be President   3

PART ONE

Making It on What I Own

1 Rockefeller Roots: The Life and Dimes   19
2 The Pocantico Kid   32
3 The Young Buck Starts Here   44
4 Dollar Diplomacy   55
5 The Polished Professional   62

PART TWO

Capital Games: The Art of Governing

6   Pointing the Finger of Power   79
7   The Unequal Branch   83
8   Governor on the Give   98
9   The *Real* Power Broker   110
10 The Prince and His Court   123
11 Banks and Bandits   135

xi

CONTENTS

12   Building with *Authority*   145
13   Monumental Errors   153
14   Politics and the Press   160
15   Critics Comforted   172

PART THREE
Nelson's Politics

16   Paying for Nelson's Politics   181
17   "No, Thank You. I Accept."   192
18   Battle of the Millionaires   201
19   Albany Fallout   211
20   Spoiling for a Fight   221
21   The Fifth Avenue Compact   230
22   Rehearsing for 1964   236
23   Odds-On Favorite   242
24   Morhouse Problems   247
25   The Governor Moves Right   266
26   The Governor Moves Left   272
27   Nelson's "Worst Investment"   286
28   Throwing Garbage   295
29   Lindsay on the Move   301
30   The Selling of the Governor, 1966   307
31   Rocky, Romney, and Dick   320
32   The Art of the Chameleon   333
33   "He's Done a Lot. He'll Do More."   339
34   The Tragedy of Attica   351

EPILOGUE: Mr. Rockefeller Goes to Washington   364

NOTES   379
INDEX   409

"I Never Wanted To Be

Vice-President of

Anything!"

New York Daily New

Nelson in a characteristic pose behind a podium he does not own yet.

PROLOGUE

The Man Who Would Be President

THERE is something about the view of Washington from the softly curtained windows of your own twin-engine jet that one misses on the hourly Eastern shuttle. Perhaps it is the whisper of the specially muffled engines or the sound-studio-like baffling of the cabin walls that creates the floating, almost timeless sensation that one associates with dreaming rather than with flight.

It was during one such flight, on a cold January night in 1964, that Nelson Rockefeller's impassive stare at the floodlit White House below was interrupted by a reporter's question. When, the newsman asked, had he first thought about being president of the United States?

"Ever since I was a kid," Rockefeller matter-of-factly replied. "After all, when you think of what I had, what else was there to aspire to?"[1]

Some six decades have passed since Nelson Rockefeller was a kid. During this time, virtually every decision he has made has been aimed at moving himself another step closer to fulfilling his aspiration. His political career has combined the best inclinations

3

his parents could instill with an almost religious devotion to duty. He has sought to blot out the stain of inherited Rockefeller wealth and has become the epitome of the new generation's commitment to public service.

For almost a quarter of a century he has carried his ambition to be president of the United States like a stigma, bearing it with a mixture of joy and pain. "It is not vitamins, but the intensity of his dreams," says a friend, "that keeps him young." Still, as a man born in 1908, he must make some concessions to the flesh. He breakfasts on a bowl of Wheatena instead of eggs, an indignity forced on him by an upward creeping cholesterol count. At night he sips Mateus rosé, a less caloric substitute for red Dubonnet, but he still can't resist his Oreos. Beyond that, he is fit. A medical lab, after studying his charts and X rays, reported: "This man is 40 years old."[2]

Like most rich men, he looks younger than he is, and he is possessed of certain eccentricities: even in a perfect stranger's house, he will straighten a crooked picture on the wall;[3] once, while flying over Mt. Rushmore at midnight, he called down to have the National Park Service illuminate the four presidents as his plane buzzed by.

His brother Laurance claims that Nelson is one of the few men he's known who can "keep his feet on the ground and his head in the clouds"[4] at the same time. A leading graphologist says that he is an "unfulfilled man."[5] It does not take a graphologist to know that.

It is possible to say, as Lincoln Steffens said of Woodrow Wilson, that "he is the most perfect example we have of the culture which has failed and is dying out."[6] It is possible to say a good many things. Nelson Rockefeller seems strangely impervious to such summings-up. "I've been thought [politically] dead so many times," he says, "that I don't think about it anymore."[7] Nelson Rockefeller just goes on, unhumiliated, insulated, frustrated.

From 1958 to 1968, for a full decade of the most turbulent politics the country has known since the Civil War, his intentions were the object of sustained and intense speculation. "He was," wrote Theodore White, "almost a force of nature, like a slumbering volcano, wreathed in clouds, occasionally emitting smoke which soothsayers attempted to interpret."[8] Three times in those years he actively sought the presidency. Once, in 1960, it seemed that he lost it because he wanted it too much. Twice, in 1964 and 1968, because he didn't want it badly enough. Along the way, he became the antithesis of Gerald Ford, that mild-mannered politician who got along by going along, who rose, in a classic example of the Peter Principle, to the highest office in the land because he was, as Richard Reeves noted, "the least objectionable alternative."[9] If anything, Nelson Rockefeller, to many in his chosen party, was always the *most* objectionable alternative. "Every movement needs a villain," said *National Review* publisher William Rusher. "For the GOP Right, Nelson Rockefeller was it."[10]

"They," said Barry Goldwater of his fellow conservative Republicans, "hate his guts." The Arizona senator also had some nonideological reservations: "I have a feeling he should never be president. He's too old, and he was born into power, so used to power, surrounded by power. I've seen that office abused too much."[11]

Still, Rockefeller tried. For years, he crawled whenever necessary in a vain attempt to be reclaimed. Too often, truth was a strategy of politics, not a habit of integrity. He was beyond arrogance, beyond cynicism, beyond ideology. As one observer wrote, he continually "knelt before the worst in the Republican Party, apologizing for offending the know nothings, mouthing the rhetoric of the people who brutalized him at the Republican Convention of 1964, and slobbering over the shell of Richard Nixon."[12] Often, his backpedaling and ex-post-facto explanations were pained and embarrassing. Still, he played the chameleon without blushing—most notably in the spring of 1975, when he told the National Urban Coalition that the reason he had declined to criticize the Vietnam war policy of Richard Nixon was that New York needed money from

Washington and that he, as governor, did not wish to harm the state's prospects for federal aid.

"You don't kick people in Washington in the shins if you expect them to do something for you,"[13] said Rockefeller—this from the only governor in the country who consistently had his own foreign policy, a well-researched series of positions often developed by the same men who, as secretaries of state, were advising presidents as to the *national* administration's foreign policy. "Are we then to assume," wondered William F. Buckley, Jr., "that anything crossing Rockefeller's lips must not be accepted as a reflection of his own thinking; that one may suppose the possibility, or probability, of an ulterior motive?"[14]

No matter. Nelson Rockefeller pushed on. Sensing, falsely, that he was winning his war for acceptance by conservative Republicans, he speculated that "the ideological differences were not as important as they seemed then, or as some of us made them out to be. We got the cheats off welfare. We cracked down on the dope pushers."[15] He might have added that he had paid his dues at Attica. "The assault on Attica was a moral disgrace," said Nixon aide William Safire, "but politically he did what our people wanted."[16]

He also gave Richard Nixon what he wanted—blind loyalty. The closest Nelson Rockefeller ever came to denouncing Nixon for the Watergate affair was in a speech to Southern Republicans, when he defined Watergate as a "tragedy for individuals." Later, to the press, he included Nixon among the individuals.[17] As for the president's White House taping system, Rockefeller declared: "I've assumed that with every president."[18]

Sometimes, in an effort to please "those people," he seemed to lose his bearings and go too far. In August 1975, during a Southern swing designed to show them that "I don't have horns,"[19] Rockefeller took to comparing George Wallace with Gerald Ford: "They are both dedicated Americans who believe in the basic values of this country, distinguished citizens and good friends of mine. . . . They happen to be of different parties and make slightly different appeals to people."

The Man Who Would Be President

Nothing worked. Once, when he was vice-president, Gerald Ford said: "Nelson, you're the one who should be in line for the presidency."[20] Then, in the fall of 1975, he was gone, off the ticket, biding his time once again, looking for the elusive opportunity to grab the big prize, complaining, perhaps rightfully, that had he been a Democrat he would have been president long ago. He said again, for public consumption, that he was relaxed about his situation, that he no longer had the ambition to be president. It all sounded familiar. In fact, he had said much the same thing seven years earlier. And at that time, Bill Moyers had replied: "I believe Rocky when he says he's lost his ambition. I also believe he remembers where he put it."[21]

As he waits, Rockefeller does so, for the first time, without meaningful office, the vice-presidency having proved to be the emasculating "standby equipment" he had always feared. For 15 years he had been governor of New York, providing, for any who cared to see, a record of activism unparalleled in the state's history, a forerunner, surely, of what a Rockefeller presidency would resemble.

The unique confluence of political and financial power, a commingling unknown in American history until his time, revealed the glories and the excesses of what in Rockefeller can only be described as a benevolent despotism. Ruling New York's politics was easy. The state's Republican Party had long been a subsidiary of the Rockefeller family, like the Rockefeller Foundation or Rockefeller University. For more than a decade the family and its friends had absorbed Republican campaign deficits; and, on occasion, Nelson could pull out of his pocket, as Lyndon Johnson would do with his popularity polls, a piece of paper, typed in blue, which reminded him—and those for whom the exercise was intended—of the precise total the party had cost the family over the years, excluding the $30 million spent on his own campaigns for governor and president.[22]

The legislature, when dominated by the Republicans, as it was for 13 of Rockefeller's 15 years, was rarely more than a rubber stamp. When recalcitrant Republicans fussed over big spending,

7

deals were struck with Democrats. Most of the state's politicians (all of whom, by nature, had vivid imaginations) were reluctant to cross Rockefeller for fear of reprisal. "Fear Plus Hate Equals Power" was the formula for success in Eugene Burdick's novel *The Ninth Wave*.[23] It was a formula which worked well for Nelson in New York. "Nothing stands in Rockefeller's way," said Senator Jacob Javits. "Nothing. He always gets what he wants."[24] Well, almost always.

He handled his critics with aplomb. Reporters who covered him regularly were treated lavishly when on tour. Some, especially those in need, received state jobs. Others coasted, confirmed in the belief that Rockefeller was too rich to steal—a popular refrain that infected Congress when he was nominated to be vice-president. "When somebody is one of the wealthiest men in the world," said House Republican Leader John Rhodes, "he's got so much money there would be no point in cheating."[25] And all the while, during his governorship, Rockefeller was pushing legislation so advantageous to the banking and insurance industries which formed the underpinning of his family's own monetary power that New York became to the financial community what Las Vegas was to the Mafia—an easy mark.

Not so, cried Nelson Rockefeller to his congressional inquisitors during his confirmation hearings in late 1974. "My power," he said, is a "myth." His family, said Rockefeller, owned only 2.06 percent of Standard Oil of California, 1.75 percent of Mobil, and 1.07 percent of Exxon, and had "no control of any kind over the management of policies of any of them." So it is an exaggeration to say that the Rockefellers "own" Exxon, or that Nelson "owns" New York. Nevertheless, as one observor noted, "what is not a myth is what any American, from pauper to president, would do if he or she got consecutive calls from Nelson and David Rockefeller. Jump. That's what I'd do and you'd do and a president would do."[26]

The same disingenuousness was applied to the Rockefellers' land holdings. Nelson ran through the list of family-owned properties, adding that "we have a place in Westchester." Of course, that place is six square miles of the most valuable real estate in the world, a private retreat with views such as the Emperor Hadrian might have had, art treasures so spectacular that Theodore White once offered to trade his East 64th Street townhouse in New York City for a single Tong Dynasty horse he had admired on the grounds of Nelson's place in Westchester.[27] After thousands of pages of hearings and countless months of staff work, all Congress succeeded in confirming was the fact that he is very rich.

Nelson Rockefeller's life has involved a sense of mission. He wanted to be an architect, but such a calling was simply not worthy of a Rockefeller. He set about the business of politics methodically. His grandfather, John D. Rockefeller the First, had done the same. "I had our plan clearly in mind," said John D. of his calculated moves to acquire control of the oil industry. "It was right. I knew it as a matter of conscience. It was right between me and my God. If I had to do it tomorrow I would do it again in the same way—do it a hundred times."[28]

It is unlikely that Nelson talks to his pillow at night about the day's adventures, as did John D.,[29] but it is certain that he feels the burden of his role in society every bit as acutely as did his grandfather. He seems to have first understood he was special while he was at Dartmouth. In a letter home to his mother he wrote:

> It is really very interesting for me to watch and see the funny way my feelings have been acting of late.
>
> All of a sudden, like the lifting of a heavy fog, I realize for the first time how unutterably selfish and thoughtless I have been getting to be. It stands out in bold relief and glares [sic] me in the face.
>
> From this very minute, I will lead a new life . . . that will not be centered around myself.[30]

Whether the world was ready for young Nelson to assuage his personal guilt at its expense will never be known. New York got him first. As governor he had a kind of nineteenth-century optimism, a conviction that any problem must, somewhere, have a solution and a means of solving it, given the proper infusion of money and effort. An admirable view, to be sure, but one which led easily to imprudence and overreaction. "Nelson's one great weakness," said a friend, "is that, because of his circumstances, he has never known *real* pain, *real* suffering, *real* defeat. As a result, his world is an unreal world, a lopsided world. He is the embodiment of the great American illusion that all problems are soluble. . . . He does not realize that there are some problems which have no answer, and that worries me when I think he might be president."[31]

A Proustian mood of nostalgic remembrances of things past appears to have consumed contemporary critics of Rockefeller's governorship. Neal Peirce said it for most when he summarized: "Thomas Dewey gave New York State government its finishing gloss of professionalism; Nelson Rockefeller took the instrument, experimented with it and reshaped it, added on appendages (some of dubious constitutionality) to make the money available to accomplish what he willed, and in the process built the most complex, fascinating, and socially advanced state government in U.S. history."[32]

There is no doubt that Nelson Rockefeller loved to build. He changed the physical face of the state more than any other governor since De Witt Clinton built the Erie Canal.[33] Nelson built schools, hospitals, roads, and monuments—none grander or seemingly more wasteful than the Albany Mall, a marble conglomeration of pompous absurdity, a gesture of grandiloquent folly. When it came to buildings or design, no detail was too trivial. It is said that he once declared one of the Mall's buildings to be out of plumb to his naked eye.

A former aide recalls his brooding over the seating arrangements for a National Governors Conference dinner. Rockefeller had commandeered the Metropolitan Museum of Art for the occasion, and he directed that a dais be set up. He was told that the hall was not large enough to accommodate a dais, but he was not satisfied. He spent a Sunday morning redesigning the table placements, eventually making room for the dais he wanted. On Monday, back in Albany, he was jubilant. "They said it couldn't be done," he told a staffer. "But I did it."[34]

What he did not do was devote the same detailed attention to some very serious areas of state concern, like prison reform and the unconscionable deterioration of the state's mental health facilities symbolized by the conditions at Willowbrook. Typically, Rockefeller had built mental health hospitals, but once the mortar was in place he lost interest. There was always enough money to put up a building, often not enough to run the program that was supposed to be functioning inside.

He declared as a philosophy of administration that he always chose the best people available and then let them have free sway —a policy that resulted in recent nursing home scandals, the alleged misuse of the state police intelligence apparatus, and a Public Service Commission that was little more than a rubber stamp for the utilities it was supposedly regulating. To accept Rockefeller's "hands-off" philosophy at face value, one must also concede the proposition that he had questionable judgment in picking commissioners.

It was not, however, until after his reign as governor, the longest of any New York chief executive since the state's first, that the ghosts of mistakes past returned to haunt him. Separate probes were conducted into the collapse of moral commitment bonding, the wholesale prosecution of rebellious inmates at Attica, and the favoritism afforded Bernard Bergman, the politically potent nursing home czar.

Rockefeller did, to be sure, establish a bold statewide housing policy; he did develop a regional mass transit system; he did convert a weak group of small colleges into a strong university system; he did pioneer an innovative water pollution and control program; and he did create an Adirondacks Park Agency and a State Council for the Arts.

Of course, he also signed a bill authorizing New York high schools to introduce a new course entitled "Communism and

Its Methods and Destructive Effects," despite the opposition of the State Education Department.[35] And on April 27, 1964, Rockefeller claimed to have told Nikita Khrushchev that he opposed coexistence between the United States and the Soviet Union because such a posture was "a very clever means of trying to pull us into close cooperation where they can then undermine the forces of human freedom."[36] On the same occasion, he was asked if the activities of Communists in the United States were not treasonable, and he answered, erroneously, that the "Communist Party in this country has been barred for that reason."[37] In a word, his performance as governor was uneven. One is reminded of Mayor Frank Skeffington in *The Last Hurrah*. On his deathbed, Skeffington is visited by the Cardinal, who says: "Ah, Frank . . . you've done grand things. Grand, grand things." To which Skeffington replies: "Among others."[38]

To accomplish his goals, Rockefeller devised a new method of financing state government. The electorate had stymied his plans by turning down his bond issue proposals, so the governor engineered an end run around the constitution. He created a myriad of autonomous state authorities empowered to float their own revenue bonds. But, these authorities were only autonomous in the sense that they did not answer to any of the normal government regulators. They *did* answer to Rockefeller, who controlled them through a personal cadre of administrative wizards. As a class, they seemed never to have heard of pilot programs. Everything was full speed ahead, with the captains of these ships bound, as indentured servants, to Nelson Rockefeller by way of personal loans and outright grants of money. In the end, they had gone too far too fast. Few had complained when Rockefeller began his back-door financing schemes. Houses for the poor were being built at record rates. It was the middle of the 1960s, the height of the Great Society, and Nelson Rockefeller was out-Johnsoning LBJ.

"Without big money," wrote William Kennedy, Rockefeller's imagination "was capable of only a frustrated sputter."[39] And even the expansion of his most innovative revenue device—

securities backed by the state's "moral" commitment—was dangerously shortsighted. A responsible executive would have either realized the practical limits of such financing and avoided straining its fragility or he would have institutionalized the delicate balance of fiscal arrangements so that the system could survive under governors whose links to the banking community were less secure. Proliferation of moral obligation bonds undermined the stability of the credit market. And the default of the Urban Development Corporation early in 1975 helped precipitate the fiscal crisis that drove New York City to the brink of bankruptcy. Only a month later, in March of 1975, the banks began a boycott of municipal securities that resulted in state receivership, a moratorium on note interest payments, and painful belt tightening.

When it all collapsed in 1975, Governor Hugh Carey would say upon taking office that he had seen "delicatessens in bankruptcy in better shape than the state of New York."[40] Rockefeller would only say that he did what he believed the people wanted.

He also did what *he* wanted, and he often pushed hard after all real hope of achieving a goal had vanished. Such was the case with his plan for a grand mall or *allée* that would link the Rockefeller-funded Lincoln Center with Central Park.[41] It is an incident that reflects the rarified atmosphere of Nelson's everyday life and his unusual method of conducting human relations.

Everyone has a favorite Nelson Rockefeller story, and the Lincoln Center mall is John Lindsay's. The plan, supported by Wallace Harrison, Rockefeller's lifelong architect friend, called for razing the buildings on 63rd and 64th streets between Broadway and Central Park West. A huge landscaped mall would open sweeping views between Lincoln Center and the park—and, if one were high enough in a building on Fifth Avenue, one could spy on the giant Chagalls that grace the Metropolitan Opera House. And it just so happened that Nelson Rockefeller's 32-

room duplex at 810 Fifth Avenue was high enough. One could stand in the living room, look over Central Park, across the proposed mall, and right up the steps of the Met. Unfortunately, two of the buildings that would have to go were the YMCA and the Ethical Culture Society headquarters. Neither would budge, and the City Planning Commission, no longer under the chairmanship of Rockefeller friend William Ballard, would not expedite the matter, let alone condemn the structures via eminent domain.

Nelson was furious, reports John Lindsay. The governor constantly harangued the mayor, urging that some way be found to undertake the project. The affair culminated in the governor's living room in the winter of 1967. Lindsay and one of his aides had gone to a breakfast meeting (creamed chicken and poached eggs, remembers former Deputy Mayor Robert Sweet, who recalls that "they said Rockefeller didn't give a damn what he ate, but what he ate was very good"[42]) and informed Rockefeller that the mall proposal was dead and buried. It was the first time that anyone in the Lindsay administration understood Rockefeller's real concern. "He walked over to the window," remembered Sweet, and said "If you just didn't have that block there, what a great thing it would be."[43] Former City Planning Commission Chairman Donald Elliott recalls that "no one had the foggiest idea"[44] that Rockefeller had always been thinking of a vista from his apartment to Lincoln Center. "I thought he was kidding,"[45] says Elliott.

He wasn't. According to Lindsay, the governor rose from the table, stomped around the room, picked up a pile of books and smashed them down, all the while shouting "I know how to build, I know how to build."

He also knew how to flatter, and one of the most conspicuous recipients of his largesse was the Democratic boss of Brooklyn, Meade Esposito. In 1972, Esposito had visited Rockefeller's Fifth Avenue apartment. He particularly admired a $5,200 Picasso lithograph of a "wise old owl." Naturally, Nelson wrapped it up and sent it home with Esposito—whose wife promptly labeled it "a nothing"[46] that clashed with her color scheme. Esposito hung the Picasso in his living room, but he might just as well have hung it around his neck. Everyone in Brooklyn knew it was there. And everyone in Brooklyn knew that it meant that Rockefeller and Esposito were on dealing terms. "Everyone" included the Republican leader of Brooklyn, George L. Clark, Jr. For years, Clark had smarted at Rockefeller's special relationship with Esposito, a closeness that left Clark in the cold.

It is likely that Rockefeller had no real perception of the slight Clark felt. Rockefeller was, after all, fairly oblivious to his own wealth, or, more properly, to others' lack of similar status. He routinely spoke of the "average taxpayer like you and me," and "the *average* guy who makes $30,000 a year."

George Clark is among those citizens of the world who are very conscious indeed of the difference between a Clark from Brooklyn and a Rockefeller from everywhere. And George Clark has a long memory. In 1975, when the vice-president was again seeking to put distance between himself and his conservative opponents, Clark was allowing as how Ronald Reagan would "sure as hell be welcome in Brooklyn." But the real irritation, it turned out, was always that damned Esposito Picasso. In 1973, when Nelson Rockefeller was trying to get the New York City Republican mayoral nomination for former Democratic Mayor Robert Wagner, the governor summoned the five New York City Republican leaders to Albany for some elbow-bending. Here, in the Executive Mansion, surrounded by other Picassos, George Clark turned on the governor for his profitable friendship with Esposito. He recited the litany of deals with the Democratic boss and finally screamed in frustration: "Governor, you even gave him a Picasso!"

Here, at last, was an irrational raving that Rockefeller could understand. The governor smiled his best "hiya fella" smile, strode across the room and put his arm around Clark comfortingly. "Hell, George," said Rockefeller. "It was only a print."

PART ONE

Making It on
What I Own

CHAPTER 1

Rockefeller Roots:
The Life and Dimes

ROOM 5600 has an Orwellian ring to it

A billion-dollar empire's enormity subdued by soft hues and the warmth of wooden walls. An aura of unreality enhanced by clouds drifting by, almost at eye level, 600 feet above the teeming streets of New York City. A mood of mystery, multiplied by the anonymity of nameless doors and unnumbered rooms lining labyrinthine corridors.

Behind those doors, 154 lawyers, accountants, investment experts, and supporting staff—complete with library, computer, cafeteria, and travel and messenger services—manage the family fortunes of John D. Rockefeller's 84 descendants and exert a profound impact on the international economy. Efficient operators greet callers simply by repeating the family phone number, Circle 7-3700, as if they staffed the switchboard for a suite of doctors' offices. The table in the modest 56th-floor reception area is routinely graced by a single magazine—*Fortune*. Housed on the floors below are the Rockefeller Brothers Fund and other family philanthropies that are the legacy of America's premier power broker. For Nelson Rockefeller, who received 25 cents a week allowance as a youth, the money managers nurture assets which total the equivalent of $1 per minute since 1627 and which generate income of about $10,000 per day.

"I have to tell you, I do not wield economic power," Nelson Rockefeller modestly maintained as the public's elected representatives first began their polite peeking into his financial affairs during the vice-presidential confirmation process. "I think that as these hearings go along, the myth or the misconception about the extent of the family's control of the economic life of this country, I hope, will be totally brought out and exposed and dissipated."[1]

But Rockefeller's easy charm and occasional arrogance, combined with the reluctance of representatives and senators to criticize too severely an incoming vice-president, made the "myth" mushroom in the minds of many and left unanswered Judiciary Committee Chairman Peter Rodino's poignant query: "Even without questioning Mr. Rockefeller's personal integrity, what does it mean to wed great, indeed immense, personal wealth to the awesome powers of the American vice-presidency and presidency?"[2]

As if in answer, attorney Joseph Rauh, Jr., of the liberally oriented Americans for Democratic Action, issued the sweeping response: "In a nation of over 200 million people, President Ford has chosen the person who will have more conflicts of interest as president of the United States than any other person he might have chosen."[3]

Decisions involving the Middle East, Israel, and oil imports would run smack into the interests of Standard Oil of California, Exxon, Marathon Oil, Standard Oil of Indiana, and Mobil Oil, in which the family's investments alone total almost 8 million shares. Interest rates and other money matters could severely affect Chase Manhattan Bank—the nation's third largest—of which David Rockefeller is board chairman and the family itself controls over 600,000 shares. Every decision affecting airlines would touch the six major carriers—including Eastern, which Laurance Rockefeller founded—in which Chase's supposedly independent trust department holds substantial stock.

Rockefeller Roots: The Life and Dimes

Presidential complaints about news coverage could also handily be directed to the bank, which shares a director with the American Broadcasting Company and the New York *Times* and votes almost 6 percent of CBS common stock through trusts. Browbeating Big Business could also be accomplished through Chase's two shared directors each with United States Steel and American Telephone & Telegraph. Criticism of the CIA or other spy bureaus could be forwarded to the family supported Itek Corp., which makes precision optical instruments and cameras. The list is endless.

Atop Rockefeller Center in mid-Manhattan, the family office supervises about $250 million owned outright by John D.'s descendants, plus another $50 million held in trusts. Of that total alone, the 84 Rockefellers were reported at last count to own 315,507 shares of Exxon worth about $21 million, 85,218 shares of IBM worth $16 million, 594,838 shares of Standard Oil of California worth $15 million, 429,959 shares of Chase worth $12 million, and 325,290 shares of Mobil worth $12 million.[1]

On top of that, lump $740 million of investments held in trusts created by Nelson's father and supervised by a supposedly independent committee, although one trust is managed by Chase. Those trusts hold another 1,972,664 shares of Exxon worth $135 million, all 1,125,000 shares of Rockefeller Center, very conservatively valued at $98 million, 2,815,310 shares of Standard Oil of California worth $70 million, 298,824 shares of IBM worth $56 million, 1,436,916 shares of Mobil worth $51 million, and 454,904 shares of Eastman Kodak worth $32 million, in addition to $10 million-plus holdings in each of the following corporations: Merck, Texas Instruments, General Electric, Minnesota Mining and Manufacturing, Montsanto, and Aluminum Company of America.

Back in Room 5600, Rockefeller Family and Associates is also advising Rockefeller University, Colonial Williamsburg, and several other charitable organizations as to where to invest about $225 million.

The Rockefeller Brothers Fund, established in 1940, is also

said to receive independent investment counsel. It is no coincidence, however, that its $170 million worth of securities and real estate includes 320,000 shares of Exxon worth $30 million and 138,000 shares of Chase worth almost $8 million. The aggregate of investments by Nelson and Happy personally, family trusts and funds, the Rockefeller Foundation and charities advised by Room 5600 include:

> 4,590,000 shares of Exxon
> 3,875,000 shares of Standard Oil of California
> 2,565,000 shares of Mobil
> 600,000 shares of IBM
> 667,000 shares of Chase Manhattan.

With assets of $13.6 billion, the Chase Manhattan Bank runs the second-largest trust department in the nation.[5] It holds—and usually votes—substantial blocks of stock in 59 major companies. Like the Rockefeller family itself, whose associates sit as surrogates on dozens of boards of directors, Chase has interlocking directorships with 79 major corporations with assets well over $25 billion. A comprehensive congressional study of operations, normally well protected from publicity, disclosed that trusts managed by Chase own 10 percent or more of the outstanding stock of Universal Oil Products, Richardson-Merrell, Varian Associates, Northwest Airlines, Purity Stores, International Basic Economy Corp., Franklin Stores, and Hammond, Inc., They also own 5 percent-plus of Jonathan Logan, Commercial Solvents, Cummins Engine, Sunbeam Corp., Texas Instruments, Bausch & Lomb, Eastern, Western, CBS, Aetna Life, Boeing Co., and United Aircraft—to name only a few.

Just how extensive the bank's impact is on the economy was illustrated by former California Representative Jerome Waldie in his assessment of Nelson's relationship with Chase. Waldie suggested that "Nelson doesn't give a damn about making money, but [investment adviser J. Richardson] Dilworth does and David does. But there was a belief that you could spend the rest of your life investigating the Rockefellers—and if you moved into David, that would be the beginning of the rest of your life."[6]

David was reminded that he was always presumed to be the most powerful Rockefeller of his generation—at least until Nelson was nominated as vice-president. "Well," he wryly replied, "I've kept my job longer, so in that sense I can't deny it. I guess," he added candidly, "that because of the combination of the name being well known and the bank being well known, if I pick up the phone or ask to see someone I'd have a better chance to get them."[7]

David's sprawling 17th-floor office at the 60-story Chase Manhattan Bank Building ("we're not here for the view," he told an interviewer) in downtown Manhattan houses a 30,000-card file of people he has met around the world. To demonstrate just how extensive his file is (it is cross-indexed by company, city, and country and is accompanied by a miniversion with 6,000 names), David modestly recalled a visit from Soviet Ambassador Jacob Malik: "I showed him the file, and he said 'let me see a card.' I showed him the card for Nikita Khrushchev."[8]

Recalling David's pleas to President Nixon for more even-handed dealings with oil-producing Arab states, Joseph Rauh observed that while "David Rockefeller can say to the big Arab countries, to Saudi Arabia, on behalf of his Aramco, that 'I can't do anything with the president of the United States to get what you want against Israel.' How could David Rockefeller say [that] if the president of the United States is his brother?"[9]

It is impossible to gauge the extent of the family's economic influence, but needless to say it is enormous. Much of its clout comes from the extensive interlocking directorates created by Rockefeller representatives. The quasi-independent Rockefeller Foundation's finance committee, which presides over about a billion-dollar stock portfolio, has included former Treasury Secretary C. Douglas Dillon. And even the Ford Foundation, whose assets range into the multibillions, fell into the Rockefeller sphere for more than a decade when John J. McCloy doubled as chairman of the foundation's trustees and board chairman of Chase. It is simplistic to equate shared directors in a company with outright control. But it is equally naïve to ignore the fact that the family's forces are represented in dozens of major firms that affect world finances and are themselves significantly affected by federal fiscal policies.

While each Rockefeller brother has his own pet projects or charities, the pattern of investment belies the heated denials that the Rockefeller family rarely acts in concert with Dilworth's baton. Referring to Room 5600 and its relationship to his relatives, Nelson earnestly explained:

> It is as though this was a service organization and they were outside clients and they were unrelated. . . . We do not operate as a corporation. We do not have activities where we sit down in a board meeting and decide will we make this investment, will we go into this market, will we do this, which is the normal activity of a corporate structure. And, therefore, I think that it is somewhat misleading to think that there is some very powerful central organization here that has many active connections all over that are coordinated, that are planned, that are administered, that are operated as a single unit with a tremendous central purpose.
>
> It is a loosely knit conglomerate of family and individuals who try to be decent citizens and who have been very fortunate in living in this society and benefiting from the society and who would like to contribute to the society itself.[10]

When Massachusetts Representative Robert Drinan was questioning the vice-president designate, he expressed the concern that family operatives could "exercise this massive wealth and economic power on behalf of the prestige of the Rockefeller name."

"Well, Father," Nelson reassured him, "you belong to a very

powerful organization which has much better discipline than the one I belong to."[11]

J. Richardson Dilworth, the perfectly proper proprietor of the family fortune, seemed swept up by his own rhetoric when he defensively declared that "both the family members and their investment advisers in the family office are totally uninterested in controlling anything. The family members are simply investors. The aim and hope of the advisers is—in a most difficult and uncertain world—over time to achieve a reasonable total return for our clients."

A lesser Rockefeller associate stated it more simply: "Our goal, like everyone else's, is to make wads and wads of money for the family."[12]

Armed even with the vice-president's unprecedented disclosures, an economist's efforts to pinpoint the scope of the Rockefeller fortune would still be no better than an educated guess. After two generations, it was subtly spread below the our face like an iceberg: funds funneled to numerous descendants and diversified firms, insulated by labyrinthine trusts and closely held companies under no requirement to disclose their assets.

What happened to John D.'s wealth was that, in addition to doling out an undetermined number of dimes, the crusty oil baron refined his crude and callous image by funneling $550 million to foundations and philanthropies, including the General Education Board, Rockefeller Foundation, Rockefeller Institute, University of Chicago, and various other religious and academic interests.

John D., Jr., in turn, continued the tradition by contributing $552 million of his own to numerous tax-exempt projects, the most notable of which were the United Nations, Colonial Williamsburg, and three national parks. Another $312 million went to his two wives, Nelson and his brothers and sister, and grandchildren. Although an almost equal amount—$317 million—was paid out in federal, state, and local taxes, JDR Jr.'s heirs avoided paying any inheritance taxes on a $150 million estate.

When he died in 1960, he had already disbursed other holdings
into trust accounts and split the remaining $150 million between
his second wife and the Rockefeller Brothers Fund.[13]

Along with his siblings, Nelson followed, and sometimes
expanded, the gift-giving theme. By the time he was nominated
as vice-president, he had already turned over $15.5 million to
various relatives. And in addition to pledging over $20 million
in art and real estate for public use, he had contributed $33 mil-
lion to various charities.

The bulk of those donations were made between 1957 and
1974 to 193 charitable, educational, and other groups ranging
from the Museum of Primitive Art—a memorial to his late son
Michael—to $656,000 to the State of New York for a swimming
pool and other improvements at the Executive Mansion in
Albany. Also on the gift list is $760,000 to supplement govern-
ment expenses on his 1969 mission to Latin America on behalf
of President Nixon, $250,000 to the Archdiocese of New York
to help finance the transportation of Michaelangelo's "Pietà" to
the United States for exhibition, $6,500 mysteriously marked
only as "United States Government," $5,000 to the Flatbush
Boy's Club in Brooklyn, and $10 to Phillips Academy in
Andover, Mass., which Rockefeller apologetically explained
must have matched a small gift from a family employee.

The benefits of Nelson's largesse were threefold: (1) for
pure public relations, they enhanced his image and continued
to erode the memory of how the money originated; (2) like the
grants from family-funded foundations, they also improved
private relations with religious, academic, and other groups; and
(3) the donation of securities instead of cash provided a double
tax benefit—deductions from his income tax, and avoidance of
the capital gains levy for which he would have been liable had
he converted the stock into cash.

Naturally, Nelson was giving away less than he was taking in.
From 1964 to 1973, for instance, his charitable contributions
totaled $14.2 million, a little over twice his $5.6 million deduc-
tion for "office, investment, and other expenses" and far less

than his $22.6 million tax tab. The federal government received $12 million in income taxes, New York State $10,000 in gasoline taxes and $819,000 in sales taxes—an incredible total, even considering how much the last two levies soared during his reign.

Until his nomination in 1974, when the Internal Revenue Service expedited an audit that resulted in an $820,000 bigger tax bill for five years, Rockefeller paid no federal income taxes at all for 1970, when his total income dipped to $2.4 million. In 1973 he paid federal income and gift taxes of $905,950 and $450,487 respectively, $629,348 in state taxes, and $295,209 in city and local taxes.

The plus side is equally sobering. In the ten years since 1964, Nelson's total income just topped the $47 million mark. The bulk of his receipts, which Rockefeller reaped to the tune of over $4 million annually, came from trust dividends ($37.9 million), capital gains ($4.6 million), dividends from his own securities ($3.2 million), and his New York State salary, which topped $82,800 during his last year as governor in 1973 (his pay from the public dropped to $65,000 as vice-president) and totaled more than $600,000 for the decade.

Nelson's 1973 income of $4.8 million included $3.4 million in trust dividends, $456,196 in dividends from his own securities, $763,014 in capital gains, and $89,384 in rentals.

Federal auditors found that of Nelson and Happy's $64 million in assets (exclusive of trusts), 52 percent was in art, 20 percent in securities, and 18 percent in real estate. In 1973, 67 percent of their income was derived from trusts, 22 percent from art sales, and 7 percent from dividends. Of their own securities, 43 percent were in Venezuelan-based agribusiness enterprises, 16 percent in oil and gas, 13 percent in the scientific and electronics industry, and 8 percent in the chemical field. Although holdings in fuel firms accounted for 21 percent of the assets of his major Trust No. 1 (mostly in Exxon and Standard Oil of California), 45 percent of the income from that trust came from the fuel industry. Similarly, in Trust No. 2, common stock holdings and income from fuel-related firms both exceeded 75 percent of total assets or income.

Asked to assess the major trust account, a Chase Manhattan portfolio manager was alarmed at the extent to which government action could affect the large blocks of oil and IBM stock. Not knowing it was Rockefeller's account or managed by Chase, the manager declared: "You'll never ever find a portfolio like that at Chase. I can only assume the man whose portfolio it is must be out of touch with the outside world . . . or, maybe, that's what I should say about the people running it. It must be run by First National City."[14]

A confidential examination by Congress's Joint Committee on Internal Revenue Taxation estimated the assets of the vice-president and his wife at $74 million—plus the $34 million estimated to be the value of their beneficial interests in trusts. Totaling the full trust holdings and those of their descendants, the net worth of Nelson Rockefeller's immediate family is estimated officially at almost $220 million.

Although Rockefeller rarely carries any money with him, the confidential audit indicated that family cash transactions are extensive and varied. Receipts from the sale of securities, art, and other assets from 1968 through mid-1974 ranged from a low of $400,372 in 1970 to a high of $9,167,813 in 1968. Purchases of such assets hit a high of $7,240,534 in 1973, compared to a six-year low of $720,546 only the year before. Also showing sharp fluctuation was the personal and household expense account, in which auditors lumped salaries, rent, maintenance, utilities, food, travel, clothes, presents, noncharitable and political contributions, and expenses for political surveys. That account ranged between $6,815,644 in 1968 and $2,426,587 in 1972. Borrowing, although avoided during several of the years examined, peaked in the 1970 gubernatorial election year, when Rockefeller took a $3.1 million loan from Chase Manhattan. The Rockefellers reported nominal deposits at the National Bank & Trust Co. of Norwich and the National Savings & Trust

Co. of Washington—about enough, in fact, to entitle them to a free toaster.

Naturally, Nelson listed several accounts at Chase. But an obscure entry in one ledger somehow made him seem more human than all his public attempts at humility. Auditors found that on August 31, 1974, his office account at the Chase Manhattan Bank was overdrawn by $5,119.

But Nelson's total balance sheet was never in the red. His total assets included $27 million worth of paintings, $5.1 million each of primitive art and porcelain, and $1 million in jewelry. Also, $770,000 worth of furniture housed in over $18 million worth of real estate, not counting the 18,000-acre Venezuela ranch that he has visited, since 1967, an average of only once a year.

Of all the landholdings, including the 32-room Fifth Avenue duplex and the Seal Harbor, Maine, retreat which boasts a Picasso tapestry in the boathouse, the most impressive, by far, is Pocantico Hills, the 3,000-acre enclave overlooking the Hudson River, 30 miles north of New York City. Quipped playwright George Kaufman: "It's what God would have done if he'd had the money."

Nelson, who shares with his brothers the fenced-in 190-acre patrolled estate-within-an-estate, first lived in Kykuit (Dutch for "lookout"), the four-story Georgian mansion, replete with Chippendale trappings, that John D. had built. In 1972 the governor built a one-story, five-bedroom Japanese style guest house of wood and stucco, "my retirement place," he said. "He has always loved Japanese things," says a family spokesman, and Nelson wasted no time showing off his new home to Emperor Hirohito when the Japanese monarch visited the United States in 1975.

Pocantico's grounds are dotted with sculptures by Picasso, Maillol, and Henry Moore. The prime gathering spot is the Playhouse, which, among other toys to amuse the family, has two indoor tennis courts complete with fireplaces.

Nelson's fondness for Pocantico and his other homes left the

Albany Executive Mansion virtually vacant during his governorship, and it became a quasi hotel for a selected clientele of long-term lodgers such as State Attorney General Louis Lefkowitz. Of course, there were always guest rooms in the *real* Rockefeller houses as well. At his Washington estate on Foxhall Road, Nelson played host to impressionable visiting politicos like Nassau County Executive Ralph Caso, who couldn't contain himself. "Imagine," he said later, "me sleeping in the bed of a Rockefeller."[15] And that was before Nelson indulged himself with a $35,000 mink-trimmed bed by Max Ernst for the refurbished vice-presidential residence.

Also contributing to Rockefeller's uniqueness as a political phenomenon was the mobility provided by a flotilla of boats and planes. Along with the 55th Street office, they saved New York State the millions of dollars it cost Nelson to serve as governor in the style to which he had become accustomed.

Some understanding of what it cost Rockefeller to be governor of New York comes from an appropriation he sought in his 1971 austerity budget. The governor agreed to continue the rent-free arrangement with the state for office space in the five-story Manhattan townhouse that is sandwiched between a beauty salon and an Italian restaurant—but he did request $200,000 annually for fuel, maintenance, and four telephone operators. He had already lavished more than $500,000 in state funds (aside from his own donations) to renovate the Executive Mansion in Albany, but he still chose to use the family aircraft instead of the Environmental Conservation Department's planes, a decision which he estimated "must have saved the state millions."[16]

As with his charitable endeavors, the Rockefeller armada fulfilled more functions than mere transportation. It was also his special brand of patronage. In 1974, for instance, a Wayfarer Ketch jet airplane carried Secretary of State Henry Kissinger and his bride, Nancy Maginnes—employed by the Rockefeller-funded Critical Choices Commission—to and from their Acapulco honeymoon.

Rockefeller Roots: The Life and Dimes

By sheer force of personality, Nelson Rockefeller, even had he been born into poverty, would probably have grown powerful and rich. But he never had the opportunity: when he kicked and screamed his way into the pine- and salt-scented air at Seal Harbor on a July afternoon in 1908, he was already a multimillionaire—the last scion of one of America's richest, most powerful families. A lucky kid.

CHAPTER 2

The

Pocantico Kid

O N the same day that Nelson was born, John D. the First was in Cleveland celebrating his 69th birthday and preparing a speech to be delivered to Baptist collegians at Western Reserve.

Two days later, both the speech and the birth shared the front page of the New York *Times* with the report of William Jennings Bryan's nomination as the Democratic presidential candidate. The announcement of Nelson's arrival, which neglected to note his name, ran five lines—the last time he was so slighted.

Unlike his four brothers and sisters, Nelson would never shun publicity behind the family's golden curtain. Rockefeller public relations men then were paid to keep the clan and its activities out of the papers, not in. As early as age 15, however, Nelson shattered that tradition. Practicing fast draws, he shot himself in the shin with an air pistol and had to be rushed to a hospital. He still bears the scar.

"Obviously a principal difference among my uncles is that he's the only one who chose a very public approach," observes John D. (Jay) Rockefeller IV, the gregarious West Virginian who lost a gubernatorial bid of his own but who subsequently captured the title of president—of West Virginia Wesleyan College. "The others chose a very private approach—with impact on the public sector."[1]

Nelson was the third child and second son born to John D. Rockefeller, Jr., and the former Abby Aldrich. He was named after his maternal grandfather, Nelson W. Aldrich, whose family descended from Rhode Island's founder. A self-made man who quit school at age 17 to become a grocery clerk in Providence, Aldrich was sent by the Ocean State to the U.S. Senate 23 years later, where he became a staunch conservative. He served for 17 years as majority leader until the Old Guard was ousted by Theodore Roosevelt.

It was Nelson's paternal grandfather, however, who was to exercise the most personal impact on the impressionable young scion. John D. descended from French Huguenots who changed their name from Roquefeuille when they fled from France to Germany to escape religious persecution. The first Rockefeller settled in America in 1723. Raised on a modest-sized farm in upstate New York, John D. Rockefeller started selling turkeys on his own at age seven and was immediately trained by his mother to turn over 10 percent of his earnings to those more needy and to save the rest.[2] The family archives, preserved in Rockefeller Center, dutifully record that by the time he was 11, young John was loaning out $50 in savings to a local farmer at 7 percent interest. After the family moved to Cleveland in 1853, he quit school to become a $3.50-a-week accountant when he was 16 years old. Four years later, he launched a commodity commission business with $900 of his savings and a $1,100 interest-bearing loan from his father. By the time he was 26, John and a partner bought out their associates in a refining firm for $72,500 and formed what was to become Standard Oil.

Seizing control of virtually every aspect of oil production across the country, he accumulated wealth with a rapidity that only contemporary technology made possible and on a scale which prompted tax and antitrust laws that would prohibit any repetition of his example.

Recalling his grandfather's strict training in religion, self-reliance, and responsibility, and his grandmother's commitment to both abolition and prohibition, Nelson was to say later that "the roots of our family ethic were deeply implanted—an ethic based on the fundamental American values which have come down through the generations since then."[3] Refined by his own rationalizations, it was an ethic that he would carry with him in his quests for the presidency, prompting such platitudes as: "Let's hear it for the Founding Fathers. I think they did a hell of a job!"[4]

The year Nelson was born, antitrust suits were being battled by his semiretired grandfather, whom Teddy Roosevelt denounced as one of the "malefactors of great wealth." Less than six years later, the Rockefeller reputation hit rock bottom in a bloody episode that was to haunt the family for years and would flare again in Nelson's mind when, as governor, he had to consider using force to break a New York City garbage strike and, later, to quell the Attica prison riot.

In 1913, dozens died when the management of the Colorado Fuel and Iron Company, of which Nelson's family was the major stockholder, massacred striking workers at its Ludlow fields. (After the president of Colorado College and a dean of the University of Denver demanded that the strikers return to work, the schools received unrestricted $100,000 grants from the Rockefeller Foundation and General Education Board.) But John D., Jr. ignored all pleas to go to Ludlow. And Nelson, 58 years later, never went to Attica.

Young Nelson was instilled with many of the same values that had been taught to his grandfather under less luxurious circumstances, and then to his father in an atmosphere of great wealth. Frugality was foremost. Nelson vividly recalls a trip out West to a national park: "We had two rooms, we children, and there was a bath between, and they had charged him for two double rooms with baths, and I'll never forget his arguing with the clerk that it was one bath and two rooms and not two baths and two rooms, and I was quite embarrassed. 'But if we don't do this,' he said, 'then other people won't feel they can do it because they might be embarrassed to do it, and people will take advantage.' It was sort of the first consumer protection approach."[5]

Nelson was trained to give 10 percent and save 10 percent of his 25-cent weekly allowance, which he supplemented by various odd jobs around the estate. "I can remember," Laurance Rockefeller said, "both of us at a very young age being given the opportunity to haul a load of manure from the farm barns over to our gardens—hauled by a large white horse. This remains in my mind as one of the more dramatic moments of gardening."[6]

The two brothers also raised rabbits. "We went to the Rockefeller Institute," Nelson recalled, "and borrowed a mother rabbit that was about to have babies, and that is how we got started in business. This is a real true story. Then, as they grew up, we wanted to separate them, you know, the fathers and the mothers. But the difficulty was that the first thing we knew, the fathers had babies. So then we went for outside advice. We were a little inexperienced, as you can see."[7] The boys subsequently borrowed a male rabbit, bred more bunnies, and sold them back to the Rockefeller Institute. It was the kind of no-risk venture that offered little challenge and may have helped discourage Nelson from a career in commerce.

Nelson and Laurance, with whom he has remained closest all his life, were big Western buffs. David still shudders at the recollection of a log cabin his two older brothers built in the Maine woods. "Winthrop and I were not allowed to go there. We were practically threatened with death if we ever walked near the place."[8]

"My brother Laurance and I were very close always," Nelson noted. "We thought Nelson and Laurance—well, we were readers of Zane Grey and Western stories, and we didn't think they were very, sort of hep names. So I was going to call him Bill and he was going to call me Dick. I always called him Bill, he never called me Dick."[9]

The log cabin was also, by imitation, Nelson's form of flattery to Abraham Lincoln, whom he has probably quoted more than any other public figure. "In terms of people I really respected—I use that word as distinct from hero," Nelson said, "I had tremendous admiration and respect for him. I remember my brother and I worked out his birchbark kettle that you put next to the fire. He and I were very big woodsmen. We had ponies in those days—we snaked the logs and built a log cabin. It was more interest and respect than I would say hero worship." "Although," he added gratuitously, "I had a great respect for George Washington, too."[10]

One may learn a great deal about a man by knowing his personal heroes, and it is interesting that Nelson Rockefeller never had any. Even as a child, he once remarked, "I'm not sure how much I was fooled by this Santa Claus stuff."[11] The lifetime list of nominees, compiled by Wallace Harrison and other friends, includes figures as diverse as Nehru, Gandhi, and General George Marshall. But all of Rockefeller's intimates agree that the list was topped by his immediate family, especially John D. the First. "I really haven't been exactly a hero worshiper type," Nelson explained. "I'm more of an activist. But I have tremendous respect for my grandparents, and my mother and father. I would have to think if you really called it heroes, it would be my two grandfathers, and my mother and father."[12]

Architect Harrison, who became close with most members of the family, also recalled that young Nelson "was one of the favorites of the old man—he got a lot of good advice from the old guy."[13] And David concurred that "certainly grandfather has always been very much of a hero."[14]

Nelson always valued his relationship with John D. Asked his advice to people who dream about being a Rockefeller, he once suggested candidly that "you should have had my grandfather as your grandfather."[15]

Sometimes, of course, the money was a mixed blessing, since it both intimidated people and created in them a lasting resentment that Nelson was taught from the outset to ignore. Even as a youngster, he was urged to turn aside taunts with a light touch.

When a local youth shouted "Hello, Mr. Moneybags Rockefeller, how many yachts do you have today?" his mother provided the easy rejoinder, "Oh, we have only 16 yachts now, but we're getting some more."[16] And then there is the apparently apocryphal story about a slow old boat that the brothers sailed around in. The craft's condition prompted a friend to ask, "Why don't you ask your father to buy you a good boat like the other boys have?" To which one of the Rockefeller lads supposedly replied: "Who do you think we are—the Vanderbilts?"[17]

Sometimes the jokes weren't so funny. At a town meeting at the Garden City Hotel in 1969, Mrs. Emma Morning of the Nassau County Welfare Tenants Coordinating Committee assailed the 5 percent public assistance budget cut. "Sir," the burly black woman bristled, "you've never been hungry yourself, and that's why you're cutting the 5 percent." Rockefeller peered over the podium and interjected: "Looks like *you've* never gone hungry!"[18]

In less hostile circumstances, he was more sober. Three days after his nomination as vice-president, Rockefeller tooled up in a maroon Mustang to Wallace Harrison's garage in Seal Harbor, which had been hastily converted into a press shack, and reminisced about bearing the most famous name in America for 66 years. Seated outside on a rough-hewn log, he explained simply: "I've got to be perfectly frank. I never felt the disadvantages. Nor did I have a feeling of guilt. I just felt that money brought with it tremendous opportunities and responsibilities. It's like a sharp tool—if you misuse it, you can get cut or hurt other people."[19]

Nelson saw a lot of his grandfather in Lakewood, N.J., Ormond Beach, Fla., and at Pocantico, where they would play "numerica" after breakfast at Kykuit, the mansion that Nelson would later call home. "I would say it's the equivalent of bingo today, and he was the banker," Nelson reminisced. "That was the best part about it. Nobody had to put up any money, you just got it out at the end."[20]

"Nelson saw a fair amount of him," David said with a detectable tinge of envy. "Nelson did admire his talents and accomplishments, and he had a tremendous impact on Nelson's life."[21]

At first blush, as author William Manchester observed after the new governor was inaugurated in 1959,

> The two men had little in common. The titan lived in stark houses, because shutters and curtains might cut off sunlight. The governor adorned the grounds around his Pocantico Hills, N.Y. home with statuary. John D. absolutely refused to deal with anyone who tried to hurry him. His grandson was ticketed for speeding. The old man declined to honor his membership in the New York Stock Exchange by appearing on the floor because he despised the turmoil. Nelson wallows in campaign hubbub and borrows a band leader's baton to add to the din. His grandfather's palate was so sensitive that he would not touch a hot dish until it had cooled. He himself bolts salami, hot dogs, and green taffy. John D. could find edification only in a Baptist pew. Nelson has the tastes of a da Vinci.[22]

But there were, as Manchester noted even then, surprising similarities that were rooted beneath the superficial differences in life-style:

> Two men, then—John D. in 1889 and Nelson taking the oath of office on his grandmother's Bible 70 years later—seem at first glance to be utterly diverse. The perceptive will note, however, that both are instinctive competitors and that each fits comfortably into his own period. John D. accepted the business cant of nineteenth-century America, and Nelson is as uncritical of current orthodoxy; he shares its abiding faith in public relations, omnipotent experts and progress by committee.[23]

Nevertheless, the former $3.50-a-week accountant who went on to dictate the cost and quantity of 90 percent of America's oil production was a tough act for the younger Rockefeller to follow. And the enduring strain of trying to follow it cut deeply into his son and those of his grandsons who even attempted the impossible task. "Your father," Abby Aldrich Rockefeller wrote her sons, "is so modest, so unassuming, and often so doubtful of his own ability that I wonder if you always realize what a tower of strength he is to me and to us all."[24]

Nelson, too, was constantly reminded of his grandfather's success and urged to curb his ebullience to conform to the code of John D. the First. "You have great admiration for your Grandfather Rockefeller," Nelson's father wrote him in a memorable letter. "Remember that one of the qualities that made him great and that not infrequently made him successful over other people, was his ability to wait and to be patient to a degree that was almost superhuman. Waiting is often hard work, much harder than working and doing, but not infrequently it is the quickest and most effective way to accomplish the desired end and it is the goal that the wise man keeps his eye on."[25]

When he was nine, Nelson was enrolled in the progressive Lincoln School in Manhattan, which could give personal attention to his tendency to transpose numbers and letters—a recurring ailment called dyslexia which was aggravated by early attempts to "cure" his left handedness, and later required him to memorize speeches to avoid stumbling over his own words. As a child, Nelson's daughter Mary once asked her older brother Rodman why their father usually passed when it came his turn in the family's responsive Bible-reading sessions. Because, Rodman replied, "Daddy can't read."

"My father didn't believe in people being left-handed," recalled Rockefeller, "and so, finally, after he had an elastic on my arm at the table and a string, and if I ate with my left hand he pulled the elastic with the string and let it snap, so I was getting identified with the right hand. This they say. I don't know. I have never studied these things, but they say this has a psychological effect if you're left-handed and you're forced to, you know—and so you can't spell. I have a little trouble with reverse reading too. I'm going to develop a sense of sympathy here in a minute."[26]

39

By age 12, Nelson had supervised the drafting of a class con-stitution which sternly advised students always to obey the class chairman. The class chairman was, of course, Nelson Rockefeller. The brothers, Laurance reminded Hugh Morrow one day, "are beneficiaries of the Lincoln School, which stressed participation and a concern for the human environment rather than reading, writing, and arithmetic." "I see it in Nelson's spelling," Nelson's press secretary replied.[27]

Later, when Nelson was in college, his father offered to return all his son's letters with misspelled words underlined, so he could look them up and learn them. Nelson politely declined but made a clever counteroffer: "I know there are various words I can't spell. I could stop and look them up in the dictionary but that would be wasting a lot of time, so instead of looking them up I'll just underline the words that I'm uncertain about and you'll know that, if necessary, I could take the time to look them up."[28] All the underlined words were spelled correctly.

Nelson entered Dartmouth in 1926. At first, his studies fol-lowed behind class socials and varsity soccer. It was not until he was appointed chairman of the Informals Committee at Dartmouth that he wrote home saying: "I've lost my feeling of incompetency, of not being able to handle a job without relying on someone else. In other words, if something has to be done . . . I feel that I'm fully capable of doing it and will know or have some idea of how to go about it without an inward fear. And, secondly, I'm losing my fear of standing up before a crowd and saying what I've got to say. . . ."[29]

Dartmouth was also the scene of his first political setback— losing the class presidency to the son of a shoemaker, and winding up as vice-president. Before making Phi Beta Kappa in senior year and producing a 45-page honors thesis on the Standard Oil monopoly, Nelson received "A" grades in every subject one term except two—politics and public speaking.

"He happened to room with my brother-in-law, John French, Jr.," Laurance would recall. "John was a superb scholar, was elected to Phi Beta Kappa in his junior year, was editor of the college newspaper, and at one point was class president. John set a fast pace in terms of campus responsibilities and campus political leadership. He and Nelson were quite different but also quite competitive. Trying to keep up with my brother-in-law on all fronts, I think, was the source of a great competitive challenge to Nelson. I believe that right in this area is where he first had to meet really tough competition and learn to lose as well as to win."[30]

Never moving into a fraternity house, he often borrowed money from his roommate and frequently failed to stay within the $1,500 annual budget allotted by his father. Nelson was an economics major. His college career was also marked by an independence and brashness which, though tempered by pragmatic restraints, were to persist throughout his presidential quest.

More than 30 years later, as he dedicated a senior citizens' housing project in upstate Plattsburgh, N.Y., Rockefeller was reminded by the window boxes on the barracks-like buildings of one of his lesser personal triumphs. "When I was in Dartmouth," he recalled, "I grew English daisies and lilies of the valley in a window box. My roommate warned me not to, but pretty soon other boys had window boxes, too. I guess the moral is, do what you think is right in this world. Others will follow."[31]

Nelson's parents continued to exert their influence, even though their son was miles from New York. Mother actually chose Nelson's Dartmouth roommate—the son of a fellow member of the YWCA board—and frequently reminded her sons that they were, in a sense, chosen people. In one letter, she expressed an abiding concern about society's "unreasoning aversion" to Jews and Negroes and urged John, Nelson, and Laurance to "put yourselves in the place of an honest, poor man who happens to belong to one of the so-called despised races."[32] When his mother reprimanded him for taking life too lightly, Nelson dramatically declared: "I shall try in a small measure to make up for the discomfort I have caused you both in the past. God alone knows how humble I feel."[33]

And, after visiting Versailles in 1928 and inspecting restoration work that was financed by the family, Nelson wrote his father that "it makes me feel proud. I only hope that I shall grow up and live a life that will be worthy of the family name. I'm sure Johnny will because he already thinks and acts exactly like you, Pa. I see the likeness . . . more clearly every day. But as for myself—well, I'm a lot different and I don't think the same way. But I hope that despite this, I'll come out on top, as it were."[34]

John D., Jr. devoted more time to admonishing his impetuous second son, urging upon him patience and responsibility and rebutting his lack of enthusiasm for an orderly business career. Deciding early which direction he did not want to take, Nelson complained:

> Frankly, I don't relish the idea of going into some business—
> not that I don't think I could make a go of it—but there is
> nothing very appealing, challenging about it. Just to work my
> way up in a business that another man has built, stepping from
> the shoes of one to those of another, making a few minor
> changes here and there and then, finally perhaps at the age of
> sixty, getting to the top where I would have real control for
> a few years. No, that isn't my idea of living a real life.[35]

Nelson solved that problem by starting at the top.

Well past the age of 60, he was asked about what he would have done for a living if he had had to go out and work. "If I had to go out and work?" he asked indignantly. "I worked all my life. I probably worked harder than . . . I was never worried. I could go out and work at anything. I could go out and dig ditches—I can do it now. I can do most anything with my hands. What I really wanted was to be an architect. If you want to know why I wasn't, it's because I didn't feel I could justify it in terms of service. I thought what would happen, would be [that] I'd get projects that the family was doing. It wouldn't be a genuine operation. I wanted to go out on my own. I've always wanted to be on my own. I've always initiated things and done the things I've initiated—never gone on boards of directors. I didn't want to be sitting there listening to someone else do something.

"I never had a long-term plan," Nelson insisted. "I have responded to opportunity which grew out of circumstances. I'm ambitious, I don't deny that. But not a long-term, carefully worked out plan that I went step by step. My life has always been one of ambition to do things, to do useful things and to do them myself—not to ride on somebody else. I was more interested in substance than form. I had no worry about doing something little if *I* was doing it and I was satisfied with what I was doing."[36]

He recalled his mother's "admonition" to associate with his superiors—"people who know more than you do, you can learn that way." But he stressed that "I wanted to be what I did do on my own. If I had to earn a living, it would have been just starting there, and the next door opens and I go in there. I've never worried about walking through a door when it opened and taking on something new."[37]

CHAPTER 3

The Young Buck
Starts Here

Less than a month after graduating from Dartmouth cum laude, and with a $2,500 bonus from father for not smoking, Nelson Rockefeller married Mary Todhunter Clark of the Philadelphia Main Line family with whom he had summered at Seal Harbor. Delaying the decision on a professional career but continuing his grooming for future service, he and "Tod" embarked on a round-the-world honeymoon highlighted by drop-ins on Standard Oil officials, poets, potentates, and political leaders like Prime Minister Ramsay MacDonald in England and the king of Siam.

Nelson returned a few months shy of his 23rd birthday with his self-reliance strengthened and his enthusiasm undiminished. Impatient as ever, he ignored the cautioning counsel of his father by becoming a trustee of the Metropolitan Museum of Art at age 24, and surprised Westchester County Republican leader William Ward a year later by accepting his first political post—membership on the county's Board of Health. It was the first time that a Rockefeller had participated directly in any such political role. But it was the beginning of a lifetime of activity for Nelson, during which he adapted his grandfather's talent for

44

attracting associates and consolidating power to the public arena, where Nelson would always function best as his own boss.

"I feel this work offers an opportunity to be of real service to the community," Nelson wrote Ward in 1932, "and although I have had no experience in this field I should be very glad to become a member of the Westchester County Health Board. I should be happy to give my time to this work." "However," he added cautiously, "I am relying on the assurance of your statement the other day that there will be no financial responsibility connected."[1]

Consciously or otherwise, the brothers divided up the world. Harold Fisher, a Brooklyn Democrat and Rockefeller-appointee to New York's Metropolitan Transportation Authority, was to observe later: "I always used to have the feeling that the family sat around and said 'Laurance is going to take care of the trees, David is going to take care of the bank, and Nelson is going to go into government' and then they were trained for that for the rest of their lives."[2]

All the while, they felt the need to justify their existence. "First generation millionaires tend to give us libraries," wrote Garry Wills, "the second and third generation think they should give us themselves."[3] Added David Rockefeller's wife Peggy, when she was asked what made her husband tick: "I think he has to prove to himself and to the world that a Rockefeller doesn't have to be a spoiled SOB." She could just as easily have been describing Nelson.

The brothers often fought, especially as children.[4] "But," Nelson said pointedly, "always, in the end, there was unity. I mean, if anyone—we'd fight among ourselves, and there was a good deal of teasing. But if anyone from the outside appeared and tried to get in on this, on one side or the other, then there was—the group came together and he'd had it."[5]

Following his honeymoon, Nelson was appointed to a minor post at Standard Oil, but he soon felt confined by the fact that he clearly ranked behind his father and older brother in the firm's hierarchy. So he also joined Chase National Bank, where he served under the tutelage of his uncle, bank president Winthrop Aldrich, and was assigned for a stretch of several months to the London and Paris branches.

When he returned, his restlessness had not subsided. One sign was his response on an official form he filled out to qualify for his $4-a-day fee as a grand juror. Under occupation, he simply wrote "clerk."

Rockefeller decided to strike off on his own, joining two friends in financing a small firm which earned fees as an intermediary in corporate deals, not unlike the commodity commission business that his grandfather had formed 72 years earlier. The new enterprise—which was so successful that, like John D. the First, Nelson bought out his partners—fulfilled two pressing personal needs. It allowed an outlet for Nelson's bursting energy which could no longer be bound by the established family businesses. And it provided an opportunity for him to prove to himself and for the record that not only was he no slouch, but he could carry the Rockefeller standard into the financial community as well as any of his relatives.

"He loves businessmen," Manhattan Republican boss Vincent F. Albano, Jr. would say after closely observing the Rockefeller style years later. "He thinks people in politics are not too bright —why didn't they go out into private industry and make it?"[6]

Under the innocuous new name of Special Work, Inc., Nelson turned his firm into a rental agency for the Rockefeller Center complex that was rising in midtown Manhattan—John D., Jr.'s personal response to the Depression, suggesting the kind of optimism that was endemic to his son. Nelson made the center bloom: he succeeded so well in undercutting competitors with below-market rates and paying off the old leases of prospective tenants that he prompted a $10 million suit from real estate mogul August Heckscher accusing the center's board of directors of unfair competition. There must have been secret smiles of satisfaction in family circles when one real estate operator compared Nelson's tactics to "John D., Sr. at his roughest."

Like the white marble Albany Mall that Nelson was to build

at ten times the $125 million cost of Rockefeller Center, the well-ordered office, commercial, theater, and broadcasting complex was to be a showcase of size so monumental as to obscure earlier family failings, with no expense spared. Even organized labor was brought into line with employee pensions and other progressive benefits that protected Rockefeller Center from any major work stoppage until 1972, when musicians struck the Radio City Music Hall. Not until the 1940s did Rockefeller Center begin running in the black, however, and Nelson learned one lesson from that. His father had financed almost two-thirds of Rockefeller Center himself; for his building exploits, Nelson engineered a back-door bonding scheme that bypassed New York State taxpayers for approval but presented them with the bill.

Art was Nelson's second love in life—he has already donated $20 million worth and still owns an incredible 1,300 pieces of nonmodern art and 2,250 of modern.[7] Unlike other large-scale collectors, he carefully culls catalogues for particularly attractive paintings and sculptures (mother "was a great friend of Matisse," he remembered) and never makes wholesale selections that wind up unopened in locked warehouses.

"The Rockefeller process of acquisition—viewed by some as thick with Machiavellian complexities and by others as a matter of simple expediency for a man in the governor's position —is all done by remote control," art critic James R. Mellon once observed. "Totally unlike any other collector," he continued, "Rockefeller has also enjoyed for years the regular services of a shadow cabinet made up of some of the country's top-level curatorial names." And "Rockefeller decisions tend to be handed down promptly, with the check—drawn on one of the innumerable Rockefeller accounts—following shortly thereafter. 'Best pay in town,' claims one dealer."[8]

It was also art that got him into trouble at Rockefeller Center. With his usual zeal, he commissioned Mexican Marxist Diego Rivera to adorn the 63 by 17 foot lobby wall of 30 Rockefeller Plaza with a fresco of American scenes. The preliminary sketch was harmless enough, but Rivera's revolutionary fervor was rekindled once he entered the newly constructed capitalist shrine. The anonymous man in the mural was suddenly replaced with the clearly recognizable figure of Lenin, his arms outstretched to a soldier and workers black and white who stood before unemployed masses waving red banners. Rivera's flat refusal to alter his artistry prompted a poem by E. B. White which concluded:[9]

"It's not good taste in a man like me,"
Said John D.'s grandson Nelson,
"To question an artist's integrity
"Or mention a practical thing like a fee,
"But I know what I like to a large degree
"Though art I hate to hamper;
"For twenty-one thousand conservative bucks
"You painted a radical. I say shucks,
    "I never could rent the offices—
    "The capitalistic offices.
"For this, as you now, is a public hall
"And people want doves, or a tree in fall,
"And though your art I dislike to hamper,
"I owe a little to God and gramper,
    "And after all,
    "It's my wall . . ."
    "We'll see if it is," said Rivera.*

It was. Through a subordinate, Nelson fired Rivera and paid him off in full with a single stroke of the pen. The unfinished figure was chipped off the wall. Years later, having either forgotten the fiasco or having become more open-minded, Rockefeller would proclaim that "art is probably one of the few areas left where there is absolute freedom."[10]

But Nelson was also in the enviable position of having creative people create what he wanted, whether it was adopting

---

* From "I Paint What I See," in *The Fox of Peapack* by E. B. White. Copyright 1929, 1957 by E. B. White. Reprinted by permission of Harper & Row, Publishers, Inc.

Picasso patterns to tapestries or adapting the blueprints of the mammoth Albany Mall to conform to his fancy of the moment. "He said to me," architect Wallace Harrison sighed, " 'I want, if it's possible, to get a great wall at the end of it . . . to get four buildings, skyscrapers.' If he wanted something, he would come out for it." Harrison also recalls Rockefeller hammering six-foot-high stakes into the sandy soil to mark the panoramic windows he wanted in his summer retreat in Seal Harbor. "He said, 'Now go make a house for them to fit in.' He didn't think it was tough."[11]

Harrison sheds more light on why Nelson never became an architect. It wasn't simply that he couldn't justify it to himself. He couldn't justify it to his mother. "His mother wouldn't let him," Harrison remembered. "She said, 'You just have too important a job to do in life.' "[12]

Meanwhile, Rockefeller was about to embark on a leapfrogging employment pattern in and out of government service with the ultimate leap destined to be into the White House. Picture an up-and-coming executive energetically climbing two ladders of success simultaneously—one foot in the private sector and one in the public.

The first public rung was to be in South America, where his road to recognition had already been paved—for good and ill—by two family fronts. First, the Rockefeller Foundation had made such strides in eradicating yellow fever and other poverty-related health and education problems that one leading Latin publisher was prompted to proclaim: "Because of the great good that the foundation has done throughout South America, that name is welcomed there as the sign of the Red Cross is welcomed and respected throughout the world."[13]

But the Rockefeller family was also blamed for the barbed-wire welcome extended the South American citizenry by branches of Creole Petroleum, the Standard Oil subsidiary whose board Nelson joined in 1935 as a minority stockholder. And when he made his first extended tour of Latin America in 1937, after taking a cram course in Spanish at the Berlitz School,

Nelson encountered bitter anti-Americanism that had been festering under the colonial yoke of companies like Creole.

He returned struck by the realization that such tactics jeopardized the very survival of foreign firms on South American soil. Lecturing Standard Oil officials on "the social responsibility of corporations" and launching local development ventures in Venezuela after a second trip in 1939, Rockefeller was spurred by what seemed like a sensible, albeit pioneering, piece of logic. What's good for the natives is good for social stability, which is good for Standard Oil, which is good for the Rockefeller family, which is good for America.

Apparently America agreed. A Rockefeller-formed brain trust, the first of many, captured the attention of President Franklin D. Roosevelt's alter ego, Harry Hopkins. Nelson was summoned to Washington, where he outlined his plans for a "hemisphere economic policy" and was offered his first federal post by FDR and the New Deal Democrats at the age of 32.

"Most of the things I've done in my life," he would explain later, "have been because I've written a memo to someone suggesting someone ought to do something."[14]

Naturally, Nelson cleared it with his family—including his father, who had not forgotten the unfriendliness toward the Rockefellers of the first President Roosevelt. And the most politically astute member of the Rockefeller clan also sought one more assurance. He flew to Utah to consult with Wendell Willkie, who was stumping for the presidency under the Republican banner. So sensitive was the mission that Nelson traveled incognito, ironically under the name of "Mr. Franklin"—a footnote that would otherwise have been lost to history except for the fact that he forgot his overcoat in a Salt Lake City hotel, which then wrote him under his assumed name.[15]

On August 16, 1940, Rockefeller was formally installed by executive order as unsalaried coordinator of the awkwardly named Office for Coordination of Commercial and Cultural Relations Between the American Republics. Stepping on toes and slashing red tape, Rockefeller forged the office into an effective tool to combat both Nazis and Communists through blacklists of enemy firms, economic and social assistance, and propaganda.

The newly created coordinator's role marked the first time that Rockefeller worked for anyone outside the family or its subsidiaries. Still, as Rockefeller recalled, "I was a dollar-a-year employee, and I guess the first salary I had was as assistant secretary of state. The reason I never got a salary from my father was because he and I couldn't agree on one. We couldn't agree on my worth. It was sort of a running thing, and we never agreed. There was no tension about it. Relations between sons and fathers in those days was a very relaxed, reverential I'd say not quite, but respectful. So he would express an opinion and I would express great appreciation and say that I would rather work for him because I loved him and wanted to help him, as distinct from the remuneration which he offered. I got $9,000 as assistant secretary of state in 1944, and that was the first time I had a salary."[16]

While trust income provided pin money, Nelson would always collect his salaries from subsequent public posts—including a $1,300-a-month pension after his 15-year stint as governor. He apparently shared the assessment of staff chief William Ronan that "I've always thought that people who turned back their salaries did sort of a demeaning thing."[17]

At the Office of Inter-American Affairs, Rockefeller exhibited the same bubbling ebullience, the same unbridled energy that would produce both bold solutions and costly mistakes through out his career. During those early years in Washington, at least he had superiors to whom he had to apologize.

Typically, Rockefeller's first run-in with the bureaucratic brass came within months of his appointment. Impatient to produce results, he plunged into a propaganda campaign that poured $600,000 worth of contrived "travel" advertisements about the United States into South American newspapers—some of them owned by Nazi sympathizers. After being sternly rebuked by Roosevelt, Rockefeller suffered a second setback: a threat to remove the information program from his office and place it under the aegis of Information Coordinator William J.

Donovan and his aide, the president's son James. Standing his ground, the 33-year-old Rockefeller survived by calling in an old chit. He enlisted support from Mrs. Anna Rosenberg, a Roosevelt intimate since Albany days and former labor relations consultant at Rockefeller Center, who intervened with FDR on Nelson's behalf.

Feeling more secure with a pipeline to the president, Rockefeller squared off next against George Messersmith, the U.S. ambassador to Mexico, who was casting a jealous eye on the relatively successful Mexican branch of the Inter-American Affairs information office. Rockefeller flatly threatened to withdraw funding for local projects already under way and shift the burden to the ambassador's budget. Messersmith surrendered.

Over the years, Nelson was to resort to the same rough tactics he employed at Rockefeller Center when confronted with any major obstacle. He expanded his office's press section under Pulitzer Prize-winner Francis Jamieson and exploited American control of the seas to keep newsprint from pro-Nazi publishers. He also supervised a slush fund for "incidentals and miscellaneous expenses" piled up by visiting Latin American journalists in Washington.[18] "You have to fight propaganda with the truth," Rockefeller would piously proclaim. "If that doesn't work, nothing will. If the truth won't work, then you're licked anyway."[19]

In addition to disseminating the truth, Rockefeller sought to foster closer ties between the business communities of the South American republics as chairman of the Inter-American Development Commission and as ranking American member of a similar commission in Mexico which successfully rehabilitated rail service. Throughout, he tapped the family fortune to fly political leaders, editors, and other image makers to private parties, an opportunity not available to career diplomats with relatively meager expense accounts.

Despite personality rifts at the State Department, Rockefeller was appointed by FDR to the newly created post of assistant secretary for American republic affairs late in 1944—another job he had lobbied to have established and expressed surprise about when he was selected to fill it. But bureaucratic infighting and resentment against Rockefeller's easy access to his superiors was to doom his advancement, a pattern that was to repeat itself when he served in two subsequent administrations.

Rockefeller remained at State just over eight months before being fired by President Harry Truman. There were several occasions during his career when his road to higher office was blocked. But this was the last time he was actually ousted from anything before he was ready to leave. The sore point was Argentina, which he had first tried to woo from the Axis camp before taking the more tolerant tack of pressing for admission of the Buenos Aires regime into the fledgling United Nations. At the San Francisco Conference, he and Harold Stassen also devised a mutual defense provision for the UN charter that ignited new controversy among career diplomats and congressmen but later proved important to the West in the form of pacts like the North Atlantic Treaty Organization (NATO). As if that wasn't enough, newly named Secretary of State James F. Byrnes was not happy with his inherited assistant and wanted his own man. Truman accepted Rockefeller's "resignation" on August 25, 1945.

"He wanted to be secretary of state," Wallace Harrison would recall three decades later. "Sometime just after they closed the Inter-American Affairs Office, he wanted very badly to be secretary of state. He found out how strong the secretary of state was in relation to his own office. Roosevelt saw Nelson climbing up to heights and power, more than anybody else. A lot of those people got so sore at him for having so much power. They pushed him out flat on his can. But goddamn it, in life you can't get all the things you want, and Rockefeller hasn't got all the things he wants—with all of it. He was perfectly content up to that time with an appointive job. I think the Department of State was probably the biggest thing he wanted and didn't get."[20]

Although, as Harrison remarks, Nelson never achieved that coveted post himself, every secretary of state since Dean Acheson had some link to the Rockefeller family or its interests.

For the first time in five years, Nelson was out of work—which meant that he could pursue his special interests privately with almost all the power and none of the red tape. Over the next few years, he founded a personal foreign aid program that for more than 30 years would straddle a fine line between philanthropy and national policy.

CHAPTER 4

Dollar Diplomacy

IN 1946, Nelson formed the American International Association for Economic and Social Development, which solicited contributions from Creole and other companies and provided seed money and training for local relief projects in South America. "I felt a deep personal concern for the Latins," recalled Rockefeller years later. "Here was where I could [help] because of the family money. That was the first time really that I did anything with it."[1]

The brothers, with Nelson in the lead, also launched the International Basic Economy Corporation. IBEC created local profit-making companies in fields as diverse as chicken breeding and housing construction. IBEC was a bootstrap operation whose ventures often made it a nonprofit outfit involuntarily. It offered Rockefeller the opportunity to unleash his imagination without the restraints of bureaucracy and accountability. When the company ran in the red, it was mostly his loss and he would accept it. The results, like Rockefeller's later record, included successes (hybrid corn seed, improved milk production, and supermarket chains, among others) and unmitigated disasters (a Peruvian sugar plantation, a Spanish tricycle factory, and a fish processing plant). "Ironically," one observer reported from Caracas, "the Rockefeller many Venezuelans speak of fondly here is far better known for his three decades of quixotic business failures and successes than for his political career or his family's large petroleum and banking interests. To Venezuelans, the former governor of New York was the 'gringo' who failed first as a philanthropist and subsequently as a farmer, rancher, fish merchant, wholesale grocer, and investor in many less publicized but equally unrewarding ventures."[2]

In addition to multimillion-dollar contributions from Standard Oil subsidiary ventures, Nelson also sought the cooperation of his brother's bank. As early as 1951, IBEC and Chase Manhattan jointly launched the Interamerican Finance and Investment Corporation, an investment banking and counselling service that was abandoned within four years. Many years later, Vice-President Rockefeller again turned to a friendly face for help. This time, on December 31, 1974, IBEC found itself unable to meet some of the provisions of a note on which it had borrowed from two insurance companies, and was also unable to comply with a credit agreement negotiated with a banking syndicate headed by Chase Manhattan. Nelson and Laurance Rockefeller persuaded IBEC's two groups of creditors to grant a temporary extension of the credit agreements and to guarantee $3 million of credit on their own. The January 6, 1975, agreement was disclosed in a two-paragraph press release a week later. It said only that IBEC's "principal interests" had agreed to the loan guarantees, although it neglected to note exactly who those interests were.

"IBEC executives say they see nothing improper in the deal between the Rockefeller-managed lender and the Rockefeller-managed borrower," the *Wall Street Journal* reported dryly. "The credit, they say, was arranged at 'arm's length,' as if strangers, rather than relatives, were arranging it."[3]

When Nelson Rockefeller loaned former U.S. Treasury Secretary Robert B. Anderson $84,000 to buy IBEC stock in 1957, there were no relatives involved. But neither did that transaction involve strangers. Anderson was deputy defense secretary when Rockefeller was President Eisenhower's special assistant for international affairs. IBEC was by then having some modest success, Rockefeller recalled, and he suggested to Anderson that he borrow some money to invest in the family firm.

Describing Anderson as "President Eisenhower's No. 1 choice to be president of the United States,"[4] Rockefeller said the former deputy secretary "was trying to make some money, and he was a good friend of mine and I liked him very much."[5] So Anderson bought 2,500 shares of IBEC in January 1957 for $60,000 and another 1,000 shares that April for $24,000 with a ten-year installment note. Eight days after his nomination as treasury secretary that June, Anderson said, "I disposed of the stock in accordance with the right of first refusal. I offered it back to Nelson Rockefeller for the same price I paid for it and he accepted. It was just a plain stock purchase."[6] There was, however, a hitch to the deal that led congressional staff investigators to question the "coincidence" of the securities transactions and IBEC's involvement in the treasury secretary's subsequent sale of oil leases.

After he bought back the IBEC stock, Rockefeller recalled, Anderson "had some other business activities which included wildcat wells, drilling operations. He was a Texan. And he had a couple of partners, Toddy Lee Wynne I think was the name of one of them, and they had lunch with me one day to see whether I would buy out some of those investments because he didn't feel he ought to own some of those investments when he was in as secretary of the treasury. And he was willing to take notes, and his partner had an idea that if it was successful, they would pay more, and if less successful, they would pay less, and I had a very good counsel who said, 'Look, you can't get into this kind of relationship with the secretary of the treasury where if his business is successful you get more or less.' So we finally said forget us, we'd like to help, but those circumstances are such that we just can't. So I did not. And he set up a corporation, and that corporation bought his interest."

Later, Rockefeller continued, "Toddy Lee Wynne came to me and asked if I would buy $150,000 now at a fixed price of that company, which owned various assets. I expressed a desire to help because he needed cash when he had to do some drilling in connection with some of the wildcat wells, and that's why he wanted to sell some of the stock, because the wells were no good if you do not drill them. About that time I got elected governor of New York, so I turned it over to IBEC, said if they wanted it they can have it. They negotiated and finally bought, I think, $150,000 of stock in this company."[7]

The company that IBEC bought into had agreed to pay Anderson up to $900,000 for his oil leases—payments that depended, in part, on the price of oil over several years.

Anderson was not the only official to whom Rockefeller touted the soundness of IBEC stock. Another was Anna Rosenberg, the former Rockefeller Center labor consultant, intimate of Franklin Roosevelt, assistant defense secretary, and public relations adviser to various Rockefeller campaigns. In 1957, she said, "we were working on his IBEC project in Venezuela, and he suggested to some of the staff that we buy stock and pay him off in ten years with 3 percent interest."[8] Mrs. Rosenberg paid Rockefeller $6,900. And then she waited for IBEC's marketing miracles to materialize. She was still waiting in 1967 when she sold her stock for $5,370.45 and, after deducting interest payments, suffered a $630 loss. Would she accept any more stock tips from Rockefeller? "No, thank you very much,"[9] Mrs. Rosenberg emphatically replied.

These IBEC transactions illustrate Nelson's unbridled assurance and carefree optimism; yet for sheer *chutzpah* and self-confidence, none of Rockefeller's postwar ventures could compare with the way in which he arranged to have the United Nations headquarters located on Manhattan's East Side. He joined with Francis Jamieson, Wally Harrison, and John Lockwood to convince real estate tycoon William Zeckendorf to sell the Rockefellers 17 acres of land—the money for the purchase to come from Nelson's father, who also needed a bit of convincing.

The story began in 1946 when Nelson generously offered the Rockefeller Center Theater for a meeting of the UN General

Assembly. "This fact was publicized," reminisced Frank Jamieson.[10] But "it became a source of personal embarrassment to Nelson because he found he could not deliver on his offer. It was an offer made impulsively in his desire to serve the UN, in which he and the members of his family had so much confidence. However, it turned out that the . . . Theater was under lease for other purposes, and Nelson was unable to work out an arrangement with his father, who owned the center. I think perhaps Nelson, in his enthusiasm, was slightly resentful of his father's inability to do so. Insofar as I was able to judge, it was inability on his father's part, with perhaps some unwillingness or slight resentment that there'd been no consultation in advance of the offer. It was basically a problem of human relations."

With the site selection committee racing a deadline, the choice narrowed to Westchester County or Philadelphia, with some minor interest in the East River parcel owned by Zeckendorf. Rough plans for a $100 million dream city on the site were already being drafted for Zeckendorf by Wallace Harrison.

When the possibility of Westchester was mentioned, Nelson asked: "Do you mean our place?"

"Well," Jamieson replied, "that would be a place, but I hadn't concretely thought of it."

Nelson didn't stop to think. Jamieson recalled that the 38-year-old Rockefeller "immediately rose to the challenge. . . . Maps of the area were sent for. They were laid on the floor, and we all looked them over. This was the first mention of the Rockefeller family estate as a potential site. It was not the first mention of Westchester. The hard facts of the matter were that it was one of the few places in Westchester where there was an undevelopd land area reasonably close to New York, susceptible to development as a UN site."

After studying the maps, Jamieson continued, "Nelson decided that he would have to take the matter up with his father to see if his father would be willing to give up all of the estate or part of it. His brothers David, Laurance, and John were consulted, and after some natural hesitation all agreed that if it seemed desirable, they would be willing to throw in their properties. I remember one rather touching or unique incident on the part of David, who had just recently redone a house which he planned to move into. He asked, 'Couldn't I give money instead?' When told that this wouldn't serve the purpose, he said all right, he'd be glad to go along."

Nelson then went to lunch with his father, who, as Jamieson remembered, "was totally unaware of the proposition—that he give up the home that he had known since his marriage and in which his children had been raised. He was to make a decision within an hour or two about whether to do so. He was agreeable."

While Rockefeller family agents sought options on adjacent acreage, in Westchester, Harrison was enlisting the support of Robert Moses and city officials to clear any obstacles to the East River site. By mid-afternoon, Nelson was focusing on two potential sites which until that morning had not been seriously considered by the selection committee. Around 8 P.M., enough land had been assembled in Westchester to fulfill the requirements of the new world organization, and Harrison had determined that Zeckendorf would part with his property for $8.5 million. Nelson phoned Senator Warren Austin, chief of the United States delegation to the UN, who suggested that representatives of the organization would rather be in New York City.

"Shortly after eight o'clock," Jamieson recalled, "Nelson's father telephoned to ask what the state of affairs on the project was. Nelson explained what had been done about Westchester and what had been done about the East River location. Nelson repeated his conversation with Senator Austin. Then, after a moment's silence—'Why, Pa! That's most generous!' and he hung up the phone.

"He turned to us and said, 'Father has authorized us to offer up to $8.5 million for the East River site as a donation from him to the UN, if it's so desired. His only condition was that the federal government agree to make this tax-free.' While the average person would assume that such a gift would be tax-free, Mr. Rockefeller made this request from experience. A gift he had made to the League of Nations had not been tax-free, so he specified that this one should be."

Harrison was dispatched to find Zeckendorf and make him the offer. He finally caught up with the flamboyant business-man at the old Monte Carlo nightclub and consummated the deal with Zeckendorf's signature on a rough city map.

John D., Jr. signed the papers the next morning, and Nelson got up after breakfast to deliver the documents to Senator Austin. As he was about to leave, reports Jamieson, "his father reached up and grabbed his coat and said rather gently, 'Will this make up for the Center Theater?' " Apparently, it did.

CHAPTER 5

The Polished
Professional

THE UN venture was heady stuff, to be sure, but Nelson had not yet satisfied his public ambitions. After occasionally communicating with Truman about foreign policy, Rockefeller was invited in 1950 to chair the new International Advisory Board that had been established by the president's Point Four legislation. Naturally, the *Partners in Progress* report concluded that a new Office of Overseas Economic Administration be created to coordinate foreign aid. Ironically, Rockefeller was undercut by W. Averell Harriman, who favored a Mutual Security Agency that would stress military aid instead. Truman opted for the Harriman plan and named him director of the new agency. And Rockefeller resigned as advisory board chairman.

Truman did make one other offer, however. The president proposed that Nelson switch parties and become a Democrat. "I don't believe in party switching," he would explain later, adding obscurely, "I really would rather pull people forward than hold people back. If I was in the Republican Party I was pulling the party forward. And if I'd have been in the Democratic Party I would have been in the position of holding people back."[1] It was obviously not the offer Nelson was looking for.

Years later, he would say the same of similar urgings from Lyndon Johnson at Camp David in 1968 and a feeler from Hubert Humphrey that same year about being the Minnesota senator's running mate on the Democratic ticket. Seven years after, frustrated by the vice-presidency, he said, no doubt ruefully, that had he switched parties he would have been president long ago.

The setback at Harriman's hands lasted only for the duration of the Truman administration. Less than a month after Dwight Eisenhower swept in the first Republican administration in 20 years, Rockefeller was named to chair a three-member Advisory Committee on Government Organization. It only took about five weeks for the committee to suggest to the president that it continue advising on an ongoing basis. Congress later okayed a key recommendation of the committee, creation of a unified cabinet-level Department of Health, Education, and Welfare, and Eisenhower selected Federal Security Administrator Oveta Culp Hobby as HEW secretary. At her request, Nelson was named under secretary and really ran the department. That was the last time he was directly under anybody except the president.

It was not, however, his last federal role. In 1954, Eisenhower thrust Rockefeller back into the bureaucratic fray as special assistant for foreign affairs, a post in which he not only clashed with old State Department foes from San Francisco days but ran into resistance from Treasury Secretary George Humphrey and Budget Director Rowland Hughes, who had already been impressed by his propensity to spend.

After running secret security seminars at Quantico and teaming up with Stassen again to press the president for an "open skies" arms agreement at the Geneva summit conference, Rockefeller was ready for a cabinet post. The cabinet, however, wasn't ready for him. He was offered under secretary of defense by outgoing Defense Secretary Charles Wilson, Rockefeller recalled, "but when Humphrey got wind of it and George told the president I'd wreck the budget with my spending, that settled that."[2]

Suffering from severe frustration, Rockefeller resigned at the end of 1955 because of "compelling personal responsibilities."[3] What was really so compelling was the rude confirmation that elective office carried a lot more clout. And that was the course he was now ready to pursue.

But first, some more studies. Rockefeller assembled influential representatives of organized labor, industry, communications, and academia to chart the best course for the country to pursue midway through the twentieth century. Later, Republican State Chairman L. Judson Morhouse, who was searching for someone who could at least run a credible race against Harriman, who had been elected governor of New York in 1954, promoted Rockefeller onto the bipartisan State Commission on a Constitutional Convention. Ironically, Harriman ended a heated deadlock over the commission chairmanship by handing it to Rockefeller and launching his political career.

Finally, on June 30, 1958, in a sticky office on the 56th floor of 30 Rockefeller Plaza, the grandson of the most prominent proponent of "public be damned" policy appealed to the public for its support. Announcing his candidacy for the Republican gubernatorial nomination, Nelson Rockefeller formally spurned the family fear of publicity and took his first official step on the path to the presidency.

"It was always something looming in the future for him," nephew Jay Rockefeller would recall later. "I've always seen that as a possibliity for him since 1959."[4]

Ever since he inadvertently shot himself in the shin, thereby gaining his first taste of publicity, Nelson Rockefeller lusted for the limelight. Perhaps because he jealously protected his privacy, he overcompensated in his public role by plunging into problem solving. Looming ahead, always, was the impossible dream.

"He's the kind of person who thinks far ahead," his brother David declared, when asked when Nelson first dreamed of the presidency. "My guess is it was early on. I suspect he's been interested in public life from a very early age. The example of grandfather Aldrich was an important factor. I don't think it was something that occurred to him the year he ran for governor. I'm sure going way back before college that he was interested in a political life. His approach to all problems—including family problems—has been political: thinking through the strategy of how you go about achieving an objective."[5]

That's why, Laurance says, he was not surprised when Nelson stepped onto the political treadmill. "Traditionally," said Laurance, "the family always participated in responsible ways, so that greater opportunity for involvement with people in the common good was a way of life. This is nothing but an extension of it. I think this has been true of Nelson's life. One thing led to another, but philosophically, psychologically, emotionally it was a continuous life process. And it wasn't a crossroad or a sudden thing. It was a life-style."[6]

If it was not a life style by then, running for president and losing three times would make it one. Winning, of course, would have made the life-style all the more worthwhile.

It was a life-style that others close to him had trouble getting used to. Nelson, Laurance said, was "extraverted, outgoing, goal oriented." But the orientation toward that goal was accompanied by privacy-piercing events like the parties at Pocantico ("I can't stand all these reporters around all the time—they never leave us alone," Nelson's first wife told a total stranger) and the confirmation hearings in 1974, which exposed the family to unprecedented probing and publicity ("Traumatic," David said of the experience[7]).

"His bag was just work," says Alton Marshall, who served as chief of staff to the governor. "And for a guy like Nelson Rockefeller to take the shit that he took? I know I couldn't do it. I think his cross or his curse is that he's got to be part of the process of searching for solutions. If I heard that phrase once, I heard it 100,000 times. Does he get his jollies by having power that people bestow rather than financial power? I'm sure."[8]

For Nelson Rockefeller it was not a matter of "rather." "He

is absolutely absorbed in his work," Marshall says. "Obviously, he doesn't have to leave to pick up the laundry or pay a light bill. He's a tough man to work for. The ideas he comes up with have to be ready for him the next morning."[9]

Ronald Maiorana, a former New York *Times* reporter who served Rockefeller as press secretary, agrees: "There is no way the man could humanly do what he does, except that the plane is waiting, the car is waiting. And when he said, 'I want something done,' you don't say 'I'll take care of it.' You get up and do it."[10]

Nelson's inauguration in 1959 followed his stunning upset over Harriman and vindication of the Rockefeller name at the polls. He had evened the score in a match of multimillionaires. And he had proved that antipathy to the Rockefellers had been mellowed by a magical attraction to the man in the street.

"If the rich are capitalism's aristocracy," author William Manchester observed, "the Rockefellers are its royalty."

His speech was consistently sprinkled with superlatives. The simplest accomplishments were hailed as "terrific" or "fantastic" or "tremendous." Searching for an even more praiseworthy adjective one day to describe the record of his regional transportation chief, Rockefeller brought down the house when he landed on "horrendous."[11] His monotonous public speaking style was always surpassed by the spontaneous, pithy remarks with which he crushed or confused his critics.

At one town meeting he hosted as governor, a man rose in the rear of an upstate auditorium and asked: "Governor, I'm a Zero Population Growth believer—how do you stand on restricting the number of children in a family to two?" Holding back a grin, Rockefeller peered at the man for a moment over the podium and replied almost apologetically: "I was the third child."[12]

Testifying before an executive sesssion of a Senate committee, Rockefeller encountered criticism from Republican William Langer of North Dakota. Not only had he voted against

The Polished Professional

Rockefeller's confirmation for the Latin American affairs post, the senator said, but he had also "been thinking of suing . . . for years. Your greatgrandfather," he told Rockefeller, "sold my father $200 worth of fake medicine."

"How long did you father live?" Rockefeller asked confidently.

"Well, he was in his nineties when he died," Langer replied.

"That," Rockefeller remarked, "wouldn't help your case much in court."[13]

To the voters he was "Rocky" or "the Rock." To a small circle of intimates, he was "Nelson." To an even more exclusive group, he would secretly be referred to as "Fang" when warmth gave way to snappishness—especially if Rockefeller was pressed about some personal or political matter he chose not to reveal.

Privately, he could afford to be gracious when it proved more effective than browbeating. Manhattan GOP boss Albano remembers that on every visit to the governor's West 55th Street office, "he always had a pot of coffee and coffee cake—and there's the great Rockefeller waiting for you."

Graciousness was obviously a growth process, however, because the story recounted by Rockefeller associate William J. Ronan of their first encounter in 1956 was singularly more stiff: "The governor-to-be took coffee, and the young lady serving some goodies along with it came over with a tray which had Danish pastry and one glazed doughnut. It was passed to me, and I took the glazed doughnut. When I did, I thought she was going to drop the tray because that obviously had been intended for Governer Rockefeller. The next day, when I appeared for the second conversation, there were two glazed doughnuts on the tray. This was the beginning of my association with Nelson Rockefeller."[14]

Despite some holes in Ronan's recollection, the doughnut episode presumably proved how well Rockefeller could accept defeat. After all, tomorrow is another day.

"He had a tremendous energy—always a sense that things are possible," said Jay Rockefeller. "It was optimism tempered by experience—a great positive sense, unlike others who through public years become more jaded."[15]

That sense of the possible probably stemmed from the fact that anything—well, almost anything—could be purchased without noticeably affecting the family fortune.

Perhaps for this reason, although Nelson was clearly aware that he was rich, he could not even imagine what it meant to be poor. Attempting to explain how much he was like the typical American taxpayer, Rockefeller observed:

"I understand bookkeeping, and I presume that this is the procedure that most Americans follow. And as I got to where I had a checking account, then I had to put the check numbers down and make the checking account balance and so forth. There were times when the account was overdrawn. . . . There are procedures which are standard procedures which I think all of us should—if we don't, should follow. Probably most people do.

"At the present time, I make up a budget at the beginning of the year based on estimated income, availability of funds for giving, for expenditures, for taxes, etc. So that in a sense [is] the same, but on a larger scale, as what I did before. I get monthly statements, so that I know where things are in relation to the budget. I review a payment of bills, relating to whatever the subject happens to be, and approve them. Then they're paid by the accounting department of the office. Since being elected governor, I no longer handle investments of my own account. I used to do that. That's an interesting and important area for anybody—is how to invest their money, wisely and so forth.

"On the giving, I follow that. I think that's about the only way. I would say the only difference is I don't write checks."[16]

Nelson never seemed to understand what money meant to other people—their money or his money—although he quickly got used to questions about it. Campaigning for the Nixon-Lodge ticket in 1960, he bumped into a Republican booster in the New York City subway. "How does it feel to be rich?" the attractive young lady asked. "Fine," Rockefeller replied with gusto. "How's it feel to be good-looking?"[17]

Later that day, he demonstrated a mind-boggling insensitivity to other people's money troubles. It was a classic scene. En route to a rally near Macy's in Herald Square, Rockefeller was confronted by a panhandler. They exchanged a few words, and then the governor ebulliently backslapped his way down the block. But the panhandler was frozen in bewilderment. "That's funny," he muttered to a passerby "I asked him for a handout, and you know what he promised me? A tax cut!"[18]

Rockefeller was just as casual about his own out-of-pocket expenses—usually because they came out of someone else's pocket. After seeing President Johnson off from the Buffalo airport one sweltering summer afternoon, Nelson walked by the sweaty motorcycle escort when one fellow shouted: "How about a round of beer, Rocky?" "Sure," the governor grinned, checked his wallet and then turned to his counsel, Robert Douglass, to glom a $10 bill. "It's become an affectation,"[19] Douglass said later. Unlike his grandfather, Rockefeller often neglects to carry dimes for the phone calls, tips, and other sundries that even the typical American can afford.

With this blithe disregard for the ordinary cares of life comes a kind of moral blindness that springs from the wedding of great wealth and systematically instilled religious beliefs. Nelson's morality is based on the misconception that someone who is good can do no real wrong, that mistakes can be excused because they were not based on evil motives, that great riches are God-given and are obviously being disbursed according to God's will. It is this kind of insulation that kept Rockefeller from Attica and his father from Ludlow, and that led to this defense by young Nelson of his grandfather's silence "in the face of the bitterest attack and slander" regarding Standard Oil:

There are two main reasons [why he kept silent]: 1. That the accusations were false and therefore would fall of their own weight when time had revealed the truth. 2. That if any public explanation of the real reasons for the great and quick success of the company were attempted it might have been made so full and explicit that it would necessarily invite other capitalists to come into the business and do likewise.[20]

That was more than mere family loyalty.

Similarly, during his controversial confirmation hearing in 1974, he encountered Arthur Goldberg, who had come to testify about the distorted campaign biography that Rockefeller operatives produced in 1970. Slapping the staid former Supreme Court justice on the shoulder and grinning broadly, the vice-presidential nominee welcomed him with a hearty "Thanks for coming!" The incredible scene of the aggrieved Goldberg being embraced by the grinning former governor provoked *Harper's* editor Lewis Lapham to opine:

> I suspect that he intended nothing cynical or disingenuous. His assumption that Mr. Goldberg would forgive him follows from his imperturbable faith in his own innocence. His misapprehension of the facts is characteristic of men who inherit great wealth. They cannot believe themselves capable of anything discreditable, and as a rule they know almost nothing about money or political reality. They have no reason to learn.[21]

An "imperturbable faith"? "That's true," Rockefeller replied unabashedly. Hasn't he ever even made a mistake? "Sure," he said, "but that's not innocence. Innocence, I suppose, relates to a crime. Making mistakes everyone does; we're all human. I expect to make mistakes. The only thing I would say about when I make a mistake is I've simply said, all right, I've made a mistake, I'll learn from that and I'm not going to do it again, rather than worry about it or feel guilty. I've never felt guilty. I mean, I do my best. If I make a mistake, okay. I've made a mistake and I learn and I'm not going to do it again. But I don't understand this guilt business."[22]

The Polished Professional

The most outgoing of the Rockefellers and trained to "surmount privilege," Nelson also followed motherly advice to seek out superiors. That practice sometimes had a positive effect: it made him a compulsive achiever as a Dartmouth upperclassman. But it also allowed him to surround himself with a layer of "experts"—not all of whom were—that further insulated him from the real world. Rockefeller said it himself after Attica, explaining: "I have always had a policy in my administration or wherever I have been to try to pick the best people I can, give them the broad policy direction, and support them in their own operations."[23] In other words, he didn't have to go to Attica because his expert—in this case Correction Commissioner Russell Oswald—was on the scene.

It was also Rockefeller's style to tap the best talent available, whether through his presumptuous freshman call on the president of Dartmouth or, later, through the 82 task forces he created over 15 years as governor of New York. Like the art collector he is, Nelson placed prized "acquisitions" in various institutions and adorned the office with his favorites.

Even Rockefeller's family became a political asset in his first campaign. Although privacy was always guaranteed by the guarded gates of Pocantico and the secrecy of his schedule, the early campaigns played upon his sense of family responsibility and how well he fulfilled the roles of devoted husband and father. And that is precisely why the shock waves reverberated so far when he announced the separation from his wife of 31 years shortly after election day in 1961. Their long estrangement ended in divorce the following March. Timid and taciturn, "Tod" was simply not a political wife. Politically, the repercussions were even greater when 14 months later, he married the charming Margaretta (Happy) Murphy, another Philadelphia Main Liner who had worked on his staff and whose former husband was a microbiologist at the Rockefeller Institute.

The second Mrs. Rockefeller was noticeably unhappy about her husband's elevation to the vice-presidency after a one-year stint as private citizen. "As a concerned citizen, I'm thrilled," she responded weakly, dutifully adding that "for me personally, it's the beginning of a new adventure."[24]

Although Rockefeller's strict Baptist upbringing generally did not extend to his social life, he perused a staff man's copy of *Playboy* once and exclaimed: "Hey! How long have they been publishing this kind of thing?" Long before his appointment of Caroline Simon as New York's first woman secretary of state inspired wisecracks from politicians who had staked out the post, Nelson took some gentle ribbing from brother Laurance, who had borrowed his Buick roadster in 1928. "I didn't know the road," he confided to Nelson later, "but I just turned your car loose on the highway and it headed for the nearest girl's college, you have it so well trained."[25] "I had two choices," recalled Rockefeller, who once taught a Sunday school class for pre-adolescent girls. "I could have become a gigolo or a governor."[26]

Cars, speed, and mechanical equipment always excited him. When he was at Dartmouth, his unrestrained desire for that Buick roadster drove him to write his father:

> I can't imagine anything more ideal than that black Buick we saw. But if you would rather get the five passenger car I would be tickled to death to have it. My honest opinion is though that the roadster would fill the ticket by far the best— taking all things into consideration.[27]

And after his father finally capitulated, Nelson sent another note:

> There's one thing I've thought of . . . I really hate to ask you. . . . Could I have two mirrors put on the wheels that are on the sides of the car? . . . I'd be glad to pay for them myself only I really can't afford it at present.[28]

Even when he was campaigning in 1958, fast cars had the same attraction. Waiting with confidant George Hinman for his plane at Westchester County Airport, Rockefeller spotted a stunning red Ferrari. "That's really what I'd like to have," he told the ex-

tremely restrained Hinman, who saw more in Nelson's statement than merely an interest in another car. "Well," he replied,
"you can take your choice. You can have your sports car or be
a governor—you can't do both."[29]

Rockefeller is somewhat more subdued now, and he spends
more time instilling responsibility in his two youngest sons, in
addition to leading them in prayer every morning over yogurt
breakfasts and watching television with them at night. He recalls
that when Nelson, Jr. was four, he wanted to help his father
arrange a display of valuable art objects at Pocantico. When
the youngster picked up a priceless vase and began carrying it
across the stone floor, a servant rushed to intervene. "But I said
to let him do it," Rockefeller remembered. "He wasn't going to
drop the vase. And even if he did, what's a vase really matter
when you're trying to teach a child to be responsible?"[30]

It was the kind of political balancing act that Rockefeller had
been performing for years never dropping the symbolic vase,
yet never reaching the far end of the corridor of power. Out sick
only three days in 25 years, he has always been endowed with
stamina more than equal to his quest. He persisted with the
kind of drive that an osteopath can prolong but only destiny can
sustain. "Nature gave me a strong body," he once explained. "I
can keep going when a lot of other people fold up. If I have
nothing else, I have plenty of vitality. Hard work like campaigning doesn't bother me."[31] And of course, it is all for a purpose, all for the ultimate goal—the presidency.

If Rockefeller should reach that goal, there will be no more
excuses. The authority of government is largely concentrated
in one man. "Power per se is good or bad depending on how it is
used," says Rockefeller. But, he continues, "Power is essential.
This nation has to have power if we are going to preserve freedom
and the opportunity for our people. If we use it wisely, it would
be for good. If we use it wrong, in a wrong way, it would be
bad."[32]

Of course, as Harry Truman once said, power is one of three
things that can ruin a man. "One's power, one's money, and one's

women," said Truman. "If a man can accept a situation in a place of power with the thought that it's only temporary, he comes out all right. But when he thinks that he is the cause of the power, that can be his ruination."[33]

It is Nelson Rockefeller's unique use of power, both public and private, that sets him apart, and about which he remains remarkably philosophical. "Do something, hopefully right," he says, "and amend it as you learn by experience to improve it."[34]

In 1974, after rejecting vice-presidential offers from Republican Richard Nixon in 1960 and Democrat Hubert Humphrey in 1968, Rockefeller amended his game plan for the presidency. He told the House Judiciary Committee considering his nomination as Gerald Ford's vice-president that "the situation has changed so with the world problems and the national problems that the action is no longer at the statehouse level. The action is in Washington and on the national scene."[35] Apparently, a vice-president was no longer "standby equipment."

Passing over his three presidential bids, Rockefeller added: "I am 66 years old. I am not starting a new career, but I have had a great deal of experience. I have just stated that I consider this a moment of tremendous change and a great many problems but also great opportunities for our country and the world and that I am anxious to serve my country in any way that I can. I have to assume that that would not preclude the presidency."[36]

Only one man in American history, Dwight Eisenhower, turned 70 while he was president. So hasn't time now run out for Nelson Rockefeller?

"Did you ever know Golda Meir, Konrad Adenauer?" the vice-president replied with a wink. "I knew them well. Great people."[37]

How long Nelson Rockefeller's lifelong dream will continue to elude him is an open question. His father lived until he was 86, and his grandfather died at age 97. As for Nelson, he predicted recently: "I expect to live to be a hundred."[38]

Patience, grandfather Rockefeller had advised. Patience. And after six decades of subdued hedonism, were there any regrets, anything Nelson Rockefeller wanted that he wasn't able to get?

"Yes," he said. "I remember bidding in an auction on a Modigliani once and losing to the Museum of Modern Art, of which I was then president; and 14 years later, another one came on the market and I was fortunate enough to get it, so it shows if you've got patience and persistence, even though you may be thwarted at one point, you can. And I'm a great believer in that."[39]

Nelson and son, Rodman, with Nelson's only "hero"—JDR, Sr.

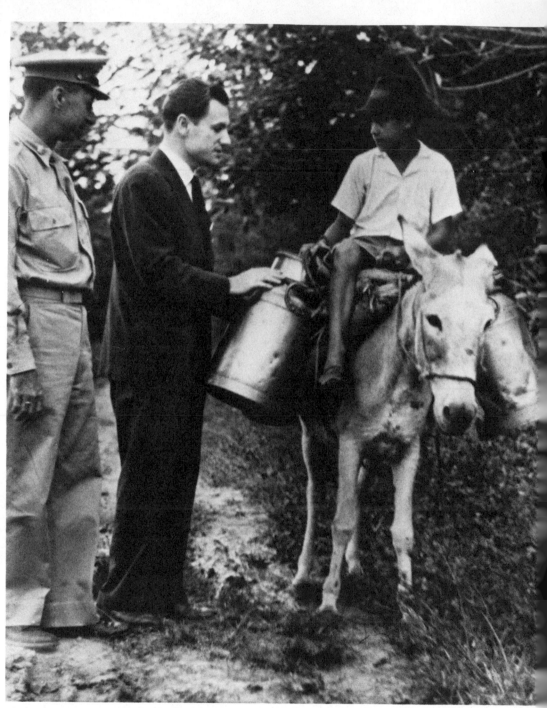

Nelson learns about Venezuela, firsthand, as wartime
Coordinator of Inter-American Affairs.

Nelson and Louis Lefkowitz, on Delancey Street,
tell a voter how it is. No baloney!

The winning team, 1958: Malcolm Wilson, Rocky,
Louis Lefkowitz, and Arthur Levitt.

New York Daily News

Though all smiles, Rocky and Dick eat each other's heart out at
breakfast, 1958. Perhaps Dick is glancing toward the future?

New York Daily News

Nelson and Jud Morhouse—"the biggest Republican in America."

New York Daily News

William Ronan smiles as Nelson accepts $74-million Triborough Bridge
and Tunnel Authority surplus check. Both men had reason to be
pleased with the financial arrangements that existed between them.

Nelson in an especially Happy moment—1963 wedding.

PART TWO

Capital Games:
The Art of
Governing

CHAPTER 6

Pointing the Finger
of Power

IN the chaotic closing days of the 1971 New York State legislative session, Albany was abuzz about a secret visit from Governor Rockefeller. The governor normally summoned lawmakers to the mahogany-paneled executive chamber and rarely met them on their own ground. So why, the wags wanted to know, did Rockefeller leave his second floor sanctuary to consult with Assembly Minority Leader Stanley Steingut one level above?

A bald and barrel-chested man whose smile resembles a smirk, Steingut had served as Brooklyn Democratic boss until 1969, when he relinquished the title of county chairman and turned over the reins to his insurance brokerage partner, Meade Esposito. Steingut's father, Irwin, had been speaker of the Assembly in the 1930s, but Stanley's lifelong dream to occupy that powerful post was shattered in 1965 after the Democrats captured control of the lower house for the first time in a decade. Republicans and rebel Democrats backed his fellow Brooklynite, Anthony J. Travia, and Steingut laid the blame for his defeat at Rockefeller's doorstep. But that was six years ago. On this June morning in 1971, Steingut was bristling over another matter—involving the same man.

Only the day before, Steingut and Rockefeller had met in the office of Perry B. Duryea, Jr., the prosperous silver-haired Long Island lobster salesman who served as Assembly speaker. Duryea needed Steingut's support for Rockefeller's Adirondack Park Agency plan, but the minority leader insisted on a personal commitment from the governor that the park agency's members would be appointed on a bipartisan basis. That much was settled in a matter of seconds.

But Rockefeller had something else on his mind. For years he had been struggling to build a bridge across Long Island Sound that linked the wealthy enclaves of Rye in Westchester County to those of Oyster Bay in Nassau County. The complaints of conservationists and a self-protective local population spurred the legislature to enact a bill that effectively stalled construction of the span. The governor promptly vetoed it. Now an attempt was under way to override that veto, and Rockefeller apparently assumed that state AFL–CIO President Raymond Corbett and other proponents of the span had enlisted Steingut's support.

No, the minority leader replied, the Democrats had taken a firm stand against the Oyster Bay Bridge. Rockefeller became enraged, accusing Steingut of making a deal for an override of his veto. As the insults intensified, the governor's counsel, Robert R. Douglass, walked to a window "as if to pray," one witness recalled. It was too late for prayer. Infuriated, Rockefeller struck Steingut, digging his fingers into the Minority Leader's chest. Stunned and shaken, Steingut denounced Rockefeller as "despicable" and stormed from the room.

The governor's visit the next morning was at Duryea's behest. Since Steingut still smarted emotionally and physically from the blow, Rockefeller rose to the occasion and came to apologize. "Yeah, I pushed Stanley," Rockefeller recalled, reenacting the incident after which Steingut half-jokingly regretted not having fallen to the floor writhing in pain—and collecting workmen's compensation. (Two years later, however, Steingut did sue New York City for $100,000 after he fractured his little toe in a pothole outside a Brooklyn polling place.)

Pointing the Finger of Power

"I pushed him with my finger in his chest," said Rockefeller, "and he took offense to it. I apologized to him afterward. There's no question of the incident. I did feel that whatever it was, that he had gone, gone, well, that he got confused. I don't like to say that anyone went back on his word. That there's been a misunderstanding over an agreement. I felt that whatever it was, there wasn't a carrying out of an understanding which I thought we had, or felt very sure we had. I was trying to emphasize my point and I guess I did so rather vigorously."[1]

"I sympathize with his character," Steingut would explain more dispassionately later. "It was unreal—that everything had to be his way. He operated government like he operated Pocantico Hills. And I understand it. It's the last feudal thing left in this country."[2]

Even Joseph Zaretzki, the former Senate Democratic leader and a frequent Rockefeller fan, recalled that dealing with the governor was a pleasure "unless he got mad. I don't think he would stomach too much real opposition to what he believes to be worthwhile. His training was that he always had his way."[3]

For 15 years, Nelson Rockefeller was the boss of New York. Nobody ever formally referred to him by that title. But having grasped public power, he ruled with an iron hand, compromising only to the extent that he would wait a little longer to get what he wanted or get it by giving away something he really never wanted at all. Regardless of party or personal ties, key critics were crushed and loyalists were rewarded. The degree of force may have varied, but the rule remained the same: it was always an "aye" for an "aye."

While he often operated from his unassuming midtown Manhattan townhouse, the Capitol in Albany was particularly suited to his style and worthy of a Rockefeller. The grandiose granite structure cost $25 million when it was finally finished after 32 years in 1899. Billed as an "intriguing blend of architecture," the Capitol's five stories incorporate Roman classical, Romanesque, neo-Greek, Gothic, Moorish, and Italian Renaissance styles.[4] The original design for a huge dome was rejected after

81

architects determined that the foundation—to say nothing of the taxpayers—would be unable to support it. From that bastion, no one in New York could state with more honesty: "L'état, c'est moi."

Nelson Rockefeller was already accustomed to the trappings of power when he entered office as a political novice in 1959. Armed with the family fortune, he parlayed the power that others had squandered into an efficient political machine that in some ways surpassed Huey Long's Louisiana.

For 15 years, in legislatures dominated by Democrats as well as Republicans, he was able to ram through bills under the guise of "public good." In fact, they were a codification of *his perception* of the public good—which ran from the boldly innovative to the radically wrong. The 15,000 laws he signed were passed by partisan politicians who, every two years, were compelled to place their political lives on the line in primaries and general election races. They became equally dependent on the public and on the governor, who was empowered to make appointments, approve projects, and both pass upon and pay bills that could be crucial to their biennial bids for reelection.

For at least the first half of his administration, Rockefeller virtually "owned" the Republican Party. Later, he decided it would be more discreet to let fat cat friends subsidize it while he forked over hefty rent checks in quadrennial installments. At the same time, he practically incorporated the debt-ridden Democrats as a wholly owned subsidiary of the GOP. Moreover, he unabashedly outbought, outmuscled, and outmaneuvered opponents in both parties to survice four tests at the polls in a state where registered Democrats regularly outnumbered Republicans.[5]

He also frequently reminded friends that although he was best known for his insatiable interest in architecture, he had begun his professional career as a businessman. And the same ruthless techniques that rented Rockefeller Center, guided his passion to serve, and furthered his quest for the presidency were what branded him as the ultimate power broker.

CHAPTER 7

The Unequal Branch

NOWHERE were those techniques more apparent than in the state legislature, a bicameral collection of 150 assemblymen and 60 state senators who were paid $15,000 plus $5,000 expenses during most of the Rockefeller regime to perform part-time public service. While the quality of the lawmakers seemed steadily to improve, there were enough cronies and incompetents to prompt pleas from the public that the post remain part time. ("I can show you some dummies," Alton Marshall once said in his midtown Manhattan office. "I can split on half a dozen right from here."[1]) Most of the lawmakers were lawyers who were in a position to profit from court patronage, the legal largesse of banks, unions, and insurance firms, and paid appearances before state regulatory agencies. Also sprinkled among the membership were businessmen, bankers, engineers, farmers, and a tentmaker.

Each Monday, during the legislative sessions that began in January and extended through the spring, they would bid good-bye to family and friends and make their lemming-like march to the decrepit capital city. If they arrived by rail, they would wind up on the east bank of the Hudson in Rensselaer—the trains didn't even stop in Albany anymore. Once there, they would check into musty downtown hotels or more lively and secluded motels on the outskirts of town. Then to their make-shift cubicles in the Capitol or more spacious but less convenient suites in the gleaming marble office building—replete with waterfall and dining room—in the mall across the street. A few hours in the red mahogany and leather Senate chamber or the gothic Assembly, and off for an evening of liquefied and lascivi-ous—if they were lucky—frolicking with fellow lawmakers, lobbyists, reporters, and private secretaries. They were perfect pawns for Rockefeller.

"He was a born diplomat," recalled former Speaker Joseph Carlino, who lost his Assembly seat in the 1964 Democratic sweep but who has remained close to Rockefeller since. "He could bring himself down to anybody's level."[2]

Unencumbered by the requirements of ordinary men and fortified with far greater energy, he often ran a one-man legisla-ture. "I worked with Democratic leaders and I had the Republi-can leaders," Rockefeller replied, in a masterstroke of under-statement, to congressmen concerned that he might similarly trample on the separation of powers as president or vice-president. "I had them totally in my confidence, took their ideas, tried to accommodate them in the development of legislation. The result of this was by the time I gave a message to the legis-lature, I was already aware of the general outline of the leaders' positions. They were aware of mine. It appeared that I was dominating but, in actual fact, that was the furthest from the truth."[3]

Anyone who has even been to Albany would blanch at the baldness of that statement. Rockefeller could wheel and deal with the best of them—and usually better—but avoided being tarred by the broad brush of boondoggle and boodle because he persuaded himself and almost everyone else that it was all for the good of the public.

Nelson also knew how to make people feel that he was acting for their *personal* good. After the Democrats assumed control of both houses in 1965, for instance, the governor proffered his plane to whisk Senate Majority Leader Zaretzki to the annual New York Congressional Delegation Dinner in Washington, and even invited Steingut to a dinner honoring the president of Mexico at Pocantico—and no one left Pocantico unimpressed.

The classic case of Rockefeller cajolery concerned another great program to meet a great problem. Early in 1968, the governor became convinced that only with a new superagency empowered to bypass politically sensitive local zoning ordinances could any low- or moderate-income housing be built. Just about everyone wanted such housing, but they wanted it somewhere else. As usual, the governor was adamant. At a news conference in the expanding bedroom community of Rockland County northwest of New York City, a local reporter persistently pressed Rockefeller about whether he favored low-cost housing near Rockland State Hospital, a mental institution where many blacks were employed. "Look," Rockefeller finally snarled. "These people are working hard and doing a good job. They have to live someplace, and there is no housing. Where do you want houses to be built—on skyhooks?"[4]

The governor unveiled the $6 billion slum rebuilding plan on February 17, releasing a storm of controversy that would continue well beyond the six weeks that preceded formal floor debate. Mayor Lindsay and other municipal leaders assailed the encroachment on home rule and accused the state administration of keeping specifics of the legislation secret. Rockefeller aide Steven Lefkowitz, son of the state attorney general and later counsel to the Urban Development Corporation (UDC), flatly denied the charge. The thrust of the critics' complaints was that the proposed authority could undertake urban renewal projects over the objections of localities. Rockefeller's response was that the "privilege" of home rule should be bulldozed when the communities were not solving their own problems. Because the din would not subside, the governor agreed on April 2 to what he called a compromise: closer state cooperation with localities would be required, but the state would retain the sweeping powers proposed originally.

One week later, Rockefeller laid it on the line. He and 18 black legislators he had invited along were flying to Atlanta for the funeral of the Reverend Martin Luther King, Jr. But before they left, the governor demanded that the Urban Development Corporation be approved that day as a lasting tribute to the slain civil rights leader. The bill sailed through the Senate but stalled in the Assembly. While the governor was marching through Georgia, time was running out in Albany.

By mid-afternoon, there were calls for a vote and the leadership thought it looked close. They were right. In what seemed like a severe blow to the governor's personal prestige, the bill was narrowly defeated, 63–69. Informed by telephone of the tally, Rockefeller became furious. But instead of conceding defeat, he became fanatically determined and ordered Al Marshall and counsel Robert Douglass "to go upstairs and get the legislators down and tell 'em I consider this a very high priority." "He didn't quit," Marshall would say later about the governor's style. "Even if he got licked, he didn't quit."[5]

For the next seven hours, with the Assembly recessed, the phone lines burned between Albany and Atlanta. Republican State Chairman Charles Schoeneck and Rockefeller aides worked over the dissidents one by one. By the time the floodlights illuminated the Capitol's eastern facade, there had been enough arm-twisting to justify the full-time services of a chiropractor. At 10 P.M. the Assembly reconvened. After 90 minutes of debate, assemblymen still suffering from shell shock approved the main bill in the urban renewal package by 86–45. Over the course of seven hours, 24 legislators had seen, or been shown, the light. The weary lawmakers okayed the final bill at 11:56—four minutes before Rockefeller's original midnight deadline.

The next morning, Rockefeller was triumphant as he signed the legislation into law. "How was the Assembly's about-face accomplished?" the governor was asked. Did he promise any favors to the lawmakers? "No," Rockefeller wryly replied. "I put it the other way around—that I would be unable to continue to do the personal favors. There was a long list, such as signing bills and appointments. Now I don't like to take this position, but I think one has to use whatever authority one has when something of major importance to the people comes before you."[6]

The very day that Rockefeller formally created the Urban Development Corporation, both houses of the legislature overwhelmingly voted to approve another measure. Introduced with bipartisan backing by Senate Majority Leader Earl Brydges and Minority Leader Zaretzki, the bill provided for retirement at half pay for lawmakers and legislative employees after 20 years of public service, including at least five with the legislature. Even sweeter was the provision that pensions would be based on the three most profitable years on the public pad. On April 10, with his righteousness and self-confidence intact, Rockefeller signed the lucrative retirement measure.

"It's going to end up on your desk and you're going to be put in a spot," Al Marshall said of such legislation. "He never bought anything that was bad. We might not have introduced a bill increasing legislative pensions," Marshall added, "but it would not be surprising if it were bandied about with the leadership in the same breath as some recommendation from Rockefeller. For instance, he might mention that 'that reminds me of the UDC bill—how are we coming on that?' If a guy isn't smart enough to ask that," Marshall declared, "he isn't smart enough to be governor of New York State."[7]

The UDC was by no means the first effort by Rockefeller to bludgeon and barter legislation into being, nor would it be the last. Another such case occurred in 1964, in the wake of what would be the greatest scandal of Rockefeller's 15 years as governor—the wholesale peddling of influence, licenses, and leniency in the politically susceptible State Liquor Authority. State Liquor Authority Chairman Martin Epstein, the frail lifelong friend of Brooklyn GOP Chairman John Crews, was already under indictment for influence peddling. Republican State Chairman L.

Judson Morhouse would be indicted the following year for his role in the bribery-conspiracy case involving the purchase of a liquor license for the posh Playboy Club off Fifth Avenue.

In the meantime, a special investigating commission appointed by the governor under the Moreland Act had recommended the most drastic revision of the liquor laws since their enactment at the end of Prohibition. Rockefeller wanted those proposals passed.

By the waning weeks of the session, it looked like trouble was brewing. The powerful liquor lobby encouraged the uncorking of a bottled-up rebellion by Republicans resentful over the governor's grandstanding. And sure enough, the recommended reforms went down to defeat. Within three weeks, however, Rockefeller interrupted his campaign for the Oregon presidential primary and summoned the legislature into special session. He demanded the enactment of bills to end price fixing, ban advertising of whiskey prices, require that distillers and wholesalers sell in New York State at prices as low as elsewhere, abolish the distance requirement between liquor stores, and effectively eliminate the free lunch by striking the requirement for kitchen facilities in taverns. On the second day of the session, a compromise package was approved, with enough Democratic votes to overcome the opposition of recalcitrant Republicans.

How did Rockefeller convince the majority of the merits of his case? Once again, he relied on a rule of thumb that President Johnson was then perfecting in the White House. "If Lyndon found out somebody really wanted something very badly," Interior Secretary Stewart Udall recalled, "he would hold it up until he could trade it off for something he really wanted."[8]

For almost three weeks after the legislature adjourned, such a bill was sitting on Rockefeller's desk. The proposal would allow the grouping of candidates of the same faction on Primary Day election machines, and it was desperately desired by Bronx Democratic boss Charles F. Buckley. The liquor legislation was something Rockefeller really wanted. So Buckley provided votes for the bar bills. And Rockefeller supplied his signature on the election law amendment.

The low esteem in which the Rockefeller regime held the supposedly co-equal branch of government was best articulated by William Ronan in a flash of frankness: "It does not make sense to have legislative leaders challenging executive initiatives. We have a tradition of strong executives, ever since Charles Evans Hughes and Al Smith. Not only does this challenging make no sense, I don't think it is really feasible. The legislative program today is too much for the legislative leaders to review, and much more so to initiate. A great deal does originate with the legislature, but the legislature . . . is more comfortable when it is not making great decisions. The attitude should be to react to initiatives and to respond to events as they occur."[9]

Because of conservative opposition from upstate Republicans —often led by the self-assured Senate majority leader, Walter Mahoney—it was not unusual for Rockefeller to have to rely sometimes on Democratic support and to horse trade with the opposite party.

One such case occurred, former Mayor Robert F. Wagner recalled, "when I called Walter Mahoney a peanut politician one time. He got very upset. It was toward the end of the 1962 session, and we came up with a vault tax to get us over the hurdle. Walter denounced it. Walter asked Bernie Ruggieri [counsel to the Senate minority] why I didn't call him. I did, and Walter said call the governor. Rockefeller said to me that I'd been picking on him. Nelson said, 'I want a letter from you saying I've done more for education than anyone else has, more for housing than anyone else has.' I said, 'I haven't lived that long— what you want is an endorsement.' 'That's what I'd like,' Nelson said. I think he wasn't going to give me the bill anyway, and he wanted to have some fun."[10]

But it was no fun nearly three years later when, for the first time since 1950, the Democrats captured control of both houses of the legislature. Their honeymoon was short-lived. For five weeks, while no bills passed and no action was taken on the budget, the Democrats deadlocked over the selection of leaders. The battle lines hardened—Assemblyman Stanley Steingut of Brooklyn and Senator Jack Bronston of Queens on one unofficial slate, Assemblyman Anthony Travia of Brooklyn and Senator Joseph Zaretzki of Manhattan on the other. Day after day, the potential leaders failed to round up enough votes to elect them.

Finally, on February 3, Syracuse Republican Senator John H. Hughes shocked the assembled lawmakers by nominating Zaretzki, who was boosted into his brief tenure as majority leader by the votes of 25 Republicans and 15 Democrats. The next day, 46 Republicans joined 35 Democrats to elect Travia Assembly speaker.

Wagner, who had backed the anti-Steingut slate, flatly declared later that "we won and Nelson helped on it."[11] Just why Nelson offered that helping hand was subject to several interpretations. Steingut would claim repeatedly that it was an effort to undermine the emerging leadership of Senator Robert F. Kennedy, who was supporting Steingut. A more compelling argument was that in exchange for Republican votes for Zaretzki and Travia, Rockefeller extracted a commitment by Wagnerian Democrats to support his unpopular proposed 2% sales tax. The levy passed later that legislative session, with the support of what would otherwise have been a surprising number of Democrats.

Wagner summed it up this way: "1965 was the most productive session—when Nelson was a liberal Republican and didn't have to make deals with fellow Republicans who were far less liberal." All in all, Wagner concluded, "You've got to rank him as one of the outstanding Governors."[12]

Two more obscure Democrats were recruited to the Rockefeller cause in a different way. One was Albert J. Hausbeck, a business executive from Buffalo. The other was Charles F. Stockmeister of Rochester. Both men were straight party-liners. That is, until the night of March 28, 1969.

With the new fiscal year only four days away, GOP Speaker

Perry Duryea was in an embarrassing bind. He was a few votes shy of the 76-member majority required to enact the governor's budget and the one-cent-on-the-dollar sales tax increase which helped bring it into balance. Desperate for Democratic defections, Duryea turned to Hausbeck and Stockmeister. The sales tax hike was okayed with two Democratic votes—theirs. The fix was in.

Within hours, their party's leaders sought to strip them of power. They also exposed the denouement of the plot. Stockmeister, who had been reelected in 1965 with the support of an anti-sales tax coalition, was to be named to the Civil Service Commission, and Hausbeck was in line for the Harness Racing Commission. The governor didn't deny it.

"First, let me say I don't believe in or make deals," Rockefeller reported two weeks later. "Let me say that what they did on the budget doesn't make me feel punitive toward these individuals in their consideration for these positions." Of Stockmeister, Rockefeller remarked later that "I had to appoint a Democrat, and I didn't see any reason just 'cause he voted for it that I should disqualify him."

Why not describe it the other way around—that the vote better qualified him, Rockefeller was asked. " 'Cause it's illegal," he snapped.[13] He hastened to add that Rochester Republicans had recommended Stockmeister for the civil service slot for several months. Why should the GOP push so hard for that particular Democrat? "Just out, probably, of the kindness of their hearts," Rockefeller replied with a smile.[14]

On July 3, 1969, as vacationers streamed away from news sources for the Independence Day weekend, the governor's office announced the appointment of Stockmeister as a $27,500-a-year member of the Civil Service Commission. Rockefeller was out of town that day. In fact, he was out of the country on his Latin American mission—having just arrived in Jamaica from the tense Dominican Republic capital of Santo Domingo.

Hausbeck was not quite so lucky. Dumped by the Democrats

in the 1970 primary, he was reelected to the Assembly on the Republican and Conservative lines. (The GOP also captured Stockmeister's seat.) He was finally defeated in the Democratic sweep of 1974.

In his 15 years as ringmaster of the Albany big top, Rockefeller utilized other techniques to tempt and turn. His favorite was the so-called message of necessity, a maneuver that enabled him to ram through legislation that most lawmakers never even had time to read. The device was designed for emergency use and allowed immediate consideration of new bills, free from the normal requirements that they age three days on legislators' desks.

Rockefeller employed that procedure with impunity. During 1970, critics charged, he introduced 130 separate messages of necessity in the last two days of the legislative session. And the following year, according to the New York Civil Liberties Union, the state budget and tax package were among the measures pushed through under the emergency powers provision. The name of the governor's game was monopoly.

"Critics said sometimes he was more interested in solving the problem than with the methodology of the problem," Marshall remembered. "Like creating the authorities. He had no problem departing from the ordinary. If another device was quicker, that's what he'd choose. To that extent, one could have called him Machiavellian. Once he decided there was a solution he would go hell bent for leather to get it. There are dreamers—like [Eugene] McCarthy. Even if they had great ideas, I don't know if they would have known how to implement them. [Nelson] traded Baltic Avenue for Ventnor Avenue and wound up with the houses on Marvin Gardens. He was capable of seeing what steps needed to be taken to get where he wanted to get."[15]

"He was trying to overcome problems," Zaretzki agreed. "Whatever he did, you can quarrel with the methods, but the results were for the benefit of the state."[16]

In more than one case, the results were also for the benefit of

Zaretzki. Early in 1972, maverick Manhattan Assemblyman Stephen Gottlieb announced that he would challenge Zaretzki in the June Democratic primary. The ailing Senate minority leader was worried, and with good reason. Gottlieb, a pipe-puffing reformer from the increasingly liberal West Side, promised to be a formidable foe. But that proved to be another broken campaign promise. Suddenly, on May 18, Gottlieb abandoned his primary bid. He blamed the cash crunch and the fact that his campaign had been undercovered in the press. He also denied that there was any city or state job in the offing for him, although he conceded that the Democratic County Committee had submitted his name to Mayor Lindsay for possible judicial appointment.

Exactly eight days later, Rockefeller rode to the rescue. He promoted the young assemblyman to a $31,325-a-year part-time post on the State Liquor Authority. The announcement stunned political insiders, and above all Gottlieb's liberal brethren. They should not have been surprised. After all, in his short-lived campaign Gottlieb had criticized Rockefeller's wrong and dangerous priorities.

"Many times," Marshall admitted with a wink, "there seemed to be some additional elements to the appointment of bipartisan people."[17]

"He was a tough young man but a very straight shooter, fearless, and he was just the kind of person I was looking for," Rockefeller said later of Gottlieb. "I asked him. He did not have to accept, and he did."[18]

Rockefeller obviously had less control over Congress, but when the occasion arose, he worked just as well with the national legislature. Such was the case in 1972, when the federal revenue-sharing measure Rockefeller had all but authored was being considered. Suddenly, its chances of passage were threatened by a political problem back home. The Republican-controlled legislature was considering a reapportionment plan, and the Democratic representatives from New York—key votes for the revenue-sharing scheme—were worried. A key vote, and the man most worried about survival in his congressional district, was Hugh Carey.

Rockefeller read between the lines. Quietly, he called on his congressional liaison, James Cannon, and New York Secretary of State John Lomenzo to secretly deny Carey's Republican rival the crucial Conservative Party endorsement.

Carey actually beat Republican John Gangemi by a slightly larger margin than the number of votes siphoned off by Conservative Franklin Jones. Had Gangemi won, he would have become the first Republican representative from Brooklyn since 1960. "Somewhere along the line, the Conservatives in Kings County had endorsed Gangemi in an informal way," recalled former Conservative Chairman William Wells. But they reversed themselves at the time of the formal endorsement and fielded a Conservative candidate. "That's how George Clark became [Brooklyn] Republican chairman, and that's how it was decided how close the Republicans and Conservatives would work in Kings County," Wells added. "It was because Rockefeller wanted revenue sharing."[19]

Rockefeller's relations with the congressional delegation were generally better during his tenure as governor than as a novice vice-president. As governor, he operated with an effective liaison staff—people, Hugh Carey said, "that normally no one could afford."[20]

There were also dinners for the Democratic delegation catered in the Senate Office Building, a practice that was interrupted after upstate Representative Samuel Stratton insisted on breaking the tradition that barred political discussions in order to rehash reapportionment. "It was obvious that Nelson was annoyed," Hugh Carey recalled, "and as a result we didn't have any more delegation dinners for a number of years. No more langouste. No more shrimp. And no more lobsters. No more filet mignon. Dinners at Foxhall always included the Republican group—they enjoyed that. We were led to believe that if we were good boys, we could get to Foxhall too."[21]

The Unequal Branch

Carey's major contact with Rockefeller was over revenue sharing. Joined by his Brooklyn congressional colleague and delegation dean, Emanuel Celler, Carey met with Rockefeller and legislative leaders the first time early in 1971.

"It didn't go anywhere till December of that year," Carey recalled, "when he called a special session because Duryea was holding firm saying that he was going to cut [the state budget] because Rockefeller didn't have the money. It was the day before Christmas Eve, and he asked if I could come to his apartment. I told him my wife had asked me to do the Christmas shopping, and I was delayed. When I got there, I was ushered in, and there was Rockefeller, Stanley Steingut, Meade Esposito, and Jerry Finkelstein. The governor said, 'Merry Christmas, we have to have help, and all your friends are here to express how urgent it is. Unless we can get an assurance that there will be a revenue-sharing bill passed this year, we're not going to be able to fund the schools and the cities and so on and so forth.' I said, well, the Congress has gone home, and I'm up here to do Christmas shopping, and I have less than a half day to take care of my family. And the governor said, 'Gee, I'm in the same boat, I haven't done a thing myself.' I said, for you it's easy. You just call up F.A.O. Schwarz and Parke-Bernet Galleries and your work is done, but I have to go borrowing and then buying. 'That's it,' he said. 'I have to borrow too.' He said without the assurance [of revenue sharing] we're going to have severe cuts to cities."

Rockefeller suggested that Carey could get Wilbur Mills to agree. If Carey could convince him to write a letter to say the bill was going to pass that year, it would have a profound impact on Duryea. Then, Rockefeller told Carey, "we could get the taxes we need on the assurance that some revenue sharing was coming."[22]

Carey left the room and telephoned Mills in Arkansas. He returned to report that "the good news is that on the state of the facts as I presented it, he would do the utmost to get a revenue-sharing bill that would give $200 or $300 million to New York this year. The bad news is that I'm not going to fly to Searcy,

Arkansas, to get this letter. Furthermore, you can't fly to Searcy. You have to fly to Little Rock and drive to Searcy. And Rockefeller said that if Mr. Cannon [James Cannon, his congressional liaison] had any Christmas plans, he'd better give them up. So Cannon was designated to go down to Washington and pick up the letter, which was typed in Mills' Washington office, and then to Searcy on Christmas Day to come back with the Santa Claus letter from Mills. And it was pushed under Mr. Duryea's nose without notice, under Mills's signature, that there would be money that year."[23]

During the subsequent squabbling in 1972 between the Nixon administration and Congress over various versions of revenue sharing, uneasy Democrats expressed the concern that after voting for the measure, they might return home to find they had been devastated by redistricting at the hands of the Republican-controlled legislature.

"In his magnanimous way," Carey remembered, "Rockefeller stood up in the St. Regis Hotel and said that, in return, [he would] say that the districting [would] be impartial and non-partisan. Whereupon I made a trip to the great computer in Syracuse and met Dick Scolaro and Charlie Webb and said I understand there is to be a exchange of views on districts, and what does it look like?

"They said the map is printed, there it is if you want to see it. I said what changes are there? They said none. I said I was told there was to be an input. They said the input is in the computer. I said, to be selfish, 'How does it look?' I remember Gary Axenfeld saying Hanley's got a good district. I said, 'How about mine?' They said, 'We can't change one block because DiCarlo told Duryea, *that district does not change.* And Duryea's more interested in [Republican legislators] DiCarlo, Kelly, Conklin, and Riccio than he is in Nelson A. Rockefeller and Hugh Carey.' Whereupon, I went down to the Syracuse Cathedral, said a few prayers, came back and said, could I speak to the speaker. And Charlie Webb said, 'Well, I'll take into consideration the changes you have in mind, but I can tell you the answer will be no.'

That was my first experience with a good sound Rockefeller contract."[24]

If every man had his price, then Nelson Rockefeller would make each an offer he couldn't refuse. Few decisions defied the pattern: the path to power and the presidency was paved with political compromise and bartered principles.

CHAPTER 8

Governor
on the Give

To Nelson Rockefeller, political patronage was simply a more productive form of the philanthropy that he had practiced as a family tradition since he was a child. Giving always had its good side. It brought obeisance. It rewarded loyalty. It improved the public image of the giver. And in public life there was one additional advantage. You were often giving away something that didn't belong to you.

A governor had lots to give away: millions of dollars of interest-free state deposits to deserving banks; fees for professional services to firms owned by party fat cats; unpaid ego-massaging appointments to co-opt image makers and enlist them in the "search for solutions"; promulgation of laws and regulations that would reap ample profits for a favored few; and, of course, the fuel that kept the party machines running smoothly and efficiently—jobs.

Rockefeller refined the patronage process to achieve maximum impact on every political level. At his disposal were resources that would arouse the envy of even a feudal prince. He was empowered to appoint almost 40,000 people uncovered by the competitive requirements of civil service—1,000 exempt, 24,000 noncompetitive, and 14,000 provisional.[1]

The governor was ever mindful of the advice of Democrat Daniel P. O'Connell, the patriarch of New York politics and last of the old-line big city bosses, who had ruled Albany County since 1919. "Uncle Dan" once explained that he would willingly pass up high-paying patronage from the state and "would rather have the charwomen and the janitors. They need the work and usually come from large families with a lot of votes and a lot of friends. The commissioner has only his and his wife's votes."[2]

By no means were all 40,000 slots filled with political appointees. But regardless of the severity of the state's fiscal condition, there was always room for a few more of the party faithful—of any party. It was a system that functioned smoothly, interlocking the political structure with the public payroll and linking its solvency to the survival of the incumbent state administration. It received little publicity, and even less criticism. The few outcries there were resulted from the increasing sophistication of the voters and sensitivity of the press, especially after the Watergate scandal.

Patronage is traditionally a practice that politicians prefer to conduct in the back rooms—of Washington, Albany, New York City, or anywhere else. On the rare occasions that the subject was impolitely pursued in public, Rockefeller cut it short with the wink, body English, or indignant glower that were his evasive response to almost any adversity.

One such occasion occurred in 1973. Applicants for summer jobs with Laurance Rockefeller's Palisades Interstate Park Commission were surprised to learn of a new requirement for employment. The commission foreman in Rockland County informed applicants that they needed green referral cards from local Republican leaders. Asked about the arrangement, Rockefeller replied with a mild rebuke to the state parks and recreation commissioner. His one-sentence statement said simply: "It is the policy of this administration to employ seasonal, temporary and permanent help on the basis of competence and qualification to do the job."[3]

The commissioner was unfazed. With no fear of being fired, he blandly replied that the department officials "welcome the assistance of the state Republican organization in finding qualified people for temporary and seasonal positions."[4] Rockefeller's rebuke appeared to have little impact. A few months later, a state parks employee upstate disclosed that he had been bounced from his post after he announced his decision to run as the Democratic candidate for Monroe County sheriff.

The state parks commissioner continued in office confident that he could ride out any attacks. After all, he was Alexander Aldrich, the governor's cousin.

Rockefeller occasionally made mistakes, too. The most outstanding was Martin Epstein, whom Nelson elevated to the State Liquor Authority (SLA) on Valentine's Day eve in 1959. It was, in fact, a gesture of affection. Not for Epstein but for Epstein's friend John Crews, the bald and beguiling Brooklyn Republican leader whose endorsement of Rockefeller for governor the year before was considered to have been crucial.

Years later, Rockefeller would be asked whether there was any information in the two State Police background reports on Epstein that cast doubt on his character and integrity. (One noted, in fact, that Epstein's name was casually dropped in testimony before a State Commission of Investigation probe into possible bribery involving the SLA.) "Carefully read, I would say you are right," he answered.[5]

Relatively few Rockefeller appointees were ever accused of outright corruption. One reason, of course, was that the $2 million he dispensed to present and former officials to supplement their state salaries were designed in part to, as he explained it, make them "independent of temptation."[6]

The staff subsidies performed one other function. For the political cognoscenti who knew, said they knew, or at least suspected that state officials were on the dole, Rockefeller's power was enhanced. Unlike themselves, he was able to operate beyond the budgetary restraints imposed both by austerity and a suspicious public. And there was always the chance that they might make the ever-expanding gift and loan list if they ingratiated themselves with the governor.

While outright corruption was kept to a minimum, critics periodically complained that the state payroll was a scandal in itself. It was laden with political leaders, and with legislators who had lost their seats; candidates quickly discovered the advantages of defeat.

Of course, patronage was nothing new to New York. A century before, under Governor John T. Hoffman, the administration in Albany had actually become another arm of the boodle barons of Tammany Hall. In 1870 a Thomas Nast cartoon depicted Hoffman uncomfortably ensconced in the seat of power, flanked by New York City Chamberlain Peter (Brains) Sweeny and Boss Tweed. The cartoon was captioned: "The power behind the throne—he cannot call his soul his own."[7] But a century later, the situation was not the same. Rockefeller was the sole power on the throne. And behind him were only his own fortune and fortitude.

Nowhere was Nelson's appointive prowess more effective than when it came to filling posts from among legislators. Such selections served two ends: they fulfilled political obligations, and they rewarded loyal lawmakers

But Rockefeller's rewarding experiences were by no means limited to legislators. Four times Rockefeller ran for governor and won. Four times his running mates ran for controller and lost to the venerable Arthur Levitt, a Democrat who has occupied that post since 1954. The four losing candidates did not stay losers long. First there was James Lundy, who was placed on the 1958 ticket as a payoff to Queens County Chairman Frank Kenna, who delivered his delegation to Rockefeller. Lundy was named chairman of the Public Service Commission. Then there was John Lomenzo of Rochester. He became New York's secretary of state, a sinecure with jurisdiction over various licensing provisions and, until recently, the convenient combination of cemeteries and voter registration. The third controller candidate was Charles Lanigan, who wound up as director of the State Office for Local Planning Coordination and then Republican state chairman. The fourth lucky loser was Edward Regan, who made the mistake of getting mad in the midst of the 1970 campaign when Rockefeller let slip that Levitt was "in like Flynn." After that, the Buffalonian with the movie star smile glumly fulfilled his fall-guy role. In 1971 he was named to a Commission on the Powers of Local Government, and he was later elected Erie County executive.

Party leaders were also sitting pretty in the patronage picture. One survey discovered that 51 county chairmen from all four New York State political parties and 44 of their relatives received some compensation from the state.[8]

Although Rockefeller's road to political success may have been paved with good intentions, nowhere was its toll on the public purse more apparent than in the New York State Thruway Authority. Ensconced in the Authority's $25,000 chairmanship since 1960 was R. Burdell Bixby, onetime law partner of former Governor Thomas Dewey and quadrennial campaign manager for the Rockefeller team. Other Thruway Authority members, who make $17,000 annually (and who, like the chairman, are part-time employees) have included former Republican State Chairman Charles Lanigan and Alton Marshall, the governor's former secretary.

Also heavily populated with the party faithful were the dozens of commissions created or continued by the governor. Included were panels which appealed to the vanity of prospective appointees, handily redirected and diffused dissent, delayed decisions on sensitive issues like aid to education and the aftermath of the Attica uprising—and, occasionally, even came up with sound solutions that political pressure or publicity kept from being pigeonholed. Since most were established to meet the first two criteria, they rarely resembled the kind of commission that the Rockefeller family was able to afford for more fruitful efforts.

The panels, which were once estimated to total over 70 simultaneously, were given a wide variety of missions. There was the Temporary State Commission of Investigation, which was created in 1958. The Commission to Commemorate the War of 1812. The Commission to Study Transplantation of Vital Organs of Human Beings. The Commission to Review the Compensation Received by Members of the Legislature and Judiciary. The Governor's Steering Committee on Social Problems. The Interdepartmental Management Improvement Council. And the Governor's Committee for Increased Use of Milk. Among others.

Rockefeller made his moves involving the commissions "like a shrewd chess player," one observer recalled.

One all-important function of the commissions was to protect the pension rights of their members. An appointment at even the most modest salary would allow some political operative to remain in the retirement system. When Charles Lanigan quit his $35,000 state planning post to become Republican state chairman, for example, he was appointed to the State Public Health Council at $1,881 a year. His successor, Richard Rosenbaum, followed a similar route. After he stepped down from his State Supreme Court seat to become the party potentate, he was appointed to the State Mental Hygiene Council, a part-time post which paid $1,500 a year.

Such politically prompted hanky-panky in employment practices was questionable under state statutes. The State Civil Service Law, at least, specifically prohibits the practice of job "recommendations" that are in any way related to "political opinions or affiliations." Relying on the loosely controlled commissions, however, Rockefeller enhanced his power by cleverly and carefully co-opting possible potential opponents. He established himself as the sun of a political solar system whose planets received his rays in direct relation to their distance from him. There were no eclipses.

So fat and secure had Republican patronage appointees become, one former official recalled, that Alton Marshall had to stun them back to reality in the midst of one gubernatorial race. "You guys have had your ass in butter too long," he exclaimed at a meeting of state commissioners and department heads. "The cabinet was semicomatose politically," the official complained. "It was totally oblivious to the fact that Nelson's reelection was responsible for their continued employment."[9]

Padding the public payroll with part-time commissioners, board members, and trustees had one saving grace: they were generally not empowered to do great harm. But also on the bargaining table when Rockefeller wanted some bill passed badly enough was a much more potent incentive to agree with the governor.

Several years ago, a reporter was trying to track down a former legislator whose old law office had closed and whose home telephone number was no longer published. Finally, he came across a state official who had been close to the lawmaker and asked his whereabouts. "Oh, John?" the official answered. "Why he's gone on to his final reward."

"That's too bad," the reporter replied.

"Oh, no," the official reassured the reporter. "He became a judge."

The bench in New York is the ultimate goal of any ambitious lawyer with political connections, and the governor was willing to accommodate for a favor. As usual, the favors sometimes rewarded friendship, but more often they rewarded an infusion of public spiritedness in a politician who had decided to support a Rockefeller program. Rockefeller's role in the process was evident in two areas. First, he was empowered to appoint judges to the Court of Claims and to the Appellate Division of the State Supreme Court without any required screening process. Second, he was authorized to fill vacancies in the judicial system ranging from the county courts to the Supreme Court and Court of Appeals, which are elective offices. It has been estimated that as many as half of the sitting state and county court judges received their present posts or their first bench berths by appointment.[10]

Rockefeller also exerted influence by negotiating with legislative leaders to approve packages of new judgeships, ostensibly to counter complaints that court calendars were too crowded.

However valid, those complaints more often originated from politically connected attorneys than from the jurists themselves.

Judgeships really were the ultimate reward for a favored few who faithfully performed for the party. Their service might have been in fundraising or running against heavy odds to protect the party line, or in supporting some legislation for which the leadership had already committed their support. Rarely were the reasons as exposed as the appointment of Stockmeister after the sales tax vote. And equally rarely were they candidly discussed.

One of the few politicos powerful enough to be blunt was Albany's Dan O'Connell. After years of probing the Democratic patriarch, Governor Dewey decided to make peace. Shortly thereafter, Uncle Dan delivered a key Democratic vote for a rent control bill. When a reporter phoned O'Connell to find out why a state senator had bolted Democratic ranks on the rent measure, a minion returned to the telephone to report that "Mr. O'Connell said to tell you that the senator votes the way he is told."[11] Of lawmakers with that kind of voting record are judges made.

From his early days in the Rockefeller Center rental office, the governor had the gift of being able to estimate, if not negotiate, the rock bottom price of any political deal. He also quickly learned that somewhere in the discussion, judgeships were likely to come up.

"The first time he was trying to create a Council on the Arts, they were trying to trade judges for ballet dancers," William Ronan recalled. "They were always trying to get more judges in the city."[12] Sometimes they succeeded. At other times the price was too high.

Former New York City Mayor Robert F. Wagner remembers receiving a phone call from Rockefeller in the spring of 1961, while Wagner was recuperating in a city hospital. "He was curious to know what was going on with judgeships," the wily Wagner said. "He said, 'There'll be so many for the Democrats, so many for the Republicans, one for the Liberals, in Brooklyn, in Manhattan, and so on, and one for you and one for me.' I asked him why we were getting two. He said, 'Well, we've got to make sure there're two good ones." I said, 'Have you got the votes?' Rockefeller said, 'I want a letter from you saying that they're needed.' Well, I hadn't been consulted and said no. And there were no judges."[13]

Rockefeller also had a hand in killing at least one judgeship bill himself. It was 1960, and the leaders had already divvied up six new judgeships in Brooklyn—three for the Republicans and three for the Democrats, who could have won all six in an election but counted on the Republicans in Albany to create the vacancies in the first place. The bill suddenly stalled when Rockefeller's arch obstructionist, Senate Majority Leader Walter Mahoney, exclaimed on the Senate floor: "Fuck the governor. I'm the majority leader of this house. No one talked to me about this bill."[14] As it turned out, Mahoney was specifically miffed because he had a judicial candidate of his own who was overlooked in the horsetrading. So the judgeship bill was amended to create another State Supreme Court slot, and the majority counsels went searching for the governor to provide the message of necessity that was required to ram the legislation through in the closing hours of the session. When they finally found him in his second-floor office at about 3:00 A.M., he had apparently heard about Mahoney's outburst and was most uncooperative. Pressed to sign the special message, Rockefeller offered only a curt comment. "Fuck Walter Mahoney," he said.[15]

One party to a more productive pact was Matthew Troy, Jr., chairman of the powerful New York City Council Finance Committee. Troy, the Queens County Democratic chairman, was later dumped, in part because he had publicly criticized the budget proposals of Abraham Beame, the diminutive mayor who exceeded even Rockefeller's pedagogic propensity to equate nods of understanding with automatic agreement. Before he was ousted in a coup in which the mayor had no small sway, Troy candidly declared that "the state patronage I get is all part of deals, usually for votes he [Rockefeller] needs in the legislature."[16]

Troy complained that "Rockefeller has such a great reputation as a square dealer, but that's not what I found out. He keeps wanting to renegotiate. I gave him Queens votes in the legislature to put a jetport in Newburgh—what did we care about Newburgh?—in return for the right to pick a Supreme Court replacement if Seymour Thaler went to jail. Well, Sy's been convicted, and I haven't heard from the governor. When I do, you can bet he'll want something else thrown in."[17]

But what was regarded admiringly by his colleagues as the juiciest single judicial deal in recent history was consummated by Troy and his Republican counterpart, the late Sidney Hein, one night in a Queens diner.

"Making deals is what a leader does," the outspoken politico crowed. "I make twenty small ones a year—trading votes in the legislature for a job or two—and a big one every two years. But the first big one shattered all my illusions about dark rooms. Sid Hein and I met in a diner on Queens Boulevard and divided up the county for the next couple of years. I insisted that we put it in writing, and I wanted him and Rockefeller to sign it—they wouldn't sign anything, but we agreed to write it out."[18] They wrote it out on May 17, 1971, and carried it out over the next six months.

The scenario started, appropriately enough, with the patronage-rich post of Queens surrogate—an early warning that where there's a will, there's a way. Veteran Surrogate John T. Clancy would resign in time for Rockefeller to elevate Louis Laurino, former counsel to the Queens public administrator, and avoid a primary. Laurino had headed Democrats for Rockefeller in the 1970 campaign and had been appointed in April to the Court of Claims. Five new Supreme Court justiceships were created by the legislature, and one additional seat became vacant because of a retirement. Three would be designated for Democrats: Borough President Sidney Leviss, the late State Senator Seymour Thaler (indicted in a bond swindle before he could be sworn in), and Civil Court Judge William Giacchio. The remaining three were for Republicans: Conservative Assemblymen Alfred

Lerner and Joseph Kunzman, who had supported a Rockefeller tax package, and Civil Court Judge Frederic Hammer. The six Supreme Court nominations, the surrogate, the Democratic district attorney and the replacement for the departing borough president all would receive bipartisan support. As would Troy in his 1973 City Council reelection race.

The classic case of the Claims Court's political role involved Fred A. Young, who resigned as chief judge of the tribunal to help run Rockefeller's abortive 1964 presidential campaign. Young was said to have been called back to campaign headquarters after he allegedly—and injudiciously—threatened a Western state GOP chairman that he would "kick him in the balls" if he continued to criticize Rockefeller's remarriage. After the campaign ended, Rockefeller gave Young a gift of $15,000 and reappointed him to the Court of Claims, again as presiding judge.

"The courts are the very bedrock of a just society,"[19] Rockefeller told the American Bar Association in 1971. To a great degree, however, his record of appointments helped erode that foundation.

Elevation to the bench and to a bevy of boards and agencies was only one of the ways Rockefeller rewarded his friends. Also at the discretion of the governor were the numerous edicts, rules, decisions, and regulations that could be issued to the benefit of the faithful or the detriment of the infidel. One such case involved Dr. Thomas Matthew, the black self-help advocate convicted of having helped himself to state Medicaid funds earmarked for his Interfaith Hospital in Queens. Matthew was a strong supporter both of Rockefeller and former President Richard Nixon, who pardoned him in 1969 after Matthew served two months of a six-month sentence for federal tax evasion. The year before, state health inspectors had complained that the food and care at Interfaith were substandard and that "there [did] not appear to be any effort made to prolonging the life of the patients."[20] At Matthew's request, however, the governor's secretary, Al Marshall, agreed to extend the hospital's certification for nine more months.

Governor on the Give

When that period expired, State Health Commissioner Hollis Ingraham concluded that Matthew had failed to live up to his promises of improvements and recommended that as of February 1, 1969, "we no longer certify this hospital for medical improvement." Rockefeller aide John Garrison agreed.[21] "The one potential problem is that Dr. Matthew is very close to President-elect Nixon and has been one of Nixon's primary examples of 'black capitalism,'" Garrison wrote Marshall. He concluded that, nonetheless, the "fact is that Dr. Matthew is operating a hospital which is so far below New York State's standards that it is a detriment to the public to be in operation."[22]

But Interfaith continued to receive Medicaid funds as a health-related facility through September 1972—four months after investigators discovered a body containing a bullet wound in the hospital's locked laundry room. Shortly after Matthew's arrest in 1973 on charges of misappropriating Medicaid funds, Queens District Attorney Thomas Mackell accused state and federal agencies of a "total lack of cooperation" with his investigation.

Yet in 1974, while Matthew was still free pending appeal of his conviction (it was overturned in 1975), Rockefeller heaped high praise on the controversial neurosurgeon. Asked what role politics played in his decision to keep Interfaith open, Rockefeller replied: "Until you told me right now that he was a friend of President Nixon's, I did not know it, so I knew nothing about that side, so politics in that sense had nothing to do with it. Dr. Matthew is one of the most brilliant, one of the most attractive, one of the most dynamic, one of the most popular black leaders in New York."[23] At least with Nelson Rockefeller.

CHAPTER 9

The *Real* Power Broker

Nelson ROCKEFELLER rarely lost a power struggle. He beat Jimmy Roosevelt and other critics while serving in South America; he defeated John Foster Dulles during the infancy of the United Nations. But it was only after his bout with one rival that the governor won the undisputed title of heavyweight power broker. His name was Robert Moses.

Moses had served five governors, accumulating clout from outside the entrenched establishment, creating the concept of public authorities that Rockefeller was to copy, building parks, playgrounds, housing projects, power plants, beaches, and bridges that cost $27 billion dollars over 44 years. But in Nelson Rockefeller, Moses met his match.

"Two men so arrogant, so accustomed to getting their own way in everything, could not long be in contact without friction—particularly when both men were grand-scale builders," Robert Caro wrote in *The Power Broker*, his monumental work on Moses. "So acute an observer as Perry Duryea says he 'could just see Rocky thinking that there wasn't enough room in one state for a Robert Moses and a Nelson Rockefeller both clicking on all six.' "[1]

The *Real* Power Broker

Moses appeared before the freshman governor in 1962 in the unusual role of supplicant, impatiently awaiting the annual extension that enabled him to continue in his Parks and Power posts beyond the mandatory retirement age of 65. But Rockefeller wasn't in the habit of offering anything automatically when he wanted something else in return. And what he wanted was the orderly transition of power on the State Park Council to brother Laurance.

"When he had brought up the matter of the extension," Moses man Sid Shapiro quoted his boss as bristling, "Nelson Rockefeller had, in his charming, gracious, assured manner, picked up a paper lying on his desk, let Moses see that it was the extension for his presidency of the Long Island Park Commission and held it up in his hand—his left hand, Moses said, dramatizing the scene with his customary vividness—while saying, referring to the chairmanship of the State Council of Parks, 'Now, Bob, don't you think now is the time for Laurance to take over?' "[2]

Moses was enraged, Shapiro continued. "Keeping one post without the other, he said, was 'out of the question'; if the governor wanted him to resign one, he would—he would resign the other, too. In fact, he would resign all posts connected with parks, the Bethpage and Jones Beach authorities chairmanships, too. In fact, perhaps the governor would also like him to resign his other state job—the Power Authority chairmanship—since he seemed to feel he had too much to do. 'Of course not,' the governor said, all he was talking about was the Parks Council chairmanship."

The stormy session ended, Shapiro recalled, with "an astonishing scene. The boss comes out of the building, and there's the governor coming out after him and tugging at his arm, really pulling at him, trying to get him to come back inside and let's discuss it. Moses pulls his arm away from him and gets inside, saying 'Come on, let's go,' and we pull away, leaving the governor of the State of New York just standing there on the sidewalk, and there are members of the public standing around and staring at this scene."[3]

Nobody runs out on Nelson Rockefeller; when Moses mistakenly followed up that meeting with a written threat to resign, Rockefeller accepted it the same day. Although he had not girded for an all-out confrontation, the governor was going to win one way or another. And Moses, so used to firing off ultimata over four decades, had obviously not counted on Nelson Rockefeller's determination to run his own show.

"For 30 years," Rockefeller ruefully recalled, "I helped Bob Moses supplement his income way back by jobs in Latin America, because I respect the guy, I love the guy, see, and I think he's done a fabulous job for New York. Twenty-seven years before he had asked my brother to be vice-chairman of the State Parks. I said, 'Look Bob, I would like to make my brother chairman of the State Parks Commission so we could go through an orderly transition. He's had 27 years of internship.' Well, Bob got very sore. I said 'Bob why are you sore?' I said, 'You picked him—I didn't.' "[4]

But Moses was worried that if he gave up one job because of age, he would soon be stripped of those that remained. "I said, 'I'm not raising questions on anything, I'm perfectly satisfied,' " Rockefeller remembered. "No, he was furious. At least he acted as though he was furious. He stalked out and he went right over to the *Daily News* thinking he'd build up the pressure. So I said, 'Don't resign, think it over!' I said, "Look, I regret it very much, but if you really feel this way, then I'll accept your resignation.' And he thought I couldn't take it. Then the third parties started coming to me saying, look, this is not fair to this great public servant, you oughtn't treat him this way, there ought to be some way to let him come back, save face and so forth. Well, I'd gone through quite a little thing myself, see, so I said all he has to do is not resign from any more things. . . . I think I got a total of 12 letters of protest. It was tragic. This was no way for him to end a great career, because he is a great public servant and I'm devoted to him and, as I say, for 30 years I'd helped him. I believe in those who've got that kind of ability who are in government, you know, getting the support the deserve."[5] (Moses says *all* he ever received from Rockefeller was $21,000 in consulting fees.)

For the next four years, Moses was left with the chairmanship of the highly profitable Triborough Bridge and Tunnel Authority, which annually produced substantial surpluses. But it was too much money for Rockefeller to overlook for long. In early 1967, the governor announced his intention to press for a $2.5 billion transportation bond issue to finance a Metropolitan Transportation Authority (MTA) to improve service on the antiquated New York City subways and commuter lines. Combining all the publicly-owned rail and bus services, it would be the first coordinated attack on the problems of mass transit on a regional basis. Among the integrated operations was to be Triborough, primarily because its revenues could help subsidize the debt-ridden rail lines.

Moses at first opposed the plan with typically damning adjectives. But after a meeting with the governor on March 9, he put aside his intense personal dislike for prospective MTA Chairman William Ronan and capitulated. The reason, it developed later, was that Moses was convinced he had a commitment allowing him to remain in a role at Triborough, where he would continue to exercise complete control over construction. The commitment, if it was ever made, was never kept.

Only days before the March 1, 1968, merger was to take effect and the Triborough Board eliminated, Ronan made his final offer. Moses could be a consultant and coordinator at $25,000 a year, with a limousine and staff. He could retain all the trappings of power but would be stripped of its substance.

"I don't know that he had any commitment from Nelson" for an influential role, Ronan would recall years later. Was there any promise of power made by himself? "No," Ronan replied.[6] Nonetheless, Moses reluctantly accepted the sinecure at the last minute.

One longtime Rockefeller aide insisted that Moses and his minions were legislated out of power because, with the master builder in his eightieth year, Moses had passed his prime. "It's an important thing to know when to get out," the aide observed. "He and Austin Tobin [of the Port Authority] stayed too long. Sometimes elected people do it, too."

There was another reason why the former power broker was defeated. "What was necessary to remove Moses from power," Robert Caro concluded, "was a unique, singular concatenation of circumstances: that the Governor of New York be the one man uniquely beyond the reach of normal political influences, and that the trustee for Triborough's bonds be a bank run by the Governor's brother."[7]

Such was the power of Nelson Rockefeller that even when he appeared to let events take their course, he was credited with the eventual destruction of his critics. Of course his power was more obvious when he moved overtly. The most significant case occurred in 1973, when the governor was preparing to hand the reins to his anointed successor, Malcolm Wilson. There was another man, however, who longed for that governorship; his name was Perry Duryea, and he was to become embroiled in a byzantine struggle with the Rockefeller administration, a struggle that further attested to Nelson's power as well as to the long reach of his retributive arm.

It began in the fall of 1972, when reports appeared concerning "mystery mailings" made on behalf of the Action Committee for the Liberal Party in marginal Assembly districts. The state attorney general was authorized to investigate.

For years, the Liberals had enjoyed a cozy relationship with both major parties although, philosophically, they were better equipped to fulfill the role of spoilers against Democratic candidates. What investigators for the attorney general discovered over the next few months was shocking only to the small portion of the public whose morality was reawakened by Watergate—and not to traditionally apathetic citizens or cynical politicians. It appeared that the mailings by the bogus Action Committee were financed by the Republican Assembly campaign committee to siphon votes from Democratic candidates. The campaign committee was controlled by Perry Duryea.

For several years, Speaker Duryea had been feuding with Rockefeller and had grown increasingly cool to the common wisdom that Lieutenant Governor Malcolm Wilson would automatically win the Republican nomination in 1974 if Rockefeller resigned or retired. Duryea had become more outspoken, challenging the governor on legislation and broadening his base from the middle to embrace the concerns of the cities, as Rockefeller edged more toward the right.

His fate was in the hands of Louis Lefkowitz, who was appointed attorney general in 1957 when Jacob Javits was elected to the Senate. A backslapping politician of the old school, Lefkowitz used to play ball on the Lower East Side, where his instincts for survival were sharpened. This time, survival dictated conflicting courses. On the one hand, teaching Duryea a lesson in discipline by turning the case over to local prosecutors would link the New York party to the same kind of Republican dirty tricks that were undermining the national administration. And to kill the case in the interests of unity and questionable constitutionality would invite charges of a cover-up.

Pressed almost daily by reporters for *Newsday*,[8] the Long Island paper that first broke the story, Lefkowitz, on June 18, finally forwarded evidence of election law violations to District Attorneys Arnold Proskin of Albany and Frank Hogan of Manhattan. To protect himself and at least hint at his own hesitations, Lefkowitz cited two related election law cases in a covering letter and concluded that "I am not unmindful" that the relevant section may be unconstitutional. Assembly Majority Leader John Kingston, who like Duryea had never taken the attorney general's requests for legislation very seriously, was furious with Lefkowitz for not killing the investigation.

On November 20, Lefkowitz asked Chief Assistant District Attorney Alfred Scotti to a November 23 meeting with the governor on the new drug law at Nelson's Fifth Avenue apartment. Before he left for the meeting, one top assistant warned Scotti that with Hogan steadily sinking, and the governor empowered to appoint his successor, an approach might be made to Scotti on Duryea's behalf. The uncorruptible prosecutor returned from the session concerned that his assistant was right.

"Either Rockefeller or Lefkowitz might have made some reference to the subpoena [for the speaker]," Scotti said, "and I believe I made the statement that testimony before the grand jury warranted [the subpoena]. I said we call 'em as we see 'em."[9]

"We spent about 99 percent of the time on narcotics at the Fifth Avenue meeting," Lefkowitz recalled. "The other 1 percent—who knows? I can't remember that coming up at all. I'm sure Rocky would have enough sense not to do that. You'd have to be a real dirty son of a bitch to indict someone," he angrily declared in his own defense. "You can cut patronage, you can no longer invite, there're lots of ways. But to indict?"[10]

In a few weeks, Speaker Duryea's political sun seemed to be rapidly dimming. Duryea, Majority Leader John Kingston, Queens Assemblyman Alfred Delli Bovi and several aides were indicted by a Manhattan grand jury. Within a month, however, the district attorney would be near death, the charges would be declared unconstitutional, and Scotti would be told by the new governor, Malcolm Wilson, that since Scotti had indicted Duryea (Wilson's rival), it was now politically impossible to appoint him as Hogan's successor.

Rockefeller flatly disputes the version of his meeting with Scotti that has been accepted as gospel in the Manhattan district attorney's office. He does acknowledge that the case was discussed, "but not by me."

It is difficult, if not impossible, to find anyone involved in New York politics who is not firmly convinced that Rockefeller engineered the entire episode. "Lefkowitz couldn't have moved without Rockefeller knowing,"[11] says Harold Fisher, Duryea's counsel for the case and a Rockefeller appointee to the Metropolitan Transportation Authority. "Certainly the members thought he could've stopped it," concluded a colleague in the Assembly.

"I knew nothing about the action taken against Mr. Duryea

until the attorney general, the attorney general of the state, told me he was going to turn over the papers to the district attorney," the governor insisted. "The attorney general of the state was of my party. He has his own responsibilities, he is elected on his own. We have a very close relationship, but a very formal relationship. He did this because of the Watergate atmosphere that exists in this country. He did it because he was not going to have any Watergate atmosphere in New York State."[12]

Rockefeller would describe the Duryea indictment and its aftermath as "the second tragedy of my political life [the first, he said, was his falling out with Lindsay]—having this situation come up between two very good friends, Louis and Perry. I didn't try to stop the thing, that would be unfair. I just tried to get absolute fairness in this thing so that there would be total objectivity." How did he accomplish that? "Just talking with the attorney general," Rockfeller replied.[13]

If Rockefeller in fact took any active role in the case, he failed; he never prevented the indictment, nor did the charges damage Duryea as much as expected. But what is so significant is that virtually every politician believed that the governor would go to such lengths to inflict punishment or retribution on a foe. More than a decade of occasional arrogance and intimidation had convinced enough prospective victims that Rockefeller was capable of that. Their conviction became more obvious later in the 1974 legislative session, when they quietly sought to cut the budget of Special Prosecutor Maurice Nadjari, who had been branded as a Rockefeller hatchet man after he hastily arrested the president of the City Tax Commission on the morning that Mayor Lindsay was slated to disclose his decision on a possible third term. Nadjari's days were numbered once the Republican reign abruptly ended. Less than a year in office and after a series of scathing court decisions against the special prosecutor, Governor Carey announced plans to dump him. Nadjari quickly countered that Carey was only attempting to cover up a probe of powerful politicians, including Democratic State Chairman Patrick Cunningham.

Nadjari was making life uncomfortable for officials of both political parties—in a continuing quest to trap influence peddlers and corrupters of the courts. A prime target of his probes and web of entrapment was powerful Brooklyn Democratic boss Meade Esposito.

Ironically, Esposito, of all his fellow Democrats, was a prime target of Rockefeller's own entrapment strategy. Ever since he succeeded Steingut in 1969, the cigar-chomping insurance broker, former bail bondsman, and high school dropout had come to symbolize Rockefeller's inveterate romancing of the state's majority party. No county in the state boasted more enrolled Democrats than Brooklyn. In reelection races where the Conservatives were eroding Republican strength, and in the legislature where solving urban ills required bipartisan support, the governor needed the Democrats to survive.

Things had been cozy enough between the two parties. The boards of banks and insurance companies—and, of course, the membership rosters of law firms—were carefully selected to obtain the most profitable mix of Republicans and Democrats.

Meade Esposito met Nelson Rockefeller for the first time at the governor's Fifth Avenue apartment one night in 1971. Summoned by fellow Democrats to discuss the state's dire fiscal straits, Esposito registered immediate disgust at the fiscal fitness of his host. "At one point," Esposito fondly recalled, "I said, 'What the hell are you doing in this fucking business?' He said, 'What the hell do you want me to do—go into the real estate business?' Then I saw some paintings. I said what the hell does this goddamned thing cost? I'm asking prices. He told me and I said, 'Your goddamned fucking wealth is obscene.' Rocky said, 'Would you mind telling that to Happy?' I told her."[14]

Others at the Fifth Avenue session, including then Representative Hugh Carey, differ about Esposito's adjectives, but they all share Carey's assessment of the result: "Rockefeller operated one party and occupied the other. Esposito thinks Rockefeller is 'a helluva guy, and if he runs in 1976, I'd have a helluva time being against him—my wife loves the guy.' Esposito once took

The *Real* Power Broker

Rockefeller and Happy to the Gun Club [Tiro A Segna, a power-packed and palate-pleasing place on MacDougal Street], and Esposito always took pride in Happy's saying, 'This is so much fun—I never met a man like you before.' He took that as a compliment."[15]

Esposito was especially useful because of Rockefeller's strained relationship with Steingut. As one Democratic lawmaker declared: "If you stood up to him, he would find a way to get around you." There were three ways to do it. "There was the petty nickel and dime stuff," Alton Marshall, Rockefeller's former secretary recalled. "Then there was a layer a lot bigger, involving personal profit. And then there was the area where one person has his own thing he'd like to see in the public arena— which is not necessarily illegal. The art of government is compromise, and on that level Nelson Rockefeller was a master. If he couldn't get a tax bill with Stanley," Marshall added, "it is not unlike Rockefeller to go to Meade Esposito and say, 'I want the votes—now what the hell do you want?' "[16]

Rockefeller found that Esposito wasn't shy about what he wanted. The governor intervened early in their relationship to encourage the Admissions Office of Upstate Medical School in Syracuse to accept Esposito's grandson. How did he do so? "By saying to the State University people," Rockefeller replied, "that it meant a great deal to Stanley Steingut."[17]

Esposito was not wooed by appeals to vanity alone. Once, he was introduced to Rockefeller at the New York Hilton during an intermission of the annual Inner Circle lampoon by City Hall reporters. He pressed the governor about the Upstate Medical "contract" and finally asked, "Do I have your assurance?" Rockefeller replied that he had. So willing was the governor to please that two weeks later Assembly Speaker Duryea called Stanley Steingut at Rockefeller's behest to report that "Meade asked Rockefeller for insurance."

The colorful Brooklyn Democrat, blurting out one night that Rockefeller even asked him to switch parties and become state Republican chairman, later boasted that "there wasn't anything

I asked him for that he didn't do."[18] Esposito deserved credit for the appointment of former Democratic State Chairman Michael Prendergast to the State Cable Television Commission, of former Buffalo Mayor Frank Sedita to the Crime Victims Compensation Board, and of Frank Rossetti, Jr. to the bench. After rejecting Rockefeller's offer to name him to the State Harness Racing Commission, a position that would provide more public exposure than most political leaders can afford, Esposito persuaded the governor to name former Brooklyn Democratic Representative Eugene Keogh to the sensitive racing post.

So close did the odd couple relationship become that Esposito even asked the governor to intervene in a legal matter. In 1973 the Brooklyn Democrat became embroiled in one of numerous investigations that failed to result in formal charges against him. This time, it involved allegations of stock manipulation surrounding a publicly traded refrigeration equipment company.

In that post-Watergate period, the political atmosphere was so sensitive that Esposito wanted to avoid even appearing before a federal grand jury. So he called Rockefeller and asked if the Republican governor would be kind enough to request that the U.S. attorney for New York's Southern District, Whitney North Seymour, Jr., a Republican, allow Esposito to file a deposition in the case instead of having to testify in person and risk embarrassing publicity. Rockefeller forwarded Esposito's request to the office of his counsel, Robert Douglass. Seymour was called but flatly refused to comply. Esposito subsequently testified before the grand jury, but was whisked in and out so quietly that denizens of the U.S. Court House in Foley Square never even knew he had been in the building.

Early in 1972, Rockefeller provided another favor, one whose immediate importance to Esposito may have been underestimated at the time. In exchange for support in Albany, the Brooklyn Democratic boss asked Rockefeller to serve as his intermediary in scheduling a secret meeting with John Mitchell, Richard Nixon's attorney general and 1972 presidential campaign director. Esposito and Mitchell "were both friends of mine,"

Rockefeller would recall later. "They were interested in meeting each other. I arranged for such a meeting over the telephone, setting up a mutually convenient time. That is all that I did. To the best of my knowledge, members of my staff had no role in setting up the meeting other than placing phone calls for me. I have no idea from any source as to what was discussed at the meeting."[19]

No idea? Well, Rockefeller should have had some inkling from reading the newspapers. And he should at least have been curious about why two powerful figures from opposite parties should be meeting in a Washington restaurant on the eve of the presidential campaign. Esposito reluctantly conceded later that he requested the meeting to help spring ousted Tammany chief Carmine De Sapio, who had been convicted in a bribery-conspiracy case, from Lewisburg Federal Prison, where he was eligible for parole.[20] If that was his mission, Esposito failed. But two other legal matters also concerned the Brooklyn leader and Mitchell, who was already running Richard Nixon's reelection campaign, was in a position to influence both of them. Brooklyn Democratic Representatives Bertram Podell and Frank Brasco were both under investigation by the Justice Department —and both were subsequently indicted and convicted for influence-peddling schemes.

"His morals are very high," the affable Esposito said of Rockefeller. "He's a Puritan."[21]

Often, Rockefeller seemed oblivious to possible conflicts. The state's loosely worded and unenforced provisions of the Public Officers Law required a filing of interest in corporations that were "state regulated" within the meaning of the statute. When he first became governor in 1959, Rockefeller disposed of his stock in Consolidated Edison because he thought "there might be a conflict." It was not until 13 years later, however, following a reporter's inquiry, that Rockefeller filed an updated report. It listed only one firm subject to state regulation—Interstate United, a food and service conglomerate whose contracts with several state-related agencies had been questioned over the years by Controller Arthur Levitt's auditors.

In 1972, however, a conflict arose that struck even closer to home. It was learned that the concession contract for the legislative dining room in Rockefeller's marble mall had been awarded to an Interstate United subsidiary—leaving lawmakers who criticized the governor in the uncanny condition of biting the hand that literally fed them. Rockefeller unloaded the stock the next day.

Nelson Rockefeller ruled the executive branch of the New York state government even more easily than he manipulated its elected representatives, and with the same goals in mind— political advancement for himself and a safe, secure financial environment in which the business establishment could prosper. That his own family's holdings would flourish or fail in direct relation to his policies as governor never seemed to bother him. The two were admittedly inseparable, and short of selling his assets wholesale, there seemed little he could do about it. William Ronan said of the inevitable conflict: "If the policies I pursued have in any way enhanced the interests of the Rockefeller family, that is only because their interests are so intimately entwined that it would be difficult to benefit New York without in some way benefiting Rockefeller interests."[22]

CHAPTER 10

The Prince
and His Court

WITH Rockefeller as governor, the interests of the state and the bankers, bosses, builders, financiers, and fatcats of all descriptions became increasingly entwined. It was as if the state had become a subsidiary of the Rockefeller family enterprises, its directors responsible only to the Prince of Pocantico and their decisions subject only to quadrennial ratification by the stockholders. It was New York Incorporated: Nelson A. Rockefeller, president.

And who were the directors? They were the "superiors" whom Rockefeller had been urged by his mother to seek out. "Only can one accomplish big things in life if you associate with big people," said Rockefeller. "And the people whom I really admire and respect are people who have ideas that I did not think of. I have got a reasonably creative mind, but I really admire the people who have the ideas and creative thoughts."[1]

In this community of "superiors," ideas should have flowed freely, but that was not always the case. Well-reasoned dissent was almost always tolerated before a decision was made; however, the official family invariably closed ranks once the governor had picked the course he intended to pursue. Attorney

General Louis Lefkowitz, one of his intimate political advisers since 1958, recalled that Rockefeller never "liked yes-men around him—in fact, some people were not invited back. You could argue with him," Lefkowitz added, "but once he made up his mind he'd like to have you shut up."[2]

Yet, Republican State Chairman Richard Rosenbaum observed, "A lot of guys yes the hell out of him—it makes you sick to your stomach."

Another intimate aide recounted a particularly irksome flaw: "he could be a bitch, and he could be totally unreasonable when he had the wrong facts. He would not go back and check directly when someone said you did or said something. Sometimes he would jump on erroneous facts and he'd be pissed off. His eyes would narrow, and instead of looking at you directly, he'd keep looking out the window—unless you sensed something was wrong and set him straight." He was not above rage, and at times would choke off criticism within the inner circle curtly and completely. "Well," he would sometimes announce arbitrarily, "I'm the governor and that's the way it's going to be." Few seemed to mind, at least publicly. Employment in the Rockefeller domain was too valued a prize.

Foremost among the inner circle of key advisers was William John Ronan, the Buffalo-born professor of public administration who was deputy city administrator of New York under Robert Wagner when he was spirited away by Rockefeller in 1956 to study the need for a state constitutional convention. "He's a bright fellow," Wagner said of his former brain truster. "He's a little tough. He doesn't have a good public relations image."[3] The public image of Ronan was that of a six-foot-two fullback whose self-confidence had soured to arrogance (after years of political battles he still insists on being called "Doctor" because he has a Ph.D.) and who tolerated no Monday morning quarterbacking by anyone less bright than himself.

Describing his hatchetman in unusually blunt terms, Rockefeller recalled the fight to tap funds of the Port Authority of New York and New Jersey for mass transit and surprised the

Senate Rules Committee by declaring: "Dr. Ronan was the only one who had the guts and the balls—I should not say that word —to challenge the entire organization, and to really go after it."[4]

After quitting as dean of New York University's Graduate School of Public Administration and Social Service, where he was making $19,000 a year, Ronan worked on the commission and campaigned with Rockefeller in 1958. The following year, at the age of 48, he was named secretary to the new governor at a $20,000 annual salary. Credited with carrying out the state's pioneering approach to regional mass transportation, he became the first $45,000-a-year chairman of the Metropolitan Transportation Authority in 1965. He was making $80,000 annually when he left the MTA in 1974 to become the unsalaried chairman of the board of the Port Authority of New York and New Jersey. It was not an unprofitable career for a public servant.

But it was an even more lucrative life as a loyal Rockefeller-phile. The rewards of such service came early. Just before he was named secretary, the new governor gave him a gift of $75,000. Over the next decade, as Rockefeller became more dependent on him and credited him with engineering the successful 1966 reelection race, Ronan received another $510,000 in loans. Those loans were forgiven on May 3, 1974, when Rockefeller also gave his alter ego another cash gift of $40,000. Why $40,000? "I assumed," said Ronan, "that he was rounding off the figure to make the total dollars $550,000. I have no idea."[5]

Ronan was only one recipient of Rockefeller's largesse. Over the years, the governor spun a web of loans and gifts that ranged from a $6,500 J. B. Stearns oil painting, *The Trial of Major Andre*, loaned to former Attorney General John Mitchell to the subsidies for Ronan and other aides.[6] Carefully timed to circumvent the state's antitipping statute, the gifts and loans purchased a kind of personal loyalty that permitted the Rockefeller team to pursue political goals with a rare singleness of purpose. The loans and gifts diminished the distractions of everyday duties: cars, maids, and larger homes bought with the Rockefeller dollars lightened the burdens of family responsibilities and made more time available to meet the governor's needs. And for most, Nelson's largesse helped eliminate potential conflicts of interest, or even the appearances of conflict. Ronan, who insisted that his hefty subsidies "had no relationship to any duties I had to perform as a state official,"[7] recalled that when he first required some cash around 1962, he lacked the kind of collateral required for a large loan.

"I think it would have been possible, very frankly, for me to have gotten a noncollateralized loan from almost any major bank in the city because of being secretary to the governor," Ronan explained. "If I walked in and asked for a loan, I am sure that I could have gotten a respectable amount. I frankly would have preferred not to do that in the position I was in."[8] Working for Rockefeller was even better than having a friend at Chase Manhattan.

After almost two decades of public service, Ronan had accumulated a $375,000 Dutch colonial home and land in East Hampton, Long Island, a $90,000 cooperative apartment at 2 Sutton Place South, $170,000 worth of industrial land in California, $150,000 in certificates of deposit and other bank accounts, and a stock portfolio (topped by 2,200 shares of Continental Copper and naturally including 1,600 shares of IBEC) valued at over $96,000. Total net worth by 1974: $880,000. And to continue to tap his talents and keep him in the style to which he had become accustomed in public life, Rockefeller recruited Ronan in 1974 as senior adviser to the family at $100,000 a year. "I've never been a sycophant," Ronan would say later. "My friendships and usefulness in terms of my politics was that I am always myself."[9] Of course it helped that being "himself" meshed so well with his patron. Rockefeller says he and Ronan are so "mentally close" that it's "almost like a marriage."[10]

Serving alongside Ronan as counsel to the 1956 constitutional convention commission was George Lyon Hinman, the bespectacled Binghamton attorney whose description of himself as "just a country lawyer" is much too modest. His relationship to

Rockefeller is like that of the "man of business" to a political duke in eighteenth century England. He is trusted, unequivocally, both by Rockefeller and by the politicians he is sent to deal with.

Being son of a state senator and friend of the Watson family of IBM fame didn't hurt either. His was the first county in the state to endorse Rockefeller publicly for the Republican gubernatorial nomination in 1958. Hinman was appointed as unpaid patronage dispenser right after the election, and he was selected as Republican national committeeman from New York the following spring. Shortly after the 1960 national convention, Hinman was also named special counsel to the Rockefeller brothers and given an office in Room 5600; he served in the practically full time post of "national and political contact, very close friend, and close adviser in personal and family affairs"[11] even beyond Nelson's term as governor. Hinman has also served on the boards of IBM and the New York Telephone Company. In 1965 he was nominated as a trustee of the State University of New York, whose chancellor, Samuel Gould, was himself a trustee of the Rockefeller Brothers Fund. Hinman has said that "the greatest triumph of the Rockefeller family is to have brought up unspoiled children."[12]

Ronan was succeeded as secretary to the governor in 1966 by Alton Garwood Marshall, a small-town Michigan native and no-nonsense ex-Marine who survived for 23 years in state service without either a civil service rating or political clout. Silver-haired and silver-tongued, Marshall started in 1947 as a $2,380-a-year budget division intern at age 26. He was secretary of the Public Service Commission when he was spotted by Budget Director T. Norman Hurd in 1961. Rockefeller named Marshall executive officer in 1965 and secretary the following year.

Beginning in 1967, the governor made the first of what would amount to five non-interest-bearing loans to Marshall over the next four years; when forgiven in 1973, they totaled $306,867. By that time, Marshall was no longer a state employee. On January 1, 1971, he had assumed the presidency of Rockefeller Center and the Radio City Music Hall. Marshall also serves on the boards of New York State Electric and Gas Corp., Westrand Industries, City Title Insurance Company, and the state's Sports Authority.

Marshall, who charmed John Lindsay's former deputy mayor, Richard Aurelio, into a special consultantship at Rockefeller Center, mused one day about what made Nelson tick. "I've often thought," he said, "that the greatest psychological impact of power would be the misuse of power. Jesus Christ, if he'd got the goddamn power and tried to set up a dictatorship or something I could understand that. But I can't understand him subjecting himself to all sorts of strain and abuse to accomplish something he thought was necessary."[13]

Marshall's successor as secretary to Rockefeller was Robert Royal Douglass, a blond and boyish-looking lawyer from Binghamton who joined Hinman's firm after graduating from Dartmouth and Cornell Law. The course he would pursue in and out of public office had been mapped by his predecessors. He was hired as first assistant counsel in 1964, when he was 33 years old, and promoted to counsel the following year. Friendly and unfazed, he practically became a member of the Rockefeller family. His children played with Nelson's youngest boys. He regularly beat his boss at golf and accepted his silver dollar rewards. He was fondly referred to as "Bobby" by everyone, including the servants at Pocantico. His was the on-the-scene counsel trusted most by Rockefeller when he agonized over the assault on Attica.

Douglass was Nelson's fair-haired boy, and it was no surprise when he succeeded Marshall early in 1971 as the second most powerful man in the executive branch of New York State government. It was also no surprise that when he resigned in the summer of 1972, just shy of his 41st birthday, Douglass returned to private practice as a partner in the prestigious firm of Milbank, Tweed, Hadley & McCloy—which happens to represent Chase Manhattan Bank. He also became counsel to Rockefeller Center and a member of its board of directors. And to top things off, he was tapped by Rockefeller as an unsalaried commissioner of the powerful Port Authority.

Another one of the Rockefeller *wunderkinder* was Henry L. Diamond, who was 38 when the governor named him New York's first environmental conservation commissioner in 1970. Diamond first ran into Laurance Rockefeller when he edited reports for the presidential Outdoor Recreation Resources Review Commission in 1959, and he had been on call for conservation duty ever since. He worked as an assistant to Attorney General Robert Kennedy in 1962 and directed the White House Conference on Natural Beauty called by Lyndon Johnson three years later. In March 1968 he was asked to join the Johnson reelection campaign staff, a move he discreetly decided to clear with his mentor. "Laurance said, 'Why the hell work for Johnson?' So I became scheduling head for Nelson Rockefeller."[14]

The bespectacled attorney with the trace of a Tennessee twang was also chairman of the Natural Heritage Trust, a state agency used to funnel $472,493—80 percent of the total it received between 1968 and 1973—from Laurance Rockefeller. After Diamond resigned, state auditors charged that the trust had made $48,714 in "improper" expenditures.[15] Included were $3,048 for Christmas parties and $18,898 in contributions to the campaign for Rockefeller's 1972 environmental bond issue. Diamond, who succeeded Laurance as chairman of the Federal Citizens Advisory Committee on Environmental Quality in mid 1973, quit his state commissionership at the end of that year to become executive director of the Critical Choices Commission. And when he did, Nelson gave him a going away (or was it welcome aboard?) gift of $100,000.

Also flourishing in Nelson's court was Oscar Ruebhausen, partner in the potent Park Avenue law firm of Debevoise, Plimpton, Lyon & Gates and chairman of Democrats for Rockefeller in the 1958 campaign. Within months after taking office, Rockefeller recruited Ruebhausen as vice-chairman of his newly created Advisory Committee on Atomic Energy. Then he named him to the City University Construction Fund, as special counsel to the commission studying the Lindsay administration, and as chairman of the Special Commission on Insurance Holding Companies. The governor even named Ruebhausen's wife to Manhattan State Senator Roy Goodman's commission that was charged with rewriting New York City's charter. So well anchored was Ruebhausen in the Rockefeller realm that Nelson established a $130,000 trust in his behalf—administered by Bobby Douglass. He was also a trustee of Herman Kahn's Hudson Institute, a member of the Critical Choices Commission, and a director of IBEC.

From 1964 to 1970, IBEC's board of directors was also graced by William L. Pfeiffer, a Buffalo-born banker and former Republican state chairman whom Rockefeller attracted early on. Pfeiffer was named to the State Racing Commission in 1969, after serving as GOP state treasurer and as manager of several Rockefeller campaigns. He has also sat on the board of Continental Copper & Steel Corp. (with William Ronan) and was a director of the Struthers-Wells Corp., whose chairman was Jerry Finkelstein, the New York City Democratic chairman.

"Bill Pfeiffer is a friend of mine for 25 years," Finkelstein fussed. "I have never asked him for a favor—I have never asked him for a contract. When you have a board, you ask people you feel comfortable with."[16]

Among Finkelstein's other comfortable relationships was that with Nelson Rockefeller. The Democratic politico provided support in Albany and Washington for revenue sharing and helped convince labor mediator Theodore Kheel to back the 1973 state transportation bond issue. The Republican governor, for his part, appointed Andrew Stein, Finkelstein's son and an aggressive East Side assemblyman, to chair the Temporary State Commission on Living Costs and the Economy—a mouthful of a title but a spacious platform for publicity. In 1972, Rockefeller elevated Finkelstein to the Port Authority. Better still, a short while later he was tapped for the prestigious board of Rockefeller Center. Finkelstein "merchandised that Rockefeller relationship all over town," an aide to Nelson later complained. "I know he does that," said Rockefeller. "But it's all part of the relationship. It's a relationship of convenience for both of us."[17]

Money—like booze, food, and fear of reformers—can always be counted on to make strange bedfellows of politicians with opposite persuasions, a fact evident in the practices and directorships of many prominent New York financial institutions. Take the Kings Lafayette Bank. Occasionally criticized for making uncollateralized loans to reputed mobsters, it was long regarded as Brooklyn's dominant Democratic bank and even numbered Kings County chairman Meade Esposito at one time among its employees. But official bank reports boasted that its chairman, John R. H. Blum, represented the Rockefeller family.

That is only the beginning. William Ronan sat on the board of Security National Bank and Metropolitan Savings Bank with William Shea, a fellow member of the Metropolitan Transportation Authority, which Ronan chaired. A Democrat, Shea was senior partner in a high-powered Madison Avenue law firm that represented Security as well as Automatic Toll Systems, a manufacturer that, since 1965, won over $4 million in contracts from the Triborough Bridge and Tunnel Authority—which is controlled by the MTA.

Another example. Al Marshall was appointed to the power-packed board of City Title Insurance Company, the firm whose directors list reads like a power broker's "who's who." "We don't deal on political lines, just with important people,"[18] says Saul Fromkes, the little colonel who runs City Title with his brother Otto. Among the important people were Stanley Steingut, who was Democratic minority leader and, later, speaker of the State Assembly; Willis Stephens, who chaired the Ways and Means Committee when the Republicans were in power; and Arthur Quinn, president of the New York Bank for Savings and finance committee chairman of Manhattan GOP Chairman Vincent F. Albano, Jr.'s county organization.

"Years ago," Albano remembers, "it was almost a religion. Personal feelings still exist on the lower echelon—the little local Democratic captain on the Lower East Side still hates his counterpart. He still thinks it's the party of the rich. [But now] there's really only one time Democrats and Republicans fight— that's election day."[19]

Connections between the family fortune and the public sector were not limited to jobs alone. During his tenure as governor, Nelson was armed with the resources to spend $5 million for a full-time staff of poll takers and pulse feelers to feed him the best advice money could buy. His single biggest such endeavor was a foundation which he established as early as 1953, long before his first gubernatorial campaign. To run it, he wanted Frank C. Moore.

Moore had served on the state payroll in several appointive posts and had been elected lieutenant governor on the Dewey ticket in 1950. He was eying the governorship race in 1954, but he resigned on September 30, 1953 (with 15 months left in his term), to take another state-related job: the presidency of an obscure tax-exempt outfit called the Government Affairs Foundation. It sounded like a front for something, and it was. The board of directors clearly telegraphed just whom it was fronting for. There was Wallace Harrison, the architect, John Lockwood, the Rockefeller family lawyer, and Louise Boyer, Nelson's executive assistant. From 1958 until the foundation was dissolved a decade later, Nelson personally poured $1,026,180 into its treasury. About half the total was donated in the form of Standard Oil stock. At the same time, the foundation gave Moore an annual salary of about $30,000, plus a $10,000 expense account.

In one period studied by the late Wright Patman, Moore's commission, which Rockefeller said was created to "improve quality and reduce quantity of government," spent 57 percent of its budget on Moore's salary and personal expenses and paid out absolutely nothing in gifts, grants, or scholarships. "It didn't do very well in reducing the quantity of government in New York State," Patman complained, and "it didn't have much luck finding other worthy outlets for its money."[20]

Sometimes it wasn't even necessary to create a separate foundation to provide for personal and political pals. The family philanthropies had long been in an ideal position to enhance the Rockefeller name. And if the potential recipients happened to be prospective political supporters of Nelson, well, all the better. In the 1970 gubernatorial campaign, almost no one could understand why Arthur Logan, the prominent surgeon, had joined a group of black Democrats defecting to the Rockefeller camp. Then Victor Gotbaum of the powerful State, County and Municipal Employees Union asserted that Logan had swapped his endorsement for the promise of a new hospital. Nothing unusual there—until the doctor himself disclosed details of the deal.

"There are individual projects which I'm interested in which the governor has given his support to," he explained. "For instance, a major new health-care complex in the West Harlem–Manhattanville area to serve the residents there who are now without adequate facilities. I think Rockefeller is about to announce some very significant financial support—as an individual. In fact, I understand it will be $2 million from the Rockefeller Brothers Fund."[21]

The family financial clout also had an important negative impact. In that same campaign in which Rockefeller disbursed more than five times the amount raised for Democrat Arthur Goldberg, his rival was said to have "spent a long, sad afternoon telephoning a list of his oldest friends asking for help in his campaign. One by one, each person on the list said no, explaining his link to the Rockefellers—membership on a hospital board or arts council financed by the Family, business loan negotiations with Chase Manhattan, and on into the night."[22]

Within months after the campaign ended, Goldberg was installed on the board of directors of Trans World Airlines by Conrad Hilton, whom he had known as a director of the Waldorf-Towers during his ambassadorial days. In some circles, it was immediately taken as a sign that the former Supreme Court justice had lost gracefully and had been forgiven—because at the time he joined the board and during his brief tenure, TWA was very much of interest to the Chase Manhattan Bank. Chase, which held 7.8 percent of the airline's common stock—

apparently the largest single block of TWA stock outstanding—
also shared five interlocking directorships with the Equitable
Life Assurance Society, which had an $87.8 million loan out-
standing to the carrier and was a 20 percent loan participant in a
lease trust agreement involving 23 jetliners.[23]

Could Goldberg have been invited onto the board without the
concurrence of its biggest stockholder? "I didn't know about
that at all," he said.[24] But about the same time he was elected to
the board, he was asked who really wields power in New York.
His response was much more revealing. "I don't profess expertise
in this subject," he explained, "which is the reason I cannot supply a list. Perhaps another reason is that I would start, and end,
with the Rockefellers."[25]

CHAPTER 11

Banks
and Bandits

LAWMAKERS and lawbreakers who share a common interest in banks take their inspiration from that terrorizer of tellers, Willie Sutton. Once asked why he robbed them, the wily Willie matter-of-factly replied: "That's where the money is."

Under any administration, banking interests pervade every aspect of the state's political structure. But during the Rockefeller administration, these links were especially sensitive. With Nelson as governor and his brother David as board chairman of the Chase Manhattan Bank, the nation's third largest, the potential for abuse was obvious. Perhaps because it was in such an exposed position, Chase often let other big-city banks carry the ball publicly for rules and legislation favorable to the banking industry.

"As superintendent of banks," Oren Root recalled, "I always had the governor's full support. Never in the three years that I was in that office did he seek to influence or direct my course of action in the discharge of my statutory duties, although I have no doubt, because of the magnitude of the stakes involved, that there were times when he was importuned to do so."

In fact, Rockefeller did not need to interfere because Root was promulgating the policies set by the new governor during his first months in office. "With the developing complexities of modern banking," Root explained, "it became increasingly clear that small unit banks were no longer equal to the demands of the times and that some relaxation of the statutory restrictions was in order. The result was a series of amendments to the New York Banking Law enacted by the legislature in 1960 and 1961 with Governor Rockefeller's support, which took steps in that direction." Root noted that he also "sponsored a bill in the legislature which would have expanded still further the areas in which banks could branch and merge. While my bill passed the Assembly, it failed in the Senate, where the opposition of the smaller upstate banks was influential. Ultimately, under one of my successors, an even more liberal bill was adopted. ...."[1]

Enough of the omnibus banking bill passed—again by virtue of a message of necessity from Rockefeller that effectively prevented meaningful opposition to develop—that one assemblyman, with an eye on Chase Manhattan's Rockefeller connection, quipped that the governor had finally "taken care of the House of David." But he had no conflicts of interest, the governor insisted, because he had sold his Chase stock before signing the bill, which allowed New York City banks to gain a first foothold in the suburbs. He seemed to have already forgotten his own observation, at the end of his freshman year in Albany, that inspired skepticism about the extent of his objectivity or the virtues of a blind trust. "An official," Rockefeller conceded, "can divest himself of all his securities and still be involved in the emotional reactions of a lifetime."[2]

Oddly enough, Nelson's biggest bank bail-out involved the Rockefeller-related Chemical Bank, which in 1969 was desperately defending itself against a takeover attempt by Saul P. Steinberg's Leasco Data Processing conglomerate. On February 18, the governor sent an emergency message to the legislature urging restrictions on bank acquisitions by firms "without related managerial experience." Just days later, Leasco's 29-year-old chairman abandoned his bid to acquire the $9 billion bank. But just for insurance, Rockefeller rammed the restrictive bill through the legislature anyway with the solid support of state banking officials.

Since Rockefeller recruited the state bank superintendents, one may presume that he appointed experts who would promulgate his policies. And every one of the five superintendents who served under Rockefeller discovered that a big dividend of his post was the promise of a profitable position in the banking industry when he withdrew from public service. No one expected banks to be regulated by consumer-oriented career civil servants immune from political pressure. But the department's domination by bankers, ex-bankers, and future bankers, and their revolving-door employment pattern, alarmed critics who were already fearful of Rockefeller's potential conflict of interest.

Rockefeller's first superintendent, G. Russell Clark, the chief administrative officer of the American Bankers Association, was appointed January 29, 1959. When Clark quit in mid-1961 to chair the National Bank of North America, he was succeeded by Root. After serving for almost three years, Root left in 1964. Within a year, he became senior vice president of the Irving Trust Company and later president of the parent Charter New York Corporation. Next came Frank Wille, Rockefeller's respected first assistant counsel and the superintendent with the longest tenure. Wille approved the formation of the state's first bank holding company—Charter New York—and left in 1970 to chair the Federal Deposit Insurance Corporation.

Rockefeller's fourth superintendent was his most controversial. His name was William Dentzer, and he was executive secretary of the State Council of Economic Advisors. The council, a group created by the governor, included two representatives of the private sector. Conveniently, they were Eugene Black, a Chase director; and William Butler, Chase's vice-president and director of economic research. But Dentzer had no personal or professional loyalty to the governor's brother's bank. And that was believed to be an underlying reason for his departure in 1972 after serving the shortest term of any bank superintendent Rockefeller selected.

During his relatively brief tenure, Dentzer formally injected himself into a Colorado antitrust suit before the U.S. Supreme Court in favor of the philosophy that potential, as well as existing, competition should be taken into account when mergers are considered. He publicized a study recommending that savings banks and other so-called thrift institutions be authorized to offer checking accounts to customers. He blocked an application to acquire the National Bank of Northern New York by Lincoln First Banks, an upstate holding company whose directors included national Republican committeeman George Hinman. And without notifying Rockefeller, he drafted an amendment to the sweeping legislation eliminating district lines and allowing banks to open branches all over the state. The amendment barred bank holding companies from chartering new banks in cities where another bank had its home office. Specifically, it prevented Chase from starting a subsidiary in suburban Garden City.

When Dentzer left in the spring of 1972, he didn't go very far away. Within five weeks, he was named chairman of the Central Certificate Service of the New York Stock Exchange.

So well prepared for Dentzer's departure was Rockefeller that he selected a successor the very same day. The governor's fifth and final appointment as the public's watchdog over the financial community was Harry W. Albright, Jr., son of a banker and former partner in the Albany law firm that represented the state's savings banks. In 1975, when the Democrats captured control of the state administration, Albright bounced into the presidency of the Dime Savings Bank of New York.

The bankers were brash about their clout in the legislature. In the waning weeks of the 1972 session, a story about a major banking industry lobbyist quietly made the rounds in Capitol corridors. The lobbyist was supposed to have boasted to brother bankers: "I don't buy legislators dinner. I buy legislators." The lobbyist flatly denied saying any such thing, but then Assembly Speaker Perry Duryea angrily "starred" pending banking bills—freezing any action on them for the rest of the session.

Banks and Bandits

Without having to brag about it, the banking industry enjoyed links to lawmakers which were at least cozy and in some cases constituted possible conflicts of interest. More than one third of the 210 senators and assemblymen owned bank stock, were directors or trustees, have handled legal affairs for banks, or have collected campaign contributions from banking industry sources.[3] Senate Majority Leader Warren Anderson, for instance, is a member of a Binghamton law firm that represented First–City National Bank. Also in the firm is GOP national committeeman George Hinman, who is a director of Lincoln First Banks. At the request of former Republican State Chairman Charles Schoeneck, whose law firm lobbied for Lincoln First, Anderson introduced a bill in 1972 that would have limited the upstate expansion of New York City banks. He insisted that the measure was only aimed at complying with the intent of the legislature to let upstate banks consolidate before the sweeping single district banking bill would take effect in 1976. State Senator John Dunne of Nassau County is a partner in a firm that did regular legal work for Chase Manhattan in Nassau and Westchester. Dunne, who explained that the firm had represented Chase before he joined it, conceded that he introduced several bills sought by the bank trust departments, some of which could hike legal fees. But he said he did so mainly for "study purposes."[4]

Among the more dramatic examples of just how rewarding public service could become was the case of Robert F. Kelly. After successfully pressing for creation of a state Cable Television Commission, Kelly was tapped for the chairmanship of that commission in 1974 at almost three times his $15,000 salary as an assemblyman. But before leaving the legislature, the Brooklyn Republican received what seemed like another bonus for his skills in the Assembly. In the 1971 session, Kelly strongly supported a bill that provided real estate investment trusts with the same tax advantages they enjoyed on the federal level—exemption from the franchise tax on banks and other financial institutions. He also introduced and backed a second bill to allow savings banks and savings and loan associations to participate and invest with any such trusts. The first bill was approved on June 2. The second passed the Assembly on April 1, but lost upon reconsideration and was tabled. Kelly personally moved to reconsider again, and on June 6 it passed by a narrow 77–66 margin. Ten months later, Kelly was named a $5,000-a-year, part-time trustee of BT Mortgage Investors, a Boston-based real estate investment trust organized by Bankers Trust Co. of New York. Chairman of the trust was William Pfeiffer, the chairman of Albany Savings Bank and former Republican state chairman. And vice-president of Bankers Trust New York Corp., the bank's parent company, was GOP State Treasurer James G. Hellmuth.

A soft-spoken man whom Rockefeller appointed to an unpaid commissionership on the Port Authority, Hellmuth also figured in an even more lucrative field for financial institutions. Every year, the state deposited hundreds of millions of dollars in interest-free accounts in politically powerful banks. Although they were supposed to be short-term demand deposits, the public's cash sometimes reposed for years in dormant accounts while the banks reaped the profits by investing or lending. The size of some deposits was based, state officials said, on the compensatory services provided by the banks, like check cashing and tax collection. But sometimes there were other compensations, too.

The largest account under the sole jurisdiction of the state tax commissioner, a Rockefeller appointee, included the multimillion-dollar receipts of the stock transfer tax. By 1972 the two banks that split the account received daily deposits that added up to over $10 million at the end of each month, at which time they were transferred to the state's general fund and disbursed quarterly to New York City.

The account was originally at the Empire Trust Co., which merged on December 7, 1966, with the Bank of New York, where continuation of the account was confirmed the following March. Hellmuth was vice-president of Empire from 1960 to 1967 and was connected with the Bank of New York after the merger. Later in 1967, Hellmuth joined Morgan and also became party treasurer. On January 1, 1968, more than half the stock transfer tax fund account was shifted to Morgan. Late in 1971, Hellmuth left his vice-presidency of Morgan to deposit himself in the same post at Bankers Trust. And six weeks later, the state switched Morgan's share of the stock transfer tax fund account to Bankers Trust, too.

The administration called it all coincidental. Taxation and Finance Commissioner Norman Gallman explained that Bankers Trust "performs a lot of accounting and bookkeeping services in connection with the stock transfer tax." As for Morgan, it refused even to hazard a guess as to why Bankers Trust found a friend in the State of New York. "The bank can't talk about its depositors," a spokesman politely replied. "We just have an in-flexible rule about customers' business."[5] Even when the cus-tomer was the taxpayers of the State of New York.

Somehow, the Rockefeller policies and projects that were supposed to be a boon to the downtrodden also managed to bene-fit the friends and fat cats who helped implement the policies or produce the projects. Nelson was not the plunderer of George Washington Plunkett's day. Rather, he represented an elite com-munity of interests which, he believed, shared his devotion to good deeds. And the interests of the architects, underwriters, and others were intimately entwined with the policies and politics of government.

Rockefeller's unprecedented expansion of mass transportation programs on a regional basis also provided two windfalls to the banks. The first was simple enough. In 1966, on the advice of the governor's secretary, William Ronan, and a designee of the legislature, William Shea, the state bailed out First National City Bank by buying the bankrupt Long Island Railroad from the ailing Penn Central. Citibank was among the biggest creditors of the Penn Central, which was paid $65 million for what state auditors said amounted to a pile of junk.[6]

The second bank boondoggle came in 1968, when the new Metropolitan Transportation Authority sought to tap the surpluses of the Triborough Bridge and Tunnel Authority to subsidize mass transit. The hitch came when the corporate trustee for Triborough bondholders, Chase Manhattan Bank, sued to block any transfer of the surpluses to the MTA because it claimed that the bond indenture would be violated. Finally, after months of fancy legal footwork, a compromise was reached. In a unique ceremony, a stipulation signed by David Rockefeller for the bondholders and Nelson Rockefeller for New York State provided that if two-thirds of the bondholders consented, the surplus could be transferred to the subways.

A sweetener was also tossed in. Triborough bondholders were offered 0.25 percent extra interest on their bonds, which would net them almost $6 million more by the time all $285 million in outstanding bonds matured in 1985. What few knew was Chase's special interest in the pact. In addition to holding $2.2 million worth of Triborough bonds in various trust accounts, the bank's own investment portfolio included $32.5 million worth—more than 10 percent of all the authority's outstanding bonds.[7]

Finally, it was a bizarre case involving Texas computer tycoon H. Ross Perot that provided living proof of the adage that success depends not only on what you know but who you know. The *what*, in the millionaire supersalesman's case, was the automation and management of New York State's multi-billion-dollar welfare and Medicaid mess. The *who* was Nelson Rockefeller.

On February 2, 1973, the state's Welfare Department dropped nine of 12 competing computer companies from the final bidding for what could become a $30 million state contract. One of the nine was Electronic Data Systems, Inc., the Texas-based firm run by former IBM salesman Perot. The next day, Welfare Commissioner Abe Lavine returned to his office to discover that his staff had made a "mistake" in rejecting EDS from the final round of bidding. He immediately ordered his staff to notify EDS that it was still under consideration. But the wiry Texas technocrat was taking no chances. Although he describes himself as "nonpolitical," officials of his firm contributed hefty sums to the 1972 Nixon campaign. And only one year earlier, Perot had personally invested $10 million in the ailing Wall Street brokerage house of DuPont Glore Forgan at the personal request of top Nixon administration officials, including then Attorney General John Mitchell.[8] All that contributed to the fact that Perot was not an obscure computer peddler when he called Rockefeller's director of state operations, T. Norman Hurd, on February 8.

The next day, Lavine arrived at Rockefeller's midtown Manhattan townhouse from Albany to meet with the governor, Hurd, and Perot. "I had to sell my wares," Perot later explained, "and I didn't want the governor to think we were just a little bitty old Texas firm that couldn't compete with IBM. I told the governor about my track record in other states, which has been proven, and he was intrigued."[9] Perot was subsequently reinstated, and was convincing enough to become one of the firms awarded a $40,000 contract to produce an automated computerized model of the welfare and Medicaid payment systems. Only a month after the first disclosure of the Rockefeller-Perot parley, Electronic Data Systems was awarded a $125,000 consultant contract without competitive bidding to help prepare a statewide registry of New York's 2.3 million welfare and Medicaid clients.

The ensuing controversy was hardly quelled by the standard Rockefeller response to criticism. Under attack by Victor Gotbaum, Queens Democratic Representative Benjamin Rosenthal, Lindsay administration officials, and editorial writers for several newspapers, Rockefeller recruited George Berlinger to set the record straight. Berlinger, a regular Rockefeller campaign contributor, was also the governor's handpicked welfare inspector general. His charge in the politically explosive Perot case was to investigate all of the allegations, with emphasis on the "motivations behind and reasons for the allegations."[10]

Dutifully seeking to reconcile contradictory testimony, the Berlinger report concluded that the governor's intervention was not improper and that the skull session he and Perot held was only to discuss the combining by Perot of income maintenance and Medicaid into a single proposal for the state.

Although Rockefeller admitted that he did not ordinarily open his office door to disgruntled contractors, he insisted that he was "very concerned and interested in seeing that the state gets the ablest people to bid on contracts."[11] But beyond politics and personal ties, there was another reason why there might have been a special interest in Perot. When he was pressed by Nixon administration pals to bail out that ailing brokerage house, Perot put up some of his EDS stock as collateral for a $50 million loan by a nine-bank consortium to finance the acquisition. The lead bank in that consortium was none other than Chase Manhattan.

Apparently contradicting a key conclusion of the Berlinger report—that Perot's rejection was not even raised at the February 9, 1973, meeting—Rockefeller had a different recollection. "We sat down," the former governor said, "and he was very disturbed because his name had been cut off the list of bidders. The bids were not in yet, and I had with me at the same meeting the head of the Social Welfare Department and questioned him. He was very embarrassed because a letter had been sent out under his signature during his absence . . . from the office canceling the bid—the invitation to bid."[12]

Rockefeller also blamed the ensuing ruckus on the opposition of labor leaders concerned that the computer contract would jeopardize the jobs of their members. "I'd never heard of his problem with the Chase bank," he explained, noting that Perot "paid off his loan anyhow."

Why even bother to become involved with the computer whiz? "I can tell you the circumstances," Rockefeller replied straight faced. "This was part of my effort to eliminate corruption from the welfare system."[13]

CHAPTER 12

Building
with *Authority*

HE'S constructed a perpetuity," complained Rockefeller's Democratic successor Hugh Carey. "The way he's set up the authorities, boards, and commissions with term appointments, it's almost beyond the reach of a governor to effectuate policy because he had these overlapping directorships in so many ways that their policy—which used to be his policy—becomes state policy without the intervention of the public. To call it a dynasty is one thing, but it's feudal."[1]

And often, physically permanent as well. Nelson Rockefeller liked to build things: big, grand, visible things—roads, schools, cultural complexes, monuments. His critics called it a "whim of iron," an "edifice complex." In addition to the $1 billion-plus Albany Mall, Rockefeller's mountain of mortar included 29 other state office buildings from Long Island to Buffalo, 200 waste-treatment plants, at least 90,000 new housing units, three new model communities, 23 new mental health facilities, 55 new state parks, 109 voluntary and municipal hospitals (constructed or expanded), and a state university system that grew from 38,000 students on 28 campuses when he took office to 246,000 students on 71 campuses when he left—an education factory to rival any in the world.[2]

All of this required big money, the kind of money the state did not have and could not raise through normal revenue sources. Rockefeller was committed to a "pay-as-you-go" fiscal policy, an accounting procedure that utilized "rollovers," inaccurate revenue projections, and complicated tax deferrals and accelerated payment schedules all designed to achieve a "balanced" budget—a constitutional requirement and, for Rockefeller, a political necessity if he was to campaign for president as a hardheaded fiscal wizard. "In truth," said Controller Arthur Levitt in 1963, "the administration is not on pay-as-you-go and never has been."[3]

To accommodate his desire to build, Rockefeller and John Mitchell, then a successful New York bond lawyer, developed a second state government consisting of some 41 semiautonomous statewide "authorities" empowered to raise their own funds through bond sales. In most instances, the constitutional demand that voters approve all bond issues was skirted in favor of bonds that had the "moral" backing of the state but not its "full faith and credit."[4]

To Rockefeller, this network of authorities was "the greatest system ever invented."[5] The people had voted down new bond issues with alacrity. The governor was now ignoring their will through a clever assortment of legislative tricks. Some politicians, notably Arthur Levitt, warned that such financing was both deceptive and dangerous, but his arguments went largely unnoticed. In 1975, Levitt would repeat his warnings to the Moreland Commission considering the collapse of the Urban Development Corporation, indicating his frustration and adding that many of the state's bankers had agreed that Rockefeller's method was "the wrong way to finance capital construction." Nevertheless, said Levitt, greed won out. The bankers hid behind the fact that the governor and legislature had decided to embark on the "moral obligation" course, since the banks, according to Levitt, were "in the business of making money through the sale of bonds."[6]

Levitt believes that it was Rockefeller's personal closeness to the banking community that permitted the system to exist. When Rockefeller left office, that relationship ended, leading to the collapse of the scheme—"like night follows day,"[7] says Levitt.

The original concept of the public authorities was that they would be self-liquidating; that is, they would be able to pay their operating expenses and debt service out of reasonable charges imposed on the users of the facilities. The public authorities were conceived as "inherently efficient agencies," said Levitt, but the original concept differed radically from what really happened. "Most public authorities," he concluded in an exhaustive 1974 report, "are not self-sufficient at all; moreover, their projects could be administered, in many cases, just as efficiently by regular state agencies."[8]

Of greater concern, said Levitt, was the fact that the state had made many "first-instance" loans to public authorities—monies that were used to get the agencies started—that "lack the capability of timely repayment."[9] As of December 31, 1974, the balance owed by the agencies to the general state treasury for the repayment of first-instance loans was $275 million, a figure that would be $150 million higher had not the state already written off that amount as "bad debts."[10]

The outstanding debt of the statewide "moral obligation" authorities is now more than $6.7 billion. And the debt of one authority alone, the giant Housing Finance Agency, is, again according to Levitt's analysis, "far greater than the full faith and credit debt of the state itself—which stood at $3.5 billion at December 31, 1974."[11]

Levitt believes that Nelson Rockefeller had no "notion of the huge burden he was placing on future generations."[12] In general, says Levitt, because the statewide authorities issue a less secure bond, interest payments are higher than they should be, and are extended over longer periods of time. And since each agency strives to meet its expenses from the fees charged for its services, those fees are higher than they would have been had Rockefeller followed the normal route of securing voter approval for "full faith and credit" bonds that would cost the state less. Before long, debt service became a major item in the state budget, as the authorities proved that they could not handle the repayment schedules out of their own funds.

The desire to meet interest and operating expenses from the fees collected invariably dictated policy regarding the facilities' use. Thus, for example, when there was talk of the state university's adopting a free-tuition policy like that of the City University of New York, the plan was immediately scuttled when institutional investors, understanding that the basis for repayment would be wiped out, refused to bid on a new issue of state school construction notes.[13]

The "perpetuity" created was controlled totally by Nelson Rockefeller. The authorities were the shock troops in his unprecedented battle to change the face of New York. At one point, public construction during his governorship operated at such a pace that authorities were slowed by competition for available contractors in the state. Rockefeller knew what he wanted: to build big and fast. William Ronan, the governor's secretary, knew how to accommodate him, having presided in 1956 over an in-depth study of public authority devices; and investment bankers and bond lawyers like John Mitchell could be depended upon to work out the details.

The authorities were used for everything: by 1972, for example, the board of the Housing Finance Agency, carefully controlled by Rockefeller, was doubling as the board for a medical facilities agency, a state bond bank, and a state mortgage agency.

To control these and other authorities, Rockefeller relied on a personal network of aides whose careers and, in some cases, their own financial well-being as well depended on his continuance in office: Edward J. Logue (Urban Development Corporation and its subsidiaries; recipient of $176,389 in loans and gifts from Rockefeller[14]); Paul Belica (a Ronan protégé who headed

HFA and its subsidiaries); Alton Marshall (a former secretary to the governor, recipient of $306,867 in loans,[15] who served on the UDC and Sports Authority boards); William A. Sharkey (another Ronan protégé, head of the Dormitory Authority); Charles J. Urdstadt (former state housing commissioner, head of Battery Park City, and board member of HFA); and the linchpin in the network, William Ronan, who watched over the others while heading first the MTA and later the Port Authority.

Ronan has a reputation of being one of the few people who fully understands the implications of the authority method of government, and he has continually dismissed Arthur Levitt as a "bookkeeper" whose criticism was "out of a less complicated time."[16] When Ronan first became Rockefeller's secretary in 1959, he also became head of the program office. That office became the training ground for staff who were subsequently placed throughout New York's public authorities in what has been called the "Wholly Ronan Empire." Of course, in turn, Ronan's dependence on Rockefeller was personal and total.

So, in addition to his normal patronage power, Rockefeller appointed various bankers and labor leaders to the authority boards in order to secure their personal and business loyalty; he also set up a pattern of appointees to his personal staff who doubled as agency heads. Some of these key aides were tied personally to Rockefeller through money; others, through loyalty, were bound to Ronan.

Uniquely, Rockefeller had his own contacts with the financial community. Wall Street had confidence in Rockefeller and confidence in his dominance of the legislature, should the time come that the state would have to make good on all those moral obligations. Whereas in many states it is an authority's relationships with the financial community that provide the security from which it conducts relations with government officials, in New York it was the governor's financial relationships that provided the security with which he controlled the authorities.

Once Rockefeller left office, his Second Government toppled like a house of cards. During a decade when the financial community had replaced the electorate as the ultimate brake on public debt, the bond brokers had proved a good deal more generous than the voters. But as Annmarie Walsh of the Institute of Public Administration has pointed out, "the game was one of diminishing returns. As the Democrats moved into Albany in January 1975, the Republicans left them a five-year projection of income and expenditures which contemplated $1.9 billion of outright appropriations to public authorities over the five-year period,"[17] a far cry from the self-sustaining panacea Rockefeller had offered 15 years earlier.

As the end drew near, the first agency to go was the Urban Development Corporation. The UDC had moved too far, too fast, without legislative or budgeting checks. Unlike the other authorities, UDC did not sell bonds backed by revenues from specific projects. All revenues were pooled and, eventually, the bad projects pulled the good ones down with them. Logue had been as cavalier as Rockefeller. The UDC budget was not even submitted for approval to the UDC board of directors.

The UDC had been created because the voters had refused to approve housing bond issues in 1962, 1964, 1965, and 1966. Rockefeller was determined to build low-income housing, and the UDC was given the power to override local zoning regulations and community opposition and build whatever it chose, wherever it chose to build it. By the beginning of 1975, it had built or begun construction on 33,600 apartments in 50 communities. It had spent $1.1 billion and was geared up to spend $900 million more.[18]

Everyone praised the social benefit of the agency when it was born, but weak vital signs were detected almost immediately. In its very first annual report in 1969, a footnote from its auditors advised that it was "not presently determinable"[19] whether UDC was going to be able to recover the costs incurred by its construction program.

Of greater concern was Logue's passion, à la Rockefeller, for cutting through red tape. He began construction on the strength of verbal commitments from the federal government for housing subsidies, and he spent money for projects which he knew might never be built. A governor's task force in 1974 reported that UDC had persistently ignored warnings that it would have trouble renting its projects. The same task force later concluded, when the handwriting was already on the wall, that 24 of the 50 projects Logue had placed in operation had "insufficient working capital provisions,"[20] i.e., they were losing money.

As the situation worsened, the banks pleaded with UDC to cut back. Logue, with the approval of Rockefeller, refused and pushed ahead. When Hugh Carey took office, UDC was spending a million dollars a day on its 500 employees and 3,000 construction workers on projects around the state. Little revenue was coming in. UDC was, in effect, broke, and it defaulted on February 21, 1975. The city's fiscal crisis followed, and by the end of 1975 the entire authorities system was in danger of collapse. In the case of UDC, as Steven Weisman has written, the "broad lesson . . . is that well-intentioned deviousness, the by hook or crook pursuit of a worthy goal, can in the long run do more damage to that goal than good."[21]

Nelson Rockefeller's system had failed. As Annmarie Walsh has concluded:

> Right up into the 1970s, he failed to see that his housing plans were overambitious and vulnerable to cutbacks in federal subsidies; that his university construction plans did not take into account the leveling off and change in habits of the college-age population; that his construction and financing plans for health and mental hygiene facilities were vulnerable to manipulation by the private entrepreneurs who ran the institutions thus made profitable; that the unsettled method of subsidizing transportation authorities—requiring new bargains to be struck between state, federal, and local budgets each year—would become an impossible drain on political and financial resources. None of these developments were perceived by the governor and his network of authority entrepreneurs. The weak spots in the system that led to this turn-

around were several: (1) the general weakness of forecasts made by typical feasibility studies, exaggerated by the optimistic ambitions of the governor; (2) the underlying dependence on federal aid for all the programs involved in housing, health, and transportation; and (3) the sheer volume of construction and debt that the system generated.[22]

"In the 1960s," says Richard Ravitch, who was brought in to clean up the UDC mess, "we forgot that resources were limited. The business of government in the 1970s will be to pay the price of the decisions of the 1960s."[23] Those decisions were largely made by Nelson Rockefeller.

CHAPTER 13

Monumental
Errors

BUILDING for the poor was one thing. Building for show was quite another. The World Trade Center was the brainchild of David Rockefeller and his Downtown Lower Manhattan Association. With Chase committed to the lower tip of Manhattan, a trade center would be yet another magnet to attract industry and business, which had strayed to midtown during the 1950s. The governor persuaded the Port Authority to undertake the project in exchange for covenants that would forever prohibit the Port Authority from investing in deficit mass transit, a prohibition that ran counter to the authority's charter to develop transportation systems within the Port of New York and New Jersey district. Later, in 1974, when the covenants were repealed in order to tap Port Authority funds for rail systems, the financial community interpreted that action as a breach of promise with the bondholders, the first tangible proof that the states of New York and New Jersey would not honor "moral commitments."

Rockefeller skillfully had the legislature pass a bill that authorized *a* trade center for lower Manhattan. Its location and size were not part of the law, but it was understood at that time that the trade center would consist of one 72-story tower plus outlying buildings on the east side of lower Manhattan.[1] Before long, with Chicago replacing New York as the city with the world's tallest building, the design was changed to something "really imposing," as Nelson Rockefeller put it. The twin 110-story towers were built, causing an enormous glut in the real estate market in lower Manhattan. In order to ensure that the World Trade Center would survive financially, Rockefeller announced, only a week after the twin-tower concept had been advanced, that the state would consolidate its offices in New York City by moving into the Trade Center, thus becoming its chief tenant—a relocation of 8,000 employees from 50 leased offices throughout the city to 51 floors of the Trade Center's South Tower.[2]

Controller Levitt opposed the plan and commissioned the engineering-consulting firm of Madigan-Hyland to compare the costs involved, relative to both the existing leases and the possibility of the state building its own new office tower. Nelson Rockefeller had once sat on the board of directors of Madigan-Hyland, the only extrafamily business on whose board he served. The original Madigan-Hyland report, recommending that the state move to the World Trade Center, was "just plain shoddy work," according to Levitt.[3] The report was redrafted, barely in time for a public hearing Levitt had ordered on the question. The conclusion was the same, and Levitt, who had the legal power to disapprove the lease between the state and the Trade Center, decided "that the die was cast, the governor wanted it and it would have been hard to go ahead with a new state office building when we actually had a report that said the Trade Center was the best option."[4] Levitt did not know until 1975, eight years after the incident, that Rockefeller had once been connected with Madigan-Hyland.[5]

As originally stated, New York was to pay $6.42 per square foot on a 40-year lease. But the cost of construction, $355 million at first estimate, had risen to $900 million by 1975, and a Levitt audit after the first year of state occupancy in 1973 indicated that the state was actually paying $9.32 per square foot for the 2.2 million square feet it then rented. The state also paid millions in "hidden costs," mainly because it had to continue payment on long-term leases at locations it had vacated in favor of the Trade Center.

In June 1975, in an apparent attempt to bring the rental down to the $6.42 per square foot figure originally negotiated, the Carey administration told the Port Authority that it would not automatically renew its option on the Trade Center space. Adding insult to injury, Governor Carey made clear that he had no intention of moving his own New York City headquarters to the Trade Center's lavish 88th floor, the area Nelson Rockefeller had personally selected as suitable for the offices of the governor of New York.

However, for sheer extravagance and waste nothing compares with the Albany Mall. It is truly Nelson Rockefeller's monument. "Misery, wretchedness, ennui and the devil," wrote architect Stanford White nearly a century ago. "I've got to spend another evening in Albany."[6] Nelson Rockefeller set out to change all that. He would make Albany a "brilliant diamond,"[7] "the most spectacularly beautiful seat of government in the world."[8]

Rockefeller established a capital-city planning commission in 1961 with Wallace Harrison, the governor's longtime friend and co-architect of Rockefeller Center, as the genius behind the design. Of course, Rockefeller was never far away. "We used to get paper napkin drawings from his Seal Harbor retreat,"[9] recalls one aide to the commission.

"What the two master builders dreamed up," wrote *Fortune* magazine, "was a modern imperial enclave, rising on a hill overlooking the Hudson River. A half mile long and almost a quarter mile wide . . . the Mall itself will contain a forty-four story office tower, four identical twenty-three story buildings, a legislative building, a justice building, a headquarters for the motor vehicle department, a cultural center (including museum and library),

155

a meeting center and a laboratory for the Department of Health
. . . the platform has a 500-foot reflecting pool flanked by two
small pools as well as lawns, trees, fountains and promenades."[10]

Easily the mall's most spectacular feature is the fact that all of
the buildings are faced in 2 million square feet of the finest
Vermont and Georgia marble, costing $20 million.[11] Rockefeller
personally selected the marble used. Critics have complained
that the mall is the greatest money waster of any 20th-century
building project. In New York City, estimated *Fortune*, construction costs average about $35 per square foot of usable space.
Mall office buildings range, however, from $120 to $230 per
square foot of usable space. The eight buildings provide a total
of 3,562,000 gross square feet, but enclose, because of incredible
design inefficiency, only about 1,665,000 square feet of usable
space—the equivalent of one giant skyscraper in Manhattan.[12]

It was obvious from the start that the people would never approve a bond issue for the mall. No one on the Rockefeller staff
ever seriously contemplated it. So the governor reached into his
bag of fiscal tricks and came out with a financing scheme so complicated that Arthur Levitt has said it is "beyond the control or
even the comprehension of the electorate."[13] Basically, the county
of Albany floats the bonds to build the mall and then leases the
whole to the state on a schedule designed to amortize the bonds
by the year 2004. Albany Mayor Erastus Corning II conceived
the idea, and he told *Fortune* that Rockefeller went for it "like a
trout for a fly."[14] Of course, once again, the circumvention of
voter approval meant a half percentage point upward difference
in the cost of the project—"a hell of a lot of money over 30
years,"[15] says Levitt, an additional cost of over $40 million.

All told, the initial estimate of $480 million has jumped to over
$1 billion. "That's what I said it would cost," remembers Arthur
Levitt. "Nelson told me I was crazy."[16]

Why the vast discrepancy? Rockefeller blames inflation, but
he also admits to poor planning, estimating, and coordination.
There was also the problem of too many architects drafting

plans. "It was a question of political expediency," said chief architect Wally Harrison.[17] "He had to get more people involved." The cost of getting "more people involved" became so excessive that Controller Levitt withheld approval of the architectural contracts until the agreements were renegotiated at a savings of $500,000.[18]

The platform for the mall, the largest construction contract in state history, drew only a single bid, and that bidder could not deliver. There was endless trouble as Rockefeller rushed the job along. Often, the 70 prime contractors and 270 subcontractors were trying to build a dozen buildings on the site all at once, climbing and falling all over each other. Levitt characterized Rockefeller's timetable for construction as "sheer madness . . . the way to bankruptcy."[19]

Another, more immediate problem was that the mall's platform lay on a bed of treacherous gelatinous blue clay that in some cases went down as far as 100 feet, a condition that required the excavation of 2.7 million cubic yards of the stuff and the driving down of 22,000 pilings to support the buildings.[20] Said Rockefeller: "The thing kept sinking into the mud."[21]

Something else that kept sinking was a promise to relocate the displaced populace in a new housing development on a site adjacent to the mall. The project was to cost $10 million, but it ran into the "Albany factor."[22] During the mall's construction, labor and material for other projects were scarce, and the cost of the new housing development doubled. "It just got way out of line,"[23] said Rockefeller, who canceled the project at the same time that he pushed his mall at a doubling of *its* cost.

Albany Mayor Corning had originally opposed the mall, holding out for a pledge of new housing for the poor blacks who would be displaced. "Do not build this magnificent monument on a foundation of human misery,"[24] said Corning in 1962— before he came up with his financing scheme and the promise of housing for the poor. As it turned out, the residents were relocated in other poor housing in Albany. In the end, it seemed that the magnificent monument could stand on a foundation of misery after all. "This is planning insanity," said urban philosopher Jane Jacobs. "It has only succeeded in destroying a good amount of viable housing and small business, and they are the base of a city's economy."[25]

Why did Nelson Rockefeller build the mall in the first place? His stated purpose was the consolidation of employees in one complex of buildings, a complex he could be "proud of." But why was new space needed? "The amount of office space," noted the Legislative Commission on Expenditure Review, "is supposed to be directly related to the number of employees and their positions. However, the amount of State office space has been increasing at a rate almost twice as fast as the number of office personnel."[26]

Another reason advanced by Rockefeller was that the mall would revitalize the downtown Albany area. It is a belief he still clings to, much as David Rockefeller continues to maintain that the Trade Center will one day spark the revitalization of downtown Manhattan he predicted a decade ago. Said Nelson to the Senate Rules Committee: "The same things are said about [the mall] as were said about Rockefeller Center when my father built it. It was Rockefeller's Folly, and it was a disaster, and so forth, and it turned out to have been the thing that saved the midtown of Manhattan, and it's been the most important development."[27]

Perhaps the answer lies deeper than politics. Psychiatrist Jules Masserman says that one of people's "Ur-defenses," most prevalent among rulers, is the delusion that "their name—and therefore themselves—will be immortalized . . . in their preserved bodies or in their indestructible granite monuments: Mussolini's 'Foro-Mussolini,' Franco's 'Valley of the Fallen,' "[28]—and Rockefeller's mall.

"He wanted something grand and monumental," says Wally Harrison of the mall. "He wanted a monument. Sure."[29]

"I may not even be re-elected," said Rockefeller shortly before the 1970 gubernatorial election. "I wanted to be President, you know, but could not get the nomination. But [the Mall] is going forward. Albany will be a great, a magnificent, capital."[30]

Before leaving office, Nelson Rockefeller dedicated his mall. He smiled broadly, his exuberance evident to all. "You know," he said, gazing at his marble mass, "if there is anything more satisfying than dedicating a new building, it is dedicating eight new buildings."[31]

CHAPTER 14

Politics and
the Press

NELSON ROCKEFELLER had great success in convincing the electorate of New York State that his politics—or his monuments—were directed toward their benefit. But his efforts to instill a similar sense of loyalty and support on the part of the press met with mixed success. He could be the most gracious of hosts and even forgo his favorite doughnut, as he did in that first meeting with William Ronan. Yet he seldom realized that reporters were not supposed to be his friends, that they were generally uninfluenced by and had little influence on the editorials of their newspapers or stations, and that their agreeing with him did not necessarily follow from their understanding of what he was trying to do or say.

His relationship with reporters regularly assigned to him was cordial, although it rarely pierced the private layer of his personality; there always seemed to be a barrier protecting the real Rockefeller. His son-in-law, Thomas B. Morgan, who became editor of the *Village Voice*, after serving as Mayor Lindsay's press secretary, tells a story about covering President Kennedy as a free-lance writer. Morgan was interviewing the president aboard *Air Force One* when Kennedy's roast beef lunch arrived.

"Did you have lunch?" Kennedy asked. Morgan replied that he had not. "Here, take this," said the president, shoving the tray across to Morgan. Then Kennedy took Morgan's notebook and pen, asked him to continue his questioning, and wrote down his own answers.[1]

Rockefeller was never that relaxed with reporters. And although he signed a sweeping shield law to assist them in protecting the confidentiality of their sources, he hardly understood their adversary role. Commenting in 1974 on conditions at the infamous Willowbrook Children's Center on Staten Island, Rockefeller noted that "when the photographers, or television people, sneak into the institution against the rules, and take pictures of the tragedy, the human tragedy which exists, the public is horrified because they are not used to seeing mentally retarded children."[2] He seemed not to understand that only because television recorded such horror did a public outcry cause conditions to improve.

During his last bid for the governorship, Rockefeller released his latest poll to several reporters aboard the campaign bus as it left the General Foods plant in suburban White Plains. The survey showed that, for the first time, the incumbent had pulled ahead of his Democratic challenger, Arthur Goldberg, by better than 2 points. "Who took the poll?" a reporter not-so-innocently asked. "Oh, you know," Rockefeller replied, "I never reveal the name of my polling organization." It had seemed like a simple enough request to the reporter though, and the response appeared to be unreasonably arrogant. In fact, election reforms passed in time for the 1974 campaign (in which Rockefeller was not running) expressly prohibit release of such secret polls.

The reporter found out that the poll was conducted by Political Surveys and Analyses of Princeton, noted in his story the governor's refusal to identify his source, and then, in passing, named the polling organization. The next morning, Rockefeller held a regularly scheduled news conference in his midtown Manhattan office. It was hot and stuffy, and he was late as usual. Finally he entered, strode to the podium, and shuffled through some papers when he noticed the naughty reporter in the front row. Rockefeller walked up to him and with a mixture of disdain and disappointment exclaimed: "Jesus, some loyal friend you are!"[3]

Rockefeller's efforts to instill loyalty were aided by another factor. The press corps that decides what everyone else reads and hears over the air is composed of individual reporters whose feelings mirror those of Americans who also have mortgages to pay off, kids to feed, and bosses to please. So Nelson's abortive national campaigns permitted them to share the self-righteousness of martyrdom without any of the blood. And the successful New York State election efforts afforded the vicarious thrill of victory.

The press corps back in Albany—which included many of the same newsmen who covered the state and national campaigns—was also like the "boys in the bus." Except the bus never moved. It was occasionally buffeted by the Republican legislative leadership and rocked by the Democrats, but it just sat there. In the driver's seat was Rockefeller on whom, in a decaying river town, reporters depended not only for news but also for diversion. Albany was also treated like a stepchild by much of the downstate press. For years, none of the three major New York City newspapers assigned a year-round correspondent to cover the state capital. Of course, there were exceptions, and reporters who either were not susceptible to such strains or who independently overcame them. But one veteran newsman recalled that Nelson, the governor—partly because he was a Rockefeller and particularly because he was Nelson Rockefeller—"played the press like a piano."

Rockefeller went through four press secretaries during his 15-year tenure as governor. Only a month after he took office in 1959, the state's Society of Newspaper Editors expressed outrage that the Rockefeller administration was "giving every indication of becoming a government-by-handout" and that state officials appeared likely to "become progressively less available for direct questioning."[4] Those conclusions were reached by a

Politics and the Press

right-to-know committee chaired by Managing Editor Albert J. Bearup of the Hearst organization's Albany *Times-Union*, who also complained that former Governor Harriman had been "much more cooperative" than Rockefeller and that "Mrs. Harriman would do practically anything" to accommodate the press.[5]

It was a difficult chapter in Rockefeller's press relations. For one thing, constant inquiries about things the Rockefellers never revealed before took some getting used to. To make matters worse, Frank Jamieson, for two decades Nelson's alter ego, was dying, and press secretary Richard Amper, a former New York *Times* man, was enough of a novice at the job to promulgate what Bearup denounced as "the ridiculous rule" that the answers to any question asked by an individual reporter would be given to all reporters—or none.

Amper, who died suddenly in 1960, was succeeded by Robert McManus, a Harriman holdover, under whom the hostility level rose so high that reporters were sometimes locked out of the press office.

His successor, Leslie Slote, was a cigar-puffing chap whose flip responses usually took precedence over substantive answers to questions posed by the press. As often as possible, sensitive subjects were dismissed with outrageous replies. "When I'm in the White House, sir, you will answer for such insolence," he informed one startled reporter. "You may say that the governor thinks the senator is a fascist pig," he told another. To the newsman who inquired why Rockefeller was riding the New York City subway during the 1967 campaign for a transportation bond issue, Slote snapped: "He hasn't got the cab fare—read the handout, for Christ sake."[6]

Slote, who became a London-based vice-president of RCA, was followed by Ronald Maiorana, a lusty raconteur and hardnosed reporter, formerly with the *Times*, who was probably the most respected of the four. He joined the staff in 1968 and started by telling Nelson what all the newsmen knew: that he was rarely responsive to questions, that his wise-guy answers made the job

163

more difficult for serious reporters, and that the flying wedge of staff men and state police constantly surrounding him was downright intimidating. Rockefeller reacted sensitively to some of those suggestions, and press relations improved.

Two others figure prominently in Rockefeller's press relations picture. One was Harry J. O'Donnell, the paunchy ex-Associated Press reporter who filled several publicity posts for Governor Thomas Dewey, the Republican State Committee and Mayor Lindsay. O'Donnell, a veteran observer of the political landscape who could divert almost any inquiry with a knowledgeable aside about ocean liners or baseball, was drafted into the press relations post of every Rockefeller state and national campaign. He left Lindsay in 1969 to become first deputy commerce commissioner of New York State, served in 1974 as Governor Malcolm Wilson's chief spokesman, and was so respected as a pro that he even continued into the administration of Democrat Hugh Carey in 1975 as director of communications.

The longest-tenured of the Rockefeller press attachés, however, was Hugh Morrow, a former *Saturday Evening Post* associate editor who went to work for Senators Irving M. Ives and Kenneth B. Keating. He joined Rockefeller's staff in November 1959 for the upcoming presidential campaign, which screeched to a halt within a month. Morrow stayed on; a trusted adviser, he remained on Rockefeller's personal payroll (he was loaned out to Lindsay in 1965) and in 1969 was appointed as the governor's communications director. Morrow continued in that role through 1974, and became press secretary to the vice-president the following year.

As Maiorana had told him, it was Rockefeller's own style that made covering him so frustrating. Schedules rarely offered details about the state or city he was in, let alone which function in Albany he was attending. And controversial questions were fended off with answers so innocuous as to be unprintable. In 1970, for instance, Rockefeller and Arthur Goldberg met in their first debate one morning at the offices of the New York *Times*, which barred other newsmen from the session. "What do you think of secret debates like this?" Rockefeller was asked as he emerged hours later. "Well," he shrugged as he slipped into his limousine, "it's a whole new ballgame, and you never know what's going to happen."[7]

One day in 1974, from the moment Rockefeller left his limousine at the dedication of a Rockefeller University addition, a reporter attempted to maneuver him close to Tricia Nixon and engage the two in a discussion of Watergate. "Rockefeller kept muttering about Mark's lost hamster," the reporter remembered. "And when he was leaving, I followed him, trying to ask him about Watergate. He turned around and gave me an icy stare that froze me in my tracks—with a message that didn't have to be articulated."

When icy stares were impractical, he could dodge controversial questions with the expertise of a slalom skier, darting between the poles and splashing wet snow on the spectators. It went just that way on a midsummer day (so much for slalom racing) in 1971, when television interviewer David Frost unsuccessfully attempted to wring from Rockefeller his prediction about the 1972 national ticket.

"Do you think that Vice President Agnew is certain to be on the ticket again?" Frost asked.

"Well," Rockefeller replied, "I don't think anything is certain in politics except that there is going to be another day and as it unfolds we will know."

"What would you say," Frost persisted, "as an incredibly shrewd political observer, what are the likelihoods?"

Unfazed by flattery, Rockefeller retorted: "You are supposed, if you are really shrewd, not to say."[8]

Because of that pattern of evasion and double-talk, Rockefeller's most newsworthy moments were, predictably, often spontaneous. In that same 1970 campaign, he was lecturing before television newsman Gabe Pressman's nighttime class at the New School for Social Research in Manhattan when he suddenly dropped a bombshell allegation. Arthur Goldberg, he said casually, in response to a student's question, had offered the chairmanship of the Metropolitan Transportation Authority to former New York City Controller Mario Procaccino in return for his endorsement. Goldberg's surprise response made it a better story. The staid former Supreme Court justice exclaimed in Buffalo: "He's full of bullshit. You can quote me—I want you to quote me." As it turned out, Procaccino endorsed Rockefeller and was subsequently appointed state commissioner of taxation and finance.

When the dissemination of news was more deliberate, leaks were a favorite Rockefeller tool. They rewarded the faithful, intimidated the independent spirits whose editors demanded to know why they were being shut out, and guaranteed more prominent space for the story. In the 1968 presidential campaign, one reporter recalled both Rockefeller and Senator Robert Kennedy played that game with the *Times*'s national political correspondent. "The Kennedy people played him like a yo-yo," said the reporter of his colleague. "His needs and their needs absolutely coincided. They wanted to be in the paper every day, and he wanted to be in the paper every day. They just leaked him stuff, and he put it right in. And of course, the *Times* wanted a story on Bobby Kennedy every day. Same thing when Rockefeller was trying to decide whether or not to go in before the 1968 convention. Again, the Rockefeller people played him like a yo-yo."[9]

Armed with early training in the public relations minefield of the State Department, Rockefeller became a master at background briefings. Like selective leaks, these briefings, held on a not-for-attribution basis, allowed him to release trial balloons without having to bear the consequences if they were shot down.

Even more useful was the private interview. "I am really going to trust you on this," Rockefeller asserted to one reporter, who recalled incredulously that he "then follows [with] a statement that is neither explosive nor revealing. Even those Rockefeller pronouncements that seem full of hot matter at the time of utterance grow cool and less satisfying when notes are read in a less heady atmosphere—or prove to have been said on the record at some earlier date."[10]

Until Rockefeller's nomination as vice-president, the subject that was closest to being taboo was his family and fortune. Part of the privacy stemmed from the fact that the previous efforts to publicize him as the model family man backfired in his 1962 divorce. Part of it was that while Nelson has always been more public than his brothers, he rigidly regarded his personal life as being outside the public domain. And part of it was because the family feared kidnappings or other terrorist tactics.

Inquiries about family relatives and their riches were referred to George Taylor, the amiable spokesman for the Rockefeller family, who cordially refused most substantive answers. Until the confirmation hearings, for instance, one of the rare official figures released was prompted by California governor Ronald Reagan's surprise disclosure that he had paid no state income taxes. When a reporter asked about Rockefeller's tax status, his press secretary only replied that the New York governor's total tax tab in each of the preceding ten years had been "in seven figures."

Shielded even more than the money were his wife and children. The charming Happy Rockefeller reluctantly agreed to respond to a few harmless questions after Nelson's nomination. But even then, as reporters were herded well behind a wooden barricade in Seal Harbor that proclaimed in luminous paint "Private Road—Keep Out," Press Secretary Hugh Morrow warned photographers against taking pictures of the Rockefellers' youngest children, Nelson, Jr. and Mark. As politely as possible, he explained that he "would have a tough time getting Nelson to cooperate with the press" if that unwritten rule were to be disobeyed. Only a few years before, Rockefeller was furious with a newsman because of a reference in his story to guard dogs and private police around Pocantico; he was equally upset because the article noted that Rockefeller had been regularly taking tranquilizers at the time.

Rockefeller could set such rules and almost always personally present his side of a story because he enjoyed easy access to the lords of the press. He personally cultivated newspaper publishers, a pattern set in his State Department days, when he wooed Latin newspaper executives by flying them up to be wined and dined in Washington, and repeated later when he recruited them to help IBEC and its subsidiaries or stuck them on state commissions, where their sinecures made them willing participants in a system that they were no longer free to analyze objectively. Family and financial links also helped. "Harry" Luce numbered Nelson among the elite inner circle of favored public officials. Laurance sat on the board of *Reader's Digest*, whose path into Latin America was paved by Nelson's wartime publishing ventures and whose editors frequently found something friendly to write about the Rockefellers.

If the reporters were wiseacres to be tolerated and toyed with, the publishers were *his* people. They were propertied, more or less cultured, and shared his stake in the stability of society. And that was precisely why criticism so puzzled him—especially from the *Times*, which was the bible of his brethren among the superrich.

"When I had to let 11,000 people go," he reminded a reporter in 1973, "the press hit me. But they were the same ones who were against new taxes. . . . This is why I don't worry anymore about what anyone says to me."[11]

Held in check by his staff, Rockefeller rarely yielded to the temptation to call editors and publishers. He would occasionally lunch at the *Daily News* with former publisher F. M. Flynn to plead a particular case, and he even called the *Post*'s Dorothy Schiff at her hairdresser's once in 1966 to feel her out on whether Franklin D. Roosevelt, Jr. would be his rival in the gubernatorial campaign. In 1975 he personally warned *Times* publisher Arthur Ochs Sulzberger that he would be slapped with a libel suit—not a threat to be taken lightly under the circumstances—if the paper printed a planned exposé that the Manhattan district attorney's office had considered prosecuting Rockefeller a decade earlier for his failure to report an alleged bribe involving a Finger Lakes racetrack.[12]

Usually, press secretaries and communications directors did most of the persuading and lambasting. When seven *Times* reporters left callback messages for Morrow in the midst of the confirmation hearings, he called *Times* editor James Reston to report that the family lawyers were too busy servicing the Congress to pander to the press. Reston reportedly promised to deploy the Washington bureau's troops more efficiently but asked: "Will you call Abe [Rosenthal] about New York?"[13]

Several years before, the governor attended a Boy Scout fund-raising luncheon in New York and was struck by the sincerity of the 17-year-old speaker who preceded him. So struck was he that he stunned the crowd by impulsively announcing that he would personally match every contribution that had been made that day. That slip of the tongue cost Rockefeller $100,000. The *Times* story the next morning was mocking, and Rockefeller was furious. He ordered Maiorana to telephone *Times* Managing Editor A. M. Rosenthal, who was apparently convinced by both the volume and substance of the press secretary's complaint to run a more favorable story the following day. But he also sent his former employee a note that concluded: "I don't like anybody to yell at me on the telephone."[14]

Why would Nelson Rockefeller, who could afford to purchase every single copy of the paper printed daily for years, even bat an eyelash about how the *Times* describes him, the Boy Scouts, or anybody else? One former intimate adviser insisted that it went beyond simple pique at being second-guessed. "He really wants approval, and where if the *Times* says it, it's got to be so," the former aide said. "His ethic was that the *Times* was read religiously and his peers read it—and that's real peer pressure."

The pressure that Rockefeller exerted on the press was not peer pressure. His press conferences exposed him as an undisputed master of manipulation. He flattered the reporters, who liked to be called by name, and he was also quite capable of intimidating others and responding with asperity. When one newsman persistently pressed him about invoking certain executive powers under the state constitution, Rockefeller bridled. "Well, if you had ever read the constitution you'd know. . . ." When another reporter began, "Governor, it's been reported that" and went on to quote a controversial story, Rockefeller retorted: "Well, who reported that—you?"

After one press conference for which Press Secretary Ron Maiorana had briefed the governor on 50 questions, Rockefeller tweaked the reporters with the observation: "You only asked 15 questions—Ron had 35 more." With needles like that, one veteran legislative correspondent said, "he was the best person at fondling and diverting the press."

"I don't think the press was ever out of control," another reporter recalled. "He got angry once about Legislative Correspondents Association cracks about the lack of Albany news conferences during the presidential campaign. He told Slote: 'They're going to have news conferences.' Monday, Tuesday, Wednesday there were 10 A.M. press conferences. And the same the following week. After six or seven, we got down in the morning to just looking at each other. He had his jaw clenched."

His favorite technique was lecturing, whether in the rarefied atmosphere of the Red Room in the state Capitol, the less formal budget briefings in the Executive Mansion, or the opulence of the playhouse at Pocantico. On a sunny fall afternoon in 1971, he summoned 350 editors and their wives—instead of less impressionable reporters—to plug for his $2.5 billion transportation bond issue. "He was proselytizing," said one witness. He was an impressive huckster—a snake oil salesman." He was also very convincing. Most editors bought the bond issue plan. But the public, suspicious because so many politicians were supporting it, rejected it overwhelmingly at the polls.

He never tried to buy reporters outright, one newsman noted, but he always sought to make the most of Rockefeller power. After the 1968 campaign, for example, he handed out silver cigarette cases to the emotionally weary members of the "flying circus" that had followed him around the country for months. One Albany reporter's wedding was even held in the Executive Mansion. He also doled out gifts, jobs, or booty to his departing secretaries. McManus was shifted to a post in the Environmental Protection Administration. Slote received a valuable Asian artifact. Maiorana was named state lottery commissioner at $44,375.

Rockefeller also extended a helping hand to reporters who were getting on in years or not getting on with their bosses. He placed Walter McDonald, a former *World-Telegram* reporter who was a frequent critic, in a Public Works Department public relations slot long enough for him to qualify for a pension after his paper folded. Douglas Dales, who was recalled from Albany by the *Times* after moving his family there, quit to become information officer for the State Police. And Art Massolo, who returned from the Peace Corps to find his job filled at the *Post*, was named as assistant appointments secretary.

"That was duly noted," one reporter recalled, adding that some of his colleagues "weren't above pulling punches because of that."

It was the quadrennial picnics at Pocantico that kept everyone talking for four more years. Reporters regularly assigned to Albany and the state political scene were invited along with their spouses to partake of the swimming pools, tennis courts, Japanese gardens, and grounds of the rambling estate, with the governor their ever-gracious host. Even Happy and the children were there to let the gentlemen of the press know how much they were trusted. It was an atmosphere designed to stifle independence, one reporter recalled: "He would admit you into his family circle, he'd show you that you were close to him, and then you'd go marching off to war together."

CHAPTER 15

Critics
Comforted

NELSON ROCKEFELLER fought seven major political wars, dozens of battles in Albany, and a key skirmish with the Congress. He resorted to the same techniques each time when combating his critics, and his fancy footwork usually dazzled opponents in or out of the political ring.

If he felt secure enough to suffer a minor defeat, he would courageously and openly fling himself into controversy. During his first term as governor, for instance, Nelson carried his opposition to a $100 million state bonus for Korean war veterans right to the annual convention of the American Legion, flatly informing the legionnaires that the money was needed for other things. More often than not, however, and especially during campaign periods, he ducked as many issues as possible, pinned specific and unpopular positions on his opponent, and occasionally made promises that he must have known he would not keep.

Predictably, Nelson was at his best in spontaneous street confrontations, where he would seem to enjoy the repartee with protesters. At one rally on Manhattan's Lower East Side in 1970, Rockefeller was greeted by a handful of hecklers—several of whom turned out to be campaign workers for his Democratic opponent—as he attempted to address the mostly Spanish-speaking crowd. Without a moment's hesitation, Rockefeller launched into a passable campaign speech in Spanish, to the delight of the onlookers. After he had captivated the crowd, he glanced at one of the hecklers, Arnaldo Segarra, winked, and said: "The trouble with you is you don't understand Spanish!"

On another day, he returned to his West 55th Street office to find himself greeted by 1,000 hostile pickets from the Civil Service Employees Association demanding that he recognize them as bargaining agent for state employees. "I haven't made my decision on this," the governor said as harried cops cleared a path for him. "You know the other organization is putting the pressure on too. I'll reach my decision soon. And I promise you I'll be very fair." Responding to a noisy challenge from one protester, Rockefeller asked, "Would your leaders like to come inside and talk with me now?" Larry King recorded the metamorphosis in mood:

> The policemen helped extract three leaders from the crush, Rockefeller moved to his office door, opening it, motioning his guests inside. He turned then, and smiled, and waved to the crowd. And a roar went up, a sudden and spontaneous sound that rose in concert with his gesture, as if he were, indeed, the concertmaster directing them. He stood a moment, raised both arms over his head as Eisenhower used to do, and then he turned to duck into the door and was gone. Behind him, in the streets, the people who had come to picket and challenge him cheered and cheered and cheered.[1]

Before long, Rockefeller was so confident of his ability to handle hostile criticism spontaneously that he institutionalized the confrontations in the form of "town meetings" held around the state—a pattern he repeated as vice-president. He cajoled, flattered, quipped, and became contentious whenever appropriate.

Typical were exchanges like the one that occurred at the Colonie Hill Inn in Hauppauge, Long Island, in late 1972. The hall was jammed with a crowd whose 500 Middle American members first listened to a series of harangues against taxes, abortion reforms, and the armed assault on Attica. But the just plain folks from Nassau County were no jury of his peers, and Nelson knew it. So when a man rose to criticize the chaos, the governor gallantly defended the right of every citizen to speak. "Yeah," another guy grumbled loudly, "the people speak and you make the decisions." "What's wrong with that," the unruffled Rockefeller retorted. "I got elected."[2]

In less hostile situations—at political receptions, for instance— he oozed with charm. Women still swoon from the Rockefeller wink. The New York *Post*'s Dorothy Schiff, at whom Nelson has winked on occasion, recalled the utter frustration felt by Democratic State Controller Arthur Levitt about Rockefeller's winning personality. "He's a menace, he's a terrible man," she quoted Levitt as saying. "But even my wife is crazy about him!"[3]

Sometimes, criticism was blunted with more subtle weapons. The most notable case, of course, was the Victor Lasky biography of Arthur Goldberg, commissioned by Rockefeller operatives and covertly financed by Laurance Rockefeller—although it appears possible that Laurance was completely unaware of it. Nelson was not unaware, however.

Rockefeller repeatedly stated that the campaign biography was first mentioned to him in mid-July 1970 by John A. Wells, a prominent New York attorney who had run Rockefeller's presidential primary campaign in 1964 and for whom Rockefeller had guaranteed a $300,000 bank loan several years earlier. But John Lockwood, the septuagenarian lawyer who had since retired as Rockefeller family counsel, had a conflicting recollection. Lockwood said that he left for a seven-week trip to Europe on June 18, 1970, which would have brought him back about the time that all the legal details of the subterfuge were already in motion. But before he left, Lockwood recalled, "there was only a suggestion that somebody, I am not at all sure I know whom, was suggesting that there should be a book about Justice Goldberg." Lockwood said he believed that Louise Boyer,

Rockefeller's former executive assistant, had raised the suggestion at that point. "My hunch is that somebody was testing the waters," he said. "I think it was well described as a 'gleam in somebody's eye.' "[4]

That gleam must have been pretty bright, however. Lasky, who described Goldberg as a "pompous windbag," said Wells "suggested" early in the 1970 campaign that he write the book and that he agreed "for the dough, baby, and I wrote it because I am a Republican."[5] Lasky was paid $10,000, spent six weeks on the project, and produced a book that Goldberg said had made his brother-in-law vomit.

Although Rockefeller, Dilworth, campaign strategist John Wells, and author Victor Lasky insisted that this was nothing but a routine business investment, the ADA's Joseph Rauh wryly observed: "If the public really believed Rockefeller business interests were handled in the casual manner of the Lasky book, New York would be treated to the unlikely spectacle of a run on the Chase Manhattan Bank."[6]

In any event, the book was a sad commentary on either the Rockefellers' business sense, political savvy, or both. Laurance, insisting that the publishing proposal was just put to him as a business venture, proved it by eventually writing it off as a $58,000 loss on his income taxes. He said he would contribute the recovery of the loss to the LBJ Memorial Grove "because I am not proud of this transaction, and I do not want to have money coming back to me from the American people."[7] Ironically, the publisher of the paperback biography appears to have had better business sense. Neil McCaffrey of Arlington House said he told Lasky that his firm would be interested in the venture "if there were a guaranteed sale, because I did not regard it as a promising commercial venture."[8] As it turned out, McCaffrey cleared $15,000 profit on the book.

McCaffrey painstakingly sought to differentiate between a subsidy—like that received from the Rockefellers—and a guaranteed sale. "Financially, it comes to the same thing, though it does make a certain difference to a publisher," he explained. "I don't mean to suggest that I think it would be dishonorable to accept a direct subsidy. But as a publisher, I prefer an arrangement like this to take the form of a guaranteed sale. In this way, our company retains the publisher's independence to perform the publisher's functions in the manner we deem best."[9]

The Goldberg book was not the Rockefellers' only literary venture, although other efforts were of a more positive nature. Nelson secretly spent about $30,000 from his personal account to purchase and promote a "decidedly pro-Rockefeller" campaign biography on the eve of his 1964 drive for the presidency. This time, there was less of a distinction between a direct subsidy and a guaranteed sale, a subtlety that apparently did not deter the publisher, the Macmillan Company. In October 1963, almost three months before the publication date, Rockefeller directed his staff to order 5,000 copies of a biography by prize-winning New York *Daily News* reporter James Desmond— about 10,000 were eventually printed in all—and later agreed to reimburse the' publisher for up to $40,000 more in advertising space and production costs to promote it in primary states.[10]

During the winter of 1973, the Academy of Political Science was fulfilling its publishing function by issuing the first analysis of Rockefeller's 15-year record; the academy had commissioned 20 college professors to write it. The generally favorable review, entitled *Governing New York State—the Rockefeller Years*, was released in mid-1974 and efficiently distributed to members of the congressional committees considering Rockefeller's confirmation as vice-president later that year.

Who financed the book? Academy President Robert H. Connery, a Columbia University professor and coeditor of the review, said it was funded from dues paid by academy members. But the academy's pursuit of the truth received a boost from another quarter as well. Just before the decision was made to publish the review, Rockefeller gave the group an $80,952 tax-exempt contribution. Connery insisted, however, that the two were unrelated. "The Rockefeller grant was for something different," he maintained. "The governor gave us some money for some monographs, maybe a book for administrative studies that have been going on for three years on the broad spectrum of state government. Meanwhile, we decided to do this as a parallel."[11] What Connery neglected to add was the source for his own opening article in the review titled "Nelson A. Rockefeller as Governor." A footnote to Connery's contribution to the review stated: "this paper is based on the New York State administrative policies studies, now in progress, sponsored by the Academy of Political Science"[12]—the very same study of "the broad spectrum of state government" financed by Nelson Rockefeller.

Often, the trappings of wealth and political power conflated in one person were overpowering, even for those trained to be unimpressed. Once, for example, an upstate reporter bucking for a promotion succeeded in getting an exclusive interview with the governor. He walked into Rockefeller's office, exchanged greetings, and then froze in awe. The governor's press secretary, immediately sensing the symptoms, not only operated the reporter's tape recorder but actually asked his questions. After the interview ended and the embarrassed newsman was safely out of earshot, the governor's spokesman tried to explain to Rockefeller what had caused him to clutch. "He's sitting not only with the governor of New York State, but also with Nelson Rockefeller," reminded the press secretary. No explanations were necessary. "Poor guy," Rockefeller said sympathetically. "You know, that's happened before."

No attempt at influencing opinion was beyond him. He flattered reporters and their superiors, commissioned biographies of both himself and his opponents, and even attempted to shape the writing of history by a group of academics. He attempted repeatedly to quiet his more vociferous critics through cajolery or "opportunities." Criticism deemed to be innocuous, he would, of course, merely ignore. And perhaps his talent for being "impervious after all these years," is what aggravated Nelson's critics most. And perhaps, too, it provided a strange kind of comfort to those whose efforts to chop him down to size were continually frustrated by his personal and political clout.

Nelson and John Lindsay divide the twin towers of the World Trade Center.

Rocky looks Right at
Ronald Reagan (top)
and Barry Goldwater.

Perry Duryea and Nelson before the axe fell.

Henry Kissinger and Nelson—always in step.

Arthur Goldberg and Nelson: who laughs last?

Meade Esposito and Nelson's Picasso: "It's only a print."

A man and his monument.

Albany Mall being built. Rocky: "The thing
kept sinking into the mud."

Nelson being sworn in as Vice-President of the United States—
moving a little closer to "real success" in American politics.

PART THREE

Nelson's Politics

CHAPTER 16

Paying for
Nelson's Politics

NELSON'S politics cost lots of money. He, his siblings, and his stepmother have already spent more to acquire and retain political power through public office than any other family in American history. Their contributions exceed the total spent personally by all previous presidents since George Washington. More in *gift taxes* was paid on their contributions to Nelson's last three gubernatorial races than his rivals were able to raise from *all* sources.

What impact could so much money have on public opinion, which, Rockefeller loftily remarked, alone determines the outcome of every election? After reciting a litany of the largesse from Rockefeller relatives, Senator James Allen said he thought "the voice of the people expressing itself on your staying in office was influenced to some extent, or at least encouraged, by massive sums spent in your behalf."[1]

"That," Rockefeller candidly conceded, "would be a fair assumption, based on the figures you have just given."[2] But, he volunteered, "I think if somebody spends his own money in a political campaign, the public's intuitive feeling is: 'Well, at least he's not spending money that somebody gave him in order to get a commitment as to what he's going to do after he's elected.' " Also, "if you have money that you've made or inherited—that you're probably not going to try and make your money after you get into office, because you've already got it."[3]

Reminded later of his remarks about outside financial support, Rockefeller was asked whether it was reasonable for the public to be just as concerned about his gift giving to present and former public officials? Side-stepping the obvious inconsistency, Rockefeller replied: "I don't think I said any such thing."[4]

The criticism that surrounded Nelson's own unprecedented spending and his family's financial favors to outsiders had its roots in the foundation of the Rockefeller fortune itself. In one way or another, most of Standard Oil's covert political influence involved Mark Hanna, the Republican boss who had been John D.'s classmate at Cleveland's Central High. It was Hanna who berated a trust-busting attorney general with the warning that "there is no greater mistake for a man in or out of public place to make than to assume that he owes any duty to the public."[5] And the boss also boasted that Standard's officials had "been most liberal in their contributions to the party, as I personally know, Mr. Rockefeller always quietly doing his share."[6]

By the time Nelson began giving on his own, the taint of the Standard Oil's dependence on influence peddlers had still not subsided. And because of such suspicions, one of his early campaign contributions was politely returned. In the spring of 1940, at the same time that he was plugging for a post with President Roosevelt, Rockefeller remembered his Republican roots and forked over $2,000 to the fledgling election effort of Wendell Willkie—far and away the largest contribution Willkie had received.

Oren Root, a fundraiser for the GOP in 1940 and later Rockefeller's superintendent of banks, recalled that when Rockefeller's windfall arrived, "at first my colleagues' and my reaction was one of elation. Upon further reflection, however, we began to worry about the possible effect of such a contribution upon our public image. While $2,000 was not a large sum for a

Rockefeller, and while it was not large by comparison with other political contributions in those days, it was very large by the standards of our simple, volunteer effort."[7]

Having assured him that his purpose was not to ask for more money, Root finally reached Rockefeller and returned half of his contribution. Root's financial relationship with Rockefeller had a revealing sequel. Nine years later, when he was running on the Republican ticket for borough president of Manhattan, he received a modest donation from Nelson. "He had explained," Root recalled, "that he would have liked to have been more generous, but in view of the fact that the Democratic Party dominated the governmental structure in New York City and in light of the many delicate relationships existing between his real estate interests and City Hall, he hoped that I would understand his wish not to give anybody an excuse to discriminate against him unfairly."[8]

Apparently, Rockefeller suffered pangs of conscience after Root's overwhelming defeat. "I was sitting one day writing thank-you letters," Root said, "when the telephone rang and it was Nelson Rockefeller. 'I have felt badly, Oren,' he said, 'that I gave you so small a contribution for your campaign. Now that the campaign is over, I would like to help you with your deficit.' " But Root "found it necessary to report to him that my campaign had ended not with a deficit but with a tiny surplus, and could I have a rain check?"[9]

Some affluent office seekers, like Averell Harriman, had family fortunes but declined to invest in themselves and others, no matter what the political profit might be. The 1974 campaign spending limits were designed to ensure that Rockefeller's observable level of personal political contributions would never be legally matched.

The biggest recipient of Nelson's munificence was the New York State Republican Party and its county and local committees. Between 1957 and 1974, they collected from him $1,031,637 in contributions that ranged from $363,000 to the GOP State Committee in 1962 to a mere $12 to the Republican Town Committee of Ossining, which adjoins his Pocantico Hills estate. "We appreciate anyone's contribution," said Town Chairman Herman Bates. "I look upon that as a neighborly thing."[10] It was only a year after he became governor that Nelson began to bankroll the Republican Party. In 1961 he gave $53,000 to the state GOP. Then $363,000 the following year. "One misconception people have is that he sustained the Republican Party," a Rockefeller confidant cautioned. "He did—by contributions to his own campaigns. But it's been independent of him since 1966." Nevertheless, during that 18-year period, Nelson gave:

Just over $1 million to his own presidential campaigns;
$412,000 to New York congressional, state, and local candidates;
$274,000 to brother Winthrop's two Arkansas gubernatorial races;
$81,000 to his own four statehouse contests;
$85,000 to the Republican Party nationally; and
$99,000 to congressional, state, and local candidates outside New York State.[11]

By far the biggest beneficiary of Nelson's own fortune—other than himself and Winthrop—was George Romney. Through more than 20 campaign committees, Rockefeller funneled at least $200,000 to his fellow governor in 1967 and 1968—a fortune for anyone other than Nelson, who poured more than $720,000 into his own 1968 campaign coffers before losing the nomination to Richard Nixon. Other big recipients have included John Lindsay ($139,000), Richard Nixon ($57,000), Senator Jacob Javits ($20,667), Westchester Representative Peter Peyser ($18,000), and former Senator Charles Goodell ($38,000). Malcolm Wilson, Nelson's successor as governor, suffered in 1974 from the stricter state campaign spending limits enacted six months after Rockefeller left office. Wilson received $34,000 from Rockefeller and lost to Hugh Carey.

A man of Rockefeller's means also had the flexibility to assist office seekers in extraordinary ways. In 1961, for instance, he contributed $3,000 to the ethnically balanced Republican New York City mayoralty ticket topped by Louis Lefkowitz. In addition, he personally loaned controller candidate John J. Gilhooley $2,500 in the middle of the campaign. Similarly, in 1963, Rockefeller contributed $3,000 to a joint committee supporting cousin Richard Aldrich for Manhattan city councilman. Right after Aldrich won the Republican primary, Rockefeller also loaned him $26,000. The family had another fundraising tool, too. Rockefeller never contributed a cent to the 1974 reelection race of Maryland Senator Charles Mathias, for example. But he hosted a reception at his Foxhall Road mansion which raised almost $10,000 for the liberal Republican's campaign.

Nelson's donation decisions were usually left to George Hinman, the courtly lawyer who, since 1960, had doubled as Republican national committeeman from New York and counsel to Rockefeller Family and Associates. "He usually makes the decision," one Hinman intimate said, "and the answer is usually no." An inkling of just how the donations are doled out was provided by Rockefeller himself, in response to a question from Senate Majority Leader Hugh Scott. "I am proud to say," Scott said proudly, "that I have received contributions from Governor Rockefeller, always legal, always recorded. I have only one item of curiosity. Why $3,000 in 1964 and only $1,000 in 1970?" "It must have been related to your margin of victory," Rockefeller replied. "It did look better in 1970," Scott conceded.[12]

As if to discourage more requests, Rockefeller said he had been asked for so much over the years that he was "totally impervious to requests for money."[13] And to prove that "I do not think I have been a sucker,"[14] Rockefeller recalled a request from Spiro Agnew, who had supported Nelson's 1968 abortive presidential bid. After Agnew resigned as vice-president in disgrace, he personally sought Rockefeller funds to finance a book. Rockefeller refused. Offering a rare example that even for him, loyalty has its limits, Nelson also denied two written appeals from presidential aide John Ehrlichman for donations to an Agnew defense fund. "From a human point of view," Rockefeller remarked, "I am embarrassed to say that I did not answer the letters."[15]

Ironically, it was the former governor's gifts to others that usually created the greatest controversy. That was also true of the family, which made about $1.7 million in contributions to candidates other than Nelson in 1968—substantially more than the reported total for the second most generous family that year, the Mellons, who disbursed $298,000.[16] Four years later, while Nelson's son Rodman sent $500 to the Nixon reelection committee, Laurance's daughter Laura and David's two daughters, Abby and Peggy, invested $19,000 in *Milhouse—A White Comedy*, the "savagely anti-Nixon film" that won Emile de Antonio a place on President Nixon's "enemies list."

As for Nelson himself, his contributions created the biggest brouhaha during his confirmation by Congress. Maine Representative William Cohen returned a $500 donation because, an aide explained, "we didn't want to create a situation where anyone would think" Rockefeller was trying to buy Cohen's vote.[17] The same year, the mixed blessing of three $5,000 checks was bestowed by Rockefeller on New York Republican Senator Jacob Javits, who, despite persistent needling from Democratic rival Ramsey Clark, finally decided not to return the contribution. Nelson was surprised, however, when Senator Edmund Muskie, a fellow member of the Commission on Water Quality, rejected his 1973 Christmas present of a $2,500 Steuben glass salmon rising to a gold fly. Rockefeller said Muskie graciously refused the fish with the observation that "your giving a gift like this for Christmas is like my giving a necktie."[18]

If it was better to give than to receive, it was also better to receive than not to receive. And even better than having a rich uncle was being blessed with several rich relatives who carried out the credo that the family that pays together, stays together—by making a capital investment in its favorite son.

Contributions to his campaigns have varied substantially from one sibling to another. In 1958, Nelson's biggest benefactor was his father, who contributed only $10,654. Six years later, family funding soared dramatically with the first donations by the Martha Baird Rockefeller trusts, which forwarded $2,157,500 to one of her stepson's national political committees. For his hotly contested third gubernatorial bid, the trusts contributed $850,000 in 1966 and another $2.3 million in 1967. Although Nelson's brothers contributed under $35,000 each in 1966, within a year his state campaign coffers were swelled with $395,000 from Laurance, $175,000 from Abby, $125,000 from John 3rd, $100,000 from Winthrop, and $50,000 from David.

For Nelson's third presidential race in 1968, he managed to spend somewhere between $5 million and $8 million without even entering a single primary. Martha contributed $1.4 million herself that year (plus gift taxes totaling $854,483)[19] and another $1.4 million through trusts. Laurance gave $244,000, John, Abby, and Winthrop each gave $100,000. Although David was noticeably absent from every one of his brother's contribution lists, he helped pay off campaign debts the following year, when he and Laurance each donated $30,000 and their stepmother contributed $80,000.

As incredible as those contributions were individually, the totals for Rockefeller's seven efforts to offer himself to the masses are even more mind boggling. Over those 17 years, he received at least:

$10.2 million from his stepmother's trusts;
$1.5 million from her personal accounts;
$1.4 million from Laurance;
$592,000 from David;
$509,000 from Abby;
$405,000 from John; and
$260,500 from Winthrop.

Add to that the $1.1 million spent on his own campaigns, another $1 million that he routed to the Republican Party in New York, and $5 million more for keeping constant tabs on the public pulse.[20] Add applicable gift taxes and what you wind up with is a grand total of at least $30 million in direct outlays to further Nelson Rockefeller's political career.

So stunning were those totals that campaign strategists sought to concoct schemes to make them less visible. That effort began as early as 1958, when Nelson's father contributed $3,000 to Democrats for Rockefeller, a recurring committee whose receipts from the Rockefellers themselves reached over $33,000 in 1970. Some $33,000 of the $40,000 collected by the Committee of Independents for the Rockefeller Team from August through November 1970 also came from Nelson's stepmother and his five siblings.[21] Covert campaign financing scams also scattered contributions in states where no disclosure was required. In 1968, William Burden, Thomas Gates, J. Irwin Miller, Arthur Watson, and John Hay Whitney were said to have provided about $100,000 each in individual contributions of $3,000 to 34 separate committees to avoid the federal gift tax. "We did have Delaware and Illlinois committees," conceded Archibald Gillies, Rockefeller's campaign finance director in 1966 and 1968. "We met all the requirements in Delaware and Illinois, but those states do not require that we open the reports in the manner that New York did."[22] Meanwhile, the financial filings in Rockefeller's home state—which, it now turns out, exposed only part of the spending picture—meticulously listed such innocuous items as $6 in receipts from the Hughes Active Citizenship Fund and an unexplained $325.14 expenditure for sponges (surely not for some soak-the-rich campaign).

"Did we every worry about where the next buck would come from?" campaign treasurer James Hellmuth asked rhetorically. "Yeah, we did. When the 1968 campaign ended, we wound up selling the furniture. When it's going well, you could get more out of your boss or Martha. When things are going badly, it's not the same thing."[23] But the biggest financial problem of any Rockefeller campaign budget was how much to expect from outside donations. "People's first reaction," Archibald Gillies recalled, was " 'Gee, why give to a Rockefeller?' We had no real comeback other than the good government responsibility—if you believe in a guy as a candidate, and that even if they could give all the money themselves it wouldn't be democratic."[24] Rockefeller's independent finance committee collected about $1.2 million of an anticipated $1.5 million in 1968—exclusive of the $100,000 which horticulturist and General Motors heir Stewart R. Mott pledged if Rockefeller would declare by March 15 and adopt an acceptable peace policy for Vietnam.[25]

"The fat cat contributors are easier to talk to," said George Humphreys, Rockefeller's sometime southern strategist and a campaign finance official for Rockefeller in 1970 and for Malcolm Wilson in 1974. "You can't raise the $25 money. I never contributed to Nelson Rockefeller's campaign, but I did contribute to Malcolm's."[26]

The formidable Rockefeller fat cats have included Frank Sinatra, developer William J. Levitt, former Treasury Secretary C. Douglas Dillon, financiers Albert Gordon, Gustave Levy, and Bernard Lasker, builder William Zeckendorf, movie mogul Darryl Zanuck, and Joseph C. Wilson of Xerox. Virtually all gave under $10,000 per campaign. Rockefeller also capitalized on the clout of incumbency to solicit hundeds of thousands of dollars in $500 contributions to the Governor's Club from officials, friends, lobbyists, and other influence seekers.

There was also another unique source of funds available only to a candidate of Rockefeller's financial clout—practical proof of the adage that the rich get richer. In 1966 alone, his main Friends of the Rockefeller Team collected almost $3.7 million in bank loans that tided him over until the family covered campaign costs. He found a friend at Manufacturers Hanover Trust ($700,000 from June 30 to August 18) and Chemical Bank ($800,000 from October 19 to 26), among others.[27]

His campaign reports every two years from 1958 to 1970 were painfully familiar to Rockefeller opponents, who helplessly witnessed a spending spree that was unrivaled in the annals of campaign financing. Hotel bills, which candidates usually settle up months after an election, were paid in advance to take advantage of a 10 percent discount—an economy attributed to Nelson himself in 1966, when his reelection machine rented 84 rooms in the New York Hilton, which is 25 percent-owned by Rockefeller Center. Hundreds of thousands of dollars would be paid to family firms, such as Wayfarer Ketch for air transportation and Greenrock for catering. Tens of thousands more would be allotted for polling and public relations, and for publicity as diverse as ads on the Armenian Radio Hour or in the Cornell *Daily Sun*. Studded with such familiar names as Joseph Canzeri (the majordomo of Pocantico), Jackie Robinson, Joan Braden, and a bevy of state public relations men briefly off the public pad, the campaign payroll soared to an unbelievable level of over 500 employees in 1970. "We spent everything we wanted to spend," George Humphreys said of the $7.2 million-plus 1970 campaign. "We stuck with the budget—we wound up about 2 percent off. At some point you get to be pissing money out the window. But when we wrote the budget, we wrote it on the basis of doing everything reasonable with the full confidence that we could fund any budget that we wrote."[28]

Why did Rockefeller campaigns cost so much? William Ronan, his closest adviser and confidant declared with disgust in the midst of one contest: "Twenty-five percent of the money in any campaign is leaked right out the window. The trouble is that you're never sure which 25 percent. Somewhere around this city there are 2 million Rockefeller buttons. Where are they? I'm damned if I know. You can stand all day on the busiest street corner in this city and not see one of them. But if you didn't have them, you'd hear from every county chairman in the state that you weren't doing anything. Some day somebody's going to have the guts to throw the buttons out."[29]

The 1974 federal election campaign act curbed contributions from a candidate for president or vice-president and his immediate family to $50,000—astoundingly, less than 2 percent of what Nelson and the other Rockefellers contributed to Nelson's 1968 campaign. As early as 1973, Nelson warily denied that he was resigning as governor to run for president because he feared that political overtones would make the $1 million which Laurance and he had each contributed to his Critical Choices Commission illegal under the new law. For Rockefeller, however, all those restrictions were less significant in light of the millions in seed money he has already sown across the political landscape. And the Supreme Court's 1976 decision to rescind personal spending limits unlocked Nelson's vast warchest once more.

While Nelson has expressed concern that public campaign financing would spur a proliferation of minor parties, he half-jokingly applauded Congress for passing new spending limits. "You will save me more money by what you have done than any other single thing that could happen,"[30] he mused, adding that "members of my family are much relieved by the legislation you all have passed."[31] While he also endorsed the concept of curtailing both the time and cost of campaigns, Rockefeller admitted with refreshing frankness that such limits offer a valuable advantage that he has enjoyed for virtually all of his political life. "I think, in fairness," he said, "one would have to say it would favor the incumbent who, by that time, is better known. That is one of the problems."[32]

On December 19, 1974, that was no longer a problem for Nelson. After years spent greasing the skids, it had cost only the price of a telephone call from Washington to Seal Harbor for him to achieve national office—although not the one he coveted.

"Political authority, the only enduring kind of political power, is not for sale in the American political system," he once insisted. "Yes, you can buy some influence, you can bribe and win sordid games, your wealth can purchase a piece of political power here or there. And we also know that with raw political power without wealth, you can buy some influence, you can bribe and win some sordid games, and you can acquire some personal wealth here and there. But great political authority in America comes only from the free gift of the people when they vote for you."[33]

That free gift, which still eludes Nelson Rockefeller, has so far cost his family over $30 million. It may cost a good deal more before his quest is ended.

CHAPTER 17

"No, Thank You. I Accept."

WENDELL WILLKIE won the 1940 Republican presidential nomination because the Eastern establishment that ruled the GOP dictated his selection. Others had wanted to become a historical footnote by losing to Franklin Roosevelt, but a measure of the lightness of the competition was the name of the man who came in second, 37-year-old Thomas E. Dewey, then district attorney of Manhattan, a post not known as a springboard to the White House.

For Nelson Rockefeller, 1960 held not much more promise of success. Richard Nixon had been Dwight Eisenhower's heir apparent since 1952, when he successfully defended his integrity in his famous Checkers speech. A race for the 1960 Republican nomination was not the track that an untested, unelected public official should run on, not even a millionaire bearing one of the nation's most famous names. Besides, if money alone could win the presidency, a man like William Randolph Hearst, who wanted the job, would have won it long before. And Hearst had, in addition to fabulous wealth, total command of a privately owned communications empire. No, the presidency was a large step away and the best preparation en route was the governorship of New York, from which seven men had sought the White House, three of them successfully.

Nelson Rockefeller announced his candidacy for the Republican gubernatorial nomination on June 30, 1958. Eight weeks later, the nomination was his. Of course, it wasn't quite that simple. In John D. Rockefeller, Sr.'s philosophy of business, Allan Nevins once wrote, "nothing should be guessed at, nothing left uncounted or unmeasured."[1] And just as his grandfather sought to remove the element of chance from the world of business, Nelson sought to remove it from politics. "I'd like to think that I was drafted," he said "but to tell you the truth I never worked so hard for anything as I did for that nomination."[2]

He had to work hard. Emmet Hughes has observed that "if there is any combination that scares Republicans it is a liberal who doesn't need their money."[3] The Eastern Republican oligarchy was at first afraid of Nelson Rockefeller. It took his money gladly; Nelson regularly contributed to the state party and was always there if extra cash was needed quickly. Taking him as governor was another matter: Nelson's own money made him independent of party control, the ultimate Republican heresy. In Chicago, in 1958, at the Advertising Club, he was referred to as Nelson Roosevelt, "another Republican who wants to betray his class and go to Washington and wreck the economy."[4] Hadn't he proved just that in Washington under Eisenhower?

At first, the Old Guard urged Rockefeller to seek another office. Tom Dewey, suspicious of charm, said "You can't win,"[5] and suggested the New York City postmastership or a congressional seat from Westchester. As each was rejected out of hand, the bidding escalated. When Rockefeller refused the U.S. Senate nomination—"all they do there is talk," he said—the Old Guard finally understood that he was serious about being governor. "Few observers realized," wrote former Rockefeller staffer Frank Gervasi in a campaign biography, "that Rockefeller's campaign . . . was a calculated first overt step up the ladder of a dream that led to the White House."[6] Some of those who did realize it, and some others who didn't, joined. Others fought.

The Eisenhower wing of the Republican Party supported Leonard Hall, a former national chairman and, to his regret during the upcoming campaign, a close friend of Sherman Adams—the man in the vicuña coat. (Said Rockefeller of the Adams case: "I'm sure Sherman Adams would agree with me that honesty in government is a basic essential. Just as important is to avoid the appearance of doing wrong, and if elected I would insist on this."[7]) In early summer, after his hopes for glory had fallen under Nelson's steamroller, Hall explained the Rockefeller magic this way: "We politicians get to be pretty good at smiling and shaking hands—hell, that's our business. But Nelson would go upstate and smile and shake hands with some leader's wife, and she'd get all watery at the knees, like he was a prince or something."[8] Hall didn't think it was funny. His antipathy toward Rockefeller led him to support Nixon in 1960, and it took 11 years for him to return to the Rockefeller orbit. In 1969 the governor appointed him to the influential state Banking Board.[9]

The conservative wing of the state party, once and always solidly behind Tom Dewey ("Dewey's brand of liberalism," *National Review* publisher William Rusher wrote in a 1971 eulogy, "would strike most conservatives today as a sort of Custer's Last Stand for the principles they believe in"[10]), supported State Senate Majority Leader Walter Mahoney. They'd gone first to Dewey himself, but the former governor, comfortably ensconced in a Wall Street law firm with the Chase Manhattan Bank as a major client, viewed a return to Albany as a comedown, not a comeback. Assembly Speaker Oswald Heck and U.S. Attorney Paul Williams rounded out the field.

The key to the early Rockefeller strategy was the appearance of no strategy at all, and a perpetuation of the myth that the incumbent, W. Averell Harriman, was unbeatable. That assumption infected the GOP like a plague as the country suffered the "Eisenhower recession." In the early months of 1958, Rockefeller's rivals did very little: "We all had our support, our bases," recalled Walter Mahoney. "We'd wait and watch it all shake out right before the convention like always. But it didn't look like a good year for Republicans anywhere, so what little we did was mainly just for exercise."[11]

Nelson Rockefeller, it seemed, was playing by the rules. In January, for public consumption, he denied any interest in the governorship, well after informing Jud Morhouse, George Hinman, and Francis Jamieson of his plans. As the Rockefeller family's public relations man, Jamieson was Nelson's closest friend outside the family, and the one intimate to oppose his race for governor—Jamieson thought Nelson couldn't win.

Nothing could shake his policy of lying low. Rockefeller even turned down a National Republican Club invitation to participate in a fortnightly series of forums titled "The Pulse of New York." His rivals accepted eagerly. It wasn't that Rockefeller didn't want the exposure. He didn't want *that* kind of exposure. Public interest in him derived from his aloofness, an above-it-all air that would dissipate only on schedule—a strategy Hubert Humphrey pursued in early 1976. "The best politics for a man in my position," said Humphrey, "is absolutely no politics at all."[12]

Nelson was not exactly a recluse, however. The chairmanship of the Commission on the Constitutional Convention in 1956 and 1957 gave him the opportunity to travel the state as a noncandidate, the kind of statesmanlike publicity that is a politician's dream. The commission also allowed him to get to know its research director, William Ronan, and its counsel, George Hinman, both to become long-term cogs in the Rockefeller campaign machine. Almost as a sidelight, as the *Herald Tribune*'s Don Irwin wrote, "the job was a cram course in the mechanics of state government and Rockefeller was an apt pupil."[13]

At the same time, the Rockefeller Brothers Special Studies kept Nelson in the news as a serious student of government. One such special study found that the United States wasn't prepared for Soviet aggression, a charge Rockefeller would repeat during the 1960 presidential campaign. President Eisenhower didn't like that kind of talk, but it got Nelson on *Meet the Press*. Still another special study that received wide play offered a six-point plan for economic recovery, including an immediate tax cut and a mini version of the New Deal's WPA. As interesting as the reports themselves were the people who took part in the studies, a veritable "who's who" of the American establishment, including Dean Rusk, John Gardner, Arthur Burns, Lucius Clay, Chester Bowles, David Sarnoff, Edward Teller, Henry Luce, and Henry Kissinger.[14] The work sessions in Rockefeller Center occasionally ran to several consecutive days, and it took months for the conclusions to be published as *Prospect for America—The Rockefeller Panel Reports* in, of all years, 1958. Nelson liked the exposure and the formula so much that he and many veterans of *Prospect for America* returned for another try 15 years later as members of the National Commission on Critical Choices, the homework committee for Nelson's 1976 run for president.

As work on the highbrow front proceeded apace, Jud Morhouse, the supposedly neutral state chairman, was taking and leaking candidate preference polls as if his political neck depended on it—which it did. The tall, crew-cut Ticonderoga lawyer knew that his days were numbered. He'd been installed as state chairman at the very end of Dewey's term as governor in 1954. No one blamed Morhouse for Irving Ives's razor thin loss to Harriman in 1954, but Morhouse knew that the next gubernatorial candidate would, by tradition, install his own man at party headquarters. All of the potential candidates had their own hacks itching for the job, all but Nelson Rockefeller. It didn't take long for Morhouse to latch on. Morhouse needed a candidate patron, and Rockefeller needed lines to the GOP organization—the perfect match.

The polls Morhouse leaked, two funded by "unknown sources," showed Nelson second only to the unavailable Dewey as the Republican with the best chance to beat Harriman. The polls also showed Rockefeller losing to Harriman by 60–40, thus confirming the other half of Rockefeller's strategy—that the nomination was worthless anyway, so why bother. The polls served an invaluable function. Morhouse would show the results to county chairmen and urge them to wait, to refrain from committing themselves officially to the other candidates they had supported for years, at least until they could see Rockefeller face-to-face. It was a strategy Rockefeller would use again in 1968 when he tried to stop Nixon by proving, via the polls, that he was the best candidate. In New York, in 1958, the strategy played out like a symphony. The chairmen waited, and the combination of charm and money, not to mention fear, worked wonders. "The guys would swoon," said Morhouse.[15]

Another swooner was Averell Harriman. A year earlier, Harriman had invited the Constitutional Convention Commission members to the Executive Mansion. According to former Assembly Speaker Joseph Carlino, Harriman turned to Rockefeller and said, "Nelson, I want to welcome you to the mansion. Take a tour . . . because this is the only time you're going to see the inside."[16] Now, in 1958, Harriman turned to the members of the Legislative Correspondents Association at their annual dinner. "The man to watch," he said, "is Nelson Rockefeller."

The Metropolitan Political Club, a group of liberal Republican insurgents in Manhattan chaired by John Roosevelt, FDR's youngest son, began a "Draft Rockefeller" movement barely two months after the club was established in November 1957. Using an old Eisenhower mailing list, the club raised approximately $27,000 (with three $1,000 contributions from real estate tycoon William Zeckendorf, public relations virtuoso Tex McCrary, and socialite Peggy Woodward) and promptly took a poll: Rockefeller on top again.[17]

Upstate, polls meant little. Rockefeller needed a way in, a way to defang his liberal image and present himself as "just folks." Later, he would accomplish the same result on the stump simply by signing autographs "Rocky." He needed a salesman, and he found just what he was looking for in Assemblyman Malcolm Wilson, a 20-year veteran with a photographic memory for names and faces—a conservative's conservative, "to the right of McKinley," said one of his legislative colleagues.

Like Jud Morhouse, Malcolm Wilson was in political limbo. Despite his long Assembly tenure, Wilson was boxed in. Oswald Heck was speaker; next in line was Majority Leader Joe Carlino, six years *younger* than Wilson. Wilson had nothing to lose by joining Rockefeller. The two had met casually over the years, but it was a late spring meeting in 1958 that brought Wilson irrevocably to Rockefeller's side. Arriving alone at Wilson's Yonkers law office, Rockefeller seated himself in an oversized green vinyl chair and talked with Malcolm Wilson for three hours. "He convinced me that he wasn't the flaming liberal some people had said," recalls Wilson, "and I told him that if he wanted the nomination he'd have to get upstate support first. City support might be enough to carry the convention, but he'd need active Republican help upstate if he was to win the general election in the fall. The surest way to get that support was to court the upstate delegates one by one."[18]

With Wilson driving his own battered Chevrolet, he and Rockefeller set out on an upstate tour that proved enormously successful. "It was just the two of us," says Wilson. "No baggage carriers, no sycophants, no PR men, nothing but us. And I paid for it personally. Not a farthing of Nelson Rockefeller's was used. When I had accumulated a debt I'd forward a statement to [Westchester County Republican Chairman] Herb Gerlach and I'd be reimbursed."[19] What Wilson failed to mention was that Rockefeller had been supporting that reimbursement kitty, the Westchester GOP organization, for years.

Wilson's great ability was to tunnel under the existing leadership structure in the upstate counties. Such was his stature that he need only announce his presence as a courtesy to the GOP county chairmen and he was free to poach delegates—the same tactic Wilson would employ in 1968 when he tried corraling convention delegates for Rockefeller's third presidential race.

Again, what worked so well in New York failed miserably elsewhere.

To the dismay of liberal Republicans, Rockefeller soon rewarded Wilson, and balanced the ticket, by handing him the lieutenant-governor nomination later that year. While he played the hayseed with Wilson upstate, Rockefeller had been telling liberals in New York City that as soon as he won the gubernatorial nomination, he would send Malcolm Wilson back to Westchester as an assemblyman. Rockefeller denies having said any such thing—about as convincingly as John Kennedy denied ever having badmouthed Lyndon Johnson before political expediency forced *him* to choose an ideological opposite as his running mate.

Personally, says former Rockefeller aide Warren Gardner, "Nelson absolutely despised Malcolm Wilson. He couldn't understand his narrow thinking. But he owed it all to Malcolm."[20] Wilson's reward was 15 years coming, but he finally became governor in his own right when Rockefeller resigned in December 1973 to seek the presidency without the benefit of public office.

The linchpin in the 1958 "upstate first" strategy was William Hill, the powerful Republican chairman of Broome County, which includes the city of Binghamton. Hill's power derived only partially from his party position. He was also president of the Binghamton *Sun*. In September 1957, Rockefeller aide George Hinman arranged for his boss and his wife to meet Hill over dinner at the Hinmans' Binghamton home. Rockefeller met Hill alone in November, and Hill went quietly to work dropping Rockefeller's name whenever it seemed appropriate, given the hide-and-seek game plan. The wraps finally came off in May 1958 when Hill published an editorial in the *Sun* endorsing Rockefeller's candidacy. All the right words were there: "new fresh vigorous leadership. He has brains, tireless energy, the broadest human sympathies. . . . He is the right man. . . . He is a winner."[21]

And he was winning. One rival who still fears Rockefeller's

long reach saw his support wither away via the threat of financial reprisal. "A lot of small towns are run by bankers," he said, "and a lot of Republican chairmen are close to those bankers. In some cases, the bankers and the county GOP chairmen are the same people. Three men I thought loyal to me came to me and said that their financial survival depended on their switching to Rockefeller. I told them to switch. Some things aren't worth the fight." In *The Power Broker*, Robert Caro quotes a veteran New York politician as saying of Rockefeller: "I bet on money —not just any kind of money but old money. New money buys things, old money calls notes."[22]

By the end of May, a month before he officially declared his candidacy, the nomination was his. The rest was anticlimax— face-saving set pieces with county leaders mourning the exits of their favorite-son front men. Stop Rockefeller movements were born and died in the same afternoon. Tom Dewey, with a few months to go as the party's top power, decreed the limits of tolerance: there would be no floor fight. On August 25, 10,000 people jammed Rochester's convention center to hail the conquering hero, the Prince of Pocantico. There wasn't even the formality of a roll call. The only real drama occurred where it always does in American politics, behind the scenes. Representative Kenneth Keating, covetous of his seniority on the House Judiciary Committee, was reluctant to accept the U.S. Senate nomination. A call to his suite at Rochester's Sheraton Hotel from Vice-President Nixon persuaded him—plus an all but flat-out promise of a federal judgeship if Keating lost.[23]

Rockefeller's acceptance speech was standard stuff. Harriman was charged with all manner of sin, from shortsightedness to vacillation and indecision. As for Rockefeller, he of course promised all things to all men. He was ready to go. In fact, he said, "I'm damn thrilled."

CHAPTER 18

Battle of
the Millionaires

THE CAMPAIGN LITERATURE had been circulating for some months. It was hilarious. It described Rockefeller as a man with a "softly persuasive voice and a sunny smile. . . . He moves with a purposeful determination to make the most of the minutes and a restful confidence that no task is too great if everybody will just 'get organized.'. . . If there had been no problems for him, he would have invented some just to keep busy. . . . On a wedding gift honeymoon around the world . . . they [Nelson and his wife] saw Mahatma Gandhi on his day of silence and got only a scribbled note to return at 5:00 A.M.; they did, and Gandhi discussed with them India's struggle for independence."[1]

A campaign manual that predated Larry O'Brien's famous compendium for John Kennedy's 1960 presidential race included everything from "Testimonial Publicity" to sample press releases to "How to Raise Money" ("raising your own money can be fun," it said[2]).

Nietzsche wrote that "One must test oneself to see if one is meant for independence and for command. And one must do it at the right time."[3] For Nelson Rockefeller, 1958 was the right time because Averell Harriman was the right opponent. Never again, thought Rockefeller, would the issue of his enormous wealth be blunted as it would now. Once overcome, it would never again be a barrier. Until it was overcome, it would represent the same kind of obstacle that Catholicism would mean to John Kennedy two years later.

"When I decided to run for office in 1958," Rockefeller recalled, "the party was bust. Harriman was governor. I have to assume that one of the reasons the party let in an independent—and I was an independent—was because they figured nobody could win, and here was somebody who could probably finance his own campaign, and therefore what's wrong with that?"[4]

Even though the Harrimans were more frugal with their fortune, it was hardly the most opportune time for the Democrats to make much hay over Rockefeller's riches. The battle of progressive plutocrats effectively blunted the barbs that would be hurled at Rockefeller in subsequent races. In 1958 his campaign cost about $1.8 million, a third more than Harriman's. Four years later, his bottom-line budget of $2.2 million was five times Robert Morgenthau's. In 1966 he boosted his sagging popularity by spending ten times as much as Democratic rival Frank O'Connor in a race that, according to official reports alone, cost the Rockefellers and their supporters almost $5 million.[5] And in 1970, Arthur Goldberg was confronted with Rockefeller's record-breaking campaign budget of over $7 million but found it difficult to criticize because Senate aspirant Richard Ottinger, Goldberg's running mate on the Democratic ticket, had, like Rockefeller, balked at placing voluntary limits on television advertising—the very expenditure that media magician David Garth had used so successfully in Ottinger's $2 million-plus primary. Ironically, it would not be until Rockefeller was being considered for an appointive post—the vice-presidency—that the political impact of the family fortune became a critical issue.

Averell Harriman and Nelson Rockefeller had been friends for years. "He and I started Sun Valley together, a private venture," recalled Rockefeller. "Luckily the railroad [the Union

Battle of the Millionaires

Pacific] took it over."[6] Both men entered public life as appointees of Franklin Roosevelt, who collected millionaires the way he collected stamps. Both men wanted the presidency. Had he won, Harriman planned a major push for the 1960 Democratic presidential nomination, with only his age as a serious problem—he would be 68 in 1960 (he was once dubbed the Adenauer of Albany), the same age as Nelson Rockefeller in 1976.

Harriman's campaign proved unexpectedly lackluster. In a bad year for Republicans, Rockefeller succeeded in personalizing the race. Most of his campaign literature never carried the word "Republican," and it was Harriman versus Rockefeller for the duration. He even managed to turn his wealth to his advantage. Sure he was worth a lot, he said, but his family had done a lot with it. The campaign headquarters fashioned a phrase that was soon reverberating around the state: "Ever hear of a Harriman foundation?" The hapless Harriman was even humiliated by his own family. Cousin John, an NYU economics professor, presented Rockefeller with a petition urging his election. It was signed by 6,000 people.[7]

The governor's political alliances appeared to be crumbling as well. Adolf Berle, Jr., a fellow New Dealer and honorary chairman of the Liberal Party—which had officially endorsed Harriman—appeared on radio and said that both Harriman and Rockefeller were "first-rate men . . . New York is lucky to have them both." The Battle of the Millionaires wasn't worth the price of admission.

Rockefeller traveled more than 8,000 miles, visited each of 62 counties, and made 135 formal speeches in 103 communities.[8] He seemed to be in perpetual motion. "In a glandular way," said one observer, "this guy is the male equivalent of Eleanor Roosevelt."[9] He discovered ethnics and went after them with relish. No bloc was too small for him to pursue. Former *Times* reporter Warren Moscow tells the story of Rockefeller's riding the ferry to Staten Island for a day's campaigning there. "Rockefeller had his shoes shined by the Italian bootblack who worked the beat," wrote Moscow. "Two days later the boot-black received at his home a personal note and a picture of Rockefeller autographed to 'my good friend Tony.' The note hailed the shoeshine as the best Rockefeller had ever had, and the candidate inquired whether Tony could possibly be available for a repeat performance on a scheduled return trip to Staten Island the following week. More than Tony's vote was involved. The incident was spread by Tony and his family throughout the close-knit Italian community, which furnished more than 40 percent of the Staten Island vote."[10]

Still, Rockefeller was not yet the master layer-on of hands that he would become. Invariably he wore rumpled suits with the sleeves too long, a bit of the common touch which probably was not intentional—Rockefeller is a notoriously sloppy dresser. On the stump, he wasn't a bad storyteller. He just told bad stories. He often tarried too long with just a few voters. To Rockefeller, they were a rare breed. "Look," said an aide on one early upstate swing, "these are the first real live voters he's ever talked to. He knows how to meet people, but he hasn't learned how to unmeet them."[11]

To say he had led a sheltered life would be putting it mildly. Immediately after the nominating convention, when he was supposed to be resting at his home in Maine, he took off in an old car with his son Steve and drove through upstate New York talking to people. "It was a fascinating experience," Rockefeller told Stewart Alsop. "Of course I'd never done anything like that before—never had a reason to, an excuse. There was one man, for example, he'd lost his job with the New York Central and he had his mother to support, and he told me he didn't know what he was going to do, where to turn. Well, that man wasn't a statistic on the unemployment rolls, he was a human being. Until you get out and talk to people that way, you feel kind of cut off, separated from reality."[12]

Attorney General Louis Lefkowitz recalls that he had to take Rockefeller down to the Lower East Side of Manhattan to show that "you're not in an ivory tower, Nelson, that you like things other people like." Lefkowitz took Rockefeller to Ratners, the famous Jewish dairy restaurant, and Rockefeller said hello to a man who refused to shake his hand. "I can't put a hello in the bank," he said.[13]

Though he learned the politician's ritual of eating blintzes, bagels, and pizza for the TV cameras, he often looked as if he would prefer to dine alone. He greeted almost everyone as "Hi-ya, fella," a habit that persists to this day and one which Larry King points out can come off as condescending "unless your name happens to be Fella."[14] But "he made crowds quiver," journalist Thomas Morgan would write later. "He demonstrated that vaunted, celebrated, feared Rockefeller personality which, like beauty in women, was both given and self-conceived."[15]

The campaign's only real issue, in the sense that it caught on in the media, was expertly exploited by Rockefeller—his charge that Harriman was a tool of Carmine De Sapio, the ruler of Democratic politics throughout the 1950s, a man who appeared sinister simply because an eye disease forced him to wear dark glasses.

Tammany bossism was an issue almost as old as New York politics itself. The Democrats had merely obliged by adding another chapter to the sorry saga at their state convention in Buffalo. Harriman favored Thomas Finletter for the U.S. Senate, a choice supported by the party's liberal elite, former Governor Herbert Lehman and Mrs. Eleanor Roosevelt. De Sapio, then fighting for recognition as the boss of bosses in Democratic politics, supported Manhattan District Attorney Frank Hogan. A bitter battle ensued. Roosevelt and Lehman condemned De Sapio publicly, Harriman was forced to abandon Finletter, and Hogan was rammed down the convention's collective throat.

Rockefeller had already learned a rule of New York politics at that time: it didn't matter what you said, as long as you said it against Carmine De Sapio. Rockefeller suggested that Harriman might like to step out and let De Sapio run for governor, since he was "sort of running the state as it is."[16]

Warming to his indictment, Rockefeller went for the jugular.

He charged that Harriman had weakened the state's crime-fighting resources as he reduced official pressure on racketeers, all a result of yielding to political pressure from Tammany Hall.[17] He said Harriman was "afraid to stand by principle" and "afraid to defy the boss system."[18] He contrasted Harriman's attitude to the position taken by Al Smith in 1922. At that time, Charles F. Murphy, then the Tammany leader, attempted to nominate William Randolph Hearst for senator over Smith's opposition. Rockefeller quoted Smith as telling Murphy: "If this convention nominates this man for senator, I will go before it and denounce you and renounce the nomination for governor."[19] (Smith won.) Harriman, said Rockefeller, wasn't fit to stand in the shadow of Al Smith. Instead, said Rockefeller, organized crime is "in business in our state" because when the governor doesn't do his job "the gates are open for organized crime to move in."[20]

The media loved it. The *Times* and the *News* endorsed Rockefeller, the latter ignoring the whole point of Rockefeller's candidacy when it editorialized that "Rockefeller is campaigning more like a man who wants to be Governor of New York, while Harriman acts more like a man who wants to be President."[21]

A fawning cover story in *Time* magazine was icing on the cake. Henry Luce, a member of the Rockefeller Special Studies panel, ruled *Time* with an iron hand. The October 6, 1958 issue praised John Foster Dulles for his "dogged fight to head off aggressive world Communism"—this time in defense of Quemoy and Matsu. The cover story on Rockefeller carried five pictures of the candidate and one of Averell Harriman, "the other millionaire," smiling beside (who else?) Carmine De Sapio. Those were the days. You knew where *Time* stood, and if you stood with it, your moral bearings would be defined neatly for you every week, packaged in quotable prose, suitable for converting the masses. The pictures of Rockefeller carried two captions. One was: "free of egotism, fears and frustrations." The other was: "Full of a desire to do big things." The first was a quotation from brother Laurance, a fact *Time* didn't signal by putting the caption in quotes. Finally, *Time*'s special brand of capitalization: Rockefeller was hailed as Modern Republican Rockefeller. Poor Averell Harriman. Not only didn't he get a campaign cover story, but *Time* called him "testy" and said that he had "shoveled generous chunks of patronage to traditionally starved upstate Democrats to get them to slave for Ave." The same *Time*, six pages further along, carried a box titled "Beware the Ban." It seems that "Harvard University's tough-minded political scientist and military theorist," one Henry Kissinger, was arguing against a nuclear test ban treaty. As an alternative, Kissinger offered a restriction on fallout: "The West and the Soviet bloc could agree to equal fallout quotas."

No paper or periodical could equal *Time*'s "objectivity," but the New York *Post* offered its readers another staple: surprise. The *Post* had endorsed Harriman but switched to Rockefeller in time for the last edition on the day before the election. The ostensible reason, as explained by publisher Dorothy Schiff in a front-page signed statement, was that "Governor Harriman's recent snide insinuation that Rockefeller is pro-Arab and anti-Israel should not be condoned by any fair minded person . . . when the head of the ticket repeats such libels he should be punished by the voters. If you agree with me, do not vote for Averell Harriman tomorrow."² Harriman responded, too late, that "I said that the Eisenhower Administration was influenced by big business throughout and that in the Middle East the change of support of Israel to neutrality was due to the influence of oil companies. I don't take back a word I have said. . . ."²³ Fair enough. Mrs. Schiff didn't take back her un-endorsement either.

In 1975, Mrs. Schiff reflected on that incident. Sitting in her huge green and white oval office overlooking the East River, the *Post*'s publisher said that she had never been for Harriman. "I'd been for Franklin Roosevelt, Jr. for governor in 1950," she said. "I spoke to Carmine De Sapio and he said 'not this time but next time you can have it for Frank.' Of course, Harriman got it and then tried to take the presidential nomination away from Adlai Stevenson in 1956. I was adamantly pro-Stevenson. Then, in 1958, at the convention, I was for Finletter for the Senate and they gave it to Hogan. But the big menace was Nixon in 1960. I wanted a 1960 alternative to Nixon. I wanted to nip him in the bud, in his own party."

The *Post* endorsed Harriman at first, said Mrs. Schiff, because "I was persuaded by certain people to come out for him. Rockefeller had met with Nixon at breakfast one day and that bothered me, so I gave the okay to Jimmy Wechsler to come out for Harriman." Apparently, Harriman's comments about Rockefeller finally outweighed Rockefeller's breakfast with Nixon. "After Harriman made his statement," said Mrs. Schiff, "I went to Baltimore for the weekend and brooded about it. On Monday I did some research and sent my statement down to Jimmy [Wechsler], who didn't kill it. He said publishers had a right to make their own endorsements."[24]

The campaign's only other drama involved a subplot, covered but not really appreciated at the time, a series of incidents that would foreshadow the Main Attraction two years later. Nelson Rockefeller was avoiding Dwight Eisenhower and Richard Nixon. He perceived, correctly, that they could only harm his cause in 1958, but he never fully understood the egos involved, especially Dick Nixon's. The vice-president had spent the fall doing what he did best, barnstorming the country speaking for local Republican candidates, plugging the idea that Democrats might not be Communists, but you had to watch them very carefully just in case. Nixon was told as nicely as possible to stay the hell out of New York. He kept his control until October 23, when he couldn't resist jetting in to Garden City, Long Island, for a speech. Nelson Rockefeller was 25 miles away at the Hotel St. Moritz, keeping a "prior engagement" at the All-American Committee dinner. Nixon's engagement was just as crucial for him. The occasion was the centennial dinner of Leonard Hall's Oyster Bay Republican Club. Nixon was counting on Hall's support for the 1960 presidential nomination, and he would need all the help he could muster if Rockefeller won the gubernatorial contest. Nixon would then find himself running against Rockefeller for president, fighting for delegates on Rockefeller's own turf. There was no way Nixon was going to skip that dinner.

The media immediately read presidential implications into Rockefeller's failure to attend. So intense was the speculation that Nixon and Rockefeller were forced to meet for breakfast the next morning in a display of party unity. Rockefeller emerged to announce that he had "no interest in the presidential nomination" and to denounce Harriman for having implied just that. Harriman "is so accustomed to running for the presidency," said Rockefeller, "that he naturally suspects that whenever two people get together they are making some kind of deal involving the presidency."[25] Chuckles all around—almost. Dick Nixon wasn't laughing. He was playing it straight. He said he didn't feel he had been "snubbed." He said he had instructed "all local candidates—I don't expect you to be at the airport or at meetings where I appear in your state if there is another meeting at which you can get an audience."[26] Even then, he was the master of the backhanded comment. Nixon's clear message was that there had better not be another meeting going on when he was around, or he had better be invited to it.

Eisenhower fared slightly better only because he wasn't so obvious. Once, when he was in New York during the campaign, Eisenhower did meet with Rockefeller, but no public appearance was scheduled to take advantage of the presence of the man Rockefeller called "one of the greatest leaders the world has ever known." On another occasion, Rockefeller did get outdoors with Ike as the president came to town to lay a wreath on Columbus Day. GOP strategists said that the visit was arranged to placate disaffected Italian-American Republicans who were upset at the failure of an Italian-American to grace the Rockefeller ticket. How far a Columbus Day wreath-laying compensated is anybody's guess. Perhaps it gave Rockefeller his margin of victory. On November 4, 1958, with Republicans dropping like flies all across the country, Nelson Rockefeller was elected governor of New York by a margin of 573,034 votes, the first of four such victories.

CHAPTER 19

Albany Fallout

No SOONER had Rockefeller won by a landslide than the talk of challenging Nixon grew louder. To the very first question on election night, Rockefeller said that he was "really not interested"[1] in the presidency. Five days later he labeled such predictions "complete fantasy."

The predictions were coming from all quarters. The *News* astrologer, Constella, said that Nixon would take on an "immediate load of heavier responsibility." Rockefeller, she said, "has a naturally lucky horoscope but his critics will be bearing down." However, she added, "his chart shows that he can ad lib his way as he goes along, for he has remarkable intuition and ingenuity."[2]

On November 22, Nixon and Rockefeller engaged in a media massage. They told the press that they had met in order "to agree to rebuild the party." They billed their temporary cessation of hostilities as a friendly pact that would leave either free to run for president in 1960. Asked afterward if the vice-president was going to sleep better or less easily, Rockefeller summoned every bit of ingenuity within him and said: "The vice-president and I have always been good friends, and I have a feeling he has slept well right through this."[3]

Not bad, but a few hours later Barry Goldwater made absolutely sure that November 22 would live as a highpoint in political insanity. Not content with the fog already enshrouding the 1960 campaign, Goldwater also provided a foretaste of the 1964 silly season. Said he on *Face the Nation*: Rockefeller must prove himself a "nonradical" as governor before he can be considered for any GOP presidential nomination—ever. Added the Arizona sage: "I'm not going to bury, so to speak, a millionaire in a poke."[4]

Speculation about Rockefeller's seeking the presidency didn't cease. Instead, it intensified—in part because the media love a fight, and the possibility of a challenge to Nixon whetted the appetite of even the most mild-mannered reporter; in part because anyone who knew anything at all about Nelson Rockefeller knew that the speculation was justified.

A week after the vice-president and the governor-elect met in their phony display of party unity, the first prognostication appeared, replete with analyses and scenarios. The story was carried in the November 28, 1958, edition of the *Daily News*, the same paper that had praised Rockefeller for his lack of presidential ambition, and it was written by James Desmond, who six years later would write a laudatory biography of Nelson.

The thesis of Desmond's 1958 *News* piece was that Rockefeller, a fresh face in the presidential politics of 1960, would be "old hat" by 1964. The article was entitled "Why '60 Is Now or Never for Rocky," and it accurately reflected the thinking of the Rockefeller camp, with one important caveat: if Nelson didn't make it in '60, he wasn't going to stop trying. Desmond dismissed Rockefeller's "for the record" disclaimers as easily as an elephant brushes off fleas. "A man of 50," he wrote,

a member of one of the world's wealthiest families whose whole adult life has been oriented to international affairs, doesn't abruptly decide to run for the comparatively provincial office of Governor unless there are higher goals over the horizon. There are, in fact, members of the American oligarchy, the combine of families representing great wealth, who will tell you, some of them without any sympathy for the idea, that the Rockefellers consented to allow Nelson to run for Governor only because he had a timetable that would put him in the White House in six to ten years.[5]

To hurry the timetable along, Desmond theorized that "any enforced delay beyond [1960] would kill Nelson Rockefeller politically." We now know that delay didn't deaden the desire, although 1960 may well have been Nelson's best chance for the presidency.

Desmond duly paid homage to the momentum generated by Rockefeller's unexpected landslide victory, quickly labeling him the GOP's "hottest property." At the same time, he pointed out that the only national Republican to speak favorably of Rockefeller and the presidency in the same sentence was Harold Stassen, hardly a sign that Nelson had a lock on the nomination.

Desmond's prescience went further. Rockefeller, he wrote, "is blessed by the fact that he has no record in office to affect his standing one way or another. Rockefeller isn't going to be judged on the record he makes as Governor the next year, if only because the voters realize that he is taking over from an outgoing administration and it would be unrealistic to expect him to change things overnight."

As governor, Nelson's first order of business was his inaugural address. He may have been in Albany, but he sounded like he was in Washington delivering his presidential inaugural. Shunning the traditional tails and striped pants in favor of a double-breasted suit and dark blue tie, he finally mentioned "New York" two-thirds of the way along. Before getting there, he issued a stirring call to the American people to rally to their destiny as leaders of the free world. It was the quintessential Cold War lecture. He pledged an unending fight against dictators: "Our neighborhood is the world," he declared. "It is divided, essentially, between those who believe in the brotherhood of man and the fatherhood of God—and those who scorn this as a pious myth."[6] Rockefeller liked that particular phrase so much that it became a staple of his stump speeches as he sought the presidency. Eventually he overworked it; "brotherhood of man and fatherhood of God" became an object of derision, and the press reduced it to acronym status. Richard Reeves wrote: "How can you tell whether Nelson Rockefeller is really running for president? Watch for the 'BOMFOGs.' "[7] Rockefeller traces his infatuation with the phrase to an incident in Cleveland, John D. Sr.'s hometown. An old woman came up to him and gave him a Bible which she said had belonged to his grandfather. In it, underlined in John D.'s unmistakable scrawl, was "Brotherhood of Man, Fatherhood of God."[8]

Most of the 1,200 persons crowded into the state Assembly chamber were startled by Rockefeller's international emphasis. The speech was interrupted by applause only once, when the governor said that the United States "is the best and strongest hope on earth for free men everywhere."

The speech was written by Emmet Hughes, one of those men who speak in prose, a brilliant political intellectual who had left Time, Inc., to become Eisenhower's sharpest thinker, the man who originated Ike's "I shall go to Korea" speech.[9] A liberal Democrat whom Bill Buckley once described as a "dove before Picasso," Hughes had grown restless in Ike's White House. He soon found an ally in the similarly disenchanted Nelson Rockefeller, and the two became fast friends. Later Hughes would receive a $150,000 loan from the governor[10] and would become Rockefeller's chief ideologue, a role he would fill, off and on, for ten years. But on election night in 1958 he was just another interested observer watching the returns in the Manhattan apartment of Time vice-president C. D. Jackson. When victory was certain, Hughes and Jackson went over to Rockefeller's campaign headquarters, where Nelson promptly took him aside. Rockefeller asked Hughes to write the inaugural, and Hughes agreed. "I'd only been to Albany one day in my entire life," recalls Hughes. "I didn't know anything about New York. The only speeches I'd written were for the president. That's all I knew."[11] Obviously, Nelson was delighted. His mind was elsewhere, too.

But Nelson was prepared to rule New York. The same task

force blitz he had used successfully in seeking the governorship was already cranking out the white papers that would tell him how to govern now that he had won. Sometimes their advice was inconsistent with what Rockefeller had said during the campaign. For example, not only had Nelson pledged not to increase taxes, but his staff had charged that Harriman was secretly planning to raise taxes if he was reelected. Now Rockefeller was about to do the same thing. In fact, new revenue was desperately needed. Like Harriman before him and Hugh Carey after him, Rockefeller took office during a national economic recession, and the state's coffers were seriously depleted. Each of these three governors sought new taxes to meet deficits they attributed to the irresponsible spending policies of their predecessors.

Rockefeller's first budget in 1959 requested five new taxes to raise a total of $277 million. That revenue, said the new governor, was needed to balance a budget up 13 percent from Harriman's final year. The Republican legislature, composed mainly of the same members who had refused for four years to give Harriman the taxes he had asked for, approved all five of Nelson's new ones, including the motor fuel tax hike that Harriman had sought since 1955.

But not without a fight. Elected politicians anxious to be reelected don't normally salivate at the thought of raising people's taxes. Upstate conservatives already viewed Rockefeller's program as something akin to "creeping socialism." His proposed tax increases confirmed their fears, and the governor offered no pacifier. Budget Director T. Norman Hurd declared tax increases a "necessity," and Rockefeller was determined to raise taxes quickly, as far in advance of the next gubernatorial election as possible. But the legislature would be up again in two years, and the legislators knew that voters could easily remember in 1960 what they might well forget by 1962.

A Republican revolt ensued, one of the few to plague Rockefeller during his 15 years in office. At first, he fought. "If they don't like [my programs]," said the governor, "they should have the courage to recommend reductions."[12] Those were fighting words, but Rockefeller soon cooled off. He learned that his role was to charm and persuade, while others (notably Jud Morhouse) played the heavy, reminding the legislature that patronage was not a right but a privilege granted to those who viewed the world as Nelson Rockefeller viewed it. Later, when a student questioned his courage, Rockefeller would refer to this early legislative scrap as proof of his manhood: "Don't talk to me about guts," the governor said. "I had the guts to ask for $200 million in new taxes right after I took office. You try that sometime and then go down to New York City to give an address and stand up and be booed for five minutes."[13]

Blaming Harriman for the necessity of new taxes put Rockefeller on a collision course with a man who would shadow him for the rest of his governorship, Controller Arthur Levitt, a Democrat who'd been elected to the post in 1954, and the only Democrat to survive the GOP's 1958 landslide. To Rockefeller, Levitt was an irritant he could safely ignore. The first two met shortly after the November election, and Levitt told Rockefeller that although he was an elected official, he considered the state controller's office to be essentially nonpartisan, a fiscal watchdog to keep the executive in check. Rockefeller smiled, nodded, and gave Levitt the same slap on the back he'd developed to perfection during the campaign.

Then he snubbed him. On New Year's Eve, Levitt found out that Rockefeller and his fellow Republican victors would be sworn in at a private ceremony at the Executive Mansion. "It was a shock," recalls Levitt, a sensitive man who angers easily over matters of protocol. "I called Nelson and told him I thought it was an affront to the office. I pointed out that the Executive Mansion was not a private fiefdom like Pocantico, but that it belonged to all the people. I also reminded him that more people had voted for me than for him. I expected him to invite me over to be sworn in with the rest. But he never asked, and he never got used to the idea of my being an independently elected official. He expected complete acquiescence. He was accustomed to getting his way, and he wasn't about to let me stand in his way."[14]

Within three months, as Levitt continued his opposition to the governor's tax program, the Republican-controlled legislature decided to slash the controller's budget. Levitt labeled the action "punishment" for his "daring to speak out,"[15] and he was undoubtedly correct—at the same time his was losing funds, the budgets of the governor's and attorney general's offices were increased significantly.

A year later, Rockefeller and Levitt were still squabbling, this time over the governor's new back-door financing schemes that would eventually become his administration's trademark. At the annual legislative dinner of the Empire State Chamber of Commerce, Rockefeller dismissed criticism of his fiscal policies and went into his standard speech, blaming the state's troubles on the deficit he had inherited from Harriman. Levitt was not scheduled to speak, but he rose and demanded an opportunity to reply. He labeled Rockefeller's plan for school board financing a "subterfuge to undermine the [state] constitution."[16] The only difference between this bit of acrimony and its predecessors was that it came in February 1960. The nation was watching Rockefeller's presidential plans with interest, and the fiscal fight at home attracted attention in papers across the country.

Levitt and his failed fiscal fight aside, Rockefeller's first two years were easily traversed. Along the way, he telegraphed a few more punches—programs and concerns, like moral obligation financing, that would characterize his governorship throughout his four terms. At base was his top management view that big government, like big business, could be run successfully with the right board of directors and the right organization.

He sought to transfer this view to New York City, which, said Norman Hurd, was "mortgaging the future to pay for the present," and he created a $350,000 state commission to make "a serious and constructive inquiry into the governmental operations of New York city."[17] McKinsey and Company participated in the project; its counsel was Whitney North Seymour,

Jr., later U.S. attorney for the Southern District of New York. Rockefeller would repeat his studies of the city throughout his tenure, each time exacerbating his relations with the mayor, whether Robert Wagner or John Lindsay. This time Wagner had the better of it. The state commission had criticized the attitude of the Wagner administration toward reform and drew inferences—too hastily as it turned out—about a certain Staten Island Democratic politician. Within 24 hours the pol had completely cleared himself, and the commission was on the run.[18] Soon the legislature's Democrats were calling for the commission's scalp. By the end of the week, the chairman and four of his aides had resigned. Generally, the legislature resented the task forces. They felt that they preempted the legislature's own committees, and an early Rockefeller bill to prevent discrimination in housing was defeated as the product of "task force mentality."

The right organization demanded loyalty and money. State employees were expected to attend fundraising dinners; later the Governor's Club was formed. Its members kicked in $500 annually, and many of the state's top officials joined. "It was expected of us," says one. "It wasn't exactly a kickback of our salary for nothing. After all, once a year we got a lunch and a tour of Pocantico. Not everyone can do that, you know." Staff loyalty was not only bought through loans from the governor but also fostered through the subtle lure of futures secured within the Rockefeller orbit. Arvis Chalmers of the *Knickerbocker News* wrote: "The cynics have said there are just two groups of people around New York's Governor—those who have a lifetime job with a Rockefeller enterprise and those who would like to have one."[19]

Rockefeller's greatest legislative failure in his early years involved his proposal to force every New Yorker to build a bomb shelter. At a cost of approximately $300 per family, it was a plan that could only be hatched in the mind of a man who had never had to worry about a rent bill. His obsession with national defense and the need to prepare for nuclear war seemed to haunt him at every turn. On a world trip during this period he visited with India's prime minister, Jawaharlal Nehru. "Governor Rockefeller is a very strange man," Nehru said later. "All he wants to talk about is bomb shelters."[20]

In an extemporaneous speech at a civil defense seminar in March 1960, Rockefeller explained the need for shelters this way: "I don't know how many of you have seen the movie *On the Beach*. I know some of my kids saw it, and I want to tell you, that is a great way to destroy people's will to resist, because they come out of that movie saying 'There is nothing we can do.'" The Russians, Rockefeller went on, had already "caught up to us in missiles, and as we sit here today we have no defense against missiles. . . . If another Berlin comes along, are we going to arrive at a point some day when the president will say: 'Well, how can we afford to stand for freedom? With the people exposed, can we run that risk?' . . . Will we be able and ready to stand, unless we know we would be able to survive? We would not, under present circumstances, as a people. We would if we had shelters. . . . Certainly we want to work out disarmament programs, but do you negotiate from weakness? No, you beg from weakness and creep on your hands and knees and accept surrender terms."[21]

Rockefeller's impassioned arguments failed to impress the legislature, and the governor was forced to drop his proposals. But he didn't drop shelters entirely. As governor and as a private citizen he could do something, and he did. With his own funds, he built a fallout shelter for the Executive Mansion, and others for his cooperative apartment building on Fifth Avenue and his estate at Pocantico. His personal shelters are still serviceable, with the canned goods replaced periodically to ensure freshness. Rockefeller also directed the building of a giant fallout shelter in Albany, a $4 million "alternative seat of government," big enough to accommodate 700 key people from various state departments. Unlike the shelters he advocated for private homeowners, the Albany bunker was designed to withstand an actual nulclear blast as well as the radioactive residue.[22]

To be sure, Rockefeller's was not a mindless, one-man hysteria. America awoke from Sputnik with a new fear of Soviet power. Those were the days of civil defense: shelter signs everywhere, air raid drills in grammar schools, and instructions on what to do in case of a one-minute alert—pray. Still, no other state felt itself in danger of imminent destruction, and Rockefeller's shelter-mania, a product of discussions with his chief nuclear war consultant—Edward Teller, father of the hydrogen bomb—offers a revealing glimpse of Nelson's single-mindedness run rampant. It is also testimony to the proposition that Rockefeller doesn't like admitting mistakes. When he left office, the Albany bunker was still in operating order, still plugged into the nationwide NORAD alert system through a communications setup among the most extensive found anywhere outside the Pentagon.

The shelter program was a domestic manifestation of a key Rockefeller presidential campaign plank: the need for U.S. preparedness in the face of Soviet hostility, and the Eisenhower administration's failure to prepare adequately for a Soviet attack. In taking on one of history's most famous soldiers in his own field of expertise, Rockefeller hardly won Ike's allegiance. Earlier, as an Eisenhower aide, he'd tried everything to win over the old general. As Stewart Alsop recalls, Rockefeller "even had a one-hole golf course built on his Washington estate in the hope—or so all of his acquaintances assumed—that the president would use the course for practice."[23] He never did.

CHAPTER 20

Spoiling for
a Fight

WHILE it is impossible to know exactly when Nelson first thought of running for president, it is safe to say that his campaign for the office began almost immediately upon his election as governor.

The campaign's first team consisted primarily of Jud Morhouse and George Hinman. Together, they made up "a sort of composite Jim Farley, with Morhouse cast in the role of contact man and front-room boy, and Hinman as the back-room boy and chief political strategist."[1]

Jud Morhouse, in his role of state Republican chairman, hit the road early. His message was simple, an updated version of the one Eisenhower had used successfully to stop Robert Taft in 1952: "Dick Nixon," said Morhouse to anyone who would listen, "is a nice guy. But he can't win."[2] Nixon's defense ignored the Morhouse jibe, and no one handled the vice-president's case better than Billy Graham. Sidestepping the issue of electability as too pedestrian a concern in a country as great and as morally righteous as the United States, Graham bluntly told his congregations that "Dick Nixon is the best trained man for the job of president in American history."[3] That was no comfort to

Rockefeller, who told a friend: "I hate the thought of Dick Nixon being president of the United States."[4]

The challenge was clear, and by autumn Rockefeller's massive personal staff was hard at work in the president business. Operating out of two brownstones on Manhattan's West 55th Street, the Rockefeller-for-president drive rivaled even the Kennedy effort. The governor's penchant for organization was exhibited anew: there was a speechwriting division, an "image" division peopled by Madison Avenue professionals, a scheduling and logistics operation, a research division, and two press offices, one to handle the routine business that flows from the office of governor, another to handle the media problems of a man seeking a higher prize.

More important than the others was the political intelligence office. To be elected, Rockefeller had first to capture the nomination. The country was divided into quarters, and the governor's agents were dispatched to test the waters. A companion, and equally crucial, operation was created to determine the amount of money that could be raised for a presidential campaign. Of course, Rockefeller could finance the entire race using family funds, but such a course would be doomed to failure. He would literally be buying the nomination—and the voter resentment that came with it. If Rockefeller couldn't secure broad-based financial support, his campaign would not only be personally costly, but the nomination, should he get it, would in all likelihood be politically worthless. To handle the financial exploration, Rockefeller assigned his brother David and the family's chief financial adviser, J. Richardson Dilworth.

The money men were well received wherever they went. They were, after all, the representatives of one of the world's most impressive financial empires. But the warm welcome was just that and nothing more. The money was solid for Nixon.

Rockefeller's other problem was Nixon's homework. The vice-president had done more than merely whip up the local politicians during his seven years' attendance at their banquets. He had cultivated the money men at the same time. Not only

Spoiling for a Fight

would Nixon surely continue Ike's "hands off business" policies, as Rockefeller might not, but he was also agreeable, or so the monied interests thought, to advice and control. Even more than Ike, who had already achieved lasting fame as a soldier, and certainly more than Nelson, who could easily get by without their help, Nixon *needed* Big Business. And Big Business reveled in Nixon's dependency. Here, as in the old days when Big Business truly dominated the party, was a poor man eager for their support.

On the political front, the public campaign—in which he became both an honorary Texan and an honorary Pawnee Indian—lasted eight weeks, from October to early December 1959. Amid a slew of "BOMFOGs," he spoke incessantly on all subjects, failing to arouse only at the annual Alfred E. Smith Dinner[5] when, among other things, he urged on America a "sense of full purpose," a "dream" without which we would become a "nation of sleepwalkers." He was always careful to praise Eisenhower, but he left no doubt that he found the president's response to the threat of Communism wanting. He quoted George Kennan's pessimistic prophecy that the United States would be unable to compete successfully with the Soviet Union but disputed Kennan's conclusion. We need only all work together, he said, quoting John Donne's *Devotions*. "No man is an Island." Finally, after quoting everyone from Socrates to an anonymous Hungarian freedom fighter, Rockefeller, at the Western States Republican Conference, challenged America to "wage unconditional peace," proceeding "from the firm base of an ever-expanding American economy, a Nation militarily strong, morally awakened, yes, and *dedicated* [his emphasis] with the old time missionary zeal to bring freedom's blessings to all mankind." We stand, said Rockefeller quoting Teddy Roosevelt, "at Armageddon, and we battle for the Lord."[6]

His audiences were charmed, but the politicians were not. In fact, poor advance work led to embarrassing situations. In New Hampshire, where the governor was pro-Nixon, party workers packed a press conference and asked tougher and ruder questions than the press. When he arrived in Chicago he was met by absolutely no one. At a press association luncheon the next day, he listed six "problems that confront America" and failed to mention the farm subsidy question, even though he was speaking in the Midwest. In Los Angeles he was forced to speak while under a portrait of Nixon.

When Rockefeller came to Texas, House Speaker Sam Rayburn, a Democrat, announced that Nelson had "friends" there.[7] Rayburn's antics confirmed the susipicions of many party pros that Rockefeller, by reason of ideology, was simply a Democrat in Republican clothing. Later, when Rockefeller withdrew from the 1960 race—the first time—Lyndon Johnson predicted that the governor might be drafted into a Democratic administration, saying that "it has been obvious for some time that there is no place in the national Republican Party for the able and progressive governor."[8]

At the time of Nelson's forays, Nixon's chief political operative was Len Hall. Hall was still smarting from 1958 and Nelson's having "stolen" the nomination that Hall felt was rightly his, so he had cast his lot with Nixon. Now, as Rockefeller scouted the country, the old fox carefully orchestrated a series of Nixon endorsements. Every time there was good news for Rockefeller, Hall would counter with better news for Nixon.

By mid-December, Rockefeller's forces were ready for an accounting. They'd spent two months testing their support. They'd generated countless headlines which had failed to generate real momentum, the kind that is translated into delegate votes. It was clear that Rockefeller would have to fight bitterly in the primaries if he were to have any chance at all of stopping Nixon. Cloaked in Eisenhower's record, Nixon would be vulnerable to Rockefeller only if the governor could succeed in repudiating the most popular Republican president of modern times, not in a general election, which would be difficult enough, but within the president's own party.

Withdrawal, Rockefeller concluded, was his only option. How to withdraw was another matter, involving the all-important consideration of living to fight another day with a good chance of winning. Here Rockefeller made a mistake. His basic misconception was the idea of "withdrawal" itself. Since he had never officially entered the presidential race, he needed to avoid the appearance of defeat. The press would accurately interpret his leave-taking as a defeat. He didn't have to do their work for them.

Rockefeller's advisers considered a "good sport" statement, pulling out and endorsing Nixon. But Rockefeller had always believed that Nixon was a "creep," as Emmet Hughes said, and he wasn't about to support Nixon for anything but early retirement. Bitterly, some aides thought that the statement should include the words "the men who control the convention and the financial powers behind them. . . ." But that was considered too harsh, and Hughes removed it.[9] George Hinman urged Rockefeller to lie low, to avoid further antagonizing the party, but the governor was determined to make his presence felt. Rockefeller told Joe Alsop that he was going to adopt a Churchillian posture, challenging Nixon to stand up for what was right.

In the end, the tough rhetoric was canned, at least for the time being. A month earlier, on November 15, Rockefeller had said, "I haven't seen any evidence of political commitments for anybody." Now, on December 26, he said that there was one person who wouldn't be getting many commitments at all, and that person was the governor of New York. ". . . The great majority of those who will control the Republican Convention," said Rockefeller, "stand opposed to any contest for the nomination. . . . my conclusion, therefore, is that I am not and shall not be a candidate for nomination for the presidency. This decision is definite and final. . . ." Quite obviously, added the governor, "I shall not at any time entertain any thought of accepting nomination to the vice-presidency."[10]

It was, recalls Emmet Hughes, the statement's author, a "double-edged" announcement.[11] And it created a frenzy in the Republican press, especially at *Time* magazine, an institution that had always looked favorably on Nelson Rockefeller. Hughes was a volunteer adviser to Rockefeller, and he was still on *Time*'s payroll as chief of foreign correspondents. "The tone of his statement," said *Time*, "was as eyebrow raising as his decision to back down. He skirted any pledge of support for his only rival, Vice President Richard Nixon. . . . Rocky's statement indicated that he was ready to serve as a witness for the prosecution of the Eisenhower Administration. . . . As far as the Democrats were concerned, nothing became Rocky's candidacy like his leaving of it."[12] Robert Elson writes that Henry Luce disagreed with *Time*'s story in a memorandum in which he said he saw "no possible reason why [Nelson] should have come out for Nixon"; *Life*'s editorial the following week reflected Luce's views. Rockefeller's withdrawal, said *Life*, was "timed to do the least harm to the Republican Party and to his own power and influence. It may even strengthen his hand."[13] Nevertheless, the flap pushed Hughes out, and he accepted Rockefeller's open invitation to join the family staff as senior adviser on public policy.

Only half of Rockefeller's withdrawal statement was correct. The decision not to seek the presidency in 1960 was not "definite and final." Events would change Nelson's plans. For the moment, however, the governor retreated to Albany, there to sulk at his misfortune, compounding his mistake by refusing an invitation from the Republican National Committee to serve as chairman or keynoter at the convention. Petulantly, he said he didn't even plan to attend the convention in Chicago in the summer of 1960.

For most of the winter and spring, events effectively silenced Rockefeller. He'd planned to barnstorm the country speaking about the nation's lack of preparedness; however, the Eisenhower-Khrushchev summit conference was scheduled for May, and he didn't want to appear to be undermining the American bargaining position. But the U-2 spyplane of Francis Gary Powers was shot down, Eisenhower bungled the obvious question concerning its mission, and the summit collapsed. In mid-

May, Jud Morhouse indicated that Rockefeller might be available for a presidential draft. On May 23 the governor issued a statement calling for the Republican Party to fully debate the events leading to and the consequences flowing from the failure of the Paris summit: "It would be false and frivolous—and ultimately damaging to both nation and party—to dismiss criticism of specific American conduct as a peril to our national unity."[14] A week later, on Memorial Day, Rockefeller had a long meeting with Emmet Hughes at his Pocantico estate. The decision to fight was taken. America had to be awakened, and Nelson Rockefeller was going to do it—let the political chips fall where they may.

On June 8, Rockefeller issued his famous "call for plain talk,"[15] as damaging a blow to the Republican Party as anything the Democrats could devise: "I am deeply convinced," said Rockefeller, "and deeply concerned that those now assuming control of the Republican Party have failed to make clear where this party is heading and where it proposes to lead the nation. Now is the time to face and weigh these facts. New problems demand new ideas, new actions. . . . I cannot pretend that the Republican Party has fully met this duty. . . . We cannot, as a nation or as a party, proceed—nor should anyone presume to ask us to proceed—to march to meet the future with a banner aloft whose only emblem is a question mark. . . ." After a nine-point program that effectively dismissed as inadequate the entire Eisenhower record, Rockefeller again asked his party to stand firmly on issues: "The path of great leadership does not lie along the top of a fence."[16]

Again the Republican press was up in arms. Rockefeller, wrote David Lawrence in *U.S. News & World Report*, is "calling, in effect, for the suicide of his own party. . . . His statement would appear to make him a more logical contender for the Democratic presidential nomination."[17] *Time* again chose to wash its linen in public. It reported Eisenhower's reaction this way: "After reading Nelson Rockefeller's blast . . . President Eisenhower remarked with a trace of bitterness in his voice: 'I see the fine hand of Emmet in this.' By Emmet he meant Emmet John Hughes, his own speech writer during the 1952 and 1956 campaigns."[18] *Time* dismissed the statement as a "firecracker [which], having made everyone jump, had left not a tremor behind."[19] That judgment was too hasty, but *Time* chief Henry Luce unwittingly gave Nelson a little maneuvering room by placing the blame for the statement squarely at Hughes's feet where, in language at least, it clearly belonged. According to Robert Elson, Eisenhower responded to Luce's assertion by saying, in effect, that Rockefeller couldn't be faulted entirely because he was being "too much influenced by a man who had no capacity for giving sensible advice."[20] "That Hughes," Richard Nixon said later, "is a dirty player and always has been. He'll pull every trick."[21]

For a moment, Rockefeller thought he saw daylight. The Nixon camp, caught off guard, had panicked. The vice-president announced that he had spoken his views on national policy, while his supporters simultaneously asserted that Nixon was perfectly correct in *not* stating his views until after the Republican Convention. Rockefeller correctly labeled these two positions "contradictory," and he accurately criticized Nixon's real performance to date. "Only three weeks ago," said Rockefeller, "the vice-president himself stated publicly, 'If I become the candidate, I intend to present to the country a new program.' This is the crux of the issue I have raised. The people, the Republican Party, and the delegates to the Republican Convention are entitled to know what a 'new program' means. They have a right to know precisely where he stands."[22]

The Nixon campaign quickly put its rhetorical house in order, and Rockefeller was unable to exploit Nixon's inconsistency or to flush him out in a way that would work to his advantage. Instead, Rockefeller became a Cassandra, spreading the message of a fading American empire wherever he went.

Between July 1 and July 19, Rockefeller declared war on his own party. He was just as contemptuous of the Democrats, but only at home, with the Republicans, was his conduct considered blasphemous. Theodore White quotes a Rockefeller friend as saying: "It's impossible. Everyone knows its impossible. Maybe only Nelson, when he's alone by himself in his shower in the morning, lets himself dream that he can be President this year; but, anyway, if he has got a chance to be President, he isn't hurting it any by attacking on the platform first."[23] That comment was representative of the Rockefeller camp's thinking. It also contains the reason for Rockefeller's continuing problems with his own party. He was hurting himself by attacking the party, no matter how he did it. He had chosen not to challenge Nixon in the primaries; party leaders and most of the rank-and-file believed, and still do, that Rockefeller had forfeited the right to attack by refusing to test himself at the polls. The governor was viewed as a poor loser, as a spoiler, and that perception would haunt his entire career.

CHAPTER 21

The Fifth Avenue Compact

AS the convention drew close, Rockefeller did nothing to erase the "spoiler" image. With all hope for the nomination lost, he determined to wage war on the party platform, a divisive, frivolous error that meant little, since platforms have never been more than a cosmetic coating which the candidate feels free to ignore if he wins. But a fight on the platform was the only match available, and Rockefeller fervently entered the bout.

On the surface, Nelson could argue that his call to his party simply echoed the concern of its leader. After the 1958 Republican election debacle, Eisenhower had created a Committee on Program and Progress to reexamine the Republican philosophy that had been so recently repudiated by the voters. The committee became Nixon's responsibility and he, in turn, had given it over to Charles Percy of Illinois, then president of Bell and Howell. Percy had worked hard to fashion a new credo acceptable to all of the party's factions while offering a new brand of Republicanism to the electorate. But a basic conflict existed. Rockefeller felt the nation was in danger; Eisenhower did not. Given the governor's White House aspirations, it is not hard to understand why the president viewed Rockefeller's sense of urgency as politically motivated. Percy and Senator John Sherman Cooper of Kentucky came to New York to paper over the differences between their version and Rockefeller's wishes. They invited Emmet Hughes to work with them but, as Hughes knew and would later recall, it was a "sucker's game," and he would have no part of it.[1]

Percy left New York without a compromise and headed for Chicago, where the convention's platform committee waited, confident that it was the body that would write Republican philosophy. To Chicago as well went Rockefeller's emissaries to the platform deliberations; Hughes, Hinman, Morhouse, Lieutenant Governor Malcolm Wilson, and William Pfeiffer, who would later run Rockefeller's 1962 and 1966 gubernatorial campaigns.

By July 21 the committee's final drafts of the platform were circulating. The working papers were substantially acceptable to the Rockefeller forces, except for their references to the sterling work of Eisenhower's eight years in office. By that evening, Rockefeller, at Hughes's suggestion, decided to fight the platform on the two substantive points the governor couldn't abide: civil rights and national defense. At the same time, Rockefeller found an opportunity to put even more distance between himself and Nixon. Asked how he would rate Nixon against Kennedy, Rockefeller apparently couldn't resist a swipe at his fellow Republican. "I think," said the governor, "the people will do that in November."[2] Later in the same press conference, he was asked if he had any "personal feeling" toward Nixon, and he answered "No."[3]

The following morning, Press Secretary Robert McManus issued a statement saying that the draft of the platform was "still seriously lacking in strength and specifics."[4] It was, remembered Emmet Hughes, "a simple little statement, but it had ten times the fallout I expected."[5]

Within hours of the Rockefeller announcement, Nixon was on the phone to Herbert Brownell, seeking a meeting with Rockefeller to end the impasse. Brownell, a longtime friend of former New York Governor Tom Dewey and a onetime attorney general and political adviser to Eisenhower, seemed the perfect middleman. Brownell reached Rockefeller, who was exultant. He told Hughes, "It didn't take long to get that message across,"[6] and said he intended to meet the vice-president at Brownell's apartment, as Nixon had suggested. Hughes thought the governor should force Nixon to come all the way to him, and Rockefeller readily agreed. Back went Rockefeller's response, relayed through Brownell to Nixon. The governor's terms resembled surrender: Nixon must call Rockefeller personally to request the meeting, and they must meet at Rockefeller's apartment, not Brownell's; the meeting must be secret and must be announced through a Rockefeller, not a Nixon, press release; the statement must indicate that the meeting took place at Nixon's request, and it must represent a detailed policy statement, not the kind of meaningless communiqué that often accompanies the termination of a summit between important leaders.[7]

Nixon agreed to all the terms, and the Rockefeller forces were jubilant. They believed they had won a significant victory. All they had really won was Nixon's lasting enmity, and, later in the decade, that would be important.

The vice-president, without telling his staff—including Press Secretary Herbert Klein, who was severely assailed by reporters for not having the muscle even to know what his own candidate was doing—arrived secretly in New York on Saturday, July 22, 1960 at 7:30 P.M. and went directly to Rockefeller's apartment at 810 Fifth Avenue, the same building Nixon would move to after losing the California governorship race in 1962. Hughes had drafted the Rockefeller position in Chicago and had teletyped the language to Rockefeller in New York. After dinner, and another Rockefeller refusal to run as vice-president on a Nixon ticket, a four-way telephone hookup was established: Percy in Chicago at the Blackstone Hotel; Hughes in Chicago at the Sheraton Towers; Nixon on the line in Rockefeller's study; and the governor on the extension in his bedroom. The four talked for three hours, with a 20-minute hiatus at 1 A.M. when the telephone operators switched shifts and the connection was broken. What emerged was the 14-point "Compact of Fifth Avenue." Seven points involved foreign policy and national defense, including the development of a strong second-strike nuclear capability at whatever cost: "There must be no price ceiling on America's security."[8] Nevertheless, Nixon was successful at excising the specific figure of $3 billion which Rockefeller wanted to include as an estimate of the cost that was not too high for national defense. On domestic issues, agreement was reached on the need for a total reorganization of the federal government, including the creation of the national security adviser post that John Kennedy would soon fill with McGeorge Bundy.

Nixon left New York at 4 A.M., and by 5 A.M. the edited Rockefeller statement was released to the press. Later in the day, basking in his "victory," Rockefeller met the press himself in Chicago. He was still unwilling publicly to support Nixon for president, hiding behind the theme of an uncommitted New York delegation whose members would all make up their own minds. And even with the adoption of his 14 points, he wouldn't say flat-out that Nixon would carry New York.

While Rockefeller enjoyed his game, all hell broke loose. In Chicago the 103 members of the Platform Committee saw their prerogatives taken from them in a classic confirmation of boss rule. Barry Goldwater expressed their frustrations and denounced the Rockefeller-Nixon deal. He called Nixon's actions at the meeting a "surrender," the "Munich of the Republican Party."[9]

At the same time, Dwight Eisenhower, the slumbering giant vacationing at the Newport Naval Station in Rhode Island, awoke. As upset as he was at the national defense plank that in effect repudiated his performance as commander-in-chief, Eisenhower was most piqued at Rockefeller's call for government reorganization. It was Eisenhower who had first advocated such an overhaul, asking Rockefeller to participate in an overall planning group that would elaborate on the idea for the president privately. Worse, Eisenhower had been planning to unveil his scheme at his last appearance before Congress—in January 1961. Then, reasoned the president, it would be his legacy to the country. His thunder stolen by Rockefeller, he was furious. As Theodore White observed: "Rockefeller had made it a partisan, factional proposal. This was treachery; this was personal theft; this was idea stealing, credit hogging. . . . Yet he could not fight the idea itself, for he devoutly believed in its necessity."[10]

Soon the platform deliberations were out of control, and all was chaos. It was left to Richard Nixon to be the leader, to bring order to the convention that would nominate him, if that nomination were to be worth anything at all. He would not order the convention to submit to the compact just to appease Rockefeller, but Rockefeller had to be appeased. Cautiously, he decided to oppose Rockefeller on only one point, civil rights. A fight on the national defense plank would alienate Eisenhower. Civil rights seemed the easiest road to travel.

The original, pre-compact plank was a moderate one by the standards of the day. It didn't support Negro sit-in strikes, as the Democrats had done in their Los Angeles platform, and at least one politician, Barry Goldwater, believes the original version could have carried the South for Nixon, and with the South the election. Rockefeller's plank offered support of the sit-ins and an end to job discrimination. "The Supreme Court," said Rockefeller, "has called for respect of the basic laws and principles of our nation 'with all deliberate speed.' The deliberateness must not be allowed to be sabotaged."[11]

Nixon twisted arms, a stronger plank was fashioned, and the platform was adopted. After all-night negotiations, it even had a national defense plank that both Eisenhower and Rockefeller could agree on.

Nixon was projected as a big man capable of the grand gesture, while Rockefeller seemed petty. "In retrospect," said one of his aides, "our performance in Chicago merely sealed Nelson's reputation as a troublemaker. He should have gone to the primaries, stated his case and then, if he lost, he should have supported his party's candidate quietly." William Miller, who would run with Barry Goldwater in 1964, goes further: "Nelson shouldn't have tried to be captain till he was on the team awhile. He should have seconded Nixon at the convention and really campaigned for him"[12]—which he didn't.

Nixon's narrow defeat has, over the years, confirmed Rockefeller's belief that he should have challenged the vice-president all the way. He believes he would have won if he'd gotten the nomination, and he is fond of pointing out that Robert Kennedy is said to have agreed with him. There are those who believe that the prematureness of the 1959 foray cost Rockefeller any chance he might have had to challenge Nixon later. No one can prove that he was premature or that he should have begun even earlier. For the record, Rockefeller said of the experience: "Why, I'd only been in politics about a year—as a professional, that is—and I had a lot to learn. I didn't even know how to talk to the pros. And those pros scared me a little, frankly."[13]

His performance in 1960, far from being viewed over time as an act of courage, has been seen as the immature action of a millionaire who always wants to have his way right now. Worse, by seeking the prize in 1960 and missing it, Rockefeller lost the political momentum he'd generated as a new face, just as James Desmond had predicted. And for all his campaigning since, he has never quite regained it.

He did run again, of course, but before 1964 could be considered seriously, there was the matter of his own reelection in 1962, and an unsuccessful try to elect a Republican mayor of New York City in 1961.

CHAPTER 22

Rehearsing
for 1964

THE FIRST BLOOD of the 1961 mayoralty race was drawn in the heat of the 1960 presidential campaign. This was a tactic Rockefeller favored, since Mayor Robert Wagner hoped to play a key role in the Democratic presidential effort and the governor wanted to knock him down a peg or two. A special unit of the State Investigation Commission was established in May 1960 to look into corruption in the city government. The unit had a budget of $500,000 and was directed by Whitney North Seymour, Jr. A yearlong investigation culminated in a 37-page final report titled *Government for Sale*.[1] Corruption, said the report, "exists at every level of city government." Seymour charged that Wagner had tried to choke off the special unit's appropriation while shrugging off large numbers of corrupt city inspectors as "little fish."[2] The *Herald Tribune* said that Seymour had "pursued witnesses with the killer instinct of flies on a cold November morning."[3] Wagner called the report "tripe" and said the unit had "gone out of business the way it started—in a blaze of mud."[4] Each of the city's district attorneys said that Seymour's "evidence" against 63 employees was not sufficient for prosecution. Wagner was hardly scratched—it would still be a race.

Rockefeller had wanted Senator Jacob Javits to run against

Wagner, but Javits refused. Louis Lefkowitz, the state attorney
general, became Rockefeller's choice. The governor had discovered ethnic politics and had concluded that the way to beat
Wagner was to run a Jew against him. The rest of the Republican ticket was ethnically balanced, and Rockefeller even tried to
induce Representative John Lindsay to run for Manhattan district attorney or controller. There was even some early talk
of a Republican-Liberal fusion ticket. The Liberals had said in
1961 that "it found many things to commend and few to condemn in Rockefeller's legislative program," but that judgment—
which would prove embarrassing to the governor when he ran
for president in 1964—proved not to be transferable to a Republican mayoral candidate in 1961.

Wagner looked at Rockefeller's ticket and borrowed a phrase
from Fiorello La Guardia, who had borrowed it from Al Smith.
Said Wagner of Lefkowitz et al.: "I could run on a laundry
ticket and beat those bums." Wagner was right. It was an uninspired campaign, the only friction coming when Rockefeller
said that "eight years of weak and vacillating Wagner . . . have
brought this great city to a sad state of affairs."[5] Twelve years
later, Rockefeller would be urging Wagner's election as mayor
to succeed John Lindsay. "He's a great New Yorker," Rockefeller would say, "highly respected by the people of all parties, a
man of high integrity and experience who can lead and heal the
city."[6] That's the way New York politics is played.

While the 1961 mayoralty was really of only passing interest
to Rockefeller, his own 1962 gubernatorial reelection was another matter. He'd suspected that Wagner might be his opponent, and that was another reason for roughing up the mayor the
year before. But, Wagner said he would not run for governor,
and Rockefeller was upset. He wanted to run against, and beat,
a Democrat of national stature. That, he reasoned, would give
him a boost toward 1964. Beating an unknown would prove
nothing. Worse, he thought, he'd have to increase his victory
margin considerably, since if he won by less than in 1958, speculation that he was slipping would be unavoidable.

A good many people were mentioned as Rockefeller opponents, including Edward R. Murrow, who was President Kennedy's choice.[7] Wagner, as head of the Democratic Party, relied on pollster Lou Harris to pick the best possible challenger. Harris had done a good job for Wagner himself in 1961, and now he came up with U.S. Attorney Robert Morgenthau. Rockefeller's worst fears were confirmed. He knew he'd win, but beating Morgenthau would mean little. So confident was the governor that he took the political risk of a separation from his first wife, Mary Todhunter Clark, only a year before the 1962 gubernatorial election. Later, his remarriage to Happy Murphy would help cripple his 1964 presidential prospects. He would find the public's displeasure inexplicable, since his divorce a year earlier had in no way injured his gubernatorial campaign.

Morgenthau spoke of the rising state debt being incurred by autonomous state agencies, but his warnings fell on deaf ears. It would take a decade and a recession for the public to see what Rockefeller had wrought through back-door financing. The governor promised not to raise taxes if reelected ("There won't be any tax increases. I won't let you down."[8]), a pledge he broke almost immediately, although he tried glossing it over by calling his new taxes "fees."

Wagner got into the act a few days before the campaign's close. He charged that in exchange for a tax he wanted for the city, he'd been asked to write a letter praising Rockefeller for "having done more for education and housing than any other governor."[9] Wagner then gave the campaign its greatest sting by saying: "I have had dealings with the governor, and I wouldn't trust him as far as I can throw him."[10]

Indulging the luxury of hindsight, it is not difficult to conclude that the 1962 gubernatorial campaign is less important for Rockefeller's victory over a lackluster opponent than for the first appearance of a Conservative Party candidate on the ballot. Of course, Rockefeller had frequently faced the wrath of upstate conservative Republicans who despaired of his spending and taxing policies. Generally, theirs was a weak voice, one which

the governor could control without serious injury to his legislative program. But a conservative *party* was more serious, representing, as it did, the institutionalization of right-wing opposition
to Rockefeller. David H. Jaquith, the Conservative candidate
for governor in the 1962 race, hardly dented the governor's
plurality. What he and his new party did do, however, was
accurately foreshadow a groundswell of antipathy toward
Rockefeller, an opposition that would cripple the governor's
presidential ambition before a Democratic candidate could
even try.

Those who founded the Conservative Party, its hard-core
ruling elite, were more than merely disenchanted with Rockefeller as governor. Many date their hostility to him way before his
governorship and can remember their first brush with him as
clearly as they can recall the date of the Japanese attack on
Pearl Harbor. William Rusher, for example, says he was against
Rockefeller "from the first time I ever saw him. It was at the
1956 Republican convention, and Rockefeller was buttonholing
people to support Jacob Javits for the Senate. That was when
there were questions about Javits' association with Communists,
and I didn't like Rockefeller helping Javits out."[11] Today,
Rusher is publisher of the *National Review* and the leading
spokesman for the creation of a new, independent national party
based on traditional conservative beliefs.

Like many conservative Republicans who learned to loathe
Nelson Rockefeller, Bill Rusher had toiled hard for Rockefeller's
Republican predecessor, Tom Dewey. There, says Rusher, was
a "real Republican. When Everett Dirksen attacked Dewey at
the 1952 GOP national convention, I booed so long and loud
that I had to go to the hospital to be treated for polyps on my
throat."[12]

Dewey had been careful to cultivate and reward the group of
young Republican conservatives who supported him. One such
Republican who would later battle Rockefeller as the manager
of Barry Goldwater's 1964 national delegate drive was F. Clifton
White. As head of the Young Republicans for Dewey for Presi-

dent, White had received his first political patronage job from the governor—assistant commissioner of motor vehicles.

It is impossible to know whether Rockefeller could have headed off future conservative trouble by playing Dewey's game of respect and reward. It is enough to recall that he hardly ever tried. While Dewey wooed the conservatives, Rockefeller ignored them. Finally, when he recognized the conservative threat as real, Rockefeller chose to fight. He tried killing their movement, both nationally and in New York, but he barely succeeded in wounding it. And once wounded, like a wild animal, its ferocity and hatred of Rockefeller increased.

Nationally, in his effort to destroy the growing conservative movement, Rockefeller supported a liberal Republican for the presidency of the Young Republicans. He succeeded in 1961, but the conservatives recaptured the YR hierarchy in 1963 and have yet to relinquish it. At home, Rockefeller's aides sought to kill the new Conservative Party during the 1962 campaign by having its nominating petitions declared invalid. Having failed, the state GOP then began a campaign to overhaul Rockefeller's liberal image—to try, as it would try again in the early 1970s, to move the governor to the right so that he would become acceptable to the GOP's conservative wing. Looking to 1964 and the presidential race, as well as to the more immediate concern of reelection, Jud Morhouse, in August 1962, sent a confidential memorandum to party leaders throughout the state setting forth "28 fiscal and business moves" designed to show Rockefeller's "conservative side."[13]

Morhouse was walking a tightrope. AFL–CIO President George Meany had called Rockefeller a "dedicated, aggressive liberal,"[14] and Rockefeller's brain trust did not want to alienate George Meany, or anyone else. So Morhouse added that his memorandum "must be used cautiously and should not be published because we do not want to emphasize the conservative side so much that we lose other votes."[15]

Here was the surest sign of interest in 1964. The Morhouse memorandum was a first step toward determining how well

Rehearsing for 1964

Rockefeller's liberal image could be fudged. As a trial balloon, it never flew. In New York, Rockefeller was unable to win over or even to check growing conservative disenchantment with his governorship. Still, the conservatives could never beat him in New York. But they could nationally, and two years later they got their first chance.

CHAPTER 23

Odds-On Favorite

I T LOOKED like a sure thing. Although his 1962 reelection victory had been uninspired, and despite the fact that he had alienated half the party in 1960, Nelson Rockefeller was the odds-on favorite to win the 1964 Republican presidential nomination. There was no one else.

Richard Nixon might have sought the prize. The narrowness of his defeat to John Kennedy in 1960, coupled with a Republican tradition of indulging "second chances" for its defeated champions, certainly earned Nixon the luxury of being considered again in 1964. But Nixon had miscalculated. He had gone home to California to cultivate his old base and had been trounced in a race for governor. The GOP's new faces, Governors George Romney of Michigan and William Scranton of Pennsylvania, were too new. Besides, they shared Rockefeller's brand of Republicanism and were ready to defer their own ambitions until their senior in New York had stepped aside.

Rockefeller's emergence as the leading contender was a new role for the governor. In the aftermath of the 1960 election, he had commanded a solid but small faction of the party. And he had spent a good deal of time prior to his 1962 awakening flexing his muscles and scrambling to make his presence known. An early battleground had been the Republican Conference Room in the New Senate Office Building. On January 3, 1961, New

York's senior senator, Jacob Javits, rose to request that his colleagues think long and hard before reelecting Barry Goldwater as chairman of the conference.

Goldwater, too, had come away from 1960 as the leader of a Republican faction. He would soon publish his "Forgotten American" manifesto in the *Wall Street Journal*.[1] Mr. Conservative was seeking to become Mr. Republican. As an opening shot at the 1964 crown, the Goldwater diatribe left little to the imagination. He described Eisenhower's party leadership as "aberrant," the result of hero worship. He said that Nixon's attempt at peaceful coexistence among the party's squabbling factions couldn't work, and that "me-too" liberalism would fail to capture many Democrats while surely alienating a good many Republicans. Goldwater also confessed that Goldwater Republicanism couldn't draw enough votes to win a presidential election. In its place he offered a new conservatism. No longer doctrinaire, it would appeal, said Goldwater, to "that dragooned and ignored individual, the Forgotten American." We are, cried Goldwater, a nation of "underdogs" who are the "silent Americans"—a theme Richard Nixon would borrow when he appealed to the "silent majority."

It was this newly visible Goldwater whom Rockefeller, via Javits, sought to slay early. Preoccupied with his own reelection in 1962, Rockefeller was seeking to stop Goldwater from getting a head start on 1964. "In light of the 1960 election results in New York," said Goldwater, "I think it is particularly inappropriate that a member of the Republican leadership of that state should seek to prescribe the pattern for political conduct of the party nationally."[2] Goldwater had the votes, and Javits, presumably on Rockefeller's orders, dropped the purge attempt.

Rockefeller retreated and shut up. By January 1962, the most that could be said for him was that he wasn't disliked any more than Goldwater or Nixon were. Sensing that the governor was treading water, Jud Morhouse, on February 27, 1962, sent a confidential memorandum to Rockefeller. He wrote that the GOP should be dominated by people from the states with big cities and, by implication, attacked Goldwater. Unfortunately for Rockefeller, who was trying to avoid controversy, Morhouse leaked his own secret memorandum to a reporter, adding that the GOP was "the party that says 'no' before it hears the question."[3] At the same time, Goldwater's supporters issued their own battle plan. They called for a conservative strategy that would downplay civil rights and play up anti-Communism. Goldwater himself rejected the statement because it spoke too bluntly to sensitive racial questions. Both the conservative game plan and the Morhouse memorandum were too strong for the world of real politics.

Rockefeller's strategy was rightward. Appeasement and rapprochement with the conservatives was the idea, and Rockefeller sought to follow it faithfully.

The evening of February 1, 1962, proved the point. The Republican National Committee was hosting its kickoff fundraiser for the 1962 congressional campaign. Various party leaders were scattered around the country. Each would speak, via a closed-circuit hookup, to the faithful everywhere. When Rockefeller's face appeared on the screen from the $3-a-plate chicken dinner in Des Moines there were boos at the $100-a-plate filet mignon dinner in Washington's Mayflower Hotel. The boos soon became applause. Nelson Rockefeller came out swinging—on the conservative side against the Democratic president. The hot issue of that time was Kennedy's plan to establish a cabinet-level Department of Urban Affairs. Kennedy had resubmitted his proposal as a reorganization plan which would go into effect automatically unless the Senate or House vetoed it. At the same time, Kennedy announced that he would appoint Robert Weaver to head the new department, the first black in history to sit in a president's cabinet.

Here was a Republican dilemma. If GOP votes killed the plan, it would appear that the Republicans were opposed to integrating the cabinet. If the plan went into effect, Kennedy would emerge as a hero to black Americans. Republicans assumed that Rockefeller would be embarrassed by his party's opposition to the plan, especially since he represented the proposition that the GOP must look to city voters for victory. What the party workers heard from Des Moines instead was an attack on Kennedy that any conservative could be proud of.

First, Rockefeller lashed out at the president's tactics: "The Democratic Administration is afraid to let its Department of Urban Affairs proposal in its present form stand on its merits," he said. "That's why they have brought in the completely unrelated race issue. What is this but political fakery?" Then, added Rockefeller, "if the president is so concerned about naming an outstanding Negro to the cabinet, why wasn't Bob Weaver appointed to the cabinet in the first place? He found a cabinet post for his brother all right."[4] Across the country, the faithful loved it. The strategy was working.

Rockefeller believed that his legion of image makers could sell anything to anyone. In short order he denounced the nuclear test ban treaty—"agreement for the sake of agreement must never become an end in itself"—and before long, in another swipe at Kennedy, the governor said that "the will to resist Communism has been eroded everywhere."[5]

Simultaneously, Rockefeller began his campaign against labeling. He unilaterally declared the terms "liberal" and "conservative" useless. Finally, he went so far as to call himself an "economic conservative and a human rights liberal."[6]

Occasionally, however, Rockefeller would forsake his courtship of conservatives. In the spring of 1962, Rockefeller said that Goldwater was "articulate, courageous, attractive, and wrong." As for the conservative Republicans who devotedly supported Goldwater, Rockefeller said: "These right-wing groups are like cattle that aren't going anywhere. They are scared and they'll fly off in any direction."[7]

By the latter part of 1962 and into the first months of 1963, Rockefeller had curbed such divisive talk, and George Hinman was traveling the country delivering calm messages proclaiming Rockefeller's party regularity. Jud Morhouse, the firebrand state chairman ever eager for a fight, was kept in mothballs at home.

Rockefeller was no longer following Morhouse's advice. He was now a confirmed devotee of the Hinman school of low-profile, party-unity politics. By the end of 1962, Morhouse resigned his party post—not because he disagreed with the campaign's strategy, which he did, but because he was the target of the first significant scandal to hit the Rockefeller administration.

CHAPTER 24

Morhouse Problems

LUCKILY FOR HIM, the Morhouse scandal never seriously harmed Rockefeller's presidential ambitions—other deeply rooted difficulties of longer standing would eventually do that. Perhaps the Morhouse trouble would have created a stir, but the scandal broke during the longest newspaper strike in New York history. Thus, at a time of real turmoil for Rockefeller at home, most of the country, which received its news of New York through the New York *Times*, was ignorant of the problem.

If ever there was one, Jud Morhouse was Nelson Rockefeller's Watergate. All the elements were there: a pattern of influence peddling by the New York State Republican chairman; large sums of money expended to ensure loyalty; and a costly cover-up that continued years later in the committee rooms of Congress.

In its simplest terms, the Morhouse story exposed the uncontrollable greed of the state's top party potentate and smeared the Rockefeller administration's reputation for being above reproach. More significantly, it revealed the inner workings of the Rockefeller family and the interrelationships of financial and political power. In fact, Morhouse's influence-peddling fees were exceeded by the hundreds of thousands of dollars of

Rockefeller largesse intended to insulate him from temptation. And finally, the inside story proves that Rockefeller was less than forthright in his recollection of the sordid episode during the congressional confirmation hearings on his nomination as vice-president.

Nelson Rockefeller first met Jud Morhouse at a Republican fundraiser late in 1955 at the Knickerbocker Club in Manhattan. Only a year earlier, Morhouse had been installed as GOP state chairman by Governor Thomas E. Dewey, a few months before the curtain rang down on 12 years of Republican rule. Already aiming for a restoration of Republican control in 1958 and re-appointment to his own job, Morhouse immediately began projecting the handsome young multimillionaire as a possible candidate.

When Rockefeller's private soundings showed he could capture both the GOP gubernatorial nomination and the election of 1958, he confided his decision to run to the two men who had encouraged him the most, George Hinman and Jud Morhouse. On June 6, 1958, Morhouse summoned a dozen GOP leaders to a suite at the Roosevelt Hotel where he displayed the pro-Rockefeller poll results and proclaimed: "I say that the organization has to go for Rockefeller—and if it doesn't I will step out as state chairman."[1]

Nineteen years after the Knickerbocker Club meeting Rockefeller's recollection of the state chairman's role was different from that of virtually every other observer. This is how it went at the Senate Rules Committee hearing on Rockefeller's nomination to be vice-president:

SENATOR ALLEN: "Was Mr. Morhouse instrumental in your getting the Republican nomination?"

ROCKEFELLER: "No sir."

SENATOR ALLEN: "He had nothing to do with that?"

ROCKEFELLER: "Well, he was state chairman, but we had a system at that time where each county had a county committee."

ALLEN: "But he supported you personally?"
ROCKEFELLER: "Not in the beginning."
ALLEN: "I see. When did that support start?"
ROCKEFELLER: "If you will forgive me for saying so, when he saw I was going to win."[2]

Contrast Rockefeller's testimony with this New York *Times* dispatch of August 25, 1958, which recognized Morhouse's ascension into the major leagues of politics: "By engineering the selection of Nelson A. Rockefeller as this year's candidate, in the face of strong, early opposition from powerful groups within the party, Morhouse has demonstrated his graduation from the amateur to the professional class in politics."

Far from joining the winning bandwagon, Morhouse helped create it. "A study of the hearing record," said Senator Jesse Helms of North Carolina in a floor speech opposing the Rockefeller nomination, "can only lead us reluctantly to the conclusion that Mr. Rockefeller deliberately set about to minimize the impact of his relationship with Mr. Morhouse and even to mislead the Rules Committee and the American people."[3]

A few months after Rockefeller's 1958 victory, he met Morhouse at a dinner under circumstances that were more mysterious than their first meeting—as was the exact date, which no one seems able to remember. This encounter in the spring of 1959 concerned a $100,000 contribution funneled through Sullivan County Assemblyman Hyman (Bucky) Mintz. There were ample reasons for mystery.[4]

On April 7, 1959, Mintz met at Manhattan's Belmont Plaza Hotel with Morris Gold, an upstate Republican official who doubled as a plumbing contractor, and John P. Maguire, Jr., who was seeking a license for the Finger Lakes racetrack.

Gold and Mintz gave Maguire the good news that the license was about to be granted, except for one missing ingredient: $100,000 in cash would have to be delivered immediately to Morhouse, who was vacationing in Florida. One day later, on April 8, Gold and Mintz went to Miami while, according to testimony at Mintz's 1965 trial, John Nilon, a promoter angling to become a racetrack concessionaire, had $100,000 transferred from the Philadelphia Trust Company branch in Ridley Park, Pa., to his account, care of the Metropolitan Bank of Miami Beach. Nilon and his brother James then also flew to Miami, checking into the Eden Rock Hotel. There, on the same day, April 8, the Nilons refused to give the money to Mintz and Gold because the racetrack's preliminary license—a requirement before the racetrack could be built—had not yet been issued. The Nilons and their money returned to Pennsylvania.

The next day, April 9, the New York State Racing Commission approved a certificate of incorporation for the Finger Lakes Racing Association, Inc., Maguire's group. On April 10, Gold flew to Pennsylvania, where he received $100,000 from the Nilons. Gold had served as a "coffee sergeant" for Mintz on the Assembly payroll and was well suited for his delivery-boy role. He hopped a plane for Florida and turned the money over to Mintz, who said he was going to the Americana Hotel to deliver it to Morhouse.

The confidential reports of congressional investigators—including the results of interviews with Morhouse, who was never called to appear before the committees considering Rockefeller's vice-presidential nomination—say that "according to Mr. Morhouse, Mr. Mintz told him that the money was a political contribution from persons who had an interest in a racetrack. Mr. Morhouse stated that while he regarded the substantial cash contribution as somewhat unusual, the Republican Party in New York State was in financial difficulty and he was not about to refuse summarily a campaign contribution."[5]

Less than a month later, on May 5, Mintz and Gold were summoned from Florida to New York, where Morhouse returned the money to them. The governor, he said, had "gotten wind" of the deal and ordered the cash to be given back. It was never disclosed just how Rockefeller learned of the racetrack fix, except that it was later alleged that the Nilon brothers contacted Joseph Pew of the Sun Oil family, then a prominent

Pennsylvania Republican, and urged him to tell the New York governor that they had made a hefty contribution and that they "didn't get what they were supposed to get."

Assistant Manhattan District Attorney David Goldstein, who handled the case, supported this version in discussions with congressional investigators. Goldstein said he had received information that the Nilons had complained to Pew and had prevailed upon him to advise Rockefeller that certain persons were not keeping their part in the deal. Gold also supposedly stated in August 1964 that when Nilon came to Monticello to pick up the money, Nilon told a Gold associate, Archie Barberia, that Joseph Pew had called Rockefeller and had asked that the money be returned. Congressional investigators note a sharp clash here with Rockefeller's version of the event. Their report concludes that "the above unconfirmed information compiled by Mr. Goldstein indicates that Governor Rockefeller may have learned of the $100,000 payment from Joseph Pew, rather than from Mr. Morhouse."

Rockefeller fixed the dinner date at which Morhouse came "to say that he had what I consider was in a shoebox, but which I am told was in a paper bag"[6]—namely the $100,000 in cash— as the June 4, 1959, party fundraiser at the Waldorf-Astoria Hotel. When it was pointed out that the money had already been returned as of May 12, 1959, Rockefeller said he assumed that it all must have happened at a mayors' dinner at the Executive Mansion in Albany on April 22, after which "Bucky Mintz went down to the Roosevelt Hotel [in Manhattan], bought a suitcase for $17.50 to put his money in and take it back to where it came from."[7]

Although he could remember the cost of a suitcase, Rockefeller became fuzzy when describing the circumstances surrounding the dinner and his fear that racetrack money was involved:

> I was indignant. Mr. Morhouse did not say "this comes from the race track people." Mr. Bucky Mintz did not say that. He said it was a cash contribution from friends of the party. Mr.

Bucky Mintz could have been given a receipt by the party for $100,000 received and it could have been put into the coffers of the party and it would have been, if I—I am not a lawyer, but if I understand—perfectly legitimately handled. My concern was, although I was new to the business, but my attorney general is very sophisticated and very bright, that this did not just sound like Mr. Bucky Mintz coming in with $100,000. To begin with, he did not have it—or at least I do not think he did. So I looked through what was said to what I thought was the case, and I said "tell that guy to get that money back and to get it back to the people who gave it to him."

Now at that point I did not know Bucky Mintz. He was an assemblyman, I think, but I wanted to be sure they got it back to the people from whom it came so that they would not find themselves in a position of feeling they had made a contribution, somebody else pocketing the money. And then this whole thing really being a very serious situation.[8]

Perhaps it was simply naïveté, but Rockefeller did not take the attempted bribe too seriously. In fact, it was not until five years later that an undercover cop assigned to the Manhattan District Attorney's Office uncovered the racetrack plot. Gold was later convicted of perjury. And only days before Mintz was convicted of bribing a detective to find out how much District Attorney Frank Hogan knew about the $100,000, his attorney posed these questions to the jury: "Now, if this was a payoff do you think the governor would say 'give it back—cover it up?' Would he let Morhouse stay on as Republican state chairman?"[9] As for Morhouse, he had already pleaded the Fifth Amendment more than 30 times before a court-appointed trustee in a federal hearing into alleged bribery involving the racetrack, which was by then bankrupt.[10]

Rockefeller recalled that until the law was later strengthened, "there was nothing wrong in what Morhouse did"[11] because he was a political rather than an elected official. The governor's recollection also included this faulty conclusion:

Morhouse Problems

I have to say that he did come to me. He could have pocketed that money. He could have put it into the account. He came to me and said exactly what I have told you, so that he was evidencing—well, now, you say there could be a crime, and I am just handed by counsel a little note that says the grand jury returned no indictment as a result of its investigation in this matter. It was investigated by the grand jury. They found no violation of New York law. I would like to be able to say to you that I caused this investigation by the grand jury because it would strengthen my position in the testimony, but I cannot remember that I did. I would assume, therefore, that the attorney general did.[12]

In fact, however, it took five years for the Manhattan district attorney to learn of the bribe attempt.

Shortly after the shoebox incident, Rockefeller realized that Morhouse required a lot more money—not that he wasn't doing well already. Official figures for 1959 show that the $17,000 from the New York State Thruway Authority post Rockefeller had given him, plus other fees, had driven Morhouse's total income up to $64,510—placing him in the top 1 percent of taxpayers in the United States.[13] Yet on December 22, 1959, at brother Nelson's urging, Laurance Rockefeller loaned Morhouse $49,000 at 3 percent annual interest, secured by stock in the Geophysics Corporation of America and the Marks Oxygen Company that Laurance had sold to the Republican leader. By May 9, 1961, Morhouse had sold back the Marks Oxygen Stock (and it had since become American Cryogenics, Inc.) for almost $80,000.[14] Laurance, who like his brother continued to refer to Morhouse as the "unsalaried state chairman," was told years later that the value of the Geophysics stock had at one point hit $240,000. "This we did not know," Laurance replied. "This is pretty dramatic and frankly this is news to me."[15]

Equally dramatic were the results of a loan from the governor himself. On September 21, 1960, Rockefeller loaned Morhouse $100,000 to purchase all his stock in the Seyah Corporation, which owned land leased to the New York Telephone Company on Long Island. Nelson's was a non-interest-bearing note which was forgiven in 1973. The property, which produced a $2,724-a-month income for Morhouse ("that was the purpose," said Rockefeller, ". . . to get him some money legitimately"[16]), turned out to include a parcel purchased later by the state for $22,000 for a railroad grade eliminating crossing and was appraised for $285,000.[17]

"I wanted to keep him from the temptations of a man who had a large family to support—college-age children, his mother-in-law and his mother living with him in his home—a wonderful opportunity, of course, for him, but, of course, it was expensive and I felt this man was under a lot of pressure in relation to money,"[18] Rockefeller would explain later.

"I was worried about an unpaid chairman of the Republican Party," Rockefeller ironically recalled. "I believe that the party should pay its chief officer, pay its officers, because I think if they don't, it opens up too much temptation on the part of others to seek to supplement the lack of income from the place his loyalty is supposed to be, which is to the party."[19]

Years later, Joe Carlino was among those who claimed to have known all along that his party's chairman had been placed on Rockefeller's personal welfare roll. "Morhouse got some kind of compensation, I'm sure,"[20] Carlino concluded even before Rockefeller's loan list was released. And, recalls Manhattan Republican boss Vincent Albano, Rockefeller lamented after the liquor scandal exploded: "The Jud Morhouse thing was only $100,000. Why didn't Jud come to me—I would've given it to him."[21]

The congressional investigators who interviewed Morhouse reported that he had told Rockefeller after the 1958 election that "because of his inability to meet his financial commitments he was going to resign as state Republican chairman and devote his time and energy to an income producing occupation." If this is true, and Rockefeller viewed Morhouse as a man who might possibly be unable to resist temptation, why didn't Rockefeller simply accept Morhouse's offer to resign? Obviously, as events had already shown—and would show again—Morhouse was too valuable to lose. So the governor and his brother did their best to keep Morhouse afloat financially. Either they didn't do enough, or he was just insatiably greedy.

Meanwhile, Rockefeller filled a vacancy on the politically sensitive State Liquor Authority with Martin Epstein, a boyhood buddy of John Crews, the Brooklyn Republican boss whom Morhouse had swung into the Rockefeller camp in 1958. (Rockefeller denies that the SLA appointment was a quid pro quo for Crews's support.) It was one of the four mistakes Rockefeller would later regret, understating somewhat "the fact that one man I appointed in 15 years turned out to be a cheat." But even then, Rockefeller recalled, "this gentleman was eulogized on both sides of the aisle in the Senate when he was confirmed, as being one of the leading citizens of Brooklyn, and one of the things that stuck in my mind was they said, among other things pointing out what a fine man he was, he raised dogs. I never did understand how that had anything to do with his capacity, but that was a point that was made on the floor of the Senate."

Unfortunately for Rockefeller, Epstein did not devote his full time to dog raising. The frail, withered man was a part-time influence peddler who continued to sell licenses and leniency from a Manhattan hospital room as he suffered from the spreading cancer that was to cost him a leg.

In 1961, meanwhile, even as Jud Morhouse was reaping the proceeds of the Rockefellers' largesse, the state chairman remained well within the grasp of temptation. The latest offer came from the Playboy Club empire whose multimillion-dollar bunny club off Manhattan's Fifth Avenue was idled by the lack of a liquor license. The hangup was the club's intention to restrict bar service to keyholders—the same concession it later won from an Illinois court. Epstein demanded $50,000 for the license and sent the Playboy operatives to see Morhouse. Not to be outdone, Morhouse demanded $100,000 plus stock options for 100,000 shares and the gift shop concessions at other clubs in several cities. When the scandal broke, he had received $18,000 in "public relations" fees.[22]

The Playboy Club fix uncorked dozens of other cases of scandal within the Liquor Authority and led to Morhouse's resignation on December 27, 1962—three months after he had been elected to a fifth term as state chairman. Thirteen days later he quit as vice-chairman of the Thruway Authority, and hours later he was called before Manhattan District Attorney Frank Hogan's grand jury. He was finally indicted on December 7, 1965.

At the same time, another Rockefeller appointee whom the former governor neglected to recall before Congress refused to waive immunity before the liquor grand jury. His name was Melvin Osterman, and he was found hiding in a closet of a Republican state committee secretary when detectives arrived at her home armed with a search warrant for the typewriter Osterman had used to write notes to Epstein. Osterman's voice was also traced from a bug in Epstein's hospital room, where they had discussed a $5,000 license "fee" for a liquor store owned by a New York socialite.[23]

There was also a bug in Morhouse's midtown Manhattan office. What it recorded were dozens of conversations, punctuated by pre-Watergate obscenities, which together leave the sordid impression of respected men abusing their political power and public trust.[24]

The time: the winter of 1963. The scene: a suite opposite Grand Central Terminal in the Chanin Building, which Morhouse shares with Aleer J. Couri, the bald and moon-faced former federal customs appraiser who parlayed political ties into a multimillion-dollar consulting company. Couri snorts nervously behind his desk, ridiculing Rockefeller's proposal to hike auto registration fees, lamenting Morhouse's role in the Playboy Club bribery plot and his resignation as Republican state chairman. Enter Walter Bligh, the bespectacled ex-secretary of the Republican State Committee.

Morhouse Problems

COURI: "What is the goof doing to himself in New York State? What baby talk. He says pay the increase in license fees and it will result in better roads and lower the insurance rates. What I'm giving now is a piece of comedy. The way that jackass is going, my friend, he couldn't get elected to the justice of the peace. Can you imagine the way the Democrats are dancing with glee over this guy's stupid operation, and all this horseshitting, all this crap is all the result of Jud Morhouse's move."

BLIGH: "Every bit of it."

COURI: "He killed himself, he killed his friends, he killed everybody around him."

BLIGH: "That's right, and all of it dishonest."

Couri complains that it was all so unnecessary, that they could have "done business" with building tycoon William Zeckendorf, a sometime Rockefeller associate, "to the tune of $200 million," but that the Playboy plot ruined everything. His only hope now is the governor's older brother.

COURI: "The fucking roof caved in, all the way down without even something holding it up. Well, let's see if David Rockefeller is going to receive him. If David Rockefeller tells him to get lost, then let's fold up, call it a bad deal."

"If I got you a big mortgage could you go down to the Chase Bank and negotiate?" Couri asks Morhouse later.

MORHOUSE: "I don't know."

COURI: "There's a doubt in your mind?"

MORHOUSE: "Yes, yes, there's a big doubt."

Couri tells friends after the conversation that he was shocked by the chairman's depression and by his admission that he can "no longer get anywhere with the Chase Bank. All he can do now is to sweat it out."

The Playboy tapes also reveal that only a year after Rockefeller loaned Morhouse the $100,000 to meet "pressing family obligations," the state chairman loaned Couri $25,000.

COURI: "Tomorrow, I'm going to give you a check with the exact interest. I'm not going to include a letter, so you'll know that's it, the exact amounts since the day you loaned it. Where are you going to deposit it, in New York?"

MORHOUSE: "I don't know, since they're tracing all my banks in New York. I think I'm going to deposit it in a bank in Massachusetts. I've done business with it a lot."

In another conversation, Bligh expresses concern that the Internal Revenue Service might come poking around about all those political cronies who "received from the state committee funds which they never reported," and Couri vaguely drops the names of other politicians like Senate Majority Leader Walter Mahoney, Assembly Speaker Joseph Carlino, Attorney General Louis Lefkowitz, and Lieutenant Governor Malcolm Wilson.

COURI: "It was on my insistence that Jud went to the governor. I wanted the governor to know and be protected. The governor appreciated it. Oh, well it's too late for me to benefit by that. It's the governor I'm thinking about. Walter Mahoney, Carlino, Lefkowitz, and Malcolm Wilson have always gotten thousands of favors through this body—that's all the more reason why you should try to avoid as much as you can for the governor to try to take it out of Hogan's hands. It's too late."

BLIGH: "I don't know, I don't know that what you said is true or not. I don't know if Walter Mahoney, or Joe or Malcolm. . . ."

COURI: "I know that Malcolm and Lefkowitz were—Marty told me."

A few days later, Morhouse is seated in Couri's office, which adjoins his own. After Couri phones former Mayor William

O'Dwyer to "drop around here and see our friend," Couri asks, "Suppose a guy like Marty Epstein kicks the bucket?"

MORHOUSE: "Where that leaves me, I don't know."

COURI: "Then they won't be able to get him to testify or say a goddamned word because he's a dead man."

MORHOUSE: "If you say so. I don't even know what shape he's in."

COURI: "The guy is an amputee, 70 years old, diabetes and a heart condition. What's holding him up?"

MORHOUSE: "You know, while he was in the hospital, everybody had him dead 100 times. They said he'd never come out of this."

Later, Bligh agrees that "Hogan was ready to move on three top guys and it was going to break because the newspaper strike was going to be over and that it had been held back until the papers were back on the street. I think the whole key to the thing is Marty."

Walter Bligh died in 1967. Aleer Couri is a wealthy semi-retired customs consultant living at a swanky suburban country club. Martin Epstein was indicted but was never brought to trial because of age and illness.

After refusing to testify, Judson Morhouse was convicted of bribery stemming from the Playboy Club plot. Senator Javits and former Governor Dewey urged leniency. And on June 14, 1966, Governor Rockefeller's secretary, William J. Ronan, wrote sentencing Judge Abraham Gellinoff of the State Supreme Court that Morhouse was "a man of honor and ability" whose social life exemplifies "effective, constructive and active participation in community affairs."

The three-paragraph "My dear Mr. Justice" letter concluded: "From my personal knowledge, Judson Morhouse has made an important contribution to the political and governmental life of this state. As you consider Mr. Morhouse's case, I wish you to have the benefit of these informed observations which I know are shared by Governor Rockefeller."[25] Ronan told the Senate Rules Committee that Rockefeller had approved the use of his name in the letter.

Two days later, Gellinoff sentenced Morhouse to two to three years in prison, after Chief Assistant District Attorney Alfred J. Scotti had assailed the former GOP chairman as a man who had "misused the vast power of his political position to satisfy his greed for money."[26] Reciting a litany of retainers from a broadcasting firm, the William J. Burns Detective Agency, S & H green stamps, Swiss watch companies, and other "consulting" fees, Scotti declared that "we have at least established that they involve the sale of political influence for money."[27] Recalling the Finger Lakes racetrack episode, Scotti concluded that "it has been established that this defendant, in seeking to enrich himself by the use of his political power, knowingly and deliberately fostered corruption in public office."[28]

One June 21, 1966, after serving six days of a two-to-three year sentence, Morhouse was released from Sing Sing prison pending appeal. After all appeals were exhausted, Morhouse applied for a pardon in December 8, 1970, to the one man who could save him from jail, the man he had helped make governor, Nelson Rockefeller. Two weeks later, as part of a traditional New York State practice, Morhouse's sentence was commuted to time already served.

Several aspects of the clemency proceedings are puzzling. First, there was the physicians' finding that imprisonment "would seriously imperil his continuing deteriorating state of health and would probably cause his death," although other state prisoners were also suffering from cancer and Parkinson's disease. Rockefeller recalled only that the Correction Department "advised me that no inmate in their care and custody at that time suffered from the combination of diseases which afflicted Mr. Morhouse."[29]

Nevertheless, there are indications that at least one of the other prisoners pardoned at the end of 1970 was released at that time in an attempt to mute the adverse publicity that would surround clemency for Morhouse.[30] On December 14, 1970, Assistant Counsel Howard Shapiro wrote to his boss, Counsel Robert Douglass, that David Wright has "terminal cancer and has a very short time to live." Notes in the official Morhouse file are filled with cryptic jottings like "Wright falling into place" and "would be doing in two cases—Wright" and "I hope we can avoid a publicity barrage on this one—but I also hope we can get a quick evaluation by Parole. On the face of it, Wright has a very compelling case." When questioned by congressional investigators, Howard Shapiro said that Wright's application for parole was submitted "out of the blue" by then Bronx District Attorney Burton Roberts. As of 1974, four years after Shapiro said that he had terminal cancer, Wright was residing in Buffalo and working as a carpenter. When House investigators traveled to Buffalo to question him, he refused to talk to them.

Another aspect of the clemency action is troublesome. When Rockefeller testified before the Senate Rules Committee, he stated that there were three independent doctors "under the leadership of the head of the state medical society," and "they went to the prison, got a waiver from him to report back to me, and wrote their collective unanimous opinions that his life was in jeopardy if he stayed there."[31]

Later, in response to a question in the House, Rockefeller conceded that on the day of the examination, "there was a very bad snowstorm and Dr. Walls, the president of the state medical society, was the only member of the three-man panel able to reach Albany to examine Mr. Morhouse. However, the other members of the panel reviewed Mr. Morhouse's medical records, reviewed the affidavits of Mr. Morhouse's physicians, and had a joint consultation by telephone with Dr. Walls following his examination and before arriving at a decision."[32]

All three were to have been transported by state plane to Albany, and the only one who made it through the snow was driven home from Albany to Buffalo by a state trooper. Rockefeller recalled that "we have never had a case where an applicant for commutation was not a member of the inmate population in the state's prison. The president of the medical society and two other members of his panel were performing a service to the state and therefore transportation was made available to them."[33]

Dr. Walter Walls agreed with Rockefeller's recollection of the incident.[34] But Walls's memory differs from that of Dr. Paul De Luca of Binghamton, one of the members of the Walls panel. De Luca confirms discussing the Morhouse examination with Walls, but places the date of their telephone consultation as after Christmas—and after Morhouse's sentence was commuted. De Luca is certain that he never signed the panel's report.

Another inconsistency concerns the affidavits of Morhouse's own doctors. They were actually dated after the application for clemency, an application supposedly based on those very same affidavits. Could Rockefeller explain that one?

"No," he replied. "My counsel dealt with this matter and has advised me that he discussed with Mr. Morhouse's counsel the fact that any medical evidence in support of the application must address itself to the question of whether Mr. Morhouse's life would be imperiled by imprisonment. My counsel also advised me that he cannot specifically recall whether this requirement resulted in a second set of affidavits being submitted by Mr. Morhouse's physicians."[35]

According to confidential congressional reports, one of the four physicians, Dr. Stanley Mandell, told congressional investigators that Morhouse had been referred to him by Dr. Harry Gordon, who in 1970 asked Mandell to prepare a letter about his patient. The letter was picked up by Gordon's chauffeur, and Mandell subsequently received several bottles of liquor from Gordon. Mandell said that Gordon was his most senior supervisor and that he regarded Gordon's request for a letter to support Morhouse's clemency application like a "young lawyer would regard a request from a senior judge." Mandell said that Morhouse had never been an advanced Parkinsonian and that when he had seen Morhouse in March 1973, he was "depressed but . . . his posture was erect and . . . he was going to work on a daily basis." Gordon told investigators that he had never seen or examined Morhouse, but based his affidavit (he was one of the four) on those by Mandell and the two others. Gordon said that he had been approached by a Morhouse friend, Alger Chapman, a former president of the Beech-Nut company and board chairman of the Squibb Corporation. Chapman had been New York State tax commissioner under Governor Dewey, had managed several of Dewey's campaigns, and had been named by Couri and others on the Playboy tapes.

Chapman told investigators that Morhouse's lawyer, Frank Raichle, had called him to say that Rockefeller counsel Robert Douglass had complained that the affidavits from the doctors "did not go to the heart of the problem" and were insufficient. The following is Chapman's interesting account as told to congressional investigators:

> Mr. Chapman recalled that upon receiving this information, he rewrote the four affidavits, working them so as to focus on the effect of incarceration on Mr. Morhouse's health. In rewriting the affidavits, Mr. Chapman said that he relied almost exclusively on a letter drafted by Sanford Morhouse [Judson Morhouse's son] intended for Judge Gellinoff. Although the letter was never sent, Mr. Chapman said that it provided him with sufficient information about Mr. Morhouse's health to prepare the affidavits. While Mr. Chapman was working on the affidavits, he said that he telephoned George Hinman, a Republican National Committeeman for New York State, an employee of the Rockefeller family and associates, a close friend of Governor Rockefeller's and a close friend and former boss of Robert Douglass, counsel to the governor. Mr. Chapman stated that he told Mr. Hinman that the affidavits were being revised to ensure that the Morhouse application would not be turned down. In addition, Mr. Chapman said that he told Mr. Hinman to tell Mr. Douglass that the affidavits were being revised and that they would be submitted in time. [Hinman, in an interview with the House staff,

confirmed that he had relayed Chapman's message to Douglass.] Mr. Chapman recalled that he took two of the affidavits, Dr. Gordon's and Dr. Mandell's, entered his chauffeur driven automobile and went to Dr. Gordon's home. Mr. Chapman said that he first met Dr. Gordon while he had been chairman and chief executive officer of Beech-Nut and that Dr. Gordon had assisted Beech-Nut in evaluating the nutritional value of its baby food. Mr. Chapman also pointed out that he had a nephew who trained under Dr. Gordon.

Rockefeller received the report from Dr. Walls on December 22, 1970. The next day, he pardoned Morhouse because he was suffering from several diseases and jail would jeopardize his life.

The House Judiciary Committee members seemed confused by the intricate tale, and the balance of the questioning of Rockefeller relative to the Morhouse commutation was left for committee counsel Jerome Zeifman. But Zeifman was unable to probe deeply because Chairman Rodino cut short the interrogation and required that written questions—with no chance for followup—be submitted. (This was the only time Rodino permitted any questioning of the nominee by a nonmember of Judiciary.)

Zeifman's written questions reminded Rockefeller that three other New York State prisoners had colostomies and that at least one also had Parkinson's disease. Zeifman pointed out that the Walkill Correctional Facility was equipped to care for such prisoners. Rockefeller merely reiterated that he had simply relied on the advice of his counsel, who had obviously reviewed all of the documents.

Five years after his commutation, Jud Morhouse was still suffering. In the words of Walter Bligh, "time and time again, up there in Ticonderoga, he must be thinking 'Jesus Christ, I was the biggest Republican in America and look what happened.' "[36]

Perhaps Morhouse had a premonition about the pardon as far back as 1963. Wan and weary, Morhouse resembled a losing high school football coach as he prepared to leave the office to walk across 42nd Street into a gray and misty February evening on his way to the Roosevelt Hotel before his return upstate.

Before departing, Morhouse discusses by phone an appointment to the Palisades Interstate Park Commission—chaired by Laurance Rockefeller—with the warning: "Everything looks okay, but I wouldn't suggest notifying him [the appointee]— the governor's office probably would want to do that." Then, matter of factly, as he places his hand over the receiver in mid-conversation, Morhouse maps an appeal to his biggest benefactor:

MORHOUSE: "I don't know what I should do with Rocke-feller. I don't want to take a little one to Rockefeller, I want to take a big one."

COURI: "That's right."

MORHOUSE: "So he's got to say to himself, 'well I owe him one last good turn, let it be a big good one.' See what I mean, he can't help but say that."

COURI: "Absolutely."

CHAPTER 25

The Governor
Moves Right

AT THE TIME, the Morhouse scandal was little more than an irritant to Nelson Rockefeller. One of the few papers publishing in New York at that point was the *Wall Street Journal*, and the *Journal*, like the rest of the country, was marveling at Rockefeller's neutralization of right-wing Republican opposition to his presidential candidacy.

The press was equating a Rockefeller-Goldwater rapprochement with a complete acceptance of Rockefeller by the Republican right. That equation would fail in the spring of 1963, but only when Goldwater himself left the field.

Rockefeller and Goldwater had a mutual admiration for free enterprise and a mutual suspicion of the New Frontier. Both were positively manic about party loyalty. In July 1962, Goldwater even went so far as to express support for GOP liberals like Jacob Javits of New York. Party unity became the theme of secret breakfast meetings at Rockefeller's Foxhall Road estate, where Rockefeller said: "I'm a hawk on foreign policy. I'm a hawk on national defense. I'm a dove on domestic issues. You've got two-thirds of me. What more do you want?"[1]

The governor and the senator dined with only two aides

present and found they shared the same suspicion—that the Eisenhower wing of the party was scheming to deny them the nomination in favor of George Romney. In fact, Goldwater had been discouraging his supporters for months. He did all he could to signal his lack of interest in the presidential nomination. No staff was added to his Senate payroll, and he cut down his out-of-Arizona speaking schedule considerably. He went out of his way to be of assistance to Rockefeller, often telephoning Republican leaders hostile to the governor to ensure that he received a decent reception when he visited their areas. "I don't want the nomination," Goldwater said. "I'm not looking for it. I haven't authorized anybody to look for it for me." Then, characteristically, Goldwater provided an out for himself should he need it later: "But who can tell what will happen a year from now. A man would be a damn fool to predict with finality what he would do in this unpredictable world."[2]

Still, Goldwater seemed safely dormant. William Miller, the upstate New York congressman who had received a $30,000 loan from Laurance Rockefeller[3] before joining Goldwater on the Republican ticket, recalls the Rockefeller-Goldwater détente with wonder. "I've never seen anyone more susceptible to a pat on the back than Barry Goldwater. He responded to all manner of flattery. Dick Nixon, when he was president, would take Barry to Burning Tree for a round of golf and Barry would be in his hip pocket for another six months."[4]

All signs pointed to a first ballot nomination for Rockefeller. But the governor was having more trouble at home in early 1963—trouble which would go largely unreported during the newspaper strike but which would later undermine his attempt to portray himself as an "economic conservative."

Rockefeller had pledged that he would offer no new taxes in his second term. Increased state activity would be paid for by revenues generated from accelerated economic movement. By January, it was clear that revenues would fall short of expectations and that higher taxes would be needed to avoid deficit spending. Both Rockefeller and T. Norman Hurd, then the governor's budget director, claim that they didn't know their problem in late October 1962, when Rockefeller made the "no tax" pledges in the course of his reelection campaign. Rockefeller asked for a $105 million increase in state charges on auto licenses and liquor. With a straight face, he called them "fees," never once admitting that they were taxes. He fooled no one. Upstate newspaper support eroded, the legislature's Republican leadership rebelled, and Rockefeller was humiliated. Eventually, the governor compromised, but the 1963 legislative session was by far Rockefeller's worst. He not only reneged on a campaign promise but also deliberately sidestepped important questions when the answers might hurt his presidential prospects. Said the New York *Times* of Rockefeller's "interest in 1964": "It was obvious from the start of the session that he would, if possible, shun issues not helpful to him politically."[5]

Unease about Rockefeller among Republican legislators was soon matched by the qualms of progressive Republicans on the national scene, who felt the governor was overcompensating toward Goldwater and the right. Their irritation reached a peak on April 9, when Rockefeller was asked to comment on the Kennedy administration's policy of restraining Cuban exiles from staging raids against their homeland. Rockefeller seemed to be suggesting that Kennedy was following a policy of appeasing the Russians by suppressing exile efforts to oust Castro. Newspaper reaction was swift. The Washington *Evening Star* said: "Governor Rockefeller . . . made it clear enough that he wants to be President. But, in our eyes, he offered no evidence that he deserves to be. His performance with respect to Cuba was a shabby bit of politicking. . . . Plainly, the Governor is trying to smear the President by expressing a 'hope' that he is not an appeaser. There is no charge and no proof—only the insinuation."[6]

At home, the reaction was no less severe. The New York *Herald Tribune*, almost a house organ of the Eastern Republican establishment, titled its editorial "Relax, Governor!" The *Trib* suggested that "Governor Rockefeller calm down. If he engages in a contest with Sen. Goldwater to see who can throw the most

The Governor Moves Right

matches into the most inflammable material, someone is going to set up an opposition line, peddling asbestos garments and fire-extinguishers."[7]

None of this slowed the Rockefeller drive. Yet it seemed clear that Rockefeller was the front-runner only by process of elimination. His strength was thin; any jolt could destroy his campaign. Few realized that just such a blow was coming, but there were signs. Republicans eager to endorse Rockefeller publicly had been dissuaded by George Hinman. Volunteers offering to establish Rockefeller-for-President clubs received a letter urging the party to remain "flexible," adding—cryptically for a man eager to be president—words similar to those Barry Goldwater had uttered months before: "No one can now foresee the situation that will prevail in 1964."[8]

Even Goodwin Knight, the former governor of California, was urged to close a Rockefeller-for-President organization in Los Angeles. The incident was reported across the country—but no one outside Rockefeller's innermost circle could account for the strange behavior.

The speculation ended abruptly on May 4, 1963, when Rockefeller announced that he had married a 36-year-old divorcee named Margaretta Fitler (Happy) Murphy—little more than a year after his divorce. The press was informed three hours after the event. Barry Goldwater heard the news from Rockefeller himself, he had been on the roof of his Washington home fixing his television antenna when he got the call. Liberals like Jacob Javits were informed by the governor's brother David—another source of irritation to progressives who felt Rockefeller was paying more attention to Goldwater than to them. Countless Rockefeller supporters were told by George Hinman, and each was assured that any adverse reaction would fade quickly. Rockefeller and his bride left the next morning for Monte Sacro, the governor's ranch near Chirgua, Venezuela, where little good was done for the cause back home as the newlyweds cavorted happily—and publicly—clad in blue jeans and sport shirts.

The Rockefellers returned to New York 17 days later, to find

269

the governor's presidential campaign all but dead and buried. Rockefeller felt he could have both the presidency and the woman he loved. He was not prepared for the reaction—in retrospect, perhaps more an expression of below-the-surface dissatisfaction with Rockefeller the candidate than of moral revulsion at Rockefeller the man.

The reaction was immediate and broad-based. Congressional mailbags overflowed with hostile comment. The clergy was livid; even the nation's most distinguished Protestant theologian, Dr. Reinhold Niebuhr, said he agreed with his cleaning woman that Rockefeller's remarriage had been "too quick."[9] No less compassionate was the Hudson River Presbytery, which admonished the Reverend Marshall L. Smith for officiating at the ceremony, claiming he was "a disturber of the peace and unity of the church."[10]

Claire Booth Luce declared that Rockefeller's actions would "cause a rise in the U.S. divorce rate."[11] Stewart Alsop wrote that Rockefeller "could have decided either to remarry or to run for president, but not both."[12] Alsop said Rockefeller should have made a nationwide "Duke of Windsor" speech and waited until 1968 to become a candidate. Another columnist suggested, perhaps wishfully, that people didn't talk about Nelson Rockefeller and the presidency anymore.

Whatever hope Rockefeller had for a softening of the reaction was short-lived. The last premarriage Gallup poll had Rockefeller leading Goldwater 43 percent to 26 percent as the choice of Republican voters for the presidency. The first postmarriage poll virtually reversed these totals. Goldwater was favored by 40 percent of the Republican electorate, Rockefeller by 29 percent. Rockefeller's remarriage had the effect of emancipating those rank-and-file Republicans who had really wanted Goldwater all along.

His marital woes had one positive effect, anyway. So generous were his relatives that the former governor is probably the first politician to have piled up a campaign surplus in six figures in losing a White House sweepstakes. After the final accounting, having spent over $3 million in the primaries, Nelson wound up with $100,000 from his sister Abby and $250,000 from brother David in his personal bank account.[13] He explained that it was because he had "more money at that time in my [campaign] account to pay all of the political expenditures which I paid than was required." Why, then, accept the $350,000? Rockefeller recalled:

It happened that I was divorced. It happened that I was remarried. It happened some members of the family were upset. I guess this happens in any family. It happened that these two were. It happened that they understood. And that as a gesture of their appreciation of what I was trying to do in the sense that I was keeping going, despite the fact that I was under bitter attack on many sides, because I had gotten remarried, this was a gesture of friendship and love and affection from two members of my family who had been upset.

I am embarrassed to say this, but it is a fact.[14]

CHAPTER 26

The Governor
Moves Left

SINCE Rockefeller was not about to abandon his drive for the Republican nomination, a new strategy was needed. Rockefeller's aides thought they saw a way back for the governor in late June at the Republican National Committee meeting in Denver. Party leaders outside the industrialized states seemed seriously to contemplate turning the GOP into a white man's party. Conservative ideology offered the guideposts. As far back as 1957, when the first civil rights bill was being introduced in Congress, the *National Review*, oracle of the Republican right, had published an editorial entitled "Why the South Must Prevail."[1] It said in part:

> The central question that emerges . . . is whether the white community in the South is entitled to take such measures as are necessary to prevail politically and culturally, in areas in which it does not predominate numerically.
>
> The sobering answer is yes—the white community is entitled because, for the time being, it is the advanced race.

When the 1963 Civil Rights Bill was introduced in Congress, *National Review* editor William F. Buckley, Jr. wrote that the individual states should be left to govern their own affairs, and that states' rights should not be abandoned—Goldwater's position exactly, as stated in "A Conservative Creed." Buckley would write in February 1964 that "I believe in potholing, rather than broadening, the highway to the voting booth,"[2] an eloquent expansion of his earlier statement that the idea that everyone is qualified to vote is "one of the great self-delusions of democracy."

If Rockefeller believed these and similar statements to be just rhetoric, he changed that view when the Young Republicans convened in San Francisco a week after their elders had met in Denver. It was this meeting which was to trigger a Rockefeller response which Republicans remember to this day.

The Young Republican caucus was of no real importance. It merely symbolized the rightward drift of the party—a movement Rockefeller could identify and challenge. Most of the YRs were for Goldwater before they got to San Francisco. A kind word for Rockefeller was heresy. Failure to support the "Liberty Amendment" (to outlaw the income tax and make up the lost revenue through the sale of unspecified government-owned industries) was proof positive of liberalism. The ultrarightists were in firm control.

The Young Republicans had acted like spoiled children, and word of their activities was widely reported. Already concerned that the party might make a real push for the white segregationist vote, Rockefeller perceived the YR convention as further evidence of a rightward tilt, and he saw in that shift a last chance to rally moderate Republicanism and secure the presidential nomination for himself.

"Nelson needed an issue," recalls one of his closest advisers "and the extreme right was it." The YR antics served as Rockefeller's excuse to abandon his neo-conservatism, much as his own remarriage had given the party's true conservatives the excuse to abandon him. Rockefeller threw down the gauntlet in the "Bastille Day Declaration" of July 14, 1963. Party harmony had been necessary to his presidential prospects before his remarriage had crippled his plans. Party discord was needed now. And that is exactly what Rockefeller created. The Hinman school of accommodation was bankrupt; the Morhouse school of confrontation was the order of the day. But Morhouse was under wraps, and it fell to Hinman, ever the faithful soldier, to fashion the Bastille Day encyclical. "When George Hinman gets mad," says Rockefeller speechwriter Hugh Morrow, "he writes Italian opera. I had to edit out words like 'fascist' and reduce the splutters and screams."[3]

First, Rockefeller had to explain why he had waited until now to denounce the Republican right:[4] "Many leaders of the Republican Party, myself included, have been working to put the party in a position to face the challenge of the 1964 election as a strong and united fighting force."

Moving on, Rockefeller said: "In making this effort toward unity for principle, it was my conviction that the activities of the radical right, while deeply disturbing in many ways, would represent an inconsequential influence on the Republican Party." Rockefeller went on to list "fundamental articles of Republican faith"—preservation of freedom throughout the world, equal opportunity for all, the federal system of government, the free enterprise system, fiscal integrity, freedom of speech and information. "Many of us," said Rockefeller, "have been taking too lightly the growing danger to these principles through subversion from the radical right."

It was time to wake up: ". . . the Republican Party is in real danger of subversion by a radical, well-financed, and highly disciplined minority." As evidence of the impending coup, Rockefeller offered the Young Republican gathering two weeks earlier in San Francisco. It was the only proof he had:

> . . . every objective observer at San Francisco has reported that the proceedings there were dominated by extremist groups, carefully organized, well-financed, and operated through the tactics of ruthless, roughshod intimidation. These are the tactics of totalitarianism.

The Governor Moves Left

Unfortunately, this cannot be brushed off as irresponsibility. For youth *is* responsible. The leaders of the Birchers and others of the radical right lunatic fringe—every bit as dangerous to American principles and American institutions as the radical left—who successfully engineered this disgraceful subversion of a great and responsible auxiliary of the Republican Party are the same people who are now moving to subvert the Republican Party itself.

. . . They are purveyors of hate and distrust in a time when, as never before, the need of the world is for love and understanding.[5]

Here, Rockefeller shifted gears, attacking the idea of a white man's party designed to lure Southern states into the Republican column:

Completely incredible as it is to me, it is now being seriously proposed to the Republican Party, as a strategy for victory in 1964, that it write off Negro and other minority groups, it deliberately write off the great industrial states of the north (representing nearly 50 percent of the country's population), that it write off the big cities, and that it direct its appeal primarily to the electoral votes of the South, plus the West and a scattering of other states.

The transparent purpose behind this plan is to erect political power on the outlawed and immoral base of segregation and to transform the Republican Party from a national party of all the people to a sectional party for some of the people. . . .

A program based on racism or sectionalism would in and of itself not only defeat the Republican Party in 1964, but would destroy it altogether.[6]

By refusing to target specifically those who had actually disrupted the Young Republican convention in San Francisco, Rockefeller seemed to be branding all conservative Republicans as radicals. He waited a full month before correcting that impression. In a letter to Jean McKee, head of the New York Young Republicans, Rockefeller wrote of his July 14 declaration: "This statement . . . is not an attack on responsible conservatism in our Party."[7]

Most Republican conservatives took the Bastille Day declaration to be just that, and the one who seemed to take it the hardest was Barry Goldwater. Twelve years later, Goldwater said of his run for the presidency: "I knew I couldn't win. The only reason I ran was to keep the party out of the hands of the Eastern establishment."[8]

The Holy War began. Goldwater left it to Senator Carl Curtis of Nebraska to reply:[9]

> It is no longer possible to remain silent in the face of such self-serving tactics by a man desperately trying to retrieve his declining political fortunes.
>
> It is my considered judgment that a man who would take such desperate and destructive measures against his own party in a gamble to gain some temporary, personal advantage has already forfeited any claim to loyalty from any part of the party organization.

Curtis's speech was reproduced for distribution to the Goldwater organizations around the country and became the standard rebuttal to Rockefeller.

The governor seemed eager for combat. He challenged Goldwater to debate (declined) and told a press conference: "The great threat is whether the radical wing, part of Senator Goldwater's following, will be able to capture its leader."[10]

"I'm not going to answer this sort of thing from Rockefeller," the senator replied. "He's using an old trick which the Democratic forces used against us for a long time, and I'm not going to fall for it."[11]

Here was the rub. Rockefeller had happily preached party unity when he seemed certain to be the nominee. Now that the tide had turned, it was no holds barred, and he was giving aid and comfort to the Democratic enemy.

On August 5, Rockefeller told an Albany press conference that he would not support Goldwater against Kennedy "if he were a captive of the radical right."

Rockefeller was happy with the exchanges, but the anticipated groundswell was not forthcoming. Expressions of support for the declaration came from New York's Senators Javits and Keating, and from Thomas Kuchel of California. But that was all. Rockefeller believed that he was fighting the good fight. Now all he heard from Eisenhower, Nixon, Romney, and Scranton was silence. The Eastern establishment that had nominated Dewey and Eisenhower was quiet. Rockefeller, said Scranton, had gone too far. It was Rockefeller, not Goldwater, who was out in the cold.

By mid-September, Goldwater's nomination seemed secure. Republican politicians avoided Rockefeller like the plague. When he traveled to Illinois, even Charles Percy was missing, and Percy, a director of Chase Manhattan (a post he resigned in early 1964 to avoid any connection with Rockefeller Republicanism), had been the informal linchpin in Rockefeller's Midwest campaign.

Rockefeller's effort had about it the unmistakable smell of political death. His attempts at landing a national-class campaign manager bordered on the absurd. He first asked Leonard Hall, a former national Republican chairman and onetime Rockefeller rival for the New York governorship. Hall said no. So did Meade Alcorn of Connecticut, another former national chairman. Back to Hall. Again, no. Finally, Rockefeller selected John A. Wells, who had managed Javits's reelection campaign in 1962. Wells then proposed that he be staff director, with Hall as the honorary campaign chief. Rockefeller offered him "a handsome retainer." This offended Hall more than anything. "Well, Nelson," he said, "I've been in the practice of law for 40 years and I haven't had to do that yet."[12] Hall then sat out the presidential nomination fight.

Rockefeller formally announced for the presidency at 8 A.M. on November 7, 1963, so that he could appear nationwide on the *Today* show. He had no real prospect of capturing the nomination.

Then, 15 days later, as in 1960 when the U–2 incident provided the excuse for Nelson's challenging Nixon, the unpredictable occurred. President Kennedy lay dead, and Rockefeller saw daylight. It was a common assumption in Washington that Barry Goldwater's presidential hopes had died with John Kennedy. It was thought that Goldwater's Southern strategy was useless against Lyndon Johnson and perhaps more important, it seemed that the industrial states, once conceded to Kennedy, were now ripe for a suitable Republican, a moderate who was not afraid of the cities.

But Rockefeller did not gain, despite Goldwater's misfortune. Too much antipathy remained. He could no longer wait for the party's leaders to come back to him; he would have to show them in the primaries. So Nelson Rockefeller began to recruit a campaign staff so extensive that it made the Draft Goldwater movement look pitiful by comparison.

The first test was New Hampshire. Rockefeller was from the East and had gone to Dartmouth. No matter that New Hampshire Republicans were generally conservative. Rockefeller had to do well there. The rules of political combat so dictated, and could not be changed.

Could Rockefeller change—again? "He's not a liberal," said Rockefeller's campaign manager, former governor Bert Teague, "and before we're through we're going to prove it."[13] Rockefeller, it turned out, had a secret weapon in New Hampshire—Barry Goldwater. Goldwater hated the factory tours and handshaking routines. Bone tired and fed up, Goldwater took a snipe at Rockefeller's love of this form of campaigning: "I'm not one of those baby-kissing, handshaking, blintz-eating candidates."[14]

The Rockefeller forces assigned bright students to dog Goldwater's every move, asking the same loaded questions at every opportunity. Before long, Goldwater was pictured as trigger-happy (he had come out for another exiles' invasion of

Cuba) and as a foe of Social Security (he proposed making it voluntary, not a particularly politic stance in a state with a higher-than-average percentage of elderly Social Security recipients). The final mistake came in late January 1964, when Goldwater said of the upcoming March 10 vote: "I don't think the outcome can possibly be convincing."[15] In a state where the only excitement is a presidential primary every four years, that deprecation did not go over well.

Rockefeller, meanwhile, was following the same handshaking route, scoring points simply by repeating Goldwater's misstatements verbatim. He seemed to make headway each time he challenged Goldwater to debate, until Senator Norris Cotton dug out a six-year-old Rockefeller letter declaring: "I cannot believe that series of debates between Republican candidates is the best way to strengthen the Republican Party."[16] The letter had been written by Rockefeller in 1958, when he was leading the pack for the New York State Republican gubernatorial nomination. The man challenging Rockefeller to debate was Leonard Hall.

The remarriage was hurting. Happy Rockefeller was hustled all over the state, the fresh girl next door. To the Manchester *Union Leader*'s publisher, William Loeb, Rockefeller was still a "wife swapper."

Going down to the wire, there were huge undecided totals in the pollsters' results. But many people had definitely decided something—they had decided against voting for either Goldwater or Rockefeller. By mid-January, the alternative was Henry Cabot Lodge. Rockefeller tried to have Lodge repudiate the write-in campaign being waged in his behalf—he spoke to Lodge in Saigon via transoceanic phone—but Lodge would do nothing of the kind. Rockefeller was furious: during the previous summer, Lodge had urged Rockefeller to run in order to stop Goldwater.

When the ballots were counted, Lodge had won, Goldwater was second, and Rockefeller third. The postmarriage strategy of proving himself by sweeping the primaries was in shambles. "The Republicans," wrote Bill Buckley, "would as soon nominate Tommy Manville as Rockefeller . . . he is in the clutch of a roaring, housewrecking, party-smashing egomania. . . . He's doing what he did in 1960 when, having failed to take it from Nixon, he degraded him. . . . He wants to rule or ruin."[17]

Rockefeller would dispute the "ruin" but not the "rule." He continued. The governor got the New Hampshire returns at his Fifth Avenue apartment. At five the next morning he was up. At seven, in a family jet, he was off to Oregon and a new challenge. Lodge was on the covers of the newsmagazines. Lodge was in the headlines. Pollster Lou Harris's first samplings of Oregon showed 46 percent for Lodge, 17 percent for Nixon, 14 percent for Goldwater, and 13 percent for Rockefeller. It looked hopeless. But as Theodore White would write: "It was as if the Red Queen in *Through the Looking Glass* had planned the elections of 1964—all should win, all should have a prize. Lodge should have New Hampshire, Rockefeller should have Oregon, Goldwater should have California—and Lyndon Johnson should have the country."[18]

Dispatched to Oregon was Robert Price, John Lindsay's campaign manager on loan to Rockefeller. In three weeks, Price developed mailing lists that swept the state. Rockefeller hit hard, for the first time using the word "mainstream," excluding Barry Goldwater, a term that would shadow Goldwater even after he won the nomination, when the Democrats used "mainstream" to great advantage. To counter Lodge, Rockefeller's forces coined the slogan "He cared enough to come." No one had to be told who didn't. On election night, Rockefeller had pulled a stunning upset. California was next. A victory there would give him one last slim chance for the nomination. Every Rockefeller resource —money and manpower—was funneled to California.

Goldwater needed another 225 votes to clinch the nomination. He had to beat Rockefeller in California. He could lose any battle but the last. And he was in trouble. Oregon had finished Lodge, and the momentum of Rockefeller's victory had established the New York governor as first in the California polls.

The Oregon pattern was followed. A professional organization was needed—Rockefeller volunteers were hard to come by —and by the time it was all over, Rockefeller had spent at least $3.5 million in California alone. A new slogan was created: "Which do you want—A Leader? or a Loner?" The pamphlet showed Rockefeller's photograph and a smaller picture of Lodge, Nixon, Romney, and Scranton, adding: "These men stand together on the party's principles." Juxtaposed was a picture of Goldwater with this text: "This man stands outside." Another part of the pamphlet was even more pejorative. The question was: "Whom do you want in the room with the H-Bomb button?" Lyndon Johnson would suggest the same in the general election.

For the first time in the campaign, Dwight Eisenhower became a significant factor. Both Rockefeller and Goldwater journeyed to the general's Palm Desert retreat, Rockefeller seeking support, Goldwater hoping for neutrality. Eisenhower faced a dilemma. He wanted to be a force for good in the party, but he didn't want to take sides. The solution, proposed by *Herald Tribune* president Walter Thayer, an anti-Goldwaterite, was to have the general contribute a signed *Tribune* article describing Ike's kind of president, a description that would fit Rockefeller without naming him.

On May 25 the article appeared—not only on the *Trib*'s front page but on the front page of the New York *Times* as well. Thayer also gave the article to the AP and UPI for simultaneous publication. Eisenhower reviewed his record in Social Security, medical care, civil rights, and a host of other areas that made Goldwater look like a member of some strange, unknown party. Appearing that evening at a college in California, Goldwater stood with an arrow under his arm and then turned so that it looked as if he had been shot in the back. On May 29, Goldwater strategist Cliff White announced that "California is not a conservative state,"[19] thereby beginning a detailed explanation of how Goldwater could be nominated without winning California.

As primary day neared, however, Goldwater's support held constant, while Rockefeller's seemed to be slipping into the undecided column. Goldwater was counterattacking, and he was scoring. Goldwater had Scranton and Romney announce that their inclusion in the Rockefeller brochure was without their consent and that they were supporting no candidate in the California primary.

Goldwater was also able cleverly to neutralize Eisenhower's article. He managed to arrange a private breakfast meeting with the former president's brother, Dr. Milton Eisenhower, on June 1, the day before the primary. Milton Eisenhower vehemently opposed Goldwater, and Goldwater's aides never misrepresented the purpose of the breakfast—which was to discuss the Critical Issues Council, a subsidiary of the National Republican Citizens Committee that Goldwater had opposed. But the mere fact of their meeting, coupled with President Eisenhower's assertion to the press; "You people tried to read Goldwater out of the party, I didn't,"[20] generated two primary day headlines giving the clear impression that Goldwater was not the pariah he had been made out to be, at least not to the brothers Eisenhower.

Afraid they were oversaturating the electorate, Rockefeller's forces virtually ceased campaigning on the Saturday before election day—just as a mass Goldwater blitz hit the print and electronic media. Campaign manager William Ronan flew home on Sunday, convinced Rockefeller would win. That was the day after Happy Rockefeller had given birth to a seven-pound, ten-ounce boy named Nelson Aldrich Rockefeller, Jr.—bouncing the remarriage issue back into the headlines. Years later, Richard Kleindienst said to Emmet Hughes: "I've told Dick Nixon, and he agrees, that the luckiest thing that ever happened to him was Nelson's baby right before the '64 California primary. It was Goldwater's terrible defeat in the general election that allowed Dick to come back in '68."[21]

The closeness of the results can be interpreted any way one wishes. The bottom line was still the same. Goldwater won with 51.6 percent of the vote to Rockefeller's 48.7 percent. By just 59,000 votes out of more than 2 million cast, Goldwater took the California primary—and the nomination.

The Governor Moves Left

Had Rockefeller won California, he might have stopped Goldwater, the top prize then being brokered to Scranton or Romney. He had been portrayed as a party wrecker and, if ever there was a time to lie low, to play the gracious loser, this was that time. But there was still a convention, still the formality, still one last chance to speak his mind—or to keep his peace.

But first, Rockefeller got behind a last minute attempt to wrest the nomination away from Goldwater and to give it to Scranton. With 600 votes solid for Goldwater, their efforts seemed hopeless. All the moderate forces could hope for was some kind of "incident" that would change the tone of the convention and give rise to a miracle.

It was a mad plan, wonderfully portrayed by Murray Kempton in the *New Republic*.[22] Comparing the convention with Chekhov's *The Cherry Orchard*, Kempton wrote: ". . . before the play had opened in San Francisco, Lopahin, the practical man, played by Senator Scott of Pennsylvania, had protested: '. . . Such odd, unbusinesslike people I never saw. You are told in plain Russian that your estate is about to be sold up and you just don't seem to take it in.' "

Gayeff, the hereditary proprietor, played perforce by William Scranton, speaks: " 'Tomorrow I must go to town. They have promised to introduce me to a certain general who might make us a loan.' "

Lyuboff Andreevna, his sister, in her one line by Nelson Rockefeller: " 'He's just raving. There aren't such generals.' "

On Tuesday, July 14, the platform was being considered. It was a long, dull evening, eight hours of boring debate. At 8:54 P.M. San Francisco time (11:54 P.M. back home in New York), Nelson Rockefeller stepped to the microphones to defend five amendments put forth by the moderate wing of the party.

Tom Braden, a syndicated columnist, former CIA official and onetime publisher of the Oceanside, Calif. *Blade-Tribune* (thanks to a loan from Nelson Rockefeller), once wrote of Rockefeller: "He is not merely 'nice.' In his second layer he is tough, and people who have had occasion to cross him in private dealings have been made immediately aware that he can be very tough indeed. . . . You might notice the toughness of Nelson Rockefeller in a curious narrowing of the eyes when he thinks someone is trying to take advantage of him, or is thinking of him solely for his money, or when things are going wrong, and someone suggests what he is working on might fail."[23]

Standing on the rostrum of the Cow Palace in San Francisco, the place where Barry Goldwater was to be nominated for the very office he himself had sought (the same Goldwater who had told Stewart Alsop "I haven't really got a first class brain"[24]), Nelson Rockefeller was tired. "He had," wrote Norman Mailer at the time, "a strong decent face and something tough as the rubber in a handball to his makeup, but his eyes had been punched out a long time ago—they had the distant lunar glow of the small sad eyes you see in a caged chimpanzee or a gorilla. . . ."[25]

He began speaking and the booing began almost immediately. The Goldwater command post sought to quiet its troops but could not. This was their day, and Nelson Rockefeller was not going to spoil it. Convention Chairman Thruston Morton and Congressman Mel Laird reminded Rockefeller of the five-minute time limit, and Rockefeller almost punched Laird in the face. Five minutes were allotted, said Rockefeller; booing didn't count. He would stand there until he could speak. "This is still a free country, ladies and gentlemen," said the governor. "Imagine," said Rockefeller years later, "if I'd won in California. There would have been an absolute donnybrook at the convention. I think it would have been so rough you just wouldn't have recognized this country because feelings would have been so bitter. It was bad enough when I lost and got up to speak. You can imagine what it would have been like had I won California and gone before that group."[26]

In characteristic understatement about adversity, Rockefeller said of that evening: "Taking a stand on the subject of extremism at the Republican convention and being roundly booed for 15 minutes was a really interesting and valuable experience."[27]

Still, Rockefeller could not sit back and do nothing. In accepting the nomination, Barry Goldwater declared that "extremism
in defense of liberty is not a vice. Moderation in pursuit of justice is not a virtue." Rockefeller said he was "amazed and
shocked."[28] Such a statement, said the governor, raises "grievous
questions in the minds, hearts, and souls of Republicans in every
corner of our party."[29]

Rockefeller did not campaign for Goldwater in any real sense.
He skipped the huge Goldwater rally on October 26, 1964, in
Madison Square Garden in order to speak at a $50-a-plate fund-
raiser for the Albany County GOP. He had announced publicly
in 1960 that he would vote for Nixon. Now, in 1964, he claimed
secrecy of the ballot and refused to say how he would vote.

After the election, Goldwater singled out Rockefeller and
Governor Romney of Michigan for special blame. Rockefeller
replied that Goldwater, as the presidential candidate, had "undermined Republican unity and threatened public confidence in the
very future of the party."[30]

Richard Nixon called Rockefeller a "spoilsport." "He got his
pound of flesh," said Nixon. "He brought on this split in the
party. Now I think he should try to heal it."[31]

Rockefeller called Nixon's statement "peevish."

Looking back, Nelson Rockefeller says of 1964: "I went
against the party. It was a terrible thing to do. But I had to make
a point."[32]

Many Rockefeller associates view the 1964 debacle as the
point of no return for Rockefeller with the Republican right
wing. Nevertheless, those 15 minutes before the Republican convention in 1964 remain his finest hour. "You know what his only
regret is," says New York County Republican leader Vincent
Albano, who was there. "Nelson was damn mad that he'd missed
prime time back East."[33]

CHAPTER 27

Nelson's "Worst Investment"

THE Republican Party was shattered. The greatest electoral margin ever given any party anywhere, 16 million votes, had wiped out every traditional GOP stronghold. No one in 1964 had the slighest notion of what the Republican Party would be like in four years. At the moment, wrote Theodore White, no formal measure could convey the "particular odor of self-doubt, self-hate and defeat that stank in the corridors of the Party from top to bottom."[1]

One would think, as did David Broder, that it was well that the conservatives had gotten it out of their system. "After the debacle," wrote Broder, "I thought, the proprietors of the defeat would have no choice but to confess the bankruptcy of their dream."[2] Not so, said Alexander Lankler, a Washington lawyer who had worked for Rockefeller's campaign. "No matter how badly mauled the party is, they will still want to control it. It may not be much, you see, but it's still bigger, more effective, and more salable than any other lobby they can get hold of."[3] Lankler was right. And Rockefeller was out.

Bruised and battered, Nelson Rockefeller came away from the politics of 1964 isolated on the far left of the Republican

Party. He had known that the country was not ready for Goldwater conservatism. Now he was being blamed for the defeat. All that was left was the chairmanship of the GOP's moderate forces, a position so dubious that *National Review* publisher William Rusher likened it to becoming "captain of the Titanic ten minutes before she went down."[4]

Once again, Nelson Rockefeller found it necessary to remove himself from presidential politics. This time, it was harder: 1960 had been a lark, a last-minute gamble, a fling, but Rockefeller had gone flat-out for 1964. It was the only time he would ever do so, and it remains his most startling loss, an unmistakable confirmation that Rockefeller Republicanism would never capture the party. Of course, he still wanted to be president, but 1964 had taken its toll, and for three years he would brood in self delusion.

"Something happens in life and you lose ambition because you have a sense of fulfillment," Rockefeller said in September 1967. "There are things that happen inside. I'm not a psychiatrist or a psychologist. I can't analyze it for you exactly. But I just don't have the ambition or the need or inner drive—or whatever the word is—to get in again."[5] "Do you remember a book called *What Makes Sammy Run?* Well, whatever factors made Sammy run made me run, too. I suppose I wanted to prove myself or something. I've run. It's behind me. . . . It's just gone, as far as I'm concerned. . . . You understand what I'm trying to say . . . really I don't want to get into it . . . you know . . . I just won't . . . I don't understand it myself."[6]

No one else did either, but it was just as well. "After the Bastille Day speech and the reception at the Cow Palace," remembers Robert Douglass, "and the Fifth Avenue Compact in 1960, most of the Republican Party to the right of left wouldn't have anything to do with him."[7] Rockefeller's political liabilities within his own party, wrote Tom Wicker in 1966, are "worse than close friendship with Mao Tse-tung."[8]

Another try for the presidency was never far from Nelson Rockefeller's mind, but a first priority, again, was survival at home. A tough gubernatorial election was slated for 1966, and the pundits were already heralding the end of the Rockefeller era. To prove them wrong, Rockefeller saw, as a first step, a GOP takeover of the New York City mayoralty.

The city and its Democratic rulers had long been a thorn in Rockefeller's side. Mayor Wagner enjoyed the annual legislative jousts with the governor, and those battles had often proved embarrassing to Rockefeller; 1965 offered a new chance to wrest control of City Hall, and a young Republican politician was dazzling the media with his charm. He was John Lindsay, once called New York's "golden *goy*,"[9] a four-term Republican congressman, almost as tall as Lincoln, with dirty-blond curls and chiseled good looks. As a legislator, Lindsay admitted that he came "close to the edge of being ineffective"[10]—he had even supported Charlie Halleck over Jerry Ford for minority leader.

"I'll tell you what kind of guy Lindsay is," says one of the former mayor's former aides. "He's the type who, when he was at St. Paul's, would go down to New York drinking with the boys, but he would be the first one to get sick. And then he would go out for the lacrosse team, instead of football." He is, says a friend, a "square saint."[11]

John Lindsay had supported Nelson Rockefeller for governor in 1958 ("I had never even met him,"[12] recalls Lindsay), but New York was never really big enough for the both of them. For one thing, Lindsay prized his independence, as Rockefeller knew. "Voters react to you intuitively," Nelson once said. "And that's the important thing John has going for him—they can *feel* his independence."[13]

Rockefeller himself first felt Lindsay's independence in 1961. Lindsay had been toying with the idea of running for mayor, but the governor had decided that state Attorney General Louis Lefkowitz should make the race. Lindsay, thought Rockefeller, would balance the ticket nicely if he would run for controller. Early in the spring of 1961, Rockefeller summoned Lindsay to his Fifth Avenue apartment. Lindsay was about to begin a speech to the Ninth Assembly District Republican Club when he took the governor's urgent call. Nat Hentoff picks up the story as Lindsay told it to him:

"John," the Governor began cheerfully, "I want you to run for controller. Would you come over immediately to meet with us?"

"Us?" Lindsay asked suspiciously.

"Yes, the rest of the ticket is here along with Javits and a few others."

Lindsay immediately decided that he did not want to face mass persuasion that evening. "I'm giving a speech," he told the governor.

"Well, can you come up immediately afterwards?"

"Nelson, it's going to be a long speech."

"That's all right. We'll be here all night."

Lindsay breathed deeply, and said firmly into the telephone, "This isn't right or fair. I'm not going to walk in on that mob."

"All right," said the governor, "We'll go into another room first and we'll talk about it."

"Nothing doing," said Lindsay. "I know damn well what's happening. Javits and Lefkowitz are desperate to find a Wasp for the ticket. Nelson, I'll be glad to have eggs with you in the morning, but I'm not coming over tonight."[14]

Further attempts were made to pressure Lindsay into running for Manhattan district attorney, but in the end his only connection with the 1961 campaign was service in the largely honorific post of campaign manager for Lefkowitz.

Rockefeller and Lindsay next clashed in 1963. Rockefeller was promoting his cousin, Richard Aldrich, for the Republican nomination for city councilman-at-large from Manhattan. Lindsay had been supporting GOP district leader Richard Lewisohn, and he continued to do so. "I don't care whose cousin he is,"[15] said Lindsay of Aldrich as he went public with the story. Lindsay charged that New York County Republican leader Vincent

Albano had hold him that he would be considered an "insurgent" if he continued to back Lewisohn. Rockefeller angrily replied at a press conference that he had never ordered Albano to "deliver" the nomination to Aldrich—although Lindsay maintains that Albano was backing Lewisohn until Rockefeller switched signals. "It was at Toots Shor's restaurant," recalls Lindsay. "Rockefeller told Albano that the party's candidate was Aldrich, and that was it."[16] At a meeting of the New York GOP County Committee, Aldrich defeated Lewisohn, 2,057 votes to 311. Lewisohn could easily have gone the primary route, charging "bossism" in the selection of Aldrich but he gracefully withdrew, saying he did not want to harm Rockefeller's chances for the presidential nomination.

"John hated him," recalls New York *Post* publisher Dorothy Schiff. "I remember him telling me at that time that Rockefeller buys everything from women to delegates and he certainly felt that Nelson was always trying to keep him down."[17]

The battle lines were drawn for the 1965 mayoralty race. Rockefeller had been primarily interested in pushing John J. Gilhooley, a Brooklynite who had been affixed to the GOP citywide ticket in 1961. The only other outstanding choices were Lindsay or Senator Jacob Javits. And the enmity between Javits and Rockefeller at that time seemed to rival that between Rockefeller and Lindsay.

Javits and Rockefeller had both stood for reelection in 1962. Javits had defeated his opponent by almost a million votes, a startling performance nearly double Rockefeller's margin over Morgenthau. Rockefeller had always feared a Javits-oriented Republican establishment attracting an independent liberal power base that would erode his own.

Rockefeller seemed to have good reason to worry. In January 1965, having again been pushed out of the spotlight—this time by Rockefeller's 1964 presidential race—the senator held a background press conference for reporters and said, though not for direct quotation, that he did not plan to support Rockefeller for president in 1968. This statement triggered a scramble for the mayoral nomination. Both Javits and Lindsay indicated that they might run if the GOP leaders would unite behind a candidate by March 1, so that there would be enough time to mount a credible campaign. Rockefeller was then in the midst of his first Democratic-controlled legislative session. He was trying to avoid antagonizing Mayor Wagner, and he was not about to accept Javits's and Lindsay's demands—there would be time enough later.

By March 1, Lindsay and Javits had both formally withdrawn their candidacies. Rockefeller charged that both had ducked out of the race, trying to fix the blame on him. A nine-month campaign wasn't necessary, said Rockefeller. What was needed was a candidate who had "the desire to run."[18] By May, Lindsay had reversed himself, and the first of the great Lindsay-Rockefeller wars began. Two monumental egos with similar political goals jockeyed for the same slice of the party pie. The campaign to come proved to be as dog-eat-dog as the job itself. Later, Lindsay would growl that being mayor is "like being a bitch in heat. You stand still and you get screwed, you start running and you get bit in the ass."[19]

As usual, the big problem was money. Before agreeing to run, Lindsay wanted a guarantee of Rockefeller financial support— roughly $500,000. "I remember John and Bob Price [Lindsay's campaign manager] came up to see me in Albany," said Rockefeller. "I guess," said Rockefeller, "John didn't want to be a part of asking me for money, so he spent his time talking to Happy, and Price and I ironed out the details for the $500,000."[20]

Lindsay wanted the money, but he also wanted Rockefeller not to tell anyone about it. He didn't want to appear to be a Rockefeller tool. "Probably what happened," recalled one friend of both Rockefeller and Lindsay, "was that Bob Price said to Rockefeller, 'We'll take the money and you be quiet about it.'" That arrangement seemed to work well until a reporter asked Lindsay if Rockefeller was helping his campaign financially. Lindsay denied, and continued to deny, getting any help, as did Price.

These point-blank denials evidently riled the governor. The balloon burst on July 5. Rockefeller had had a "little interview" with Emmet Hughes at Pocantico, and the untold tale of Lindsay's candidacy was now told in Hughes's *Newsweek* column.

The company line, as written by Hughes, was that Rockefeller had to address his initial appeals to Javits because he was senior to Lindsay in the party, but that the governor had opposed an early candidacy by either man. "For some two months, beginning in late 1964," Hughes reported, "the governor kept pressing the senator. One early February day in Washington, Rockefeller (and two of his aides) left a long quiet lunch with Javits quite convinced that the senator, at last, was persuaded to run. He was wrong: by Sunday, February 28, Rockefeller learned that Javits had finally decided against the race, and on that day the governor held his first long conference with Lindsay."[21] Hughes insisted that Rockefeller played a decisive role in moving Lindsay back into contention by exercising leadership and promising that the Rockefeller family fortunes would "guarantee the covering of $500,000 of campaign expenses."[22]

Why did the *Newsweek* story emerge? One theory was that Rockefeller was trying to pressure Lindsay into supporting him for governor the following year in case Javits challenged his control of the party. Several weeks earlier, on May 15, powerful State Senator John Hughes of Syracuse had written Javits a letter that was quickly circulated among Republican leaders. The Syracusan predicted that "a campaign in which the governor runs for reelection will bring nothing but disaster. It gets down to a rather basic decision whether the party should be irrevocably damaged because of one person . . . the fact is we are totally lacking in leadership and the governor cannot lead since there are very few who will follow. He has no right to take the party, the legislature and many local officials down with him."[23]

In any event, Lindsay quickly denied the *Newsweek* story, accurately labeling it a "plant" while lying about its veracity. Soon after, Lindsay was asked if he would accept the $500,000 if it were offered. "I don't think so," said Lindsay. "I don't think it would be right to accept that amount of money from two or three people."[24] Two weeks later, Lindsay said he would not participate in any "dump Rockefeller" movement, and the Rockefeller family eventually coughed up just about the entire half million.

The tension between the two continued through the campaign. Lindsay rejected the help of "national" Republican figures, a category that he expanded to include Rockefeller, but accepted the assistance of Senator Javits, whom he classified as a "city" figure.[25] On election night, as the first Republican mayor since Fiorello La Guardia claimed victory in a New York City mayoralty race, Lindsay aides unsuccessfully sought to block Rockefeller from the view of television cameras focused on the banner-bedecked stage. "I had a hell of a time getting in there," recalls Rockefeller.[26] But he did, and he walked right up to Lindsay, who visibly reddened when Rockefeller put an arm around him and said, "Well, *we* did it."[27]

At the very least, Lindsay should have been sensitive to Rockefeller's justifiable pride. After all, it was Lindsay himself who said: "There are some techniques which you've just got to remember. One of the main ones is that when you're campaigning you have to ask and thank, ask and thank, again and again. For money. For support of all kinds. No matter how sophisticated they are, people like to be asked, and they like to be thanked. Some politicians have no compunctions about continually asking. It still kills me to do it, but that's a rule you have to learn."[28]

Later, Lindsay explained his public denials of aid from the Rockefellers. "It was not in their interests or in my interest to have that widely broadcast and become the dominant theme of the campaign," Lindsay bitterly complained. "Maybe Nelson figured that if he was responsible for that much money, he owned you. Money is power, and people are afraid of it."[29]

In all, the Rockefeller family financed about 20 percent of Lindsay's successful mayoralty campaign. Nelson himself pumped $90,000 of the $500,000 family total into the Republican-Liberal Committee for Effective Candidates. But the price of their support was actually 60 percent higher: they were forced to pay another $300,000 in gift taxes on the donations to Lindsay committees.

"I wouldn't call it an investment," Rockefeller explained with the hindsight of a decade. "It was a campaign contribution. Well, not all investments work out. I didn't do it as a personal investment. I did it because I thought he was the best person to be mayor of the City of New York on the Republican side who had a chance of getting elected."[30]

"Well," Rockefeller recently added, "that didn't get us off to the best start."[31] And according to Hugh Morrow, Rockefeller's longtime aide who had been loaned to Lindsay during the mayoral campaign, "That $500,000 was one of the worst investments in the history of American politics as far as Nelson Rockefeller was concerned."[32]

CHAPTER 28

Throwing Garbage

MORROW was right. Once Lindsay was in office, the underlying tension between governor and mayor escalated, heightened by the inevitable conflict in their official roles, but often brought to a boil simply because of the personalities involved.

Lindsay had inherited long-neglected problems, and he immediately sought to solve them with the same kind of bold solutions that had become a Rockefeller trademark. But the city needed money and was forced, by law, to seek the state legislature's approval for almost every levy. The 1966 legislative session became heated, as the city sought more state aid. There followed a conciliatory Christmas message from Lindsay to Rockefeller, a message which further stamped the handsome young mayor as the spokesman for the cities, an emerging force on the national political scene who could interfere with the political plans of more established national leaders—like governors.

Paranoia became the watchword. Lindsay used the occasion of a nationally televised interview in November 1967 to say that while Rockefeller had ruled himself out of the running for the presidency, "should he change his mind, I think it would be a good thing for my party and for my country."[1] That statement, combined with some "Draft Rockefeller" clubs being organized by Lindsay strongman Sid Davidoff, was interpreted by Rockefeller as a deliberate attempt to put him on the spot. Only the month before, while Rockefeller was promoting liberal Republican harmony behind the candidacy of Michigan's George Romney, Lindsay had held a private briefing for Washington reporters, saying Illinois Senator Charles Percy would be the strongest nominee.

The same Nelson Rockefeller who had forced the capitulation of Richard Nixon in 1960 and hurled back the jeers of the GOP rank and file in 1964 was now, in 1967, taking on the likes of Sid Davidoff, then a coat-holder for the mayor. "How paranoid can he get,"[2] said a friend of the governor.

The following February, the ties between Rockefeller and Lindsay rotted along with some 100,000 tons of garbage that piled up during a nine-day strike by the city's sanitationmen. Lindsay had been irreparably tarnished on his very first night as mayor when the Transport Workers Union struck the city's subway system. He had given in to union leader Mike Quill's demands then, but he was determined to stand firm this time.

A week earlier, union members had thrown eggs at their president, John DeLury, for agreeing to a settlement worked out by two mediators appointed by Lindsay. DeLury had no choice but to follow his membership and was soon jailed for violating the no-strike provisions of the state's Taylor Law. Meanwhile, Lindsay refused to negotiate while the union was on strike. To do so, he said, would be yielding to "blackmail." DeLury's answer, a well-worn labor phrase, was: "No contract, no work."

To which Lindsay countered: "Now is the time, and here is the place, for the city to determine what it is made of; whether it will bow to unlawful force, or whether it will resist with all the strength and courage that 8 million people can find within themselves. . . . If the city submits to this reckless, unprincipled use of power, seldom again will a municipal labor contract be agreed to on its merits."[3]

Throwing Garbage

On the morning of February 8, after the Health Department had declared a state of emergency, Lindsay had breakfast with the governor and asked that the National Guard be called out. "I told him," Lindsay said later, "that it would have helped the city and possibly the country if the people in the slums could have seen the men of the National Guard—*their* National Guard, by the way—working constructively with their hands instead of patroling the streets with rifles at the ready."[4]

Rockefeller refused Lindsay's call for the Guard, telling reporters that "my grandfather called out the National Guard in a strike, and a lot of people got killed. I don't want that to happen again." Ten days later, when the strike was settled, at an Albany news conference, Rockefeller was asked if he was afraid of possible rioting if the troops had been called out. "Well," said Rockefeller, "did you, by any chance, see Rap Brown on television. . . . He said, 'This is what we're waiting for. We want the troops. We want to overthrow the government. We want to have rioting. We want to fight the soldiers. Bring them on!' "[5]

Rockefeller went on to say that there was a very real possibility of a general strike if he had called out the Guard. Six years later, he repeated this reasoning to the Senate Rules Committee as it considered his nomination for vice-president, adding, "I think this could have spread to a racial war, and I could visualize these National Guardsmen, if you will forgive me for saying so, who are young men from offices and architects and so forth, trying to pick up these huge garbage cans, and they would all have had hernias. And they would have been suing the state for years."[6]

Of all these reasons, the threat of a general strike and the general hostility toward Rockefeller that would likely follow his calling out the Guard were apparently controlling. The governor was angling for the 1968 presidential nomination. He had assiduously courted New York's labor leaders for years, successfully winning their support for governor in 1966. He was not ready to jeopardize that delicate relationship just to please John Lindsay.

"How do you figure Rockefeller," one of Lindsay's aides asked Nat Hentoff. "Does he really think he's going to get the Republican nomination this way? George Meany and Harry Van Arsdale can't help him there." "I'm afraid," added the mayor himself, "I'm screwing up someone's political plans."[7]

Apparently so. Rockefeller effectively removed Lindsay from dealing with the strike. All day long on February 8, Rockefeller conferred with John DeLury, conveniently released from jail for the negotiations, while Lindsay cooled his heels in an upstairs conference room in the governor's New York office on West 55th Street. The talks dragged on into the evening, DeLury and Rockefeller and his aides dining on a spread of steak sandwiches, french fries, salad, and apple pie, all wheeled down the street from the Gotham Hotel. "The best meal I had since I went to jail," said DeLury.[8]

Jail itself was the best thing to happen to DeLury in a long time. He became an instant hero to his membership. Of course, DeLury wanted a few privileges, like a private telephone and a bedboard for his back—both granted. More importantly, DeLury wanted to be jailed alone, without his fellow union leaders. John Lindsay recalls that DeLury came to him privately and said: "John, for God's sake, can you arrange for me to go to jail alone? Don't send any of my colleagues in the union, because I have to be the martyr. Otherwise I'm ruined."[9]

Lindsay agreed, and DeLury served his 15 days alone. Meanwhile, the city's press was urging the mayor to hold his ground. "Stand fast, Mr. Mayor," said the *Daily News*, analyzing the strike this way: "Instead of backing the mayor by calling up National Guardsmen, to show sanitation union head John DeLury who was boss, the Rock tried to harvest some political hay."[10]

The roles seemed reversed. "It's a wild situation," said Victor Gotbaum, head of the municipal employees union. "Rockefeller passes punitive labor legislation [the Taylor Law] and then lets union leaders out of jail; Lindsay favors mediation and now asks for a pound of flesh."[11] Said Lindsay, "I am shocked that Governor Rockefeller has capitulated to the union that is striking unlawfully against 8 million New Yorkers."[12]

Finally, after a humiliating rejection from legislative leaders when he asked to address them in a joint session, Rockefeller negotiated a settlement with the union—which the city had to underwrite. Lindsay denounced Rockefeller for "cowardice," for "capitulating to extortionist demands," and for "corrupting the fundamental rights of the people of New York."[13]

Shortly before Rockefeller would announce the outlines of the agreement, the governor tried to calm the situation by meeting with the mayor. Lindsay stubbornly refused. "What if I order you as your governor to meet with me?" Rockefeller asked. "Good night, Nelson," said Lindsay and hung up.[14] "Rockefeller and Lindsay are conceded to have reached general agreement in only one area," wrote Edward O'Neill of the *Daily News*. "They'd like to bury each other. In garbage."[15]

The reaction of Rockefeller's fellow Republican leaders was swift—and predictable, since it was an election year. Barry Goldwater said that the strike had "killed Rockefeller politically. . . . He thought more of a union leader's vote than he did of the health and welfare of the people."[16] Rockefeller did not reply, although he did respond to a question asking his reaction to Richard Nixon's criticism of his handling of the garbage crisis.

"Well," said the governor, "I could tell you a story that might be applicable." He told about the manager of a Peruvian mine high up in the Andes. While the manager was down at a bar in Lima, he got a cable from his superintendent saying that the workers had a rope around his neck and were going to hang him if he didn't get them a wage increase. So the manager sent for a telegram blank and wrote out a wire in which he said: *Tell those so-and-sos they can't intimidate me.* So, Rockefeller noted, "It depends on where you are."[17]

Soon the New York *Times* entered the fray, portraying Lindsay as the "hero" for refusing to capitulate, and labeling

Rockefeller's actions a "setback" to his presidential ambitions. The *Times* quoted "one Republican politician in Washington" as saying: "It may be that Nelson is just not a lucky man. Four years ago it was divorce and remarriage. This time it's Lindsay and garbage." But, asked the *Times*, will the voters be as angry in August (convention time) or November (the general election) as they are in February?[18]

CHAPTER 29

Lindsay on
the Move

BY the time Nelson Rockefeller's third try for the presidency
had fallen apart, there were more than enough reasons for its
demise; the garbage strike was only one liability, and a small one
at that. Nevertheless, Rockefeller was furious at the press. "The
Times," says Malcom Wilson, who at the time of the strike was
Nelson Rockefeller's lieutenant governor, "completely misrepresented the situation. Lindsay was portrayed as a knight in shin-
ing armor by his Boswells, the editorial board of the New York
Times, and we heard from our advance men around the country
that the Times, from which all the other papers take their cues,
was killing the presidential drive."[1]

Barely four months after the garbage strike, Lindsay and
Rockefeller were embroiled in another test of wills. New York's
junior senator, Robert F. Kennedy, had been killed on the night
of the California presidential primary. His successor would be
chosen by the governor to fill the remaining two years of
Kennedy's term.

It took Rockefeller three months to fill the vacancy, primarily
because of the Lindsay problem and the attendant disruption to
the party's various factions that would be caused by the appoint-

ment of *anyone*, a ruffling of the waters which Rockefeller preferred to put off until after the Republican National Convention.

Lindsay was reportedly told that he could have the post, but that he must request it so that Rockefeller would not have to bear the responsibility for having handed the city back to the Democrats. Lindsay was immediately mentioned as a possibility, along with a host of other candidates, including former HEW Secretary John Gardner, who was being supported publicly by David Rockefeller and whose Common Cause would later be funded by the family. Gardner declined, however, reaffirming his commitment to his new post with the Urban Coalition. By June 13, Lindsay had said that he had not "closed the door" to the Senate post. He denied that he would not accept it, adding that it had not been offered.

"The thing is," said Lindsay to Nat Hentoff, "Nelson doesn't realize that if he did offer it to me and I turned it down, that wouldn't hurt him or the man who does eventually accept the appointment. My answer would be that I have to support the mayoring business, that the action is here. Sure, I'd turn it down. I've told Nelson that in power, complexity, and responsibility, my job dwarfs even his and that he ought to keep that in mind. But he still thinks I might accept, and that makes him fearful. I know what he's thinking. 'If I do make you a senator, would you still come up to New York this summer and walk through the ghettos?' He's afraid there might be a riot while he's running for president and he wants me in the city to cool it for him. . . ."[2]

Finally, in a television interview in Little Rock on June 29, Rockefeller stated flatly that he would consider Lindsay only if the mayor asked him for the position. Lindsay's aides, who were caught in an uncomfortable situation, said that it was up to the governor to ask the mayor. The next day, Lindsay, under pressure, announced that he would not ask for the appointment. The Senate seat was eventually given to Charles Goodell, an obscure representative from upstate Jamestown. Ironically, Goodell was opposed by Lieutenant Governor Malcolm Wilson, who believed that he and Goodell shared the same politically conservative positions and that Goodell would unbalance the ticket if Wilson ran for governor in 1970.

Lindsay sought reelection in 1969, receiving only half the governor's 1965 financial support in a heated Republican primary campaign against Staten Island Senator John Marchi. Lindsay lost, but he retained the Liberal Party line and mounted an independent bid for a second term against Marchi (nominally backed by Rockefeller as the Republican choice) and organization Democrat Mario Procaccino. (After Lindsay bowed out of the 1973 mayoral race, Rockefeller coughed up a mere $5,000 for Marchi's second mayoral bid. Brother David, decidedly more involved in those "delicate relationships" between real estate interests and City Hall, doled out $5,000 each to Marchi and Democrat Abe Beame.[3])

Lindsay divided his opponents in 1969, winning reelection with 43 percent of the vote and moving ever closer toward the Democratic camp. Then, slowly, Lindsay began pressing another thorn into Rockefeller's political hide. He had united the state's six largest cities through their mayors; the Big Six were Albany, Buffalo, Rochester, Syracuse, Yonkers, and New York, all fighting for common goals. In creating this coalition, Lindsay effectively diluted the traditional upstate-downstate rivalry in the legislature. After the mayors symbolically marched up State Street in Albany to the Capitol, they won state revenue sharing in 1970 for the first time from the Republican-dominated legislature and from Rockefeller, who could not afford to alienate the cities' constituents as he campaigned for an unprecedented fourth four-year term. After all these legislative concessions, the crusher came in October when Lindsay endorsed Rockefeller's Democratic rival for governor, Arthur Goldberg.

Shortly after his victory, Rockefeller decided to lock horns with Lindsay again. Party loyalty could no longer stand in the way, since it was obvious that Lindsay had turned his back on the GOP. The governor named a commission to probe New

York City government. Lindsay quickly retaliated with his own commission to investigate the efficiency of New York State government. The result was another draw.

Name-calling reached its peak during the 1971 legislative session. Reelected lawmakers and the state administration, secure for another four years, slashed the city's budget requests, further infuriating Lindsay. "He's inept," said the governor of the mayor. "He's not responsible for what he's saying. He's emotionally upset. The poor man has been under a lot of pressure." To which the mayor retorted: "We've been raped, but we're being charged with prostitution."[4]

A few months later, on a bright August morning, Lindsay formally relinquished his role in the Republican Party before a packed press conference at Gracie Mansion. He would carry the urban message wherever he could be effective, marching onto the campaign trail under its standard if necessary. Toe by toe, Lindsay began to test the presidential waters. Rockefeller, ruled out of the 1972 sweepstakes by virtue of Richard Nixon's incumbency, must have watched with a mixture of mature reflection and envy. On one occasion at least, the governor passed up the opportunity to assail Lindsay, perhaps because he surely would have been branded a hypocrite. No, said the governor, when asked if Lindsay should resign the mayoralty in order to run for president; incumbents, especially those in New York, traditionally seek higher office without being required to quit their public posts.

Lindsay fared dismally in the early primaries and soon dropped out of the Democratic presidential race. As he buckled down for his last 20 months in office, another conflict with Rockefeller was brewing. In September 1972, the governor named Maurice Nadjari to supersede the five district attorneys in New York City in order to investigate corruption within the criminal justice system.

On April 1, 1973, the morning John Lindsay was supposed to announce his plans for the upcoming mayoralty race, the zealous special prosecutor's office swooped down on several Lindsay administration officials indicted in a parking ticket fixing scheme. The mayor's aides could never be convinced that the timing was coincidental. But the affair was academic—Lindsay announced that he would not seek a third term.

After years of feuding, both Lindsay and Rockefeller left elective office only weeks apart. Each had been a little diminished by their open displays of jealousy, envy, and paranoia. Who was at fault? "It was 50–50," said one confidant of both men. "They should share the responsibility."

On the one hand there was Nelson Rockefeller, the millionaire accustomed to getting what he wanted. He had learned to compromise, but for him that still meant getting what he wanted only a little more slowly. He did not favor yes-men, but he despised no-men carrying their case to the public. He was used to loyalty and felt betrayed by the man he had supported heavily for mayor. Rockefeller also wanted two things that his money could not buy outright. One was youth, which Lindsay had. The other was the presidency, which Lindsay also wanted.

On the other hand there was John Lindsay, a handsome, Yale-educated aristocrat. Independent and stubborn, he was surrounded by a coterie of aides whose independence and stubbornness exceeded his own. He had felt himself to be the new kid on the block, the kid who had taken on the neighborhood bully, even though the bully had recognized him as a potentially formidable foe and had offered to join forces. Neither would ever win, nor would they stop fighting.

"I could never have a substantive discussion with him," says Rockefeller. "Substance wasn't his thing. I happen to be a nut on substantive discussions. I love it. This is what interests me about government. I think John figured out what was the right thing for him to do, and I think that the political judgments interested him much more than the substantive judgments. I think a fair analysis would be that his first interest was politics. I really think that was the basic problem."[5] Not so, says John Lindsay. "My greatest joy was getting into substance."[6]

What about politics? One politician recalled even before their pique peaked that "Rockefeller knows you win some and you lose some. Lindsay wants to win them all."

Rockefeller insisted not only that he do most of the winning but also that the game be played according to his rules. "I'm sorry John, but you'll just have to learn to compromise," the governor told the mayor during one of their private budget negotiations. Rockefeller then extended both hands before him, the left perhaps 18 inches above the right. My left hand, said the governor, is the governor. My right hand, said the governor, is the mayor. "Compromise like this, John," said Rockefeller, lowering the left hand about an inch as he raised the right hand all the way up. The mayor flushed; the muscles along his jaws twitched as he left the room. Rockefeller leaned back in his chair and grinned.[7]

"Tom Dewey told me never to have a Republican governor and a Republican mayor," says Rockefeller. "He said it was an impossible combination and I didn't listen to him."[8]

CHAPTER 30

The Selling of the Governor, 1966

"IT WAS the greatest vindication of my life," says Nelson Rockefeller of his 1966 gubernatorial victory. "Everyone told me I was finished [including brother David, who told Nelson, 'You have a hole in your head'[1]], that I couldn't stand again and hope to win a third term as governor of New York. But I believed that I could and I went out and froze those other people. That was a tremendous satisfaction. For the second time, I had had the courage to stand in the face of total opposition for something I believed in."[2] Unstated by Rockefeller, added by a close friend, was the fact that the 1966 election was also a "vindication of his life with Happy, of his marriage. If he had lost, they would have had to live the rest of their lives thinking that she had ruined his political career."[3]

As a comeback, Rockefeller's 1966 performance was a dazzling achievement, the quintessential "back from the dead" campaign, a marvel that would stand as some sort of record for two years, until Richard Nixon would stage the most remarkable comeback in the history of American politics.

Going into the 1966 campaign, Rockefeller's own polls showed that only 21 percent of the people were willing to vote for him for governor. "Husbands have left home with higher ratings than that, governor," said Rockefeller's pollster. "You couldn't get elected dogcatcher."

Before preparing for the Democrats, however, Rockefeller had to deal with Jacob Javits. The senator had long resented Rockefeller's firm control of the party. State Senator Hughes was urging Javits to take on Rockefeller, and clearly the time had come for the governor to flatter Javits and bring him back into the fold. Thus, on October 26, 1965, in Ithaca, Rockefeller announced that Javits was "our favorite son from New York for the vice-presidential spot" on the Republican ticket in 1968.[4]

Javits decided to play hard to get. A favorite son, he pointed out, could only be a candidate for president, not vice-president. Rockefeller, said Javits, had made a "self-contradictory statement."[5] Undeterred, Rockefeller next asked Javits to be his 1966 campaign manager. Javits's acceptance would have foreclosed his own candidacy, so the offer was rejected. "You never know with Jack Javits," said the governor, "just what he's going to do."[6]

What Javits did do was to go "inventorying" (his word) in April 1966 to see if there was sufficient support for him to take the gubernatorial nomination from Rockefeller at the party convention. (New York was then one of the few states that did not pick candidates in open primaries, a condition remedied in 1967 by the legislature.) The convention system virtually ensures renomination to an incumbent, and Javits found that New York Republican politics in 1966 was no exception.

The Javits problem was finally resolved with Rockefeller announcing his support for the senator as the state's favorite son for president, which meant really that Javits was now free to run for vice-president. Just to make sure everyone got the point, Rockefeller used an appearance by Governor Romney on May 23 in Garden City to endorse the team of Romney-Javits. Romney had not been informed and was startled; Javits beamed and immediately committed himself to the reelection of Rockefeller as governor.

The Selling of the Governor, 1966

Having deftly avoided an internal challenge to his renomination, Rockefeller turned to the general election. Given his low standing in the polls, Democrats virtually fell over each other in the scramble to run against him. Finally, City Council President Frank O'Connor, a former Queens County district attorney, was chosen. O'Connor was a shy man, genuinely fearful of shaking hands with new people. He had perhaps $600,000 to spend, and the only professionals in his organization were several Kennedy aides who seemed afraid of what might happen if O'Connor actually won. In fact, New York *Post* publisher Dorothy Schiff is not alone in suspecting that Senator Robert Kennedy had engineered O'Connor's selection precisely because he was afraid of competition from a Democratic governor of stature.

The only excitement in the O'Connor campaign came at the convention that nominated him. O'Connor himself was chosen by the bosses without trouble, as was the remainder of the ticket. Still, the Democrats were sensitive to the "bossism" charge, so they conspired to have Stanley Steingut's Brooklyn delegates cast their ballots after a majority already had been voted for O'Connor—a ploy easily pulled off by simply having the roll of delegations called in reverse alphabetical order. From then on, O'Connor could honestly say that he had been nominated without the votes of Boss Steingut.

On the next morning, a small, orderly antiwar picket line formed around Buffalo's War Memorial Auditorium, an attempt to mar the appearance of Vice-President Hubert Humphrey before the convention. Suddenly, the Buffalo police arrested two of the pickets, one of them a young telephone operator on her lunch hour. A few Democratic reformers rushed to the police station to remind the Buffalo cops that the Democratic convention had just endorsed the right of peaceful dissent. They threatened to carry the issue to the floor, thereby embarrassing Buffalo Mayor Frank Sedita, who was angling for the nomination for lieutenant governor. Sedita rushed from the convention to the courtroom, discovered that the telephone operator had dated his son, and persuaded the judge, who happened to be his brother, to dismiss the case.[7]

If the Democrats had been half as ingenious in dealing with Rockefeller, they might have won. Actually, says Attorney General Louis Lefkowitz, "anyone but O'Connor would have beaten Rockefeller."[8] O'Connor may well have been an inept campaigner from the start, but Rockefeller was leaving nothing to chance. Big numbers told the tale. The Rockefeller organization, for instance, churned out 27 million pieces of literature and other paraphernalia.

Rockefeller was indefatigable on the stump. In ten months, he visited every county in the state. He made 380 speeches, often renouncing any further ambitions by pledging that he had taken himself out of national politics, "completely and forever, without reservation."[9] He never lost stride, always taking the offensive, never permitting an awkward moment to mar a day of campaigning.

Once, in Harlem, close to election day, at the height of the racial tension surrounding the issue of a Civilian Complaint Review Board for the New York City Police Department (Rockefeller opposed the creation of such a board, which was heavily supported by black and minority groups), the governor passed the Apollo Theater, where the marquee read "James Brown Revue."

"I know him," said Rockefeller. "Stop the bus."[10] Rockefeller and his party walked a block back to the theater, where they were ushered backstage. Looking out from the wings, it was obvious that the James Brown in question was the singer, not the football player. "I know that fellow, too," said Rockefeller. When an aide noted that all that was needed to whip up a really hostile reception was a couple of boos, the governor replied: "I like to play my hunches."

At that point, Rockefeller's friend, bandleader Lionel Hampton, walked out to Brown, talked to him, and then waved Rockefeller on. The governor walked to the center of the stage, put his arms above his head in a boxer's winning gesture, received a big round of applause, and walked off the stage. Not content with that, he shook hands with aisle seat holders on the way out, moving on quickly when his hand was ignored.

No stone was left unturned. Campaign literature was devised for every possible interest group and region in the state. Rockefeller's building programs had won the allegiance of the building trades unions, and there were signs on many construction sites that read: "Protect Your Job—Vote Rockefeller." Peter Brennan of the building trades (later Richard Nixon's secretary of labor) and Harry Van Arsdale, president of the New York City Central Labor Council, both endorsed Rockefeller's re-election bid—leading Murray Kempton to say of the building trades leadership: "They would build gas ovens if it was steady work."[11]

Rockefeller and his personal emissaries, led by George Hinman, were careful to flatter just about every opinion maker they could find. In New York City, both the liberal *Post* and the conservative *Daily News* endorsed the governor.

But the real story of Rockefeller's phenomenal victory was his electronic campaign, a forerunner of his 1968 presidential strategy and a model for all major American political campaigns since. It was, wrote the *National Observer*'s James Perry, "the almost perfect political campaign,"[12] a new way to merchandise a candidate. The only thing that wasn't new was the Rockefeller campaign song; the words "Rockefeller for President" were scratched out in favor of "We need Rockefeller more than we ever did before."

The biggest slice of the Rockefeller budget was always reserved for television time. "Governor Rockefeller for Governor," the 1966 slogan, was emblazoned in blue and white on practically every barn and billboard in the state. Tom Losee, Nelson's campaign communications director, estimated that 10-second spots before and after the old Huntley-Brinkley news program cost $600 each, a rate that rose to $2,900-a-minute in prime time. "By my own count, 3,027 Rockefeller commercials were shown on New York's 22 commercial television stations,"[13] wrote James Perry in his *The New Politics*, the best account to date of the way candidates are sold to the electorate. Over one month, it was estimated that the commercials bombarded more than 80 percent of the families in the state at least eight times.

Early polls had proved, as William Ronan said, that "the governor just wasn't popular. People didn't like him anymore."[14] An early start was needed, a whole new selling job was required. "Because the routine of day-to-day public relations apparently had been unsuccessful," said Ronan, "we had, first of all, to tell the people what had been accomplished. I wanted to find a series of methods to show what had been done. This, I felt, was one way of overcoming the disability of higher taxes. I thought people would accept the taxes if they could see what had been done with the money . . . so we undertook a precampaign approach. . . . Since people were down on the governor, we decided to sell his accomplishments without using him at all."[15]

Here was a radical departure, the first time a candidate would not be speaking for himself. Rockefeller was a bar of soap, all right, and the first rule for selling soap is the selection of the proper advertising agency.

"We moseyed around the field and we found Jack Tinker," said Ronan. "We liked their different approach. It was offbeat and it had been successful in restoring some products."[16] Tinker and Partners was the firm that had convinced Braniff Airlines to paint its planes in pastels and had given Alka Seltzer sales a shot of effervescence. Mary Wells, then at Tinker, made the agency's presentation to the Rockefeller campaign only days before leaving to establish her own advertising firm. The Tinker agency, which had never worked for a political client before, was signed on in April 1966, fully five months before the Republican State Convention.

Tinker quickly decided to "sell" those issues that directly affected the lives of New Yorkers—highways, higher education, local schools, health, the minimum wage, pollution. The first Tinker commercial set the tone of the early phase of the campaign. It was a 60-second spot titled "Fish Interview." It showed a hand wearing a press hat talking to a fish puppet and ran, in part, like this:

> REPORTER: "You, sir."
> FISH: "Uh huh."
> REPORTER: "How do you feel about Governor Rockefeller's Pure Waters Program?"
> FISH: "His pure what?"
> REPORTER: "Pure waters."
> FISH: "Oh, oh yeah."
> REPORTER: "This program sir, is wiping out water pollution in New York within six years. [Not so, as it turned out.]"
> FISH: "Well, it was pretty smelly down here."[17]

Campaign manager William Pfeiffer viewed the "Fish Interview" with a number of party leaders. "The politicos said it was no damn good," recalls Pfeiffer. "They're so used to the staged stuff, to the candidate standing there talking. You had to wait out the Tinker commercials to find out what they were all about. The politicos thought they were just a waste of time. That's when I knew we had done the right thing."[18]

Another commercial, "Road to Hawaii," showed a stretch of road whipping by as the voice-over said, "If you took all the roads Governor Rockefeller has built, and all the roads he's widened and straightened and smoothed out . . . if you took all of these roads, and laid them end to end, they'd stretch all the way to . . . Hawaii [sound of breakers and Hawaiian music]. . . . All the way to Hawaii . . . and all the way back."[19]

Most of these commercials were also produced for radio, and there were accompanying bumper stickers. For example, the "Road to Hawaii" theme was repeated in a bumper sticker that read: "12,000 miles of Better Roads. Pothole-haters for Rockefeller." It was the perfectly integrated candidate selling job.

Still another commercial played to Rockefeller's record in

education. The TV spot opened on a pickup basketball game with five good, tall, fast players and one short, fat, inept kid. The message was obviously addressed to the fat kid:

> Hey, kid, want to go to college? Maybe you catch the eye of some coach, get yourself a scholarship. No, you don't have to be nine feet tall to get a scholarship, or a blooming genius either. Why, if you can get *into* college, you can get the money to help you *go* to college. From New York State. Two hundred thousand new state scholarships and grants are sitting there waiting, every year. Two hundred thousand new chances to make it, every year, even for you, shorty . . . tubby . . . butterfingers. The man who did it, the man responsible for those new scholarships is Governor Rockefeller. Who was no Bob Cousy himself.[20]

Governor Rockefeller appeared in none of these early commercials. His voice wasn't even used. A few worried Rockefeller staffers were urging that the governor be used in some way. So, reports Tinker's Myron McDonald, "we did make a 15-minute film of the governor called 'Governor Rockefeller, the Man.' We sent a crew of people up to the 'Camp,' as it is called, in Maine, which had the governor and little Nelson and Mrs. Rockefeller for a week of 'roughing it.' I put our people under strict orders to take the worst possible pictures of this operation. I'd never seen the Camp. They came back, and the worst possible pictures they could take of the camp came out looking like the Orangerie at Versailles. We did not use the 15-minute film."[21]

Market research dictated the distribution and frequency of the Tinker commercials. The campaign staff isolated the "heavyweight" counties, those with the most voters. Phase 1 of the three-phase TV campaign covered the period July 5–September 12. During those weeks, the schedule called for running 37 one-minute commercials every week in New York City and 18 every week in each of the most populous areas upstate. As a result, the precampaign commercials—all emphasizing Rockefeller's accomplishments, but never once picturing the governor himself—were shown 700 times before the Republican convention even opened.

A major political advantage of the commercials, beyond acquainting the public with the "Massive Rockefeller Record" (sometimes shortened to "The Massive Rockefeller Record: A Ruthlessly Condensed Version"), is that it really did effectively steal the tax issue from O'Connor. The TV spots were showing the people how their tax dollars were being used, and initial poll results showed that the strategy was working.

Still, Rockefeller was trailing, if only because people were *too* used to him and wanted a fresh face. It was time to get rough, to attack O'Connor directly. This was the message from the field. In an internal memorandum dated September 27, 1966, campaign aide John Deardourff told the hierarchy at the Hilton Hotel headquarters that Rockefeller's best issue in the western part of the state was the portrayal of O'Connor as a "typical New York City politician supported by the Tammany Hall Crowd, the same backward and irresponsible elements of the Democratic Party who virtually bankrupted New York City." In general, wrote Deardourff, "a greater anti-O'Connor thrust is likely to pay much larger dividends than anything else which could be done."

Ten and 20-second commercials were prepared attacking O'Connor and his record. Typical was this one: "Frank O'Connor, the man who led the fight against the New York State Thruway is running for governor. Get in your car. Drive down to the polls and vote."[22] This was a distortion, if not an outright lie. The fact was that, as a state senator, O'Connor did not "lead" any fight against building the Thruway. His actual position was that the Thruway should be *free*. There was little time for O'Connor to explain that very significant distinction, and, of course, Rockefeller did not want to explain it.

Finally, as in all campaigns, the name-calling became heated when a "gut" issue was involved. In New York, in 1966, the gut issue was narcotics and crime. During the 1966 legislative session, Rockefeller had proposed a sweeping narcotics program which was designed to pursue and jail pushers while forcing addicts into mandatory treatment. So strong was the measure that it worried many civil libertarians, and Frank O'Connor opposed the program. The first Rockefeller TV commercial to take advantage of O'Connor's "soft" stand said: "If you walk home at night, or if there's a teenager in your family, you should be worried. Governor Rockefeller is worried. As much as half the crime in New York is caused by addicts. That's why the governor has sponsored a tough new law. . . ."[23] The next spot hit O'Connor directly: "If you want to keep the crime rates high, O'Connor is your man."[24] The man speaking those words was Nelson Rockefeller himself. And that message was a long way from the "Fish Interview" and "Road to Hawaii."

O'Connor could never retaliate. During the week of October 18, for example, Rockefeller's commercials were seen in 91 percent of all television homes in New York City (and 5.6 out of 6 million New York homes had television). Not just seen once in each home, but seen an average of 9.8 times—saturation to the nth degree.

What little O'Connor television there was paled by comparison. And much of the footage was not usable. It took a whole day, for example, to film O'Connor discussing urban problems in front of a tenement. When the film was produced and viewed for the first time, a staffer saw what everyone had missed— the graffiti scrawled on the doorway.

O'Connor presciently attacked Rockefeller's "back-door" financing schemes—the practice of floating bonds through public authorities in order to circumvent the constitutional requirement that bond financing first receive voter approval. But no one was paying attention.

When it was all over, Rockefeller had 2,690,826 votes to 2,298,363 for O'Connor. The margin of difference was Franklin D. Roosevelt, Jr. Running on the Liberal Party line, Roosevelt polled 507,234 votes, ballots that almost certainly would have gone to O'Connor if the Liberals had supported him.

FDR, Jr.'s role in the campaign—and the general question of Rockefeller's relationship with the Liberal Party—have long been the subject of suspicion and speculation. Franklin Roosevelt, Jr. had wanted the Democratic nomination. It is said that FDR, Jr. was the very kind of politician Robert Kennedy did not want to build up in New York—a rival with a name as prominent as his. Others conjecture that Roosevelt was a gift to Rockefeller from Liberal Party boss Alex Rose, a candidate who would draw votes from the Democratic nominee, thereby ensuring Rockefeller's reelection.

To be sure, the Liberals had to stretch in order to take Roosevelt as their nominee. "Young Roosevelt," as he was invariably known, was the same fellow who had once worked for Dominican Republic dictator Rafael Trujillo, who called Hubert Humphrey a draft dodger in West Virginia, and who, having been elected to Congress in 1949 as the candidate of the Liberal Party, turned on his party only two years later.

If Roosevelt was a strange choice for the Liberals, the party's relationship with the governor was even stranger. Rockefeller had long been personally close to such Liberal Party leaders as David Dubinsky and the late Adolf Berle; Rockefeller's first wife, Tod, was an enrolled Liberal. The Liberal Party's Bible had long been the New York *Post*, which endorsed Rockefeller in 1966 as well as in 1958. The Liberals would also help Rockefeller in 1970, perhaps inadvertently, perhaps deliberately.

The Liberal Party was born in 1944, out of anti-Communism, that most conservative of passions. The Liberals had some success in New York politics, often way out of proportion to their share of the electorate. By 1964 the party was more middle-of-the-road than liberal. Its campaign platform urged the "economic and diplomatic isolation of the Castro tyranny" and recognized "the necessity of giving the President authority to grant military aid wherever the interests of freedom demand it." There was no plank on American civil liberties.

Of course, these positions were right up Nelson Rockefeller's alley. But it is a more concrete act that still fuels the controversy over a Rockefeller–Liberal Party conspiracy. Nelson Rockefeller was literally responsible for keeping the Liberal Party alive as an entity capable of appearing on the ballot. On April 21, 1960, in the midst of the closing days of the legislative session, GOP leaders agreed to furnish enough votes to approve a bill that would permit the Liberals—or any other small party (though the Liberal Party was the only one around at the time)—to function legally in counties where it didn't have sufficient strength to organize county committees. The bill circumvented a Court of Appeals decision which invalidated Liberal Party electoral participation in such counties.

In return, the Liberals agreed to oppose those Democratic candidates who would challenge incumbent Republican legislators from New York City when they came up for reelection that fall. The Liberals also helped sustain the Republican legislative leadership by withholding their support from the Democratic adversaries of Senate Majority Leader Walter Mahoney and Assembly Speaker Joseph Carlino. The Republicans had legislated Liberal survival. They could just as easily have legislated Liberal death. If there is a better reason for Liberal friendship with Rockefeller's GOP, no one has detected it.[25]

In the earliest stages of the 1966 campaign, Alex Rose apparently began believing some very weird polls which showed Roosevelt beating O'Connor and Rockefeller. Curiously, Rose immediately began to dull some of the luster of his own candidate. In a series of conversations with reporters that is probably unique in New York political history, Alex Rose reflected on his candidate for governor. Rose had rejected Roosevelt's claim to the 1965 gubernatorial nomination because, he said, "I was disappointed in his congressional career. His ambition got the better of him. He immediately began running for governor. I didn't like it. It was as if I hired a young fellow to work in the

318

union, and he went around telling everyone he wanted to run for president of the International."

Having admitted that he had been "down" on "young Franklin," Rose then said: "I recognized in the past few weeks that in the past I had dealt with a boy and now I was dealing with a man. He must have decided to become a real Roosevelt. He's grown up, especially since his mother's death."[26] Roosevelt, it seemed, had spent time in Liberal purgatory. Rose was now making sure no one believed that "young Franklin" had suddenly achieved a direct line to God. As political endorsements go, Rose's comments about his own candidate were on the cool side of lukewarm.

No one has yet *proved* collusion between the Liberals and Rockefeller in 1966, but there will aways be enough coincidence to spark debate.

CHAPTER 31

Rocky, Romney,
and Dick

NINETEEN SIXTY-SIX was also interesting as a mirror of Rockefeller's relationships with his fellow Republicans. Of course, the governor and the mayor were already feuding, so not much was expected from John Lindsay. "He delivered less," says Rockefeller confidant Robert Douglass. "John Lindsay didn't lift a finger for us."[1]

If the Lindsay problem was expected, the dance Nelson Rockefeller did with Richard Nixon was absolutely fascinating. Rockefeller was trying hard to dissociate himself from all national Republicans, but the gubernatorial race was close, and a case could be made for help from Nixon, directed primarily to upstate conservative strongholds. William Safire, a go-between in the delicate negotiations between Rockefeller and Nixon, tells the story in *Before the Fall: An Inside View of the Pre-Watergate White House*:

> The relationship between Richard Nixon and Nelson Rockefeller in 1966 was that of a mongoose and a cobra temporarily called upon to work side by side. They had fought

before and would fight again, but while Rockefeller was running an uphill race for reelection and Nixon was running around the country supporting Republicans, they agreed to a truce so they could oppose some common enemies. . . .

On Monday, October 31, Jack Wells called me into his corner office at the New York Hilton and laid it on the line:

"Dick Nixon is going to be speaking Wednesday night in Syracuse on behalf of a couple of congressional candidates. Bill Pfeiffer and I think it would be a good idea for Dick to come out with a strong endorsement of Rockefeller."[2]

Safire carried the request back to Nixon in Lodi, New Jersey. "I've been consistent in campaigning only in those areas that requested me," Nixon told Safire. "Would Nelson be willing to admit that he had changed his mind, and asked me to speak up for him in New York? Let me sleep on it."

Nixon called Safire at home at 8 A.M. the next day, one week before the election. He wanted to be used strongly if he were to be used at all. Safire picks up the story:

Nixon recognized Rockefeller's difficulty in admitting that he had changed his mind and asked Nixon to campaign for him. With the *Daily News* poll showing Rockefeller trailing O'Connor, this reversal would appear to be a desperation move. Nixon was willing to "voluntarily" come out for Rockefeller provided he was certain that (a) his endorsement would be received with enthusiasm by Rockefeller and Javits, and (b) Rockefeller would help Nixon elect Congressmen in Iowa by helping to finance an Iowa telecast. . . .

I told Nixon I thought Rockefeller would rather spend the rest of his life on a ranch in Venezuela than agree to all of this, but it would be an interesting discussion and was worth a try.

Jack Wells called a meeting in a Hilton room at 10 A.M. Present were Governor Rockefeller, Bill Pfeiffer, William Ronan, with Senator Javits joining us toward the end. . . .

The governor sat on the edge of a desk, his legs dangling, looking at the floor glumly. I finished. There was a pause, and Rockefeller said incredulously: "Iowa!" . . .

"Iowa," said Rockefeller again. . . . Then he added that he didn't want a controversy about Nixon at the end of the campaign.

Pfeiffer suggested that I ask Nixon simply to speak up for the state ticket in Syracuse "without being asked."

I asked Rockefeller what his reaction would be to that endorsement. Rockefeller sighed and said, "Delighted." . . . "Isn't there anything else we have to worry about?"[3]

"Nixon," concluded Safire, "was not pleased but, in good grace, he went to Syracuse and—in Murray Kempton's words— sketched 'his profile in political courage by mentioning Rockefeller's name. . . .' "[4] Nixon had been the good soldier. It would not be long before he and Rockefeller would battle once more for the presidential nomination.

Written off as a presidential candidate only two years earlier, Nelson Rockefeller, the party wrecker, was suddenly a major figure on the national scene simply because he had won reelection when his defeat had been expected. His goal was still the White House, but Rockefeller was keeping a low profile, waiting to see how the GOP would right itself after the 1964 debacle. "I am not a candidate for president," said the governor. "I am determined not to be used as an instrument to split the unity of progressive Republicans behind a candidate who can win in 1968."

Rockefeller knew that the only way he could possibly get the Republican nomination was by doing and saying exactly what he was doing and saying—that he was not interested. His press secretary, Les Slote, tired of answering the same question over and over again, found an explanation that seemed to satisfy everyone. Rockefeller, said Slote, was not a *political* candidate at all. He was an *existential* candidate.[5] He could not become a real candidate by trying to be one because that would wreck the party.

He could become a candidate only by *not* trying to be a candidate.

In place of himself, Rockefeller "let George do it." After himself, George Romney was the best man Rockefeller could think of for the presidency. Romney was progressive, the governor of a large industrial state, seemingly bright, easily advised. And he could be used. Long after Romney's campaign began to fade, Nelson Rockefeller continued to support him, cleverly propping him up, thereby foreclosing the potential candidacies of other progressive Republicans until Rockefeller could decide what to do—which in the end meant running himself.

Thus, two weeks after the 1966 election, Romney flew to Puerto Rico, there to meet with Nelson Rockefeller at the Dorado Beach Hotel, one of the Rockefeller family's lavish resorts. Their agreement was simple: Rockefeller would provide all possible support to Romney, both public and private—research, speechwriting, staff, and money, some $200,000 when the totals came in.

Romney manned "the point," and everyone was happy—even Richard Nixon, who, like Rockefeller, understood the desirability of offering the press a front man to take the heat. "I want him to get the exposure," said Nixon.[6] Thus it came to pass that the missionary—Mormon George Romney—was fed to the cannibals.

Romney was no more a darling of the Republican right than was Rockefeller, of whom Barry Goldwater had said: "Rockefeller dumped Nixon and me, so I just frankly can't see how any Republican can support him."[7] Romney had repudiated Goldwater in 1964 and had run on his own for governor of Michigan. Goldwater's principles, said Romney, "do not square with the principles for which the Republican Party stands on the basis of its past record and heritage."[8]

Actually, attacking Goldwater in 1964 was a common denominator for much of the party—including the ever-cautious Richard Nixon. "Looking to the future of the party," Nixon had said in 1964, "it would be a tragedy if Senator Goldwater's views as previously stated were not challenged—and repudiated."[9] To this, Goldwater replied: "He is sounding more and more like Harold Stassen every day."[10]

Still, Nixon was different from Rockefeller and Romney. Having been brazen with his rhetoric, he repented after Goldwater was nominated, tirelessly campaigning for Goldwater in more than 20 states in 1964. Ever the GOP's best "good soldier," Nixon toured for the congressional candidates in 1966, traveling over 30,000 miles, hitting 82 districts, often at his own expense and never with more than two staffers, Pat Buchanan and William Safire.

Nixon's forays were rarely covered in the press. When they were, said Safire, they "barely made the furniture pages in the New York *Times*."[11] The press was not to blame. After all, wasn't Richard Nixon politically dead? Theodore White borrowed from Dickens's *A Christmas Carol* in order to convey the political reality: "Marley was dead: to begin with. There is no doubt whatever about that. The register of his burial was signed by the clergyman, the clerk, the undertaker, and the chief mourner. . . . Old Marley was as dead as a door-nail."[12]

No matter, reasoned Richard Nixon, the world champion attender to detail: he was picking up valuable IOUs, redefining the ancient political ritual of "touching base" wherever he went. Recalls one midwestern congressman: "If Dick passes through town, he telephones from the airport. If I'm not in, he'll likely chat with someone on my staff. And I'm not particularly close to Nixon. Rockefeller? I've seen him on television."[13]

Nixon was not loved, and most of the party, including Dwight Eisenhower, was convinced that he could not win. But he was acceptable, and in the end that would make all the difference.

Meanwhile, Nelson Rockefeller was relatively quiet, trying his best to be all things to all men. At various points during the 1968 campaign, the governor claimed that he was ideologically close to both Richard Nixon ("he's a moderate and I'm a moderate") and Ronald Reagan ("there is no ideological gulf between us"[14]). Later, in the heat of battle, he would deride Nixon.

"Nixon's the one, all right," he told an audience in Springfield, Illinois, "the one who lost it for us in 1960."[15] For the most part, however, as Larry King observed, "he was playing his political cards so close to his vest they might fade on his shirt."[16]

Rockefeller's fence straddling extended beyond personalities to issues. For example, in his annual State of the State message for 1968, he sounded every bit as conservative as Ronald Reagan, calling for a balance between "what is do-able and what is desirable." Five months later, the governor would battle for creation of the Urban Development Corporation, as liberal a concept of the role of government as has ever been advanced in the United States.

It was a foreign issue, the Vietnam war, that gave Rockefeller the opportunity to raise evasion to an art form. The governor had been a hawk on the war since its inception. Late in the 1964 campaign, he had advocated bombing the North.[17] "Winning the fight for freedom in Vietnam is essential to the survival of freedom in all of Asia," Rockefeller told an Oregon primary audience in 1964. "The administration should make clear that it supports the existing government in Saigon, and should cease from criticizing it. . . ."[18] From 1964 until 1968, however, he consistently told the press that he had "no position" on Vietnam.

A blistering internal policy debate on Vietnam occupied Rockefeller's foreign policy advisers in late 1967. The antagonists were Henry Kissinger, the hawk, and Emmet Hughes, the dove. Hughes felt he had weaned Rockefeller from his support of the Johnson war effort. "But then," recalls Hughes, "Romney made that 'brainwashing' statement, and it would have seemed that we were victims of the same sort of thing. So nothing was done, and Henry won by default."[19]

The New York *Times* took to calling Rockefeller "Nelson the Silent." The following exchange at a March 1968 press conference indicates why:

QUESTION: "Governor, could you please outline for us your views on the war in Vietnam?"

ANSWER: "Surely. My position on Vietnam is very simple. And I feel this way. I haven't spoken on it because I haven't felt there was any major contribution that I had to make at the time. I think that our concepts as a nation, and that our actions have not kept pace with the changing conditions, and therefore our actions are not completely relevant today to the realities of the magnitude and the complexity of the problems that we face in this conflict."

QUESTION: "Governor, what does that mean?"

ANSWER: "Just what I said."[20]

There is, Rockefeller once said, "a technique when you don't want to be committed to something of talking around it. I've done it myself."[21]

For two months in 1968 the governor sounded like a dove. This was the period between Robert Kennedy's assassination and the Republican convention, a period when Rockefeller was trying to capture Kennedy's constituency, barnstorming the country calling for a "New Leadership." He bought full-page newspaper ads and television spots aping the rhetoric of the peace movement.

As Rockefeller held back, bobbing and weaving only when he saw fit to greet the public, George Romney was proving his apparent incompetence for the office of president of the United States. Ohio Governor James Rhodes said of the Romney effort: "Watching George Romney run for the presidency was like watching a duck trying to make love to a football."[22]

George Romney could not make it with the press. Neither understood the other. Romney, for example, had billboards in New Hampshire that read "The Way to Stop Crime is to Stop Moral Decay." He couldn't understand why the press laughed at that slogan, and the press could not understand what Romney meant by moral decay. On and on through 1967, Romney would be candid with the press and have occasion to regret that candor the next day. He was not catching on.

What finished him, just as it would finish Lyndon Johnson a short while later, was the war. Pressed for a statement at every turn, Romney avoided taking a clear position. ". . . If the Michigan executive has a major weakness today," wrote David Broder in the New York *Times* as early as 1966, "it is probably his fuzziness on national and international issues. His advisors say adequate briefings at the proper time can overcome the problem, but his lapses are embarrassing."[23]

Romney never improved. The press wanted to talk Vietnam, and Romney acted as though he didn't even know where it was. In Hartford, Connecticut, on April 7, 1967, Romney finally gave a Vietnam speech, a speech that had been edited by the Rockefeller forces in New York to make it more "hawkish." Still, Romney had said *something*, and it might have served him well had Lyndon Johnson not shrewdly praised the Romney plan as embracing much of his own thinking. Romney was thus denied the opportunity to be an independent voice on Vietnam, and he slipped in the opinion polls almost immediately. By September, Romney's hometown newspaper, the *Detroit News*, had denounced him, adding that only Nelson Rockefeller could save the GOP.

A few weeks later, Romney joined the shipboard junket of the National Governors' Conference. As the boat left port, a copy of *Time* magazine was placed under every door. On the cover were Rockefeller and Reagan, the Republicans' "dream ticket" said *Time*. *Fortune* magazine had recently praised Rockefeller and his "Record to Fit the Times," calling the New York governor "a consummate latter-half-of-the-twentieth century politician, a man in no sense overwhelmed by an era of radical change but rather a step ahead of it."[24] Now the press plaudits were rolling in. *Newsweek*'s James Cannon, later to join Rockefeller's staff and now director of the Domestic Council, wrote that "Rockefeller is a man whose first love is governing," quoting an unnamed "humorist" as saying that Rockefeller is "the only man in the country whose fallback position is the Presidency."[25]

Riding along, as always, with the favorable press attention were the public opinion polls. By late fall, Gallup had Rockefeller beating Johnson 52 percent to 35 percent, a performance well in excess of Romney's, the man Rockefeller was supporting. And the man Rockefeller continued to support.

The do-nothing strategy had worked well, and the governor was not about to blow his chances for the nomination by actually seeking it, at least not in late 1967. Dutifully, Romney continued to go about the country, a pathetic figure now, dogged everywhere by reporters. When the pressure became unbearable at home, he went abroad, to Paris and the rest of Europe, often claiming that the Continental correspondents were misquoting him even as their portable tape recorders proved they were not. He even went back to Vietnam—all to no avail.

The New Hampshire primary was approaching, and Rockefeller put up still more money to test the sentiment in the first primary state. Surprise! Richard Nixon, who had been quietly working while the press watched Romney stumble, was the favorite of New Hampshire Republicans by 64.2 percent to 12 percent for George Romney. One of those present when the secret poll results were analyzed summed up Romney's problem: "I guess the poll shows that New Hampshire Republicans think George Romney is too dumb to be president of the United States." On February 28, George Romney left the field. It had not been a pleasant experience.

All eyes were on Rockefeller. Still, he waited. He was worried —and for good reason. At the same time that Gallup's voter preference poll showed him crushing Lyndon Johnson, a companion poll indicated that GOP county chairmen, the nucleus of those who would actually nominate the Republican standard-bearer in Miami, favored Richard Nixon over Nelson Rockefeller by five to one.

Rockefeller's only concession to the obvious pressure was a statement issued the day after Romney's withdrawal in which he reaffirmed, in the same sentence, his dual position: "I am not going to create dissension within the Republican Party by contending for the nomination, but I am ready and willing to serve the American people if called."[26]

Three weeks of intensive soul-searching followed, as the

party's elders trooped to New York, beseeching him to make the race. He was loving every minute of it. Clearly, Rockefeller wanted the presidency; just as clearly, he could either reach for it or sit back and let it come to him. The latter choice was a gamble he might well lose, since vacuums do not remain unfilled for long in American politics. The central problem, as usual, was that the party's local leaders did not want him.

On March 21, 1967, Nelson Rockefeller held a press conference to announce, in effect, that nothing had happened. Three hundred newsmen gathered to hear what the New York *Times* promised would be a declaration of candidacy. What they heard, instead, was just the opposite. The reason, said Rockefeller, was simple enough: "Ideally, the Presidential candidate of each of our two major parties should reflect as broadly as possible the will and the spirit of each party and its leadership across the country. By this criterion, I could not truthfully claim such a Republican following today. Quite frankly, I find it clear at this time that a considerable majority of the Party's leaders want the candidacy of former Vice President Richard Nixon."[27]

Was this a clever ploy, or had Rockefeller seriously given up all hope? First, it is clear that his reason for not running was true, an accurate measure of party sentiment at that time. Second, he knew that if he were still to have a chance for the prize, some event—like the U 2 incident in 1960 or John Kennedy's assassination in 1963—would have to intervene to encourage his candidacy. Otherwise, Nixon would have to slip up somewhere down the road. As it happened, Lyndon Johnson announced that he would not seek reelection a week after Rockefeller had more or less pulled himself out of the race. And a week after that, Martin Luther King, Jr. was assassinated, with rioting and bloodshed to follow. Here was a way back into the presidential sweepstakes. The Ides of March had forced a change in the politics of 1968. Nelson Rockefeller waited a month and then declared himself "in."

As in past campaigns, the governor had already announced the creation of a special task force to assist him in making known his positions on the great issues of the day—a necessity, said Rockefeller, in "a time of crisis and confusion probably without parallel in our history." All the familiar faces were there: Henry Kissinger, Emmet Hughes, Oscar Ruebhausen.

Having battened down the intellectual front for the battle to come, Rockefeller, on April 30, announced his "active candidacy" for president. The first response was overwhelming. Massachusetts held its primary that very day, and a massive "write-in" gave Nelson the state's 34 delegates on the first ballot.

A great start, followed by a great stop. The party's chieftains still opposed Rockefeller. The primaries had never been the route to success for the governor, so he would avoid them. He would appeal directly to the people, using the advertising techniques that had worked so well in the 1966 gubernatorial race in New York. The public opinion polls would be his primary. He would prove that only he could win in November. The party would have to accept him. After all, didn't all parties want a *winner* before an ideologue?

In three months, he traveled 66,200 miles, speaking at rallies of voters "outdoors" and meetings of delegates "indoors." He was two different people. "Outdoors," among the people Gallup and Harris would survey, Rockefeller spun his Bobby Kennedy *shtick*, like this: "As I have been saying and promising across the land from Vermont to Texas, these crises can end only with a truly New Leadership, and this New Leadership has to begin by proclaiming an end to the Old Politics."[28]

"Indoors," Rocky *was* the Old Politics, speaking smoothly, rattling off statistics, trying his damndest to be a real Republican, to be one of *them*. It wasn't working. After one typical trip to Tennessee, R. W. Apple, Jr. of the New York *Times* wrote: "Nelson Rockefeller arrived in Tennessee with twenty-eight delegates sewed up for Richard Nixon, and he left with twenty-eight delegates sewed up for Nixon."[29]

Okay, concluded the Rockefeller strategists, hit the "outdoor" strategy harder. A $4.6 million media blitz was launched, including $1.5 million for the insertion of full-page ads in 41 cities every week. The ads, which detailed Rockefeller's positions on the issues, were primarily written in the Tinker advertising agency, the same company that had put together the Rockefeller campaign commercials in 1966. "Who says there's no place for a rich man in politics?"[30] quipped William F. Buckley.

A funny thing happend. At Miami, just one week before the convention, the Gallup poll put Nixon *ahead* of Rockefeller, against either Humphrey or Eugene McCarthy, by 2 to 5 percentage points. Two days later, Rockefeller leaked the results of the Harris poll, which contradicted Gallup. At the convention itself, Rockefeller leaked his own poll showing that he was the stronger candidate in the industrial states where the electoral votes were concentrated—a last gasp that moved no one. Rockefeller had set his own ground rules, and Gallup had bankrupted the strategy. The 1968 campaign was over for Nelson Rockefeller. He who lived by the poll, died by it.

Richard Nixon, the safe, acceptable candidate, was nominated for president on the first ballot. After the normal scurrying about, he chose Governor Spiro Agnew of Maryland, an early supporter of Nelson Rockefeller, as his running mate, "a statesman of the first rank," said Nixon. On the day of his selection, three Atlanta pedestrians interviewed on television defined Spiro Agnew in three different ways:

"It's some kind of disease."

"It's some kind of egg."

"He's a Greek who owns that shipbuilding firm."

Spiro Agnew himself told the convention that "I have a deep sense of the improbability of this moment."[31]

Nixon spoke to the convention and stole straight from Barry Goldwater. He spoke of the "forgotten Americans, the nonshouters, the nondemonstrators." He spoke of the need "to quit pouring billions of dollars into programs that have failed." He stole from Martin Luther King ("I have a dream"), saying "I see a day" eight times—a day when, for instance, "Americans are once again proud of their flag." Finally, Nixon expressed his faith in dreams:

I see [a] child tonight. He hears a train go by. At night he dreams of faraway places where he'd like to go. It seems like an impossible dream. But he is helped in his journey through life. A father who had to go to work before he finished the sixth grade sacrificed everything he had so that his sons could go to college.

A gentle Quaker mother, with a passionate concern for peace, quietly wept when he went to war, but she understood why he had to go. . . . [After all, he would say in the summer of 1974, "my mother, she was a saint."]

And in his chosen profession of politics, first there were scores, then hundreds, then thousands, and then finally millions who worked for his success.

And tonight he stands before you, nominated for President of the United States of America.[32]

"You'll like Dick," wrote Frances Hodgson Burnett in *Little Lord Fauntleroy*. "He's so square."

Perhaps so, but Richard Nixon always knew who his enemies were. William Safire tells the story of flying with the president-elect on *Air Force One* at a time when the cabinet was being selected. Nelson Rockefeller had been suggested for several posts.

"At Treasury," said Safire, "what about David Rockefeller—no, you can't have two Rockefellers in the Cabinet."

" 'Is there a law,' Nixon asked without changing expression, 'that you have to have one?' "[33]

CHAPTER 32

The Art of
the Chameleon

FOR Nelson Rockefeller, the election of 1968 was a very special tragedy. Nixon's victory had been more than a triumph of personality; it had been a triumph of ideology. In winning the White House, Nixon had buried the Eastern Republican establishment, which had shunned him as an outsider. The Eastern wing had been damaged by the nomination of Goldwater in 1964 and the subsequent domination of the party apparatus by his conservative followers. Surely, reasoned the Eastern liberals, that too would pass—in 1968.

The Eastern establishment had clung to the belief that while others might rule the GOP, they could never capture the country. Now Nixon had done just that. The "can't win" tag could now more aptly be ascribed to Nelson Rockefeller than to Richard Nixon. The conservatives—the moderate conservatives, at least—had the White House. The time had come for Nelson Rockefeller to move irrevocably rightward. He had long been outside the mainstream of his party. He was now outside the mainstream of the country as well. And he knew it.

Rockefeller spent the remaining years of his governorship trying to have it both ways—a chameleon approach which he mastered without shame. Richard Nixon had recognized this ability in its embryonic form during the 1968 election. Analyzing his rival's predicament, Nixon had told an aide: "If I were Rocky's adviser, I would tell him to make a strong pitch for fiscal responsibility and strengthening the dollar. That would be an unexpected move. Instead, I think he's going to go for a major statement on the cities and call for all-out spending programs. In the same breath, he'll probably promise to balance the budget."[1]

Nixon was not far from the mark. Rockefeller's home-front performance seemed to change with the political winds. In 1968, seeking to soften his liberal image, he had called for balancing the "do-able with the desirable." In 1969, with a conservative administration controlling the federal government, Rockefeller had gone further. He warned of a "grave financial crisis." Although no budget that is $1.2 billion over the previous year's can be labeled an austerity budget, Rockefeller called for a halt to new programs and an across-the-board cut in state spending of 5 percent.

By the next year, an election year, Rockefeller had changed his thinking again. He had positioned himself on the right and now, facing a Democratic challenge, he would move back to the left. In his 1970 message to the legislature he was his old liberal self. Without blinking an eye, he called for new programs for school breakfasts and subsidies of mass transportation fares. All of a sudden, according to the governor, this was "a time for faith, for vision and for courage. More and more people—and especially young people—are questioning hypocrisy and injustice in our society." It took Rockefeller 21,840 words to blame Congress for cutting federal taxes in an "election year mood," thus necessitating his liberalism at home. For good measure, Rockefeller called for liberalizing the abortion statute and lowering the voting age to 18. He asked for a 10 percent cost-of-living increase in welfare and more aid for the aged, blind, and disabled. He also proposed a study of state drug laws regarding marijuana and an evaluation of the penalties for its use. He called for a new Department of Environmental Conservation, a new Department of Parks and Recreation, and a new Department of Correctional Services.

The Art of the Chameleon

That was in 1970. In 1971, having won reelection and still desiring to move with the country's rightward drift, Rockefeller was back before the legislature calling for "belt tightening." This time his 30-minute speech was interrupted only twice for applause. Many "important and desirable" programs, said the governor, would have to be deferred because the state now lacked the resources to solve its problems. He said he had eliminated $403 million in budget requests by his department and agency heads, and he called on the federal government to enact revenue sharing. As Nixon had prophesied, Rockefeller was calling for cutbacks at the very time he was asking for more money for the cities. "Unless we reverse the downward spiral," said Rockefeller in 1971, "particularly evident in so many urban areas, we will be faced with a breakdown of essential services."

To the critics who watched in horror as he flitted all over the fiscal landscape, Rockefeller had a ready reply: "It doesn't make you a liberal to spend money you don't have. It just makes you a damn fool."[2]

To meet his program costs, whether they were products of his liberal or conservative spending years, Rockefeller had to rely on taxes. It is hardly surprising that an analysis of his taxing proposals by the Congressional Reference Service indicated that in each gubernatorial reelection year (1962, 1966, and 1970), there "were no proposed tax changes." Yet, during his 15 years in Albany, New Yorkers saw their taxes rise by over 300 percent, significantly above the national average. "Rocky's grandfather gave away dimes," said one critic. "Nelson seems determined to get them all back." Rockefeller's budgets increased fivefold during his tenure, and the burden of taxation fell most heavily on the individual taxpayer, through income and sales levies. It was common in New York to hear a merchant quote a price with the addendum "and 7 cents for Rocky."

A report by the House Judiciary Committee concluded that New York State relied on personal income taxes for 50 percent of its revenue, compared with an average of 28 percent for the other 49 states.[3] This, of course, was no accident. Rockefeller has long believed that the burden of taxation should be removed from businesses and the "junior executive" levels in order to keep and attract industry to New York ("the whole future of our growth depends on management"[4]). He continually offered stimulants for business expansion. Corporations and small businesses were given tax relief, and tax write-offs were offered for research and development. To encourage investment in new plants and expansion of existing ones, tax write-offs were authorized for this purpose at twice the rate of federal schedules.[5] In 1971 the governor exclaimed: "I am proud to say that in the past 11 years there has not been a single new business tax in New York State"[6]—a taxing policy to warm even Barry Goldwater's heart. Meanwhile, the burden of taxation fell, in Rockefeller's words, "on the average person like you and me."

While he skillfully manipulated the home front, Rockefeller began to genuflect before the national party. For the first time, his national position remained consistent for five years: he was an unabashed supporter and, in public at least, admirer of Richard Nixon.

When Nixon came to live in New York after his 1962 loss in the California gubernatorial race, he might as well have been an immigrant who couldn't speak the language. He was systematically ignored and excluded. His advice was not sought; he was an alien. Though Nixon lived in the same building as the governor, the two never socialized. In fact, it was with a great deal of personal satisfaction that the president-elect received Nelson Rockefeller in the Nixon apartment shortly after Election Day in 1968. Without ever having been included in New York Republican circles and without the state's electoral votes, Richard Nixon had won. Try as he might, even Nelson Rockefeller could not ignore the fact.

Rockefeller had contributed only $3,000 to the 1968 Nixon Victory Dinner, but in 1972 he was chairman of the New York Committee to Reelect the President, and a more substantial contribution was solicited by former Commerce Secretary Maurice Stans. Having already donated $50,000 to Nixon campaign committees in 1971, Rockefeller said, "I asked my brothers and sister if they would like to make a contribution and mentioned to them my pledge of $50,000. Each of them decided to make similar contributions."[7]

On March 29, 1972, just one week before stricter federal spending and disclosure requirements took effect, Rockefeller family lawyers delivered 68 checks from Nelson, Abby, John, and Laurance to the Finance Committee for the Reelection of the President. Included were $3,000 checks from each of the four Rockefellers to 16 Delaware and Illinois committees that were obscurely described as the Good Government League, Committee for Civic Betterment, and Citizens for Reasonable Government. Checks for $2,000 each were also sent to the United Citizens of Delaware for a Prosperous America. On June 12, 1972, David donated $50,000 in 17 checks to Nixon campaign committees in 13 states.[8]

In 1972, after spending much of his political career in a vain attempt to destroy him, Nelson Rockefeller rose to renominate Nixon in Miami: "We need this man of action, this man of accomplishment, this man of experience, this man of courage, we need this man of faith in America. . . ."[9] The words would not be enough this time, so the Nixon-in-'72 New York campaign was managed superbly by Nelson Rockefeller's smooth-running technocracy. When the dust had cleared, New York had given Nixon the largest electoral majority of any state in the nation. He missed carrying New York City by only 82,000 votes. It was a triumph of staggering proportions—but, of course, the election nationwide had been much the same for Nixon. Rockefeller, it turned out, had not done anything particularly extraordinary. And he would not be rewarded. If the governor harbored any private desire to serve in the Nixon cabinet, he let no one know of it.

In fact, during all of the Nixon presidency, the only significant assignment Rockefeller handled for the president was the now infamous 1969 trip to South America. "Anti-Americanism" was so rabid that Rockefeller avoided three countries on his

NELSON'S POLITICS

itinerary and openly predicted more "Castros" in South America. President Kennedy had broken diplomatic relations with the military dictatorships that had ousted democratic regimes; Rockefeller was now urging "the pragmatic concept that diplomatic relations should not constitute moral approval, and that our dislike of a regime must not deprive the people of that country of the economic aid they need."[10] Rockefeller conceded that representative government was a worthy ideal but concluded:

> Democracy is a very subtle and difficult problem for most of the other countries in the hemisphere. The authoritarian and hierarchical tradition which has conditioned and formed the cultures of most of these societies does not lend itself to the particular kind of popular government we are used to. . . . For many of these countries, therefore, the question is less one of democracy or a lack of it than it is simply of orderly ways of getting along.[11]

Woodrow Wilson had once declared that he was going to the South American republics "to elect good men."[12] Nelson Rockefeller seemed less concerned with the goodness of hemispheric leadership or the legitimacy of its claims to power than in its stability.

338

CHAPTER 33

"He's Done a Lot.
He'll Do More."

STABILITY in New York meant Rockefeller as governor. "Satisfaction" had erased ambition, he had said prior to jumping into the presidential race in 1968. Now, as Garry Wills put it, "he took another look at his soul and found all satisfaction lies in achievement." So a fourth gubernatorial campaign commenced. With it came a temporary suspension of his new conservatism.

"Four years ago," wrote the *National Observer*'s James Perry in October 1970,

> I suggested that Nelson A. Rockefeller's winning campaign for governor was the most astute, the most professional, the most imaginative, and perhaps the most ruthless the nation has ever seen.
>
> And I further suggested that we probably would never see another like it.
>
> Wrong. Wrong. Wrong.
>
> Rockefeller is running for governor once more this year—and this campaign is the most professional, the most astute, and the most carefully organized....

The TV commercials were again handled by Jack Tinker. They were more restrained than in 1966, concentrating on the theme: "Rockefeller: He's done a lot. He'll do more." The governor reported spending $6.8 million (of which $4.9 million came from Rockefeller and his family), but a more reasonable estimate, given the loopholes in the reporting laws at that time, would probably be much higher. Some of that money was used at the very end of the campaign. Rockefeller's forces feared overconfidence and a low turnout, so 400,000 simulated telegrams were sent to upstate voters saying: "I need your help. Unless you vote this Tuesday the organized Democratic Party of New York City could take over your state government. . . . I need your support for good government."[2]

A $3.2 million media campaign blitzed 95 percent of the viewing families in New York City alone, hammering "He's done a lot. He'll do more" into the heads of every family at least nine times.[3]

Rockefeller's outlay for television, which by itself was almost $600,000 more than what Democrat Arthur Goldberg spent in his primary and general election campaigns combined, boosted the governor's budget to over $7.2 million—including $584,000 for a primary in which, as usual, he had no opponents.[4] That year, when brother Winthrop had allocated only $1.3 million for his Arkansas reelection bid (he lost) and Democratic Senate aspirant Richard Ottinger was forced to defend his $2.7 million race, Nelson Rockefeller ran the most expensive nonpresidential contest in American history.

The 1970 campaign was the most expensive race for the family as well. Almost $5 million was pumped into Nelson's fourth and final gubernatorial campaign, the bulk of it from the trust's contribution of over $3.4 million, followed by:

$644,000 from Laurance,
$464,000 from David,
$194,000 from Abby,

"He's Done a Lot. He'll Do More."

$144,000 from John, and
$54,000 from Winthrop.[5]

Laurance's largesse makes it difficult to believe the official family explanation that he invested in the negative campaign biography of Arthur Goldberg only as a business venture because he had reached his self-imposed limit on political contributions.

Once again, in 1970, the Democrats were outmanned. Rockefeller had 380 full-time employees, compared with 35 for the Democratic ticket. ("Wealth always gives a politician an edge,"[6] says Nelson.)

And, as usual, the Democrats were hobbled with a poor candidate. Former Secretary of Labor, Supreme Court Justice, and UN Ambassador Arthur Goldberg seemed an ideal choice to challenge Rockefeller.[7] Try as they might, however, the Democrats could not make a *mensch* of Arthur Goldberg. Try as he might, Goldberg could not loosen up. He was not approachable, he was not a regular guy. He was not *simpatico*, a quality which Nelson Rockefeller, despite his wealth, seemed able to convey to everyone he met. Goldberg was as studied as a legal brief. He seemed to *be* running for Supreme Court justice rather than governor.

He was used to praise and deference. Campaigning was hard for him. When asked by reporters how he should be addressed (a query that would normally evoke a "just Mr. Goldberg" reply from a clever politician who knows that the press is leary of titles), the candidate replied: "Call me Mr. Justice."

Flying back to New York from Indiana, where he had received a labor award, Goldberg made his point: "You know, if I ran for governor of Indiana, or Iowa, I'd win in a walk—but in New York no one has any respect for anyone." John Lindsay had to borrow from W.C. Fields to explain Goldberg's lack of charisma: "I spent a week with Arthur Goldberg last night."

Goldberg had won the nomination armed with an Oliver Quayle poll that just about equated Goldberg with God. Quayle

341

concluded: "Right now, it is only possible for the Democratic Party to capitalize on Rockefeller's negative job rating by running Arthur Goldberg against him."[8] Quipped political writer Richard Reeves: "That poll will probably be displayed one day in a small roadside museum alongside the scripts of old Milton Berle shows."[9]

Goldberg scored Rockefeller's fiscal "gimmickry," but again, no one was listening. He blasted Rockefeller's Public Service Commission and Rockefeller's appointment of the former chairman to a $30,000-a-year post as a consultant when the PSC chairman himself was only getting $37,275.[10] He accused Rockefeller of misusing statistics—particularly by claiming that 7,400 new businesses had located in New York during his administration without acknowledging that 13,000 had left.[11] He attacked Rockefeller for suggesting that the Democratic Party had been captured by "extremists" (the governor had accused the Republicans of the same thing in 1964), an attack Rockefeller made because he had concluded that the election would be won in blue-collar and ethnic areas that responded to that kind of harangue. Goldberg cited Rockefeller's campaign pledges constantly: "The drug addict will be as rare as the tuberculosis patient in ten years. You know who said that? Nelson Rockefeller. Well, there are somewhere between five and ten times as many addicts now as there were then."[12]

All of which prompted *Time* magazine to conclude that the Goldberg campaign had moved from "disastrous to mediocre."[13]

One possible reason for Goldberg's incredibly inept campaign could be that Rockefeller had successfully co-opted his rival— or at least softened his resolve to fight hard. In May 1970, just a month before Goldberg's expected primary victory over Howard Samuels, the governor invited the former justice and his wife to Pocantico for dinner.

"We just had a social session as two civilized beings ought to have," said Goldberg after he followed up on Rockefeller's casual invitation of "Let's get together." And Rockefeller Press Secretary Hugh Morrow concurred that it was simply "what gentlemen about to go into combat would do."[14] But several top Goldberg supporters were stunned that he would casually dine with the Republican governor on the eve of their campaign. One aide to the Democratic candidate said he was "convinced that Goldberg could never thereafter go after him and play rough. By inviting him up there, Rockefeller said to Goldberg 'You're a nice little Jewish boy from Chicago, and you've done well for yourself. But if you think someone with all this is going to let you take it away, you're over your head.' "

Later that year, a reporter covering the campaign mentioned to Rockefeller the possible appointment of a troubleshooter to cut red tape and answer citizens' complaints. A few days later, Goldberg disclosed his own interest in such an appointment.[15] "See," the reporter told Rockefeller on their next encounter. "Goldberg is going to appoint an ombudsman." "You're wrong," Rockefeller replied only half-jokingly. "Goldberg said he is going to be an ombudsman. Hell, if that's all he wants, I'll appoint him."[16]

The Rockefeller campaign had of course begun early. A year before the election, the *Times* reported that Rockefeller was campaigning as if the election were next week. "It is," said a Rockefeller staffer at that time, "like a country mobilizing for war,"[17] which was not a bad description. Rockefeller does not come to lose. For him, elections *are* the moral equivalent of a war. Besides, as he told a friend, he was moving early in order to "keep ambitious heads from popping up all over the place this year."

Nelson Rockefeller won in 1970 by 716,061 votes, not by going to the right, although he did do that, but by clinging desperately to the center. "To be perfectly frank," said Rockefeller in 1970, "I'm interested in enough votes to elect me. And my position has always been to be in the middle and to stretch my arms out to either side."[18]

In order to know just how far his hands should extend, Rockefeller had his own polls. "The polls," said campaign director R. Burdell Bixby, "tell us better than our instincts what it is the people are concerned about."[19] The pollster who told the candidate what the people were concerned about was Lloyd Free, who believes that voters are "ideological conservatives" when they think about the general role and purpose of government, but "operational liberals" when it comes to specific proposals to solve specific problems. Free identified "the pivotals" as those voters who could swing either way, and he found that half of them lived in New York City, half upstate. The difference between the city pivotals and the country pivotals was a constant problem, but Rockefeller managed to appeal to both groups.

On the stump, he was everywhere. A young Goldberg staffer met the governor at a Pulaski Day parade in Buffalo and said: "Hello, Governor, it seems I only meet you at parades." "Son," said Rockefeller, "parades are my business."[20]

The Rockefeller campaign had 31 divisions for nationalities, and the governor seemed to have some connection with every one of them. Rockefeller asked a Greek group: "How many of you remember I was Spiro Agnew's first choice for president?"[21] Another time, he told a Jewish audience: "My ancestors may have been Jewish. We're not really sure."[22]

Bit by bit, what Democratic Party leaders had presumed would be Goldberg's solid support among Jewish voters began to crumble: In October, industrialist Charles Bassine of Spartan Industries accelerated the erosion. He mailed 100,000 letters describing Rockefeller as "our strongest and loyal friend" and warning the Jewish community not to "be tempted to vote for Goldberg on the basis that he is a Jew and, therefore, presumably more sympathetic to Israel." The Rockefeller camp disclaimed credit for the dual-edged endorsement and declared: "This letter does not come from Rockefeller headquarters nor was it distributed with the approval or knowledge of anyone at the headquarters."[23] Exactly one year later, after Rockefeller's reelection, Bassine became a trustee of Rockefeller University.

For Catholics, there was the old question of parochial school aid. Despite Supreme Court rulings striking down all attempts to provide public assistance to parochial schools, Rockefeller continued to hold out the hope that New York could somehow get around the law. He urged the legislature to repeal the so-called Blaine Amendment, "replacing it with the less restrictive language of the federal Constitution on separation of church and state." He knew such a measure, even if enacted, would not alter the situation, but he conveyed concern and interest to the Catholic electorate, and was rewarded for it at the polls.

Backstopping the stump engagements was the now typical two-phase TV campaign. The first phase was the Record, the second, Pledges, mostly promises to do "something" about crime and narcotics and the other issues that Free's polls said were of most concern to the voters. He did not attack Goldberg as he had O'Connor. On the other hand, as Alton Marshall, then secretary to the governor, said, "You almost *have* to end up with *some* question of your opponent's credibility. People wouldn't want their soap opera to end without some suspense."[24] So the television campaign ended with a series of questions for the undecided voter that were designed to attack Goldberg's credibility.

At the same time, a massive direct-mail effort was underway. Based on information from commercial mailing lists, polls, and especially state records (the Rockefeller campaign had, by computer, the ability to sift every letter ever received by a state agency expressing a New Yorker's concern about any problem), the campaign organization had accumulated and computerized details on the lives and worries of as many as 75 percent of the state's voters. Specially tailored letters were targeted to many of these people. Some 30 million pieces of literature were prepared, everything from conventional ethnic appeals to brochures detailing what Rockefeller had done for every group and region in the state. For cooking buffs, the campaign even sent out a card with a recipe for Happy Rockefeller's coffee cake.

Not everything was simple. There was one delicate situation for Rockefeller. He was trying to walk a tightrope between the U.S. Senate candidacies of Republican Charles Goodell, whom he had appointed only two years before, and Conservative James Buckley. Rockefeller gave about $38,000 to the Goodell campaign and, with the noticeable exception of an attack on Goodell's Vietnam troop withdrawal plan (Rockefeller said it "can only undermine the effectiveness of the president's bargaining position"[25]), he never had an unkind word for his official running mate. Of course, sometimes his normal exuberance got the better of him. At one point he issued a press release which said: "Today's New York *Times* quotes me as describing Senator Charles Goodell as 'the brightest, ablest man that I know on the political scene.' Clearly, what I meant to say was that Senator Goodell is *one of* the brightest, ablest men that I know on the political scene."[26]

By the time the campaign was in full swing, Rockefeller was able to muster a statement saying "I'm voting for Goodell myself and nobody has any question about it, and I'm leader of the party."[27] True enough, but the governor omitted any words of restraint directed to the hundreds of Republicans who were actively working for the election of Buckley. In fact, Rockefeller seemed to be running with both men; the state was flooded with two sets of campaign buttons, one saying "Rockefeller-Goodell," the other "Rockefeller-Buckley."

Just to be sure that all the bases were covered, Rockefeller wanted Spiro Agnew to campaign for him in the upstate conservative area surrounding Syracuse. His request reportedly amazed President Nixon, who recalled the way Rockefeller had wanted to use him in 1966. Said Nixon: "Isn't that something! They're really reading the tea leaves, aren't they?"[28]

Nothing better illustrates Rockefeller's desire for a broad base of support than the way in which organized labor was won over to the governor's side. Rockefeller had always had generally good relationships with organized labor. Victor Riesel had written before the first gubernatorial campaign in 1958 that the state's labor hierarchy, which had an abundance of rhetoric for other candidates, was mum when it came to Rockefeller. From the beginning of his tenure in office, Rockefeller used his appointment power to flatter and cultivate labor's leaders. The president of the New York City Central Labor Council, Harry

Van Arsdale, was appointed to the honorific Task Force to Study the State's Power Needs and Resources in 1959.[29] Other labor leaders were appointed to similarly innocuous posts throughout Rockefeller's governorship, and special task forces and panels were created in the State Labor Department for the sole purpose of providing room for union representation.

Of course, there were other, more tangible reasons for labor's love for Rockefeller. New York always had the highest state minimum wage in the country. Unions that endorsed him were treated well, and the lesson was learned by other labor organizations. For example, in 1963, just after he'd won reelection with the first-time support of the Patrolmen's Benevolent Association and Uniformed Firefighters Association of New York City, Rockefeller asked the legislature for a law establishing the principle that firemen's and patrolmen's pensions after 20 years be computed on the basis of the worker's total earnings during his last year on the job. The legislation finally passed in 1967, and the principle soon spread to the transit police, housing police, corrections officers, and sanitationmen. (The *Daily News* said that Rockefeller's action was the "principal spur behind the rocketing costs of pensions."[30])

Above all, Rockefeller was a builder, and the construction unions, the backbone of unionism in New York, never forgot the man who gave them jobs. And Rockefeller never tired of reminding them of it. "He got us the jobs," says Peter Brennan, the construction union leader who served a stint as Richard Nixon's labor secretary.[31] "There was always guys who didn't want to go for him, so I'd take them around and show them the buildings he was responsible for, the work he was responsible for. Hell, they could see the buildings. I didn't have to do any more persuading after that. In the construction industry it's either feast or famine. We had a pretty good feast when Rockefeller was around."

Nineteen-seventy was the year of the Big Payoff. Arthur Goldberg had been a friend of labor all his life. He'd been a union lawyer for 20 years before his appointment as secretary of labor by President Kennedy. And still, organized labor in New York State went for Rockefeller. Why? "We always knew what the score was with Rocky," says Brennan. "Goldberg was an unknown quantity. He never would build as much as Rockefeller. That's for sure. Hell, he was criticizing the building. He wanted the money to go to the poor."[32] Adds George Meany, president of the AFL–CIO: "Nelson is satisfied with his own share, and he don't try to keep the other fella from getting his. He doesn't have that mean streak you find in some of these Republican businesmen."[33]

In fact, Meany might have added, he's got rather a kind streak in him—at least when it comes to powerful labor leaders. When Meany's wife collapsed at a Rockefeller dinner party, the vice-president sat at her hospital bedside until doctors determined she had not had a heart attack.

The New York State Federation of Labor met for its annual convention at the Concord Hotel in the Catskills in the first week of September 1970. The convention was being rigged for an endorsement of Rockefeller. In advance of the convention, the executive committee of the state AFL–CIO had voted, 16–8, to recommend such an endorsement. Eleven of the 16 votes came from men representing the construction and building trades. (Although the building trades accounted for only 17 percent of organized labor in the state, they held nearly half the executive committee seats, largely because of their aggressiveness and the indifference of most of the federation's other unions.)

Still, the Goldberg forces thought they would have a fair chance on the floor when the entire convention voted. Unfortunately, because of the partisanship of State AFL–CIO President Ray Corbett, a Rockefeller supporter from way back, the Goldberg forces could not even get a list of the delegates accredited to the convention. A list of delegates was needed if a roll call was to be honest, but Corbett stalled. At the same time, Harry Van Arsdale was rushing three busloads of electoral workers to the Concord to pack the hall. And, mysteriously, according to a reporter for the Buffalo *Courier-Express*, a box

"slightly smaller than a shoebox"[34] full of delegate badges ma-
terialized. Impartial observers swear that the convention hall—
which can accommodate 3,000 people—was filled with at least
2,500 bodies on the evening of the vote, this despite the fact that
only 1,303 delegates were registered.

As the time for the vote approached, Goldberg partisans, led
by Victor Gotbaum of the municipal workers union, rose to
demand a roll call. Corbett immediately called for a standing
vote on the question and declared that the ayes had it—Nelson
Rockefeller was the federation's choice. Gotbaum went hoarse
screaming on the floor for a roll call. Corbett shut off his micro-
phone. A Rockefeller supporter moved for adjournment, and
Corbett adjourned the convention without taking a vote. All the
microphones went dead, and the house lights were turned off.

That was when the ashtrays started flying. The hall became
bedlam, illuminated only by the spotlights of the CBS camera
crew. Gotbaum confronted Van Arsdale, who said, "What are
you getting so excited about?" To which Gotbaum replied:
"You stole it from us, Harry."[35]

Even Rockefeller's aides were shocked. Next morning, Corbett and the executive committee declared an unprecedented
one-month recess, during which time all actions of the convention were to continue in effect. When the convention reconvened, the result was the same—without much fuss. It was all
over by then, and no one—not even Gotbaum—had the stomach
for another ashtray-throwing scene.

Gotbaum felt that Rockefeller had executed a deliberate and
cynical plan of catering to the needs and desires of the building
trades in order to get his "labor support." The governor, said
Gotbaum, "is a man with no ideology. He's not a guy who's
turned his back on principles; he's never had any. This is where
I differ with a lot of people. They talk about going from left to
right as though he was a liberal, left-wing Republican. This is
pure, arrant nonsense. Rockefeller is a tabula rasa; he's a clean
slate. You can put anything on his table and if the mood of the
times calls for it, he'll eat it and digest it."[36]

349

Rockefeller thereafter claimed "the backing of organized labor," frequently reporting that he had the endorsement of "83 unions with membership of over 1.3 million."[37] How the governor arrived at that figure is not exactly clear. Rockefeller seemed to have invented a "new math" all his own. For example, one of his press releases claimed the support of 30,000 members of the International Union of Dolls, Toys, Playthings, Novelties, and Allied Products; attached to the press release itself was a statement from the union which placed its membership at only 20,000, some of them residents of Canada.

Before turning rightward again, Rockefeller decided to take a postelection vacation in Puerto Rico. Peter Fishbein, Arthur Goldberg's campaign manager, had the same idea. Fishbein booked a first-class seat aboard an Eastern Air Lines flight, but when he arrived to claim his ticket he was told that first-class had been oversold and that he would have to fly coach. "Just then," recalls Fishbein, "Rockefeller and Lefkowitz and Wilson and a whole entourage swept up. The governor had booked all of first-class. He spotted me and we talked for a few minutes, and I said that such were the fortunes of war. He had won the election and was flying first-class. We had lost and I was flying coach. 'Listen,' he said, 'win or lose, I'd go first-class on this plane.' "[38]

CHAPTER 34

The Tragedy
of Attica

FOR Nelson Rockefeller, the years following 1970 were ones of retrenchment. The state budget had soared 400 percent in a decade and, in 1971, for the first time in 20 years, revenue was so scarce that the state had to draw on the tax revenue stabilization fund. Tax collections were $400 million below expectations. There was a $1.5 billion budget gap, and the people had been taxed-out; starting with his first year in office, sales, income, gas, cigarette, and liquor levies had been increased 13 times. Rockefeller cut back, but he also attacked, finding a ready target in the welfare rolls. He had already put through the legislature a one-year residency rule for welfare recipients even after such a requirement had been struck down as unconstitutional by the U.S. Supreme Court in January 1972. (Ironically, eight years earlier, Rockefeller had criticized Barry Goldwater for proposing the same idea. And in 1960, Rockefeller had vetoed an identical measure, saying, "The time a person has lived among us is no measure of his needs."[1])

Undaunted, Rockefeller said that "laws designed for good social purposes" may actually have the effect of "undermining public morality." He singled out welfare and introduced legislation to require welfare recipients to pick up their checks in person. Twenty-three percent of those who would normally have received checks in the mail didn't show. "They didn't show," said Rockefeller, "because they either had a job, or they lived in Puerto Rico or some other country or some other state."[2]

From there, as Watergate unfolded, it was a short jump to "I decided to get the cheats and chiselers off the taxpayers' back," a remark that drew great applause from an audience of Arizonans who also heard the governor say that Barry Goldwater, "this great man," has become "a symbol of integrity and the soul of frankness." And from there into Moral Lecture No. 1. "There has been a growing tendency to cut corners," said Rockefeller—who never had to—"to think that it's smart to beat the system; whether it's fixing a ticket [as in the Lindsay administration]; cheating on exams [could he be referring to Ted Kennedy and the Harvard Spanish exam episode?] or lying to the public [Richard Nixon, perhaps?]; padding expense accounts or [here he goes again] chiseling on welfare."[3]

The heartland loved it. He crippled the Urban Development Corporation's most potent weapon, the power to override local zoning regulations. He signed a bill restoring the death penalty, hailing it as "a major deterrent";[4] he'd already passed tough "no-knock" and "stop-and-frisk" laws during his first flirtation with conservatism in 1964. And he called for harsh, mandatory sentences for drug dealers and users, again ignoring evidence that such legislation would not deter the traffic in or the use of narcotics.

In fact, the stringent drug laws imposed by Rockefeller in 1973 offer a good illustration of the way in which the governor mixed politics with policy. Rockefeller had done little about New York's drug problem during the early years of his governorship. Finally, in 1966 he proposed a "new" program, an "all-out war," that would "wipe out" narcotics addiction. But from 1967 to 1971, according to the Legislative Commission on Expenditure Review, fewer than 150 addicts were deemed "cured" by the state program. As the public's outrage grew, Rockefeller's rhetoric escalated. And in 1973, he fashioned a new plan that called for harsh mandatory prison sentences allowing little, if any, chance for parole. His original proposal was so severe that a nineteen-year-old who shared a small amount of hashish with a friend would be subject to a more severe sentence than a convicted murderer.[5]

Rockefeller justified the law by explaining that "about 135,000 addicts were robbing, mugging, murdering day in and day out for money to fix their habit, and it was costing the people of New York up to $5 billion."[6] At that rate, Rockefeller's alleged army of addicts would have had to commit something on the order of 49,275,000 robbings, muggings, and murders a year, which would mean that the average New Yorker would be robbed, mugged, and murdered approximately seven times annually.

The exaggerated statistics were only part of the politics of fear. "How can we defeat drug abuse before it destroys America?" he asked rhetorically in the New York *Law Journal*. "I believe the answer lies in summoning the total commitment America has always demonstrated in times of national crisis. . . . Drug addiction represents a threat akin to war in its capacity to kill, enslave, and imperil the nation's future; akin to cancer in spreading deadly disease among us; and equal to any other challenge we face in deserving all the brainpower, manpower and resources necessary to overcome it. . . . Are the sons and daughters of a generation that survived the Great Depression and rebuilt a prosperous nation, that defeated Nazism and Fascism and preserved the free world, to be vanquished by a powder, needles and pills?"[7]

Virtually every law enforcement and legal organization in the state opposed his plan. The New York City bar association said that his proposals were "conceptually barbaric, incompatible with the entire structure and approach of New York's modern Penal Law, and in some respects preposterous to the point of unconstitutionality. More important from a pragmatic standpoint, they appear unworkable,"[8] a conclusion seemingly borne

353

out by the evidence. Governor Hugh Carey's Law Enforcement Task Force has recommended that the legislature correct some of the most "egregious aspects of the 1973 drug law" in order to "provide sentencing alternatives to the present mandatory minimum sentences so that the courts can exercise discretion to fit the punishment to the crime."[9]

None of the criticism bothered Rockefeller. Supreme Court Justice Burton Roberts, a former Bronx County district attorney, called the governor's proposals "pure and simple gimmickry" to satisfy the "blood lust"[10] of the public. The New York *Times* called the plan "little better than a politically attuned harangue that threatens to make a bad situation worse."[11]

When he signed his measures into law, Rockefeller attacked his critics without mercy, calling them a "strange alliance of vested establishment interests, political opportunists and misguided softliners."[12]

What his critics had argued for was a greater emphasis on apprehension and treatment, a realization that certainty of punishment, not severity, is the only real deterrent to crime. Rockefeller would have none of it, although he knew and understood that axiom of penology better than most. "If your chances of getting caught and sent away are only 2 percent, why worry?"[13] he said in September of 1973. It was his critics' point exactly, but one which he wouldn't follow to its logical conclusion. National politics dictated a firm response—penalogical rules be damned—and he positively beamed when he hailed his new laws as "the toughest anti-drug program in the nation."[14]

Of course, he had already proved his toughness and shown his muscle at Attica. His actions during that crisis are the best indication we have of the way he might handle a military conflict if he were president.

For five days in September 1971, 1,200 inmates laid siege to the New York state prison at Attica. Thirty-nine correctional officers and civilians were held as hostages. An assault was undertaken to recapture the prison in which 39 inmates and hostages were killed, the highest casualty toll of any disturbance in U.S. penal history and, according to the official commission appointed to review the situation, the "bloodiest one-day encounter between Americans since the Civil War."

"The degree of civilization in a society can be judged by entering its prisons," said Dostoyevsky. Attica, according to the Rockefeller-appointed commission headed by Dean Robert McKay of the New York University Law School, was a walled fortress where security was the only objective: "In general, inmates were subject to daily humiliation and degradation . . . the promise of rehabilitation was a cruel joke. If anyone was rehabilitated, it was in spite of Attica, not because of it."[15]

Tensions between inmates and guards had been building during the summer of 1971. An inmate manifesto setting forth a series of moderate demands, and including a commitment to peaceful change, was sent to Correction Commissioner Russell Oswald and Governor Rockefeller in July.

A brief fight between two inmates on September 8 resulted in their being taken from their cellblocks to isolation. This action precipitated angry name calling and vows of revenge, since the inmates were convinced that the two were being taken away to be beaten. On the next day, some prisoners refused to return to their cells after breakfast. A lieutenant who intervened was attacked and knocked to the floor. By 10:30 A.M., the rebellion had spread and the prisoners controlled four cellblocks. Two of these were retaken quickly, but the authorities lacked sufficient forces to storm the remaining seized portions of the prison. Commissioner Oswald arrived by 2 P.M. and decided to continue the negotiations that had begun almost immediately. There followed three days of talks over the prisoners' 28 demands, most of them calling for reform in prison conditions, coupled with amnesty for those participating in the revolt.

From the outset, Rockefeller believed that the rebellion was led by "revolutionaries,"[16] a premise the McKay Commission disputed. The governor told the commission that he had "followed these developments with great interest and considered that, if tolerated, they posed a serious threat to the ability of free government to preserve order and to protect the security of the individual citizen. Therefore, I firmly believe that a duly elected official . . . would be betraying his trust to the people he serves if he were to sanction or condone such criminal acts by negotiating under such circumstances."[17]

Seven months later, Rockefeller elaborated: "Now one of the techniques that is being used by revolutionary forces today, not only in our country but in the world, is to take hostages and then, at the threat to kill the hostages, [they try] to achieve political objectives which are in violation of all of our laws. Now, if this procedure is successful and had it been successful there, in my opinion this thing would have spread like wildfire, and it would have destroyed our capacity as a free government, destroying the ability of our structures as a government to effectively preserve freedom."[18]

The McKay Commission found that "rather than being revolutionary conspirators bent only on destruction, the rebels were part of a new breed of younger, more aware inmates, largely black . . . unwilling to accept the petty humiliations and racism that characterize prison life."[19]

Rockefeller left the uprising in the hands of Oswald. To aid him, Rockefeller dispatched his own secretary, Robert Douglass, to Attica. "I was only an observer," says Douglass. "Russ was calling the shots. He was in complete control."[20]

By Sunday, September 12, negotiations had broken down almost completely, and the impartial observer team had requested that Rockefeller come to the prison, even if such a trip were only a symbolic gesture that would establish "greater credibility with the inmates." The governor refused. According to Tom Wicker, who was one of the observers, "Inmate rhetoric . . . had suggested that [the prisoners] clearly understood that Governor Rockefeller was The Man with the power. Obviously, they wanted him to treat them with some respect, as if they too were men worth negotiating with. . . ." If Rockefeller didn't come, said one inmate leader, it would just confirm "what [we] knew in [our] guts, that he *doesn't* care."[21]

The observers tried again. Still, Rockefeller refused. Here was the man who had won a 1964 primary with the slogan "He Cared Enough to Come," a man who had once said "I fancy myself an excellent negotiator. I love it. It is, I think, my one natural talent."[22] Of course, it is entirely possible that Rockefeller's presence would not have altered the situation. Then again, the master campaigner might have been useful. At the very least, his presence would have given the negotiators more time. There was always time to assault, said Representative Herman Badillo, there was always "a time to die."

Even Commissioner Oswald tried to persuade the governor to come to the prison—on three separate occasions. ("I thought," said Oswald, "that it might be appropriate for someone as warm and understanding as the governor to walk that last mile."[23]) "When the governor refused Oswald's request that he come," said the McKay Commission, "he was spurning the recommendation of the man on whom he had relied to bring about a peaceful resolution, and departing from his usual policy of giving full support to his appointees."[24]

In a 1975 interview, Rockefeller said that by the time of Oswald's request, "his judgment was no longer valid,"[25] an interesting statement which raises the question of why Rockefeller then permitted Oswald to continue running the show, up to and including the final assault.

The McKay Commission concluded that "the Governor should have gone to Attica, not as a matter of duress or because the inmates demanded his presence, but because his responsibilities as the State's chief executive made it appropriate that he be present at the scene of the critical decision involving great risk of loss of life, after Commissioner Oswald had requested him to come."[26]

As usual, Rockefeller was worried about implications far beyond New York's borders: "If I said I'll go . . . if we did this in our state, what happens to the framework of order in our country?"

In a rare moment of candor before the House Judiciary Committee during its hearings on his nomination to be vice-president, Rockefeller confessed that he did not go to Attica because he would be seen on "the world television cameras" as "the man who failed in this thing."[27]

To which Representative Elizabeth Holtzman would later reply: "A man who is more concerned about his television image than about trying to prevent death is not qualified in my judgment to assume the moral leadership of this country."[28]

On the morning of September 13, 1971, the morning the assault on Attica was to take place, it was raining in New York City. The governor was to meet with William Ronan and others to discuss the upcoming transportation bond issue. The group gathered in the library of Rockefeller's Fifth Avenue apartment, waiting for the governor to come down from Pocantico.

Finally, Rockefeller arrived, showing off a new raincoat to those waiting in the library. He announced that he had made a decision about Attica, that "it was a matter of principle," recalls one person present that morning. "The governor said it was a question of 'knuckling under' or 'preserving our traditions of justice.'"

Rockefeller was standing, talking expansively now, while the others remained seated. He said he had considered every alternative, that Happy had even suggested drugging the food, but he was fearful that one inmate would not eat and that that inmate would then take reprisals. (At various other times, Rockefeller himself had inquired about the possibility of drugging the inmates' water. Others on the governor's staff had asked about the feasibility of a supersiren or giant floodlight to incapacitate the prisoners, and the idea of dropping hundreds of gallons of water on the inmates from helicopters was also discussed. All of these suggestions were considered impractical: they would disable the police as well as the prisoners, and none could work quickly enough.)

The gathering adjourned to the dining room for breakfast as Rockefeller took a call informing him that the assault was about to begin. The governor told the group that he had been assured that every precaution would be taken to avoid harm. He said that the police were going to be using a new kind of gas that would put everyone to sleep. Transportation Commissioner Theodore Parker, a former Army general, asked Rockefeller what the gas was, and the governor picked up the phone linking him directly to the scene. He asked, got a reply, and called out the name of the gas by chemical formula. "Hell, governor," said Parker, who deciphered the name, "that's just tear gas."

"He was listening intently," recalls another man present that morning. "We were all trying to read his face. He smiled and we heard him say 'Thank god.' They were starting to bring out the hostages. Then it was clear that he was being told about the casualties. He had been rooting like a kid at first, you know, saying 'get them all out.' Now his face was changing from buoyancy and becoming more leaden. He had thought the assault would be orderly and safe. It wasn't. The governor was now seated in an armchair, and the rest of us got up and left without bothering to say good-bye."

Despite instructions to the contrary, corrections officers — believed to be too emotionally involved to act with restraint — were permitted to assault the prison along with the State Police. No nonlethal weaponry was available, and the guns and ammunition used were such that they made inevitable the killing and wounding of innocent people. In six minutes, according to the McKay Commission, 2,200 lethal missiles were discharged, many of them from shutguns with "double-zero" buckshot which, upon firing, scatters in a fanlike pattern that is 2.5 feet wide at 50 yards from the muzzle.[29] (The use of such ammunition was specifically prohibited in the "model" plan for handling prison disturbances that the State Police had drawn up years before.) The McKay Commission concluded that excessive force was definitely used.[30]

As bad as the assault was, the reprisals carried out by the police in its aftermath were far worse.

By 10:10, less than half an hour after the first shot, the inmates were being herded back to their cells. They were required to clasp their hands behind their heads as they made their way through the debris of the assault. Most were still choking from the gas. The corrections officers had taken over, in charge again after four days of frustration. Many state policemen joined them as they pushed, kicked, and slugged the inmates. When a jam of bodies gathered around the steps leading out of the ward, the inmates were ordered to crawl—face down, hands still behind their heads—farther into the next yard.[31]

"The prone inmates," wrote Tom Wicker, ". . . were ordered, in small groups, to stand up and strip. Not just clothes, but religious medals, eyeglasses and false teeth had to be removed in preparation for body searches. The corrections officers with their clubs had a special preoccupation with the inmates' watches. Some they smashed on the inmates' wrists; some they tossed up in the air and hit like fungoes; some they threw on the ground and stomped." Dr. John Cudmore of the National Guard "had to stop another corrections officer from clubbing an inmate whose bleeding head the doctor was treating. A National Guardsman helping to carry out a wounded man was unable to stop several troopers from hitting the inmate with their clubs while he lay on a stretcher. The inmate screamed, and a trooper shouted, 'Fuck you nigger, you should have gotten it in the head!' "[32]

Before they could reach their cells, the inmates had to make their way through a long tunnel. Corrections officers stationed themselves on either side of the passageway. As each inmate ran or stumbled by, wrote Wicker, "the correction officers, public employees of the state of New York, agents of law enforcement, hit him with their clubs. If he took his hands down, he was stopped and beaten in place. If he fell, they took turns hitting him while he was down. Shouts of 'nigger' and 'motherfucker' rang through the echoing corridor. One guard chased an inmate all down the line, hitting him as he ran."[33]

Special treatment awaited the inmate leaders. Frank Smith was marked with a chalked "X" and made to lie on his back across a recreational table, and a football was placed under his chin. He was told that if the football fell he would be killed.[34]

Russell Oswald conceded that there had been beatings, but considered the tunnel gauntlet "more in the nature of an old fraternity hazing" which he could "understand."[35]

In the months following the Attica rebellion, only inmates were prosecuted. It took more than four years and a special commission appointed by Governor Hugh Carey to determine officially that "criminal acts of brutality to inmates occurred," and that the state's prosecution had been so warped by "imbalance" and "serious errors in judgment" that a special prosecutor was necessary to consider the possibility of obtaining indictments against law enforcement officers and state officials.[36]

In *A Time To Die*, Tom Wicker reflected on Attica:

... the involvement of Nelson Rockefeller had been extraordinary. For once, the hand of established power in America had been seen directly at work. Usually, the headlines traced deaths and destruction to no higher sources than obscure Southern governors or big city police chiefs or pompous generals and their rows of ribbons; and the forces beyond them could be but dimly glimpsed, and impersonally at that—the "military industrial complex," "the imperialists," "the money men." But at Attica one of the richest men in the world, possessing as much of the power of wealth as anyone could, had been seen in direct command also of the political and military powers of the state. At Attica, there had been a rare and chilling glimpse of the real thing at work—power itself, as well as the agents of power.[37]

What did Nelson Rockefeller think? ". . . Frankly," said Rockefeller of the forces at Attica, "I think [they] did a superb job."[38]

Later, the governor would say that he had made a mistake—he should have ordered his men in sooner. He also admitted one fault—he had not realized how serious the prison situation had become. "One of the things I regret most," said Rockefeller, "is my own lack of perception of the tremendous need which existed."[39] Perhaps that lack of perception was due to the fact that he had never visited a state prison during nearly 13 years as governor.

Nearly everyone lost at Attica. The dead, of course; the surviving prisoners and their cause of reform; the police and other officials who at least suffered a loss of credibility, if little else; and Russell Oswald, who was never quite the same again. The governor eased him out as correction commissioner 18 months later, giving him another job at a reduced salary in order to keep him in the state pension system. Russell Oswald was given a testimonial dinner. The governor did not come.

About the only person who did not lose was Nelson Rockefeller. He put it all behind him, and maybe even scored a few points with the Nixon crowd, as William Safire said.

Slightly more than two years after Attica, Nelson Rockefeller resigned as governor of New York after 15 years in office. Re-election to a fifth gubernatorial term was a risky proposition. He had tried for the presidency three times using the governorship as his launching pad. He would now try from the vantage point of private citizen, knowing, of course, that he could still command his state's delegates at a Republican National Convention. He would follow a familiar pattern, creating the Commission on Critical Choices from which he could speak out on current issues. He said he was not a quitter but had come to realize that "New Yorkers' best interests are affected by problems over which we do not have control in the state." He fooled no one.

A year later, three years after Attica, Nelson Rockefeller was nominated for vice-president by Gerald Ford. He tried hard to sidestep controversial issues during his confirmation hearings. It was better, he reasoned, to admit mistakes than to defend his actions. So it was perhaps inevitable that Nelson Rockefeller would humble himself regarding Attica. "If Attica would happen again," said Rockefeller, "I would think that . . . the proper way to proceed" would be "to go ahead . . . without weapons."[40]

Again, he fooled no one, but the matter was dropped. Rockefeller's "Bay of Pigs" would not prevent his becoming vice-president of the United States.

Mr. Rockefeller Goes to Washington

ON his own turf, Nelson Rockefeller was unbeatable. His combination of wealth, influence, political savvy, and sheer unadulterated gall enabled him to dominate the politics of a state as few men ever have. Yet the national scene always brought out the worst in him. The New York Nelson was bold, innovative, crafty, combative; the national Nelson—at least in his first three presidential campaigns—was indecisive, erratic, and inept. Loyal to a fault to his supporters at home, he was little more than an outside agitator to the party at large. In New York he almost never lost; going national he lost often—and sorely.

When Gerald Ford nominated Nelson Rockefeller to be his vice-president on August 20, 1974, the prevailing wisdom was that the dynamic Rockefeller would easily outshine the president, who had inherited the office from Richard Nixon two weeks earlier. But the prevailing wisdom was wrong. Away from his home base, Nelson could not outshine even Ford's dim light, and he advanced neither the president's nor his own political fortunes.

Oddly enough, Rockefeller sought the vice-presidency before the vice presidency sought him. In October 1973, while Nelson was still governor of New York, Spiro Agnew pleaded *nolo contendere* to a felony and resigned the vice-presidency in disgrace. For one frantic week, Rockefeller went after the second spot, until the president finally settled on the Michigan congressman who offered what Nixon needed most—blind loyalty. Actually, in choosing Ford, Nixon might have been doing Nelson a favor—if only the governor had realized it. Instead, Nelson reasoned that he would have his best shot at the White House if the president could finish out his term. "Nobody wanted Nixon innocent more than Nelson Rockefeller," said Theodore White, "but it wasn't in the cards and Nelson looked silly supporting him all the way to the gallows."[1]

Why, first as governor in 1973 and then as a private citizen in 1974, did Rockefeller want the vice-presidency so badly? His brother, Laurance, had said years before, "Harry Emerson Fosdick once preached a sermon entitled, 'Life Is Making the Most of Second Best.' I believe life taught Nelson that sermon."[2] But Nelson, who insisted earlier that he wasn't "cut out to be a No. 2 type of guy," clung to another motive. "I am not going to kid you," he told the Washington press corps at the time he ruled himself out of contention as Gerald Ford's 1976 running mate, "that I came down here with no thought of the presidency in mind."[3] Once, after constant questioning, Nelson had blurted out that yes, he still wanted to be Number One, that he had accepted the vice-presidency hoping it would lead to the White House. "What," he said, "do you think I'm doing here?"[4] Apparently, after 15 years in Albany and three unsuccessful campaigns for the top spot, being "standby equipment" wasn't so bad after all. Gerald Ford had been standby equipment, and look what happened to him.

But before Nelson could dream of the presidency, he had to be confirmed to the lesser post. At first, the process appeared easy. The rationale for supporting his nomination seemed to be that the president needed all the help he could get and that Rockefeller unquestionably had a firm grounding in domestic and foreign affairs. Rarely did anyone ask whether that experience was good or bad, least of all the media. The nation's top two weekly newsmagazines attempted to assemble a wealth of information about the nominee on short notice but conspicuously omitted certain salient facts and questions that might have provided some perspective. Columnist Nicholas von Hoffman tartly described the reportage in *Time* as worthy of the Second Coming. *Newsweek*, he complained, neglected even to note that Rockefeller sat on the Foreign Intelligence Advisory Board or to question the value of the Albany mall or the way it had been financed. Neither, von Hoffman concluded, "presumed valid grounds for serious criticism."[5]

During the first four days of Rockefeller's confirmation hearings Senate Rules Committee members gingerly poked into the more obvious aspects of Nelson's affairs, neglecting to question the nominee about the more than $2 million he had doled out to public officials. But after the committee recessed on September 26, news of the gifts and loans leaked onto front pages across the country. Rockefeller adviser William Ronan described it as "the Chinese water torture leakage: drip, drip, drip, out of the committee."[6]

Eventually, Nelson was forced to confront the basic issue. Wealth, he conceded, "is almost everywhere a potential source of power. That seems to be in the nature of things: wealth almost always gives a person an edge." But "wealth only leads to true political power . . . when it has been transmitted by our constitutional arrangement into public authority." Why? Because "it is the magic and majesty of our constitutional order that all of the sources of private power are in the long run tamed and domesticated."[7]

"Would my family background somehow limit and blind me,

so that I would not be able to see and serve the general good of all Americans?" Rockefeller asked rhetorically. "Let us remember that we are all limited to some extent by our backgrounds, that all American politicians must rise above the limitations of their private backgrounds. Poverty too can blind a man or a woman. Some never rise above the hungry resentments of early hardships."[8]

That did it. There were a few more damaging disclosures, a few of which even drew blood, but no more potentially mortal wounds to the Rockefeller colossus. Robert Douglass, who served as Rockefeller's congressional liaison during the confirmation process, recalled: "In mid-October we were taking an awful pasting on the [Goldberg] book, the loans and gifts, without an opportunity to get a forum, and the conservatives were starting to make noise. There were enough ingredients in that volatile mix that if Ford hadn't stuck with him, I was worried that if someone wanted to torpedo him there were a lot of slippery bananas around. But when we got through that and reappeared, I never worried about him not making it."[9] After eight days of hearings and 47 witnesses in addition to the nominee (who himself testified for 11 hours and 54 minutes), the Senate Rules Committee voted 9–0 on November 22 to recommend confirmation.

"Never," said Rockefeller, "has anybody's life been examined with as great care and thoroughness as your committee has seen to it that this was done." "I believe," concurred brother Laurance, "that you have more information on my brother than any living American in history."[10]

In fact, however, the congressional interrogation of Rockefeller and his friends was surprisingly sloppy. Even the token efforts were impeded by the brief, artificial time limits on questioning imposed by Senate Rules Committee Chairman Howard Cannon and, later, by House Judiciary Committee Chairman Peter Rodino, and by the fact that at least one key witness to the Rockefeller family's economic clout—brother David of Chase Manhattan—was never called before either committee.

At least the Senate committee scored a point for candor. Its December 3, 1974, report recommending Rockefeller's confirmation noted:

> The Committee made no attempt to establish the nature and magnitude of the personal wealth of the nominee's brothers and sister nor how this wealth in combination serves to enhance the economic influence of the Rockefeller family. Neither was this information disclosed by the nominee, by any other member of the Rockefeller family, or by any close associate. Also not investigated were the specific holdings and interlocking relationships of foundations, closely held corporations, university portfolios, banks, and other institutions which have long been identified with the Rockefeller interests.[11]

"Throughout the hearings," wrote Lewis Lapham in *Harper's*, "the committee mistook Mr. Rockefeller's manner of self-assurance for firmness of political purpose, his command of the issues for proof of political vision. In his anxiety to make a good impression on the committee, he resembled a prep-school boy seeking to explain himself in the headmaster's study. Not only did he give the committee every record that it asked for, but he agreed with almost every criticism the senators cared to make. When Senator Pell suggested that he forbear from giving money to government officials, Mr. Rockefeller responded with a dutiful pledge 'to cut it out.' "[12]

What eluded most committee members was the notion that Nelson might not be above making a buck. They failed to recognize how all-pervasive were the potential conflicts of interest, and how Rockefeller's generous gift giving could corrupt both the giver, who seemed to believe he was beyond the ordinary restraints of government, and the recipient, whose accountability to the public was clearly compromised. The investigators were not helped by the fact that Rockefeller refused to come up with a complete gift list to nonofficials and his brothers disclosed only those gifts made to public officials while in office. Rockefeller insisted throughout that he expected to be repaid by the public officials, a position that prompted New York Representative Elizabeth Holtzman to complain that "it is hard to accept his story when we have seen that only one out of ten public officials to whom he made loans ever made repayment of any kind, whereas all but one of the 26 persons who never held public office repaid their loans in whole or in part. The improbability is compounded when we realize that Mr. Rockefeller, at least in the case of Mr. Ronan (who got loans of $550,000), never even inquired as to whether repayment was possible."[13]

Finally, under tough questioning from California Representative Jerome Waldie during the House Judiciary Committee hearings, Rockefeller admitted that he practiced a pattern of giving gifts before and after a person held public office, making loans in the interim which would be forgiven later, in order to avoid conflicts with New York's so-called antitipping law.

WALDIE: "Am I describing correctly a process that you engaged in with intent to avoid the narrow definition of the law precluding gifts to employees?"

ROCKEFELLER: "No, sir."

WALDIE: "Why, then, governor, did you not collect a single loan that was forgiven, or why was there no interest charged on any of these loans during the period of public service? Why were they always forgiven and converted into a gift subsequent to public service? Why did you not convert them into a gift during the public service?"

ROCKEFELLER: "Because there was a law in the state of New York that said that gifts from an employee—"

WALDIE: "That is exactly what I have said."

ROCKEFELLER: "All right."[14]

Waldie continued, attacking the notion that the Rockefellers had made sacrifices for public service. "You are not," he said, "even entitled to anything except the responsible feeling that you have performed that which you are obliged to perform for the people of this country. You have not performed anything [exceeding] that [which] an individual who works 40 hours a week in a paper mill in Antioch, California, who goes home at night and takes care of a Cub Scout troop, and works on the weekends contributes and sacrifices for public service."[15]

Sensing the rising tension, acting committee chairman Jack Brooks called a coffee break. Instead of retreating, Rockefeller bounded up to the second tier of seats in the committee room to confront Waldie, whom he had never met before, and confessed: "You know, fella, you're right." Even Waldie, who was familiar with the acting style of California Governor Ronald Reagan, was impressed. "That took guts," he said subsequently, and "after that, I was totally diffused."[16]

The full House approved the nomination by 287–128 on December 19. Among those favoring Rockefeller was a large contingent of black legislators who heeded the advice of Representative Shirley Chisholm. "Let us not establish a standard for this nominee to which we ourselves would not be subjected," she said. "Let us instead, especially the concerned Democrats, lay aside partisan views in this critical hour, and confirm this seasoned, savvy, and able, although not perfect public servant."[17] So savvy was the vice-president that three months later he named Thaddeus Garrett, Chisholm's administrative assistant, to his staff.

Shortly after the House vote, almost four months after he was nominated, Nelson Rockefeller took the oath of office as vice-president. "It's been a fabulous experience," said Rockefeller, "it really has."[18]

During his first week on the job, Rockefeller was put on the Senate payroll, was paid 20 cents per mile for his flight from Tarrytown, New York, to Washington as the nation's first commuting vice-president, and was briefed in boring detail about the emoluments that go with being an employee of the U.S. Senate. The new vice-president cut short one prolonged explanation of the insurance and other options open to him by saying: "Okay, okay, I'll take the best."[19]

Of the man who had appointed him, Rockefeller had nothing but praise. An "extraordinary man . . . totally secure inside and relaxed, which is unusual. I've never seen him ruffled. His patience is unbelievable. . . ."[20] This nation must live under a star because Ford is the right man for this time. . . ."[21] I'm delighted, I couldn't be happier."[22] Asked about his working relationship with the president, Rockefeller put two fingers together and said: "We're like that."[23] But he had no illusions. He had, he said, known every vice-president since Henry Wallace, "and they were all frustrated, every one of them. . . ."[24] I don't expect anything. This, I think, is my greatest strength."[25]

Rockefeller's first impulse as presiding officer of the Senate was to run that show as he had run the New York State legislative circus. He found that unlike the tamer beasts of Albany, the lions of Washington were not eager to jump through his hoop.

The first controversy of 1975 was over a motion for cloture in a debate to change the Senate's filibuster rule. In a naïve attempt to expedite a decision, Rockefeller ignored calls for recognition from Senators James Allen of Alabama and William Brock of Tennessee and ordered the roll call to proceed. He was quickly taught a lesson about senatorial courtesy.

"It says so right here in the precedents of the Senate," the vice-president replied to an astounded Barry Goldwater. "The chair may decline to respond; the chair may decline to answer a parliamentary inquiry."[26]

"That is correct," Goldwater countered. "That is what it says, but I never thought I would see the day when the chair would take advantage of it."[27]

It was not like the old days in New York. Tempers didn't cool until two months later, when a carefully orchestrated ritual permitted five senators and the vice-president to mark a cease-fire. Rockefeller apologized for any "discourtesy" he may have shown the Senate, adding, "If I make a mistake I like to say so. I'm a very simple person."[28]

Not simple enough so far as Donald Rumsfeld was concerned. The White House chief of staff had sought control of the powerful Domestic Council, an organization that had done much to shape domestic policies under Richard Nixon. Rockefeller wanted the council under his wing, as tangible proof of President Ford's stated promise that Rockefeller would have a major role in domestic affairs. In New York, the matter would have been settled without trouble. In Washington, Rockefeller was forced to go to Ford to resolve the issue. The vice-president won, but in the end, as a further indication of the essential powerlessness of the No. 2 spot, Rumsfeld pared the Domestic Council's budget so severely that Rockefeller's vision of the council as a long-range think tank was crippled. In short order, even under the direction of Rockefeller aide James Cannon, the Domestic Council became moribund, serving the Ford administration by preparing position papers on such weighty affairs of state as the federal government's view of poisoning coyotes.

Undaunted, Rockefeller bypassed the council, developing a new federal energy program by tapping the brainpower available to him outside the government—in this instance, Edward Teller, who had developed the plan while working on a project for Rockefeller's Commission on Critical Choices.

Here again, Rockefeller was thinking big. As he had created a largely autonomous system of public authorities for New York State, he now envisioned a $100 billion Energy Independence Authority to develop the nation's energy resources. Rockefeller's proposal split the Ford administration. The president's economic aide, William Seidman, sent Ford a toughly worded memo just before Ford backed the EIA (likening it to the Manhattan Project) which clearly implied that the federal government was biting off more than it could chew.[29] Others who opposed the plan were Federal Reserve Board Chairman Arthur Burns, Council of Economic Advisers Chairman Alan Greenspan, and Treasury Secretary William Simon. Greenspan charged that the proposal "creates a large potential for real and perceived corrupt practices."[30]

Mr. Rockefeller Goes to Washington

An earlier opponent was Russell Peterson, director of the President's Council on Environmental Quality. Peterson had confronted Rockefeller and Teller at a Critical Choices Commission meeting, urging a conservationist approach to the problem. "In my view," said Peterson, "most of the current energy debate is missing the critical choice. The debate is focused on energy supplies, primarily: where will our energy come from? . . . this is the American 'can do' attitude at work. But a focus on supply ignores the really critical choice, which is, in my opinion, how much energy shall we plan to consume?"[31]

Rockefeller called on Teller to rebut Peterson. "I will give you the gist of what I want to say," said Teller, "in the first minute. In fact, in two words: can do." To which Rockefeller replied: "Hear! Hear!"[32] Rockefeller's energy proposal languished in Congress, with about as much chance of passage as a resolution in praise of New York City's fiscal integrity.

Rockefeller clearly was taking his lumps within the administration and with the Congress. His chairmanship of the panel investigating CIA abuses hardly improved matters, although it did give him an opportunity to reassert his hawkish foreign policy views, which were perfectly congruent with those of the Republican right-wingers he was still trying to appease.

Rockefeller was an unlikely choice to probe the CIA, so close had been his associations with the agency over the years. During the 1950s he headed the Eisenhower administration's equivalent of the supersecret "Forty Committee"[33]—the group of high government officials charged with overseeing CIA clandestine operations. During the Nixon administration, he served on the Foreign Intelligence Advisory Board and received regular briefings on covert American operations abroad.

One such briefing, on the election of the Marxist Salvador Allende as president of Chile, was attended by Rockefeller in December 1970, a briefing Rockefeller was reportedly reminded about by CIA Director William E. Colby shortly after he was nominated to be vice-president. The reminder was prompted by press disclosures of covert CIA activities against Allende both before and after his election, and by Colby's concern that Rockefeller might be questioned about them by Congress. Colby had nothing to worry about.

"What did Nelson Rockefeller do when the news broke this fall about covert CIA actions which led to the overthrow of the Allende government?" Representative Holtzman asked rhetorically. "Did he call William Colby, the director of the CIA, to get the details of CIA activities; did he call William Colby to express concern over the torture of people by the new junta? He called William Colby only to learn whether he really used the word 'destabilization.' A man who is concerned with semantics when confronted with enormous abuses of power and human rights should not, in my judgment, be confirmed as vice-president."[34]

Despite this background—or, some cynics said, because of it—Rockefeller was given the job of investigating the snoopers. From the start, he left no doubt that he believed that what was good for the CIA was good for the nation. Asked whether confidence could be restored in the agency, Rockefeller replied: "Surely, otherwise this country couldn't be in existence anymore."[35] He insisted that "the public is going to be satisfied on this one if the facts are obtained and if they are then made available and corrective action is taken."[36] Having thus defined the criteria for a successful inquiry, he then failed to meet them. In the end, not all the facts were obtained, nor were all the facts that were obtained made public. The most notable omission was any discussion of alleged CIA assassination plots against Castro, Diem, and Lumumba, among others.

Nevertheless, Rockefeller was proud of his work. "No stones are left unturned," he said of the panel's final report, "no punches pulled."[37] What it all amounted to, said Rockefeller, was that "there are things which have been done which are in contradiction to the statutes, but in comparison to the total effort, they are not major."[38] To which Chairman Frank Church of the Senate Intelligence Committee retorted: "I don't regard murder plots as a minor matter."[39]

Compared with the Rockefeller report, the congressional committees investigating the C.I.A. have gone further, with less bias. Rockefeller's probe is viewed by many as a whitewash, an inevitability predicted in a cartoon by *Newsday*'s Tom Darcy which portrayed Rockefeller and the C.I.A. in conversation with their arms around each other: "We *must* have a bit of a fight, but I don't care about going on long," said Tweedledum. "What's the time now?"

Tweedledee looked at his watch, and said, "Half past four."

"Let's fight till six, and then have dinner," said Tweedledum.

Rockefeller's public performance on other issues was not much better. He had already offered a novel motive for supporting the Vietnam war (to keep the dollars flowing to New York) and for the declining federal interest in urban minority problems (nobody forced the blacks to migrate from the farms).[40] Now, when Congress refused more money for Saigon as Vietcong troops closed in, Rockefeller charged that the legislators would have blood on their hands if the Communists took over, since a million South Vietnamese would be liquidated in the process.[41]

He seemed to be making headway—at least with Barry Goldwater. The two spent several uninterrupted hours flying to Taipei for the funeral of Chiang Kai-shek. Goldwater promptly declared that "Rocky and I see more eye to eye on foreign policy than I and Ford do."[42] In fact, said Goldwater, "I think [Rockefeller] makes me look like a dove, to tell you the truth."[43]

Maybe so, but Rockefeller was still the enemy. In 1968, Ohio Representative John Ashbrook had said: "Nelson Rockefeller is the jackal in our camp. If he climbed a flagpole and sang 'Yankee Doodle Dandy' I still wouldn't support him."[44] Seven years later, little had changed. Rockefeller journeyed south in yet another vain effort to convert GOP conservatives. In South Carolina, one Republican said of his appearance: "You might say he changed some of our minds from 'hell no' to just plain 'no.'"[45] In the minds of conservatives he was still, to use William Rusher's words, Gerald Ford's "deadliest mistake."[46]

By the fall of 1975, conservative opposition had reached a

crescendo. Ford was dragging in the polls, Ronald Reagan was forcing the president ever rightward, and Nelson Rockefeller was trying desperately to hang on. The big issue was federal aid for New York City, and Rockefeller wasn't about to appear too liberal—not until he finally understood that he could not run with Ford under any circumstances. At that point, he flip flopped, championing the city and publicly disagreeing with the president as he tried to regain his credibility with whatever remained of his constituency back home.

Finally, on November 3, he decided to remove himself from consideration for the 1976 vice-presidential nomination. Some concluded that he jumped before he could be pushed. It really didn't matter. He had been driven from the ticket just as assuredly as if he had been fired, and the press conference he called to explain his action did him more good than anything he had done in politics in years.

His performance before the Washington press corps was vintage Rockefeller. He looked tired and older—finally. His jowls were clearly visible. But before long, it was all there again: the wink, the grin, the arched eyebrow, the self-mockery, and the Rockefeller slump—when Nelson Rockefeller feels that the press is eating out of the palm of his hand during a stand-up routine, he begins to drape himself over the lectern as if he were making love to it. He was brilliantly uninformative, but at last he was a martyr, and his abdication performance drew rave reviews. "Nothing so became Nelson Rockefeller in the vice-presidency of the U.S. than his renunciation of it,"[47] said *Time*, which added the incredible notion that Rockefeller was, if anything, "overqualified" for the presidency. Mary McGrory noted that Rockefeller "always looks best leaning into right-wing boos."[48] To Tom Braden, the columnist who had received financial help from Rockefeller and the one writer who seemed to be speaking directly for the vice-president, Nelson was "sick and tired of being chivied about by men of far lesser experience and knowledge."[49]

Mr. Rockefeller Goes to Washington

The truth was that after six decades of defending the family name, of fighting for the public's free gift of political authority, and of seeking the approval of his superiors, Nelson Rockefeller had become almost numb to criticism. He would listen, but he did not hear.

"After what I've been through, I don't react anymore," Rockefeller once explained. "I don't have visceral reactions. Sometimes I use righteous indignation as a legitimate way of saying things you couldn't say in a quiet conversation. If you're stirred up, people will accept it—like the Virginian: 'When you say that, smile.' "[50]

Nelson Rockefeller is a man who, in his own terms, is a failure. After all, said Nelson of the presidency, "I'm a politician. That is my profession. Success in politics, real success, means only one thing in America."[51] It is not unlikely that he feels maligned and misunderstood, that he thinks himself a great man and shares with Thomas Carlyle the belief that this "is an age . . . that denies the existence of great men; denies the desirability of great men. Show our critics a great man . . . [and] they begin to what they call 'account' for him, not to worship him, but take the dimensions of him—and bring him out to be a little kind of man."[52]

So Nelson Rockefeller waits, hoping that somehow he will not remain a "might-have-been"—a Daniel Webster, a Henry Clay, a Robert Taft. When he resigned New York's governorship he was asked how history would treat him; specifically, if his record would stack up with that of Theodore Roosevelt, whom he had always admired. "I'm less worried about history, to tell you the honest truth," said Rockefeller, "than I am about the future. But I do, would like to recall, as a little closing here, to let you know that my mind is always thinking about problems, in trying to understand them, I did sit in [Teddy Roosevelt's] lap once in our home, and he had been over in Africa and been bringing back big game alive, and I had been thinking a lot

377

about it, and so I said, 'The one thing I can't figure out is how did you bring the giraffes back on those flat cars when you went through a tunnel?'

"And he was marvelous and warm and friendly, and he said, 'We had a pulley and we'd pull their heads down before we went through the tunnel.' So that I was trying to figure those problems out even in those days."[53]

These days, Nelson Rockefeller tends to be philosophical, much as he was in 1967 when he said that he no longer wanted the presidency. Politics is change, he said then, summing up in his unquenchably optimistic way: "You want something and work for something and you can't win it. Then you make up your mind you're not going to have it, you relax about it—and then it comes up again."[54]

NOTES

Prologue

1. Nelson Rockefeller has no recollection of ever saying any such thing. In fact, he had even considered issuing a personal denial to the editors of *Newsweek*, where the quote appeared on September 2, 1974, shortly after his nomination. The authors traced the quote back to a profile by *New York Times* reporter Francis X. Clines, then to another story by James Clarity (who had since been assigned to the *Times*'s Moscow bureau), and finally to Robert Phelps, a respected former *Times*man and now an editor of the *Boston Globe*. "About a week after Christmas 1963," Phelps recalled, "I had asked for a private interview. We were on an airplane, and I sat down and talked to him. I remember the plane circling over Washington and seeing the lights. I asked him that, and that's the quote. I'll stand by it. It's accurate."

2. Hugh Sidey, "Rockefeller in the Boiler Room," *Time*, August 11, 1975, p. 18.

3. Interview with Louis Lefkowitz, New York, January 1975.

4. Laurance Rockefeller, written response to authors' questions, March 1975.

5. Daniel S. Anthony, "The Handwriting on the Wall. A Graphologist Looks at Our Leaders," *New York*, June 30, 1975, p. 36.

6. Lincoln Steffens, quoted in Garry Wills, *Nixon Agonistes* (Boston: Houghton Mifflin, 1970), p. 589.

7. Penelope McMillan, "Mr. Rockefeller Goes to Washington," *New York Sunday News Magazine*, March 9, 1975, p. 21.

8. Theodore H. White, *The Making of the President—1968* (New York: Atheneum, 1969), p. 224.

9. Richard Reeves, *A Ford, Not a Lincoln* (New York: Harcourt Brace Jovanovich, 1975), p. 148.

10. Interview with William Rusher, New York, April 1975.

11. Mary McGrory, "Barry and Rocky," *New York Post*, March 3, 1975.

12. Richard Reeves, "The Nationwide Search for Nelson Rockefeller," *New York*, September 2, 1974, p. 8.

13. *New York Times*, May 2, 1975.

14. William F. Buckley, Jr., "Rocky's Motives," *New York Post*, May 24, 1975.

15. Reeves, "Nationwide Search," p. 8.

16. Ibid.

17. Mary McGrory, "Rocky's out of Step," *Washington Star*, December 16, 1973.

18. *New York Times*, July 18, 1973.

19. *New York Times*, August 29, 1975.

20. Bill Moyers, quoted in Kirkpatrick Sale, *Power Shift: The Rise of the Southern Rim and Its Challenge to the Eastern Establishment* (New York: Random House, 1975), p. 303.

21. Richard Reeves, "Rocky (Is, Is Not, May Be) Running," *New York Times Magazine*, November 26, 1967, p. 156.

22. See Chapter 16 for a discussion of campaign financing.

23. Eugene L. Burdick, *The Ninth Wave* (New York: Dell, 1956), back cover.

24. Reeves, "Nationwide Search."

25. *Newsweek*, September 2, 1974.

26. Richard Reeves, "The Resistible Return of Nelson A.," *New York*, October 7, 1974, p. 9.

27. Interview with Theodore H. White, New York, September 1975.

28. John D. Rockefeller, quoted in Matthew Josephson, *The Robber Barons* (New York: Harcourt Brace, 1934); excerpted in Earl Latham, ed., *John D. Rockefeller: Robber Baron or Industrial Statesman?* (Lexington, Mass.: D. C. Heath, 1949), p. 37.

29. Ibid.

30. Nelson Rockefeller, quoted in Wills, *Nixon Agonistes*, p. 212.

31. Stewart Alsop, *Nixon and Rockefeller* (Garden City, N.Y.: Doubleday, 1960), p. 142.

32. Neal Peirce, *The Megastates of America* (New York: W. W. Norton, 1972), p. 25.

33. Jack Newfield, *Bread and Roses Too* (New York: E. P. Dutton, 1971), p. 195.

34. Interview with Richard Marron, Albany, March 1975.

35. *New York Times*, April 22, 1961.

36. *New York Times*, April 27, 1964.

37. Ibid.

38. Edwin O'Connor, *The Last Hurrah* (Boston: Little, Brown, 1956), p. 396.

39. William Kennedy, "Rocky Is 64, Going on 35," *New York Times Magazine*, April 29, 1973, pp. 16ff.

40. Interview with Hugh Carey, New York, March 1975.

41. *New York Times*, December 6, 1966.

42. Interview with Robert Sweet, New York, December 1975.

43. Ibid.

44. Interview with Donald Elliott, New York, December 1975.

45. Ibid.

46. *Newsweek*, October 21, 1974.

Chapter 1

1. U.S. Congress, Senate, Committee on Rules and Administration, *Hearings on the Nomination of Nelson A. Rockefeller of New York to be Vice President of the United States*, 93rd Cong., 2nd sess. (Washington, D.C.: Government Printing Office, 1974), pp. 20, 23.

2. U.S. Congress, House, Committee on the Judiciary, *Hearings on the Nomination of Nelson A. Rockefeller to be Vice President of the United States*, 93rd Cong., 2nd sess., serial no. 45 (Washington, D.C.: Government Printing Office, 1974), p. 2.

3. Ibid., p. 472.

4. All reports of Rockefeller family holdings are presumed to be bare minimums. They are based on official data submitted to congressional investigators in autumn 1974 and reflect market values at that time. Nelson's holdings were placed in a blind trust after he was confirmed as vice-president.

5. U.S. Congress, House, Committee on Banking and Currency, Subcommittee on Domestic Finance, *Commercial Banks and Their Trust Activities: Emerging Influence on the American Economy*, staff report, 90th Cong., 2nd sess. (Washington, D.C.: Government Printing Office, 1968), vol. 1.

6. Interview with Jerome Waldie, New York, January 1975.

7. Interview with David Rockefeller, New York, March 1975.

8. Ibid.

9. House Judiciary Committee, *Hearings*, p. 525.

10. Ibid., pp. 254–255.

11. Ibid., p. 235.

12. Charles B. Smith, quoted in G. William Domhoff and Charles L. Schwartz, "Probing the Rockefeller Fortune: A Report Prepared for Members of the United States Congress," H. Rept. 1066, November 1974, p. 26.

13. Statistical information on the wealth and finances of the Rockefeller family was obtained from figures supplied by the family to the authors and to congressional committee staffs, as well as from confidential analyses by those committees.

14. Dan Dorfman, "Inside Chase Manhattan: First Look at Rocky's Net Worth," *New York*, September 30, 1974, p. 30.

15. Interview with Ralph Caso, New York, August 1974.

16. House Judiciary Committee, *Hearings*, p. 1026.

Chapter 2

1. Interview with John D. Rockefeller IV, Buckhannon, W. Va., January 1975.

2. U.S. Congress, Senate, Committee on Rules and Administration, *Hearings on the Nomination of Nelson A. Rockefeller of New York to be Vice President of the United States*, 93rd Cong., 2nd sess. (Washington, D.C.: Government Printing Office, 1974), p. 12; Rockefeller Family Archives, Rockefeller Center, New York.

3. Senate Rules Committee, *Hearings*, p. 13.

4. Richard Reeves, *A Ford, Not a Lincoln* (New York: Harcourt Brace Jovanovich, 1975), p. 148.

5. Nelson Rockefeller, televised interview by David Frost, New York, July 20, 1971.

6. Laurance Rockefeller, written response to authors' questions, March 1975.

7. Nelson Rockefeller, interviewed by Frost.

8. Interview with David Rockefeller, New York, March 1975.

9. Interview with Nelson Rockefeller, Washington, D.C., March 1975.

10. Ibid.

11. Statement by Nelson Rockefeller. From *CBS Reports: The Rockefellers*, broadcast by CBS television, December 28, 1973. © CBS, Inc. 1973.
12. Interview with Nelson Rockefeller, Washington, D.C., March 1975.
13. Interview with Wallace Harrison, New York, May 1975.
14. Interview with David Rockefeller, New York, March 1975.
15. Nelson Rockefeller, interviewed by Frost.
16. Joe Alex Morris, *Nelson Rockefeller* (New York: Harper, 1960), p. 16.
17. Joe Alex Morris, *Those Rockefeller Brothers* (New York: Harper, 1953), p. 21.
18. *New York Times*, March 8, 1969.
19. Interview with Nelson Rockefeller, Seal Harbor, Me., August 1974.
20. Nelson Rockefeller, interviewed by Frost.
21. Interview with David Rockefeller, New York, March 1975.
22. William Manchester, "Nelson Rockefeller's Moral Heritage," *Harper's*, May 1959, p. 26.
23. Ibid.
24. Morris, *Rockefeller Brothers*, p. 19.
25. Morris, *Nelson Rockefeller*, p. 66.
26. Nelson Rockefeller, interviewed by Frost.
27. Laurance Rockefeller, written response to authors' questions, March 1975.
28. Morris, *Nelson Rockefeller*, p. 65.
29. Ibid., p. 37.
30. Laurance Rockefeller, written response to authors' questions, March 1975.
31. Thomas B. Morgan, *Self Creations: 13 Impersonalities* (London: Michael Joseph, 1966), p. 122.
32. Morris, *Nelson Rockefeller*, p. 77.
33. Ibid., p. 51.
34. Ibid., p. 59.
35. Ibid., p. 50.
36. Interview with Nelson Rockefeller, Seal Harbor, Me., March 1975.
37. Ibid.

Chapter 3

1. Nelson Rockefeller to William Ward, December 14, 1932, Rockefeller Family Archives, Rockefeller Center, New York.
2. Interview with Harold Fisher, New York, July 1974.
3. Garry Wills, *Nixon Agonistes* (Boston: Houghton Mifflin, 1970), p. 32.
4. Nelson "was restless at the table and he frequently felt called upon to amuse his sister and brothers by clowning or making remarks that they thought were funny," reported Morris in *Nelson Rockefeller*. "Eventually, his seat at the table was moved so that he was not close to certain of his brothers."
5. Statement by Nelson Rockefeller. From *CBS Reports: The Rockefellers*, broadcast by CBS television, December 28, 1973. © CBS, Inc. 1973.
6. Interview with Vincent F. Albano, Jr., New York, July 1974.
7. Rockefeller Family Archives.
8. *New York Times*, May 18, 1969.
9. E. B. White, *The Fox of Peapack* (New York: Harper and Row, 1928), pp. 20–21.

10. Nelson Rockefeller, "The Governor Lectures on Art," *New York Times Magazine*, April 9, 1967, pp. 28ff.

11. Interview with Wallace Harrison, New York, May 1975.

12. Ibid.

13. *New York Mirror*, October 9, 1940.

14. Interview with Nelson Rockefeller, Washington, D.C., March 1975.

15. Rockefeller Family Archives.

16. Interview with Nelson Rockefeller, Washington, D.C., March 1975.

17. Interview with William Ronan, New York, February 1975.

18. *New York Daily News*, July 13, 1942.

19. Inez Robb, "Rockefeller: All American," *New York Journal American*, November 22, 1940.

20. Interview with Wallace Harrison, New York, May 1975.

Chapter 4

1. Interview with Nelson Rockefeller, Washington, D.C., March 1975.

2. H. J. Maidenberg, "Rockefeller in Venezuela," *New York Times*, November 24, 1974.

3. *Wall Street Journal*, March 26, 1975.

4. U.S. Congress, Senate, Committee on Rules and Administration, *Hearings on the Nomination of Nelson A. Rockefeller of New York to be Vice President of the United States*, 93rd Cong., 2nd sess. (Washington, D.C.: Government Printing Office, 1974), p. 645.

5. Ibid.

6. Interview with Robert B. Anderson, New York, October 1974.

7. Senate Rules Committee, *Hearings*, pp. 645–646.

8. Interview with Anna Rosenberg, New York, October 1974.

9. Ibid.

10. This account of the United Nations land acquisition is based on "The Reminiscences of Francis Jamieson," a manuscript on file with the Columbia University Oral History Research Office and based on an interview tape-recorded in 1952.

Chapter 5

1. Interview with Nelson Rockefeller, Washington, D.C., March 1975.

2. James Desmond, *Nelson Rockefeller: A Political Biography* (New York: Macmillan, 1964), p. 144.

3. Ibid., p. 153.

4. Interview with John D. Rockefeller IV, Buckhannon, W. Va., January 1975.

5. Interview with David Rockefeller, New York, March 1975.

6. Laurance Rockefeller, written response to authors' questions, March 1975.

7. Interview with David Rockefeller, New York, March 1975.

8. Interview with Alton Marshall, New York, February 1975.

9. Ibid.

10. Interview with Ronald Maiorana, New York, February 1975.

11. Francis X. Clines, "Events from the Personal Life and the Career of Rockefeller," *New York Times*, August 21, 1974.

12. Gene Spagnoli, "Only the White House Can Scratch His Itch," *New York Daily News*, December 12, 1973.

13. Joe Alex Morris, *Nelson Rockefeller* (New York: Harper, 1960), p. 153.

14. Senate Rules Committee, *Hearings*, pp. 924–925.

15. Interview with John D. Rockefeller IV, Buckhannon, W. Va., January 1975.

16. Senate Rules Committee, *Hearings*, p. 149.

17. "Rockefella," *New Yorker*, November 5, 1960, pp. 46–47.

18. Ibid.

19. Interview with Robert Douglass, New York, February 1975.

20. Morris, *Nelson Rockefeller*, p. 46.

21. Lewis Lapham, "Victory for the Big, Dumb Money," *Harper's*, February 1975, p. 38.

22. Interview with Nelson Rockefeller, Washington, D.C., March 1975.

23. Senate Rules Committee, *Hearings*, p. 126.

24. *Time*, September 2, 1974.

25. Morris, *Nelson Rockefeller*, p. 78.

26. D. Norton-Taylor, "Nelson Rockefeller: A Record to Fit the Times," *Fortune*, June 1, 1967, pp. 96ff.

27. Morris, *Nelson Rockefeller*, p. 64.

28. Ibid., p. 65.

29. Interview with an eyewitness to the conversation.

30. Charles Dumas, "What Next for Rocky?" *New York Daily News*, June 27, 1972.

31. Frank Gervasi, *The Real Rockefeller* (New York: Atheneum, 1974), p. 29.

32. Senate Rules Committee, *Hearings*, p. 83.

33. Merle Miller, *Plain Speaking* (New York: Berkley/Putnam, 1973), p. 384.

34. Senate Rules Committee, *Hearings*, p. 603.

35. U.S. Congress, House, Committee on the Judiciary, *Hearings on the Nomination of Nelson A. Rockefeller to be Vice President of the United States*, 93rd Cong., 2nd sess., serial no. 45 (Washington, D.C.: Government Printing Office, 1974), p. 151.

36. Senate Rules Committee, *Hearings*, p. 35.

37. Interview with Nelson Rockefeller, Seal Harbor, Me., August 1974.

38. Senate Rules Committee, *Hearings*, p. 182.

39. David Frost, *The Presidential Debate—1968* (New York: Stein and Day, 1968), p. 110.

Chapter 6

1. Interview with Nelson Rockefeller, Washington, D.C., March 1975.

2. Interview with Stanley Steingut, New York, February 1975.

3. Interview with Joseph Zaretzki, New York, February 1975.

4. *The New York State Capitol* (Albany: New York State Office of General Services, 1974).

5. Enrollment figures for 1970, Rockefeller's last New York State race, totaled 2,957,908 Republicans, 3,566,252 Democrats, 107,372 Conservatives, and 109,311 Liberals.

Chapter 7

1. Interview with Alton Marshall, New York, February 1975.
2. Interview with Joseph Carlino, New York, August 1974.
3. U.S. Congress, Senate, Committee on Rules and Administration, *Hearings on the Nomination of Nelson A. Rockefeller of New York to be Vice President of the United States*, 93rd Cong., 2nd sess. (Washington, D.C.: Government Printing Office, 1974), pp. 99–100.
4. *New York Daily News*, December 14, 1973.
5. Interview with Alton Marshall, New York, February 1975.
6. *New York Times*, April 11, 1968.
7. Interview with Alton Marshall, New York, February 1975.
8. Stewart Udall, quoted in Martin and Susan Tolchin, *To the Victor . . .* (New York: Random House, 1971), p. 250.
9. William Ronan, quoted in Alan G. Hevisi, *Legislative Politics in New York State* (New York: Praeger, 1975), p. 217.
10. Interview with Robert F. Wagner, New York, March 1975.
11. Ibid.
12. Ibid.
13. Interview with Nelson Rockefeller, Washington, D.C., March 1975.
14. *New York Times*, July 4, 1969.
15. Interview with Alton Marshall, New York, February 1975.
16. Interview with Joseph Zaretzki, New York, February 1975.
17. Interview with Alton Marshall, New York, February 1975.
18. Senate Rules Committee, *Hearings*, p. 214.
19. Interview with William Wells, New York, October 1974.
20. Interview with Hugh Carey, New York, March 1975.
21. Ibid.
22. Ibid.
23. Ibid.
24. Ibid.

Chapter 8

1. Martin and Susan Tolchin, *To the Victor . . .* (New York: Random House, 1971), p. 96.
2. Sam Roberts, "The Last of the Old-Time Pols," *New York Sunday News Magazine*, November 3, 1974, p. 34.
3. Nelson Rockefeller, "Hiring Policy," public statement, April 3, 1973.
4. *New York Times*, April 4, 1973, p. 67.
5. U.S. Congress, House, Committee on the Judiciary, *Hearings on the Nomination of Nelson A. Rockefeller of New York to be Vice President of the United States*, 93rd Cong., 2nd sess., serial no. 45 (Washington, D.C.: Government Printing Office, 1974), p. 250.
6. U.S. Congress, Senate, Committee on Rules and Administration, *Hearings on the Nomination of Nelson A. Rockefeller of New York to be Vice President of the United States*, 93rd Cong., 2nd sess. (Washington, D.C.: Government Printing Office, 1974), p. 583.

7. Morton Heller, *The Art and Politics of Thomas Nast* (New York: Oxford University Press, 1968), plate 115.

8. *New York Post*, June 18, 1973.

9. Interview with Hugh Morrow, Washington, D.C., March 1975.

10. Interview with Cyrus Vance, New York, February, 1975.

11. Roberts, "Last of the Old-Time Pols."

12. Interview with William Ronan, February 1975.

13. Interview with Robert F. Wagner, March 1975.

14. Alan G. Hevisi, *Legislative Politics in New York State* (New York: Praeger, 1975), p. 112.

15. Ibid.

16. Richard Reeves, "Matty Troy and the Politics of Lying," *New York*, March 5, 1973, pp. 45ff.

17. Ibid.

18. Ibid.

19. New York State, Governor, *Public Papers of Nelson A. Rockefeller, 53rd Governor* (Albany, 1971), p. 1762.

20. House Judiciary Committee, *Hearings*, p. 1056.

21. Ibid., p. 1190.

22. Ibid., p. 1191.

23. Ibid., p. 1056.

Chapter 9

1. Robert A. Caro, *The Power Broker* (New York: Alfred A. Knopf, 1974), p. 1071.

2. Ibid., p. 1074.

3. Ibid.

4. Interview with Nelson Rockefeller, Washington, D.C., March 1975.

5. Ibid.

6. Interview with William Ronan, New York, February 1975.

7. Caro, *Power Broker*, p. 1141.

8. Some of the information in this account of the Duryea episode was developed with the help of Edward Hershey, the *Newsday* reporter who covered the case.

9. Interview with Alfred Scotti, New York, May 1975.

10. Interview with Louis Lefkowitz, New York, February 1975.

11. Interview with Harold Fisher, New York, July 1974.

12. U.S. Congress, House, Committee on the Judiciary, *Hearings on the Nomination of Nelson A. Rockefeller to be Vice President of the United States*, 93rd Cong., 2nd sess., serial no. 45 (Washington, D.C.: Government Printing Office, 1974), p. 129.

13. Interview with Nelson Rockefeller, Washington, D.C., March 1975.

14. Interview with Meade Esposito, New York, April 1975.

15. Interview with Hugh Carey, New York, March 1975.

16. Interview with Alton Marshall, New York, February 1975.

17. Nelson Rockefeller, written response to authors' questions, March 1975.

18. Interview with Meade Esposito, New York, April 1975.

19. House Judiciary Committee, *Hearings*, p. 1386.

20. Interview with Meade Esposito, New York, April 1975.
21. Ibid.
22. House Judiciary Committee, *Hearings*, p. 953.

Chapter 10

1. U.S. Congress, Senate, Committee on Rules and Administration, *Hearings on the Nomination of Nelson A. Rockefeller of New York to be Vice President of the United States*, 93rd Cong., 2nd sess. (Washington, D.C.: Government Printing Office, 1974), p. 616.
2. Interview with Louis Lefkowitz, New York, February 1975.
3. Interview with Robert F. Wagner, New York, March 1975.
4. Senate Rules Committee, *Hearings*, p. 559.
5. U.S. Congress, House, Committee on the Judiciary, *Hearings on the Nomination of Nelson A. Rockefeller to be Vice President of the United States*, 93rd Cong., 2nd sess., serial no. 45 (Washington, D.C.: Government Printing Office, 1974), p. 959.
6. Ibid., pp. 213, 1179.
7. House Judiciary Committee, Hearings, p. 975.
8. Ibid., p. 974.
9. Interview with William Ronan, New York, February 1975.
10. Unpublished manuscript by Steven Brill.
11. Interview with George Hinman, New York, February 1975.
12. Michael Kramer, "Are These the Best Money Can Buy?" *New York*, January 14, 1974, p. 6.
13. Interview with Alton Marshall, New York, February 1975.
14. Interview with Henry L. Diamond, New York, April 1975.
15. *New York Times*, May 14, 1975.
16. Sam Roberts, "The City Politic: The Only Time the Two Parties Fight," *New York*, September 16, 1974, pp. 12ff.
17. Unpublished manuscript by Steven Brill.
18. Roberts, "Only Time."
19. Interview with Vincent F. Albano, Jr., New York, July 1974.
20. *New York Daily News*, December 21, 1966.
21. Fred Powledge, "The Marketing of Nelson Rockefeller," *New York*, November 30, 1970, p. 45.
22. Richard Reeves, "Who Really Runs New York City?" *New York*, January 4, 1972, p. 28.
23. U.S. Congress, House, Committee on Banking and Currency, Subcommittee on Domestic Finance, *Commercial Banks and Their Trust Activities: Emerging Influence on the American Economy*, staff report, 90th Cong., 2nd sess. (Washington, D.C.: Government Printing Office, 1968).
24. Interview with Arthur Goldberg, Washington, D.C., May 1975.
25. Reeves, "Who Really Runs New York City?" p. 28.

Chapter 11

1. Oren Root, *Persons and Persuasions* (New York: W. W. Norton, 1974), p. 149.

2. *New York Times*, December 16, 1959.

3. Sam Roberts, "Banks and the Legislature: They Go Together," *New York Daily News*, March 26, 1973.

4. Ibid.

5. Sam Roberts, "Report State Funds Follow GOP Big to New Bank Job," *New York Daily News*, March 13, 1972.

6. David Leinsdorf, *Citibank: A Preliminary Report by the Nader Task Force on First National City Bank* (Washington, D.C.: Center for the Study of Responsive Law, 1971), p. 337.

7. U.S. Congress, Senate, Committee on Rules and Administration, *Hearings on the Nomination of Nelson A. Rockefeller of New York to be Vice President of the United States*, 93rd Cong., 2nd sess. (Washington, D.C.: Government Printing Office, 1974), pp. 948–949.

8. *New York Daily News*, May 21, 1973.

9. William Sherman, "Rocky Keeps Pal in Running for $30 Million," *New York Daily News*, May 21, 1973.

10. *New York Daily News*, August 10, 1972.

11. Francis X. Clines, "Governor Defends Intervention in Contract Bidding," *New York Times*, May 22, 1973.

12. Senate Rules Committee, *Hearings*, p. 214.

13. Ibid., pp. 214–215.

Chapter 12

1. Interview with Hugh Carey, New York, March 1975.

2. *New York Times*, December 12, 1973.

3. *New York Times*, April 7, 1963.

4. See New York State, Office of the Controller, Division of Audits and Accounts, *Public Authorities in New York State*, December 31, 1974.

5. *New York Times*, December 12, 1973.

6. *New York Times*, November 18, 1975.

7. Interview with Arthur Levitt, New York, May 1975.

8. New York State, Office of the Controller, *Public Authorities*, p. 2.

9. Ibid.

10. Ibid.

11. Ibid., p. 3.

12. Interview with Arthur Levitt, New York, May 1975.

13. Michael Harrington, *Toward a Democratic Left* (Baltimore: Penguin, 1969), p. 85.

14. U.S. Congress, House, Committee on the Judiciary, *Hearings on the Nomination of Nelson A. Rockefeller of New York to be Vice President of the United States*, 93rd Cong., 2nd sess., serial no. 45 (Washington, D.C.: Government Printing Office, 1974), p. 36.

15. Ibid.

16. Interview with Arthur Levitt, New York, May 1975.

17. Annmarie Walsh, *The Public's Business* (Twentieth Century Fund, forthcoming).

18. See Steven Weisman, "Nelson Rockefeller's Pill: The UDC," *Washington Monthly*, June 1975, pp. 35–44.

19. Ibid., p. 39.
20. Ibid., p. 40.
21. Ibid., p. 44.
22. Walsh, *Public's Business.*
23. Weisman, "Rockefeller's Pill," p. 44.

Chapter 13

1. Downtown Lower Manhattan Association, "World Trade Center: A Proposal for the Port of New York," January 27, 1960.
2. *New York Times*, January 19, 1964.
3. Interview with Arthur Levitt, New York, May 1975.
4. Ibid.
5. Ibid.
6. Eleanor Carruth, "What Price Glory on the Albany Mall?" *Fortune*, June 1971, p. 92.
7. *Albany Times-Union*, May 27, 1962.
8. Carruth, "Albany Mall," p. 92.
9. Ibid.
10. Ibid., p. 94.
11. Ibid., p. 95.
12. Ibid.
13. Neal Peirce, *The Megastates of America* (New York: W. W. Norton, 1971), p. 35.
14. Carruth, "Albany Mall," p. 94.
15. Peirce, *Megastates*, p. 35.
16. Interview with Arthur Levitt, New York, May 1975.
17. Interview with Wallace Harrison, New York, May 1975.
18. *New York Times*, May 25, 1967.
19. *New York Times*, December 11, 1968.
20. Carruth, "Albany Mall," p. 166.
21. Wolf von Eckhardt, "Rocky's Monumental Error, or the Billion-Dollar Misunderstanding," *New York*, April 20, 1970, p. 26.
22. Ibid.
23. Ibid.
24. Ibid.
25. Carruth, "Albany Mall," p. 167.
26. New York State, Legislative Commission on Expenditure and Review, "Office Space for New York State: Program Audit 1/1/72," January 17, 1972, pp. 5–8.
27. U.S. Congress, Senate, Committee on Rules and Administration, *Hearings on the Nomination of Nelson A. Rockefeller of New York to be Vice President of the United States*, 93rd Cong., 2nd sess. (Washington, D.C.: Government Printing Office, 1974), p. 217.
28. Jules Masserman, quoted in Eckhardt, "Rocky's Monumental Error," p. 26.
29. Interview with Wallace Harrison, New York, May 1975.
30. Eckhardt, "Rocky's Monumental Error," p. 24.
31. *New York Times*, March 13, 1970.

Chapter 14

1. Interview with Thomas B. Morgan, New York, March 1975.

2. U.S. Congress, Senate, Committee on Rules and Administration, *Hearings on the Nomination of Nelson A. Rockefeller of New York to be Vice President of the United States*, 93rd Cong., 2nd sess. (Washington, D.C.: Government Printing Office, 1974), p. 139.

3. Interview with Nelson Rockefeller, New York, October 1970.

4. Peter Kihss, "Governor Scored on News Policies," *New York Times*, February 4, 1959.

5. Ibid.

6. Larry King, "The Cool World of Nelson Rockefeller," *Harper's*, February 1968, pp. 31–40.

7. Interview with Nelson Rockefeller, New York, October 1970.

8. Nelson Rockefeller, televised interview by David Frost, New York, July 20, 1971.

9. Timothy Crouse, *The Boys on the Bus* (New York: Ballantine, 1974), p. 79.

10. King, "Cool World."

11. William Kennedy, "Rocky Is 64, Going on 35," *New York Times Magazine*, April 29, 1973, pp. 16ff.

12. Interview with Hugh Morrow, Washington, D.C., March 1975.

13. Ibid.

14. Interview with Ronald Maiorana, New York, February 1975.

Chapter 15

1. Larry King, "The Cool World of Nelson Rockefeller," *Harper's*, February 1968, p. 40.

2. William Kennedy, "Rocky Is 64, Going on 35," *New York Times Magazine*, April 29, 1973, pp. 16ff.

3. Interview with Dorothy Schiff, New York, May 1975.

4. U.S. Congress, Senate, Committee on Rules and Administration, *Hearings on the Nomination of Nelson A. Rockefeller of New York to be Vice President of the United States*, 93rd Cong., 2nd sess. (Washington, D.C.: Government Printing Office, 1974), pp. 879–880.

5. Interview with Victor Lasky, New York, October 1974.

6. Senate Rules Committee, *Hearings*, p. 1029.

7. U.S. Congress, House, Committee on the Judiciary, *Hearings on the Nomination of Nelson A. Rockefeller of New York to be Vice President of the United States*, 93rd Cong., 2nd sess., serial no. 45 (Washington, D.C.: Government Printing Office, 1974), p. 894.

8. Senate Rules Committee, *Hearings*, p. 862.

9. Ibid., p. 868.

10. Memorandum from Hugh Morrow, December 12, 1963.

11. Sam Roberts, "Pro-Rocky Book Followed 81G Gift," *New York Daily News*, November 4, 1974.

12. Robert H. Connery and Gerald Benjamin, eds., *Governing New York State: The Rockefeller Years* (New York: Academy of Political Science, 1974), p. 1.

Chapter 16

1. U.S. Congress, Senate, Committee on Rules and Administration, *Hearings on the Nomination of Nelson A. Rockefeller of New York to be Vice President of the United States*, 93rd Cong., 2nd sess. (Washington, D.C.: Government Printing Office, 1974), p. 553.

2. Ibid.

3. Statement by Nelson Rockefeller. From *CBS Reports: The Rockefellers*, broadcast by CBS television, December 28, 1973. © CBS, Inc. 1973.

4. Nelson Rockefeller, written response to authors' questions, March 1975.

5. William Manchester, "Nelson Rockefeller's Moral Heritage," *Harper's*, May 1959, p. 26.

6. Ibid., p. 27.

7. Oren Root, *Persons and Persuasions* (New York: W. W. Norton, 1974), p. 134.

8. Ibid., p. 135.

9. Ibid.

10. Interview with Herman Bates, New York, November 1974.

11. Unless otherwise noted, information on Rockefeller campaign financing comes from official reports filed with the Senate Rules Committee and the House Judiciary Committee, and therefore should be presumed to be base figures.

12. Senate Rules Committee, *Hearings*, p. 618.

13. Ibid., p. 599.

14. Ibid., p. 600.

15. Ibid., p. 200.

16. Herbert E. Alexander, *Financing the 1968 Election* (Lexington, Mass.: D.C. Heath, 1971), p. 180.

17. Interview with Richard Fallon, November 1974.

18. Senate Rules Committee, *Hearings*, p. 558.

19. Herbert E. Alexander, *Money in Politics* (Washington, D.C.: Public Affairs Press, 1972), p. 48.

20. Senate Rules Committee, *Hearings*, p. 553.

21. Campaign reports filed with the Office of the Secretary of State, New York State.

22. Interview with Archibald Gillies, New York, April 1975.

23. Interview with James Hellmuth, New York, April 1975.

24. Interview with Archibald Gillies, New York, April 1975.

25. Alexander, *Money in Politics*, p. 62.

NOTES

26. Interview with George Humphreys, New York, April 1975.

27. Campaign reports filed with the Office of the Secretary of State, New York State.

28. Interview with George Humphreys, New York, April 1975.

29. Tom Buckley, "The Three Men Behind Rockefeller," *New York Times Magazine*, October 30, 1966, p. 134.

30. U.S. Congress, Senate, Committee on Rules and Administration, *Hearings on the Nomination of Nelson A. Rockefeller of New York to be Vice President of the United States*, 93rd Cong., 2nd sess. (Washington, D.C.: Government Printing Office, 1974), p. 618.

31. Senate Rules Committee, *Hearings*, p. 554.

32. Ibid., p. 161.

33. Ibid., p. 509.

Chapter 17

1. Stewart Alsop, *Nixon and Rockefeller* (Garden City, N.Y.: Doubleday, 1960), p. 106.

2. William Manchester, "Nelson Rockefeller's Moral Heritage," *Harper's*, May 1959, pp. 25-31.

3. Interview with Emmet Hughes, Princeton, N.J., April 1975.

4. Ibid.

5. Nick Thimmesch, *The Condition of Republicanism* (New York: W. W. Norton, 1968), p. 107.

6. Frank Gervasi, *The Real Rockefeller* (New York: Atheneum, 1964), p. 19.

7. *New York Times*, July 1, 1958.

8. Alsop, *Nixon and Rockefeller*, p. 39.

9. New York State, Governor, *Public Papers of Nelson A. Rockefeller, 53rd Governor* (Albany, 1969), p. 983.

10. William Rusher, "Thomas E. Dewey, R.I.P.," *National Review*, April 6, 1971, p. 358.

11. Interview with Walter Mahoney, Buffalo, N.Y., April 1975.

12. *Newsweek*, January 12, 1976, p. 21.

13. Gervasi, *Real Rockefeller*, p. 206.

14. Ibid., p. 189.

15. Alsop, *Nixon and Rockefeller*, p. 109.

16. Interview with Joseph Carlino, New York, August 1974.

17. Interview with Mort Lawrence, executive director (1958) of the Metropolitan Political Club, New York, March 1975.

18. Interview with Malcolm Wilson, White Plains, N.Y., April 1975.

19. Ibid.

20. Interview with Warren Gardner, New York, May 1975.

21. William H. Hill, "Nelson Rockefeller," *Binghamton Sun*, 1958; reprinted by the Metropolitan Political Club.

22. Robert A. Caro, *The Power Broker* (New York: Alfred A. Knopf, 1974), p. 1068.

23. Interview with Kenneth Keating, Washington, D.C., August 1964.

392

Chapter 18

1. New York Republican State Committee, *Meet Nelson Rockefeller*, undated 1958 campaign pamphlet.

2. Rockefeller for Governor Clubs, *Organization Manual*, undated 1958 campaign pamphlet. The state director of the Rockefeller for Governor Clubs was Marty Snyder, who had been Dwight Eisenhower's World War II mess sergeant.

3. Friedrich Nietzsche, *Beyond Good and Evil* (Chicago: Henry Regnery, 1955), p. 47.

4. Interview with Nelson Rockefeller, Washington, D.C., March 1975.

5. Herbert E. Alexander, *Money in Politics* (Washington, D.C.: Public Affairs Press, 1972), p. 35.

6. Interview with Nelson Rockefeller, Washington, D.C., March 1975.

7. *New York Daily News*, October 31, 1958.

8. Frank Gervasi, *The Real Rockefeller* (New York: Atheneum, 1964), p. 220.

9. William Manchester, "Nelson Rockefeller's Moral Heritage," *Harper's*, May 1959, pp. 25ff.

10. Warren Moscow, *The Last of the Big Time Bosses* (New York: Stein and Day, 1971), p. 157.

11. Warren Weaver, "The Political Evolution of Nelson Rockefeller," *New York Times Magazine*, February 16, 1964, pp. 11ff.

12. Stewart Alsop, *Nixon and Rockefeller* (Garden City, N.Y.: Doubleday, 1960), p. 41.

13. Interview with Louis Lefkowitz, New York, January 1975.

14. Larry King, "The Cool World of Nelson Rockefeller," *Harper's*, February 1968, p. 37.

15. Thomas B. Morgan, *Self Creations: 13 Impersonalities* (London: Michael Joseph, 1966), pp. 115, 118.

16. *New York Daily News*, August 28, 1958.

17. *New York Times*, October 8, 1958.

18. *New York Times*, October 17, 1958.

19. Ibid.

20. *New York Daily News*, October 17, 1958.

21. *New York Daily News*, October 28, 1958.

22. *New York Post*, November 3, 1958.

23. *New York Daily News*, November 4, 1958.

24. Interview with Dorothy Schiff, New York, May 1975.

25. *New York Times*, October 25, 1958.

26. Ibid.

Chapter 19

1. Theodore H. White, *The Making of the President—1960* (New York: Atheneum, 1961), p. 68.

2. *New York Daily News*, January 4, 1959.

3. *New York Daily News*, November 24, 1958.

4. Ibid.

5. *New York Daily News*, November 28, 1958.

6. New York State, Governor, *Public Papers of Nelson A. Rockefeller, 53rd Governor* (Albany, 1959), p. 11.

7. Richard Reeves, "Rocky (Is, Is Not, May Be) Running," *New York Times Magazine*, November 26, 1967, pp. 30ff.

8. Chalmers Roberts, "Rockefeller-Watching," *Washington Post.*

9. *New York Times*, July 5, 1961.

10. *Newsweek*, October 21, 1974.

11. Interview with Emmet Hughes, Princeton, N.J., April 1975.

12. *Knickerbocker News*, March 5, 1959.

13. Peter Maas, "Nelson Rockefeller: Does He Have a Future with the G.O.P.?" *Saturday Evening Post*, September 15, 1962, p. 69.

14. Interview with Arthur Levitt, New York, June 1975.

15. *New York Times*, April 6, 1959.

16. *Knickerbocker News*, February 5, 1960.

17. Emmet O'Brien, Gannett News Service dispatch, February 17, 1960.

18. Ibid.

19. *Knickerbocker News*, August 11, 1959.

20. *Newsday*, December 12, 1973.

21. *Vital Speeches*, April 15, 1960, pp. 411–413.

22. Phil Tracy, "The Albany Bunker," *Village Voice*, February 15, 1973.

23. Stewart Alsop, *Nixon and Rockefeller* (Garden City, N.Y.: Doubleday, 1960), p. 97.

Chapter 20

1. Stewart Alsop, *Nixon and Rockefeller* (Garden City, N.Y.: Doubleday, 1960), p. 164.

2. Paul Martin, Gannett News Service dispatch, January 21, 1959.

3. *Albany Times-Union*, October 15, 1959.

4. Nick Thimmesch, *The Condition of Republicanism* (New York: W. W. Norton, 1968), p. 109.

5. New York State, Governor, *Public Papers of Nelson A. Rockefeller, 53rd Governor* (Albany, 1959), p. 1148.

6. Ibid., p. 1174.

7. Larry King, "The Cool World of Nelson Rockefeller," *Harper's*, February 1968, p. 37.

8. *Knickerbocker News*, December 28, 1959.

9. Interview with Emmet Hughes, Princeton, N.J., April 1975.

10. New York State, Governor, *Public Papers* (1959), p. 1028.

11. Interview with Emmet Hughes, Princeton, N.J., April 1975.

12. Robert T. Elson, *The World of Time Inc.* (New York: Atheneum, 1973), p. 461.

13. Ibid., p. 462.

14. New York State, Governor, *Public Papers* (1960), p. 1029.

15. Ibid., p. 1044.

16. Ibid.

17. *U.S. News & World Report*, June 20, 1960.

18. Elson, *Time Inc.*, p. 465.

19. Ibid.

20. Ibid., p. 466.

21. Richard J. Whalen, *Catch the Falling Flag* (Boston: Houghton Mifflin, 1972), p. 153.

22. New York State, Governor, *Public Papers* (1960), p. 1051.

23. Theodore H. White, *The Making of the President—1960* (New York: Atheneum, 1961), p. 185.

Chapter 21

1. Interview with Emmet Hughes, Princeton, N.J., April 1975.

2. New York State, Governor, *Public Papers of Nelson A. Rockefeller, 53rd Governor* (Albany, 1960), p. 1137.

3. Ibid., p. 1139.

4. Ibid., p. 1166.

5. Interview with Emmet Hughes, Princeton, N.J., April 1975.

6. Ibid.

7. For a full account of the Rockefeller-Nixon meeting, see Theodore H. White, *The Making of the President—1960* (New York: Atheneum, 1961), pp. 196–198.

8. The full text of the "Fifth Avenue Compact" may be found in the *Public Papers* (1960), pp. 1167–1169.

9. White, *Making of the President—1960*, p. 199.

10. Ibid., p. 200.

11. New York, Governor, *Public Papers* (1960), p. 1164.

12. Interview with William S. Miller, Buffalo, N.Y., April 1975.

13. Larry King, "The Cool World of Nelson Rockefeller," *Harper's*, February 1968, p. 36.

Chapter 22

1. For a discussson of this report, see *New York Times*, July 17, 1961.

2. Ibid.

3. *New York Herald Tribune*, July 18, 1961.

4. *New York Times*, July 18, 1961.

5. New York State, Governor, *Public Papers of Nelson A. Rockefeller, 53rd Governor* (Albany, 1961), p. 1327.

6. Arvis Chalmers, "New Ballgame Now for Rocky and Wagner," *Knickerbocker News*, spring 1973.

7. Alexander Kendrick, *Prime Time: The Life of Edward R. Murrow* (Boston: Little, Brown, 1969), p. 482.

8. *New York Times*, November 5, 1962.

9. *New York Times*, November 1, 1962.

10. Ibid.

11. Interview with William Rusher, New York, April 1975.

12. Ibid.

13. *New York Times*, September 21, 1962.

14. William Manchester, "Nelson Rockefeller's Moral Heritage," *Harper's*, May 1959, p. 27.

15. *New York Times*, September 21, 1962.

Chapter 23

1. Robert D. Novak, *The Agony of the G.O.P.* (New York: Macmillan, 1965), p. 25.

2. Ibid., p. 37.

3. Ibid., p. 59.

4. New York State, Governor, *Public Papers of Nelson A. Rockefeller, 53rd Governor* (Albany, 1962), p. 1179.

5. *New York Times*, September 17, 1963.

6. Warren Weaver, "The Political Evolution of Nelson Rockefeller," *New York Times Magazine*, February 16, 1964, pp. 11ff.

7. *Newsweek*, May 14, 1962.

Chapter 24

1. Joe Alex Morris, *Nelson Rockefeller* (New York: Harper, 1960), p. 317.

2. U.S. Congress, Senate, Committee on Rules and Administration, *Hearings on the Nomination of Nelson A. Rockefeller of New York to be Vice President of the United States*, 93rd Cong., 2nd sess. (Washington, D.C.: Government Printing Office, 1974), p. 600.

3. *Congressional Record*, December 5, 1974.

4. Most of this account of the racetrack case is from the testimony of former Manhattan Assistant District Attorney David Goldstein during hearings before the House Select Committee on Crime (92nd Cong.) on the influence of organized crime on sports.

5. Morhouse was interviewed at his Ticonderoga, N.Y., home by congressional committee staff; he was never called to testify before a committee session.

6. U.S. Congress, House, Committee on the Judiciary, *Hearings on the Nomination of Nelson A. Rockefeller of New York to be Vice President of the United States*, 93rd Cong., 2nd sess., serial no. 45 (Washington, D.C.: Government Printing Office, 1974), p. 210.

7. Ibid.

8. Senate Rules Committee, *Hearings*, p. 605.

9. *New York Herald Tribune*, February 24, 1966.

10. *New York Times*, April 28, 1965.

11. Senate Rules Committee, *Hearings*, p. 606.

12. Ibid., pp. 606–607.

13. House Judiciary Committee, *Hearings*, p. 249.

14. Senate Rules Committee, *Hearings*, p. 583.

15. Ibid., p. 904.

16. Ibid., p. 583.

17. Ibid., p. 588.

18. Ibid., p. 601.

19. House Judiciary Committee, *Hearings*, p. 249.

20. Interview with Joseph Carlino, New York, July 1974.

21. Interview with Vincent F. Albano, Jr., New York, August 1974.

22. *New York Times*, May 4, 1966.

23. Handwritten and typed transcripts of the taps and bugs, on file with the New York County District Attorney's Office, were introduced as evidence in a last-ditch appeal by Morhouse.

24. Ibid.

25. William Ronan to Abraham Gellinoff, June 14, 1966.

26. *New York Times*, May 18, 1966. Scotti also reminded the jurors that Rockefeller had assured holders of liquor licenses that there would be no reprisals if they cooperated in the investigation.

27. *New York Times*, May 18, 1966.

28. Ibid.

29. House Judiciary Committee, *Hearings*, p. 1197.

30. The doctors and other participants were interviewed by congressional staff investigators, and a copy of the staff report was obtained by the authors.

31. Senate Rules Committee, *Hearings*, p. 115

32. House Judiciary Committee, *Hearings*, p. 1198.

33. Ibid., p. 1404.

34. See note 30.

35. House Judiciary Committee, *Hearings*, p. 1197.

36. New York County District Attorney's Office, wiretap transcripts.

Chapter 25

1. Interview with William Rusher, New York, April 1975.

2. *New York Times*, April 15, 1963.

3. *Time*, December 16, 1974.

4. Interview with William Miller, Buffalo, N.Y., April 1975.

5. "A Poor Session at Albany," editorial, *New York Times*, April 6, 1963.

6. *Washington Evening Star*, April 9, 1963.

7. *New York Herald Tribune*, April 10, 1963.

8. Robert D. Novak, *The Agony of the G.O.P.* (New York: Macmillan, 1965), p. 116.

9. *New York Times*, May 10, 1963.

10. *New York Times*, May 25, 1963. For other comments, see *New York Times*, May 9-10, 1963.

11. Claire Booth Luce, "Without Portfolio—Governor Rockefeller's Remarriage," *McCall's*, September 1963, pp. 29ff.

12. Stewart Alsop, "Affairs of State: Is Nelson Rockefeller Dead?" *Saturday Evening Post*, October 12, 1963, p. 18.

13. U.S. Congress, Senate, Committee on Rules and Administration, *Hearings*

on the Nomination of Nelson A. Rockefeller of New York to be Vice President of the United States, 93rd Cong., 2nd sess. (Washington, D.C.: Government Printing Office, 1974), p. 657.

14. Ibid., pp. 657–658.

Chapter 26

1. Arnold Foster and Benjamin K. Epstein, *Danger on the Right* (New York: Random House, 1964), p. 219.
2. Ibid., p. 256.
3. Interview with Hugh Morrow, Washington, D.C., March 1975.
4. New York State, Governor, *Public Papers of Nelson A. Rockefeller, 53rd Governor* (Albany, 1963), pp. 853ff.
5. Ibid.
6. Ibid.
7. Ibid., p. 890.
8. Barry Goldwater, televised interview on *Tomorrow*, NBC, January 20, 1975.
9. *New York Times*, July 15, 1963.
10. *New York Times*, July 18, 1963.
11. Ibid.
12. Stephen Hess and David S. Broder, *The Republican Establishment* (New York: Harper and Row, 1967), pp. 132–133.
13. Warren Weaver, "The Political Evolution of Nelson Rockefeller," *New York Times Magazine*, February 16, 1964, pp. 11ff.
14. Robert D. Novak, *The Agony of the G.O.P.* (New York: Macmillan, 1965), p. 307.
15. Ibid., p. 313.
16. Ibid., p. 318.
17. *National Review*, May 19, 1964.
18. Theodore H. White, *The Making of the President—1964* (New York: Atheneum, 1965), p. 117.
19. *New York Times*, May 30, 1964.
20. *New York Times*, June 2, 1964.
21. Interview with Emmet Hughes, Princeton, N.J., April 1975.
22. Murray Kempton, "They Got Him," *New Republic*, July 25, 1964, p. 8.
23. Stewart Alsop, *Nixon and Rockefeller* (Garden City, N.Y.: Doubleday, 1960), p. 52.
24. Stewart Alsop, "Affairs of State: Is Nelson Rockefeller Dead?" *Saturday Evening Post*, August 24, 1963, p. 18.
25. Larry King, "The Cool World of Nelson Rockefeller," *Harper's*, February 1968, p. 31.
26. Interview with Nelson Rockefeller, Washington, D.C., March 1975.
27. David Frost, *The Presidential Debates—1968* (New York: Stein and Day, 1968), p. 105.
28. *New York Times*, July 18, 1964.
29. Ibid.

30. *Knickerbocker News*, December 15, 1964.
31. *Albany Times-Union*, November 6, 1964.
32. Interview with Nelson Rockefeller, Washington, D.C., March 1975.
33. Interview with Vincent F. Albano, Jr., New York, July 1974.

Chapter 27

1. Theodore H. White, *The Making of the President—1968* (New York: Atheneum, 1969), p. 31.
2. David S. Broder, "The Struggle for Power," *Atlantic*, April 1966, p. 64.
3. Ibid.
4. Interview with William Rusher, New York, April 1975.
5. Richard Reeves, "Rocky (Is, Is Not, May Be) Running," *New York Times Magazine*, November 26, 1967, pp. 30ff.
6. Charles McCarry, "Win with Rockefeller," *Saturday Evening Post*, February 24, 1968, p. 81.
7. Interview with Robert Douglass, New York, February 1975.
8. Tom Wicker, "The Unhappy Warriors," *Atlantic*, April 1966, p. 80.
9. Stephen Hess and David S. Broder, *The Republican Establishment* (New York: Harper and Row, 1967), p. 313.
10. Ibid.
11. Jack Newfield, *Bread and Roses Too* (New York: E. P. Dutton, 1971), p. 177.
12. Interview with John Lindsay, New York, April 1975.
13. Nat Hentoff, *A Political Life: The Education of John V. Lindsay* (New York: Alfred A. Knopf, 1969), p. 42.
14. Ibid., pp. 44–45.
15. Richard Reeves, "Rockefeller and Lindsay Feud," *Life*, June 25, 1971, pp. 54–56.
16. Interview with John Lindsay, New York, April 1975.
17. Interview with Dorothy Schiff, New York, May 1975.
18. *New York Herald Tribune*, March 22, 1965.
19. A frequent complaint of Lindsay's, which he repeated in *The Edge* (New York: W. W. Norton, 1976), p. 125.
20. Interview with Nelson Rockefeller, Washington, D.C., March 1975.
21. Oliver Pilat, *Lindsay's Campaign: A Behind-the-Scenes Diary* (Boston: Beacon Press, 1968), p. 115.
22. Ibid., p. 116.
23. Ibid., p. 117.
24. Ibid., p. 118.
25. Hess and Broder, *Republican Establishment*, p. 315.
26. Interview with Nelson Rockefeller, Washington, D.C., March 1975.
27. Hess and Broder, *Republican Establishment*, p. 315.
28. Hentoff, *Lindsay*, p. 26.
29. Interview with John Lindsay, New York, April 1975.
30. Interview with Nelson Rockefeller, Washington, D.C., March 1975.
31. Ibid.
32. Interview with Hugh Morrow, Washington, D.C., March 1975.

Chapter 28

1. *Nation*, December 4, 1967.
2. Ibid.
3. *New York Times*, February 8, 1968.
4. Nat Hentoff, *A Political Life: The Education of John V. Lindsay* (New York: Alfred A. Knopf, 1969), p. 202.
5. New York State, Governor, *Public Papers of Nelson A. Rockefeller, 53rd Governor* (Albany, 1968), p. 929.
6. U.S. Congress, Senate, Committee on Rules and Administration, *Hearings on the Nomination of Nelson A. Rockefeller of New York to be Vice President of the United States*, 93rd Cong., 2nd sess. (Washington, D.C.: Government Printing Office, 1974), p. 669.
7. Hentoff, *Lindsay*, p. 204.
8. *New York Daily News*, February 9, 1968.
9. *New York Post*, October 24, 1975.
10. *New York Daily News*, February 10, 1968.
11. *New York Daily News*, February 9, 1968.
12. *New York Daily News*, February 11, 1968.
13. Richard Reeves, "Rockefeller and Lindsay Feud," *Life*, June 25, 1971, pp. 54–56.
14. Ibid.
15. *New York Daily News*, February 10, 1968.
16. *New York Daily News*, February 21, 1968.
17. New York State, Governor, *Public Papers* (1968), pp. 923–924.
18. *New York Times*, February 18, 1968.

Chapter 29

1. Interview with Malcolm Wilson, White Plains, N.Y., April 1975.
2. Nat Hentoff, *A Political Life: The Education of John V. Lindsay* (New York: Alfred A. Knopf, 1969), pp. 211–212.
3. U.S. Congress, Senate, Committee on Rules and Administration, *Hearings on the Nomination of Nelson A. Rockefeller of New York to be Vice President of the United States*, 93rd Cong., 2nd sess. (Washington, D.C.: Government Printing Office, 1974), p. 491; *New York Daily News*, October 31, 1973.
4. Richard Reeves, "Rockefeller and Lindsay Feud," *Life*, June 25, 1971, pp. 54–56.
5. Interview with Nelson Rockefeller, Washington, D.C., March 1975.
6. Interview with John Lindsay, New York, April 1975.
7. Reeves, "Rockefeller and Lindsay."
8. Interview with Nelson Rockefeller, Washington, D.C., March 1975.

Chapter 30

1. Nick Thimmesch, *The Condition of Republicanism* (New York: W. W. Norton, 1968), p. 115.
2. Interview with Nelson Rockefeller, Washington, D.C., March 1975.

3. Richard Reeves, "Rocky (Is, Is Not, May Be) Running," *New York Times Magazine*, November 26, 1967, pp. 30ff.

4. Stephen Hess and David S. Broder, *The Republican Establishment* (New York: Harper and Row, 1967), p. 316.

5. Ibid.

6. Ibid.

7. See Jack Newfield, *Bread and Roses Too* (New York.: E. P. Dutton, 1971), p. 168.

8. Interview with Louis Lefkowitz, New York, January 1975.

9. *Congressional Quarterly*, July 21, 1967, p. 1249.

10. *New York Daily News*, December 12, 1973.

11. Newfield, *Bread and Roses Too*, p. 196.

12. James Perry, *The New Politics: The Expanding Technology of Political Manipulation* (New York: Clarkson N. Potter, 1968), pp. 121–122.

13. Ibid., p. 107.

14. Ibid., p. 111.

15. Ibid., p. 112.

16. Ibid., p. 113.

17. Ibid., p. 116.

18. Ibid., p. 117.

19. Ibid., p. 118.

20. Ibid., p. 119.

21. Ibid., p. 120.

22. Ibid., p. 129.

23. Ibid., p. 131.

24. Ibid., p. 132.

25. Michael Kramer, "The One Boss Rocky Can Count On," *New York*, April 19, 1973, p. 6.

26. Ibid., p. 13.

Chapter 31

1. Interview with Robert Douglass, New York, February 1975.

2. William Safire, *Before the Fall: An Inside View of the Pre-Watergate White House* (Garden City, N.Y.: Doubleday, 1975), pp. 28, 29.

3. Ibid., pp. 30–31.

4. Ibid., p. 32.

5. Theodore H. White, *The Making of the President—1968* (New York: Atheneum, 1969), p. 228.

6. Ibid., p. 53.

7. Richard Reeves, "Rocky (Is, Is Not, May Be) Running," *New York Times Magazine*, November 26, 1967, p. 44.

8. Robert D. Novak, *The Agony of the G.O.P.* (New York: Macmillan, 1965), p. 428.

9. Ibid., p. 433.

10. Ibid., p. 435.

11. White, *Making of the President—1968*, p. 51.

12. Ibid., pp. 41–42.

13. Larry King, "The Cool World of Nelson Rockefeller," *Harper's*, February 1968, p. 34.

14. *New Republic*, June 1, 1968.

15. Garry Wills, *Nixon Agonistes* (Boston: Houghton Mifflin, 1970), p. 208.

16. King, "Cool World," p. 32.

17. Tom Wicker, *JFK and LBJ* (New York: William Morrow, 1968), p. 217.

18. Jack Newfield, *Bread and Roses Too* (New York: E. P. Dutton, 1971), p. 202.

19. Interview with Emmet Hughes, Princeton, N.J., April 1975.

20. New York State, Governor, *Public Papers of Nelson A. Rockefeller, 53rd Governor* (Albany, 1968), p. 987.

21. King, "Cool World," p. 38.

22. White, *Making of the President—1968*, p. 54.

23. Ibid., p. 40.

24. *Fortune*, June 1, 1967.

25. *Newsweek*, December 18, 1967.

26. New York State, Governor, *Public Papers* (1968), p. 968.

27. Ibid., p. 984.

28. "Why I Want the Job," *Look*, August 20, 1968.

29. R. W. Apple, Jr., quoted in White, *Making of the President—1968*, p. 236.

30. *National Review*, July 2, 1968.

31. Lewis Chester, Godfrey Hodgson, and Bruce Page, *An American Melodrama: The Presidential Campaign of 1968* (New York: Viking, 1969), p. 482.

32. Ibid., p. 498.

33. Safire, *Before the Fall*, p. 33.

Chapter 32

1. Richard J. Whalen, *Catch the Falling Flag* (Boston: Houghton Mifflin, 1972), p. 153.

2. Neal Peirce, *The Megastates of America* (New York: W. W. Norton, 1972), p. 23.

3. U.S. Congress, House, Committee on the Judiciary, *Analysis of the Philosophy and Public Record of Nelson A. Rockefeller*, 93rd Cong., 2nd sess., October 1974, p. 30.

4. Ibid., p. 15.

5. *Congressional Quarterly*, July 21, 1967, p. 1250.

6. House Judiciary Committee, *Philosophy and Public Record of Nelson A. Rockefeller*, p. 27.

7. U.S. Congress, House, Committee on the Judiciary, *Hearings on the Nomination of Nelson A. Rockefeller of New York to be Vice President of the United States*, 93rd Cong., 2nd sess., serial no. 45 (Washington, D.C.: Government Printing Office, 1974), p. 1194.

8. Ibid.

9. Theodore H. White, *The Making of the President—1972* (New York: Atheneum, 1973), p. 243.

10. Tad Szulc, introduction to *The Rockefeller Report on the Americas* (Chicago: Quadrangle, 1969), p. ix.

11. *The Rockefeller Report on the Americas* (Chicago: Quadrangle, 1969), p. 58.

12. Garry Wills, *Nixon Agonistes* (Boston: Houghton Mifflin, 1970), p. 434.

Chapter 33

1. Garry Wills, *Nixon Agonistes* (Boston: Houghton Mifflin, 1970), p. 216.

2. Neal Peirce, *The Megastates of America* (New York: W. W. Norton, 1972), p. 50.

3. Robert H. Connery and Gerald Benjamin, eds., *Governing New York State: The Rockefeller Years* (New York: Academy of Political Science, 1974), p. 38.

4. Herbert E. Alexander, *Money in Politics* (Washington, D.C.: Public Affairs Press, 1972), p. 35.

5. U.S. Congress, House, Committee on the Judiciary, *Hearings on the Nomination of Nelson A. Rockefeller of New York to be Vice President of the United States*, 93rd Cong., 2nd sess., serial no. 45 (Washington, D.C.: Government Printing Office, 1974), p. 266.

6. *Empire State Report*, December 1974, p. 46.

7. *New York Post*, October 20, 1975.

8. Richard Reeves, "This Is the Battle of the Titans?" *New York Times Magazine*, November 1, 1970, pp. 23ff.

9. Ibid.

10. *New York Times*, March 14, 1970.

11. *New York Times*, October 22, 1970.

12. Reeves, "Battle of the Titans?"

13. Ibid.

14. Interview with Hugh Morrow, Washington, D.C., March 1975.

15. *New York Times*, April 12, 1970.

16. Gene Spagnoli, "The Rocky Years," *New York Daily News*, December 13, 1973.

17. *New York Times*, October 27, 1969.

18. Reeves, "Battle of the Titans?"

19. Fred Powledge, "The Marketing of Nelson Rockefeller," *New York*, November 30, 1970, p. 40.

20. Reeves, "Battle of the Titans?"

21. Ibid.

22. Ibid.

23. *New York Post*, October 30, 1970.

24. Powledge, "Marketing of Nelson Rockefeller," p. 46.

25. *Albany Times-Union*, September 26, 1969.

26. New York State, Governor, *Public Papers of Nelson A. Rockefeller, 53rd Governor* (Albany, 1969), p. 1433.

27. Reeves, "Battle of the Titans?"

28. William Safire, *Before the Fall: An Inside View of the Pre-Watergate White House* (Garden City, N.Y.: Doubleday, 1975), p. 319.

29. New York State, Governor, *Public Papers* (1959), p. 713.
30. Peirce, *Megastates of America*, p. 51.
31. Interview with Peter Brennan, New York, August 1975.
32. Ibid.
33. Joseph P. Goulden, *Meany* (New York: Atheneum, 1972), p. 401.
34. Sheldon Zalaznick, "You Stole It, Harry," *New York*, October 12, 1970, p. 36.
35. Ibid.
36. Powledge, "Marketing of Nelson Rockefeller," p. 45.
37. Ibid.
38. Interview with Peter Fishbein, New York, February 1975.

Chapter 34

1. New York State, Governor, *Public Papers of Nelson A. Rockefeller, 53rd Governor* (Albany, 1960), p. 188.
2. Pete Hamill, "Rocky's Hand," *New York Post*, October 29, 1973.
3. Nelson Rockefeller, address to Trunk 'n Tusk Dinner, Phoenix, Ariz., October 15, 1973.
4. *New York Times*, September 12, 1973.
5. New York City, Bar Association, Committee on Criminal Courts and Procedure, *1975 Legislative Bulletin*, no. 1, p. 5.
6. Edward Jay Epstein, "The Great Rockefeller Power Machine," *New York*, November 24, 1975, p. 67.
7. Ibid., p. 71.
8. New York City, Bar Association, *1975 Legislative Bulletin*, no. 1, p. 3.
9. *New York Times*, June 20, 1975.
10. *New York Post*, January 15, 1973.
11. "The Politics of Drugs," editorial, *New York Times*, January 9, 1973.
12. Nelson Rockefeller, press release from the Executive Chamber, Albany, N.Y., May 8, 1973.
13. Nelson Rockefeller, *Address to the 69th Annual Meeting, American Political Science Association*, Fairmont-Roosevelt Hotel, New Orleans, La., September 5, 1973, p. 19.
14. Nelson Rockefeller, press release from the Executive Chamber, Albany, N.Y., May 8, 1973.
15. New York State, Special Commission on Attica, *Attica: The Official Report of the New York State Special Commission on Attica* (New York: Bantam, 1972), p. 4; hereinafter referred to as the *McKay Report*.
16. Ibid., p. 321.
17. Ibid., p. 319.
18. Nelson Rockefeller, televised interview with John Hamilton, WNEW, New York, April 6, 1972.
19. *McKay Report*, p. 105.
20. Interview with Robert Douglass, New York, February 1975.
21. Tom Wicker, *A Time to Die* (New York: Quadrangle, 1975), pp. 202–203.

22. Larry King, "The Cool World of Nelson Rockefeller," *Harper's*, February 1968, p. 38.

23. *New York Times*, April 29, 1972.

24. *McKay Report*, pp. 323–325.

25. Interview with Nelson Rockefeller, Washington, D.C., March 1975.

26. *McKay Report*, p. 325.

27. U.S. Congress, House, Committee on the Judiciary, *Hearings on the Nomination of Nelson A. Rockefeller of New York to be Vice President of the United States: Supplemental Dissenting and Separate Views*, 93rd Cong., 2nd sess., H. Rept. 93–1609, p. 43.

28. Ibid.

29. Wicker, *Time to Die*, p. 274.

30. U.S. Congress, House, Committee on the Judiciary, *Selected Views and Positions of Nelson A. Rockefeller: An Analysis*, 93rd Cong., 2nd sess., November 1974, p. 82.

31. Wicker, *Time to Die*, p. 287.

32. Ibid., p. 288.

33. Ibid., p. 290.

34. Ibid., p. 291.

35. Russell G. Oswald, *Attica: My Story* (Garden City, N.Y.: Doubleday, 1972), pp. 289–290.

36. *New York Times*, December 22, 1975.

37. Wicker, *Time to Die*, p. 306.

38. *New York Times*, September 14, 1971.

39. *McKay Report*, pp. 78–79.

40. U.S. Congress, Senate, Committee on Rules and Administration, *Hearings on the Nomination of Nelson A. Rockefeller of New York to be Vice President of the United States*, 93rd Cong., 2nd sess. (Washington, D.C.: Government Printing Office, 1974), p. 128.

Epilogue

1. Interview with Theodore H. White, New York, September 1975.

2. James Cannon, "Rocky: He Who Runs Least Runs Best," *Newsweek*, December 18, 1967.

3. *New York Times*, November 7, 1975.

4. Interview with Nelson Rockefeller, Washington, D.C., March 1975.

5. Nicholas von Hoffman, "Rocky in Medialand," [*More*] *Magazine*, January 1975.

6. Interview with William Ronan, New York, February 1975.

7. U.S. Congress, Senate, Committee on Rules and Administration, *Hearings on the Nomination of Nelson A. Rockefeller of New York to be Vice President of the United States*, 93rd Cong., 2nd sess. (Washington, D.C.: Government Printing Office, 1974), p. 511.

8. Ibid., p. 510.

9. Interview with Robert Douglass, New York, February 1975.

10. U.S. Congress, House, Committee on the Judiciary, *Hearings on the Nomination of Nelson A. Rockefeller of New York to be Vice President of*

the United States, 93rd Cong., 2nd sess., serial no. 45 (Washington, D.C.: Government Printing Office, 1974), p. 909.

11. Senate Rules Committee, *Report*, December 3, 1974, p. 28.

12. Lewis Lapham, "Victory for the Big, Dumb Money," *Harper's*, February 1975, p. 38.

13. House Judiciary Committee, *Report*, December 17, 1974, p. 46.

14. House Judiciary Committee, *Hearings*, p. 213.

15. Ibid., p. 215.

16. Interview with Jerome Waldie, Washington, D.C., February 1975.

17. House Judiciary Committee, *Hearings*, p. 679.

18. *Newsweek*, December 30, 1974.

19. John Osborne, "Rocky at Work," *New Republic*, January 25, 1975, p. 12.

20. *New York Post*, June 10, 1974.

21. Nelson Rockefeller, televised interview on *Agronsky and Company*, WNET, October 22, 1975.

22. *New York Daily News*, August 3, 1975, p. 57.

23. *Time*, January 20, 1975.

24. *New York Daily News*, August 3, 1975.

25. *Time*, January 20, 1975.

26. *Congressional Record*, February 26, 1975, pp. S–2633.

27. Ibid.

28. *New York Times*, April 25, 1975.

29. Robert Scheer, "Rocky's Energy Caper," *New Times*, October 17, 1975, p. 10.

30. Ibid.

31. Ibid.

32. Ibid.

33. Interview with Nelson Rockefeller, Washington, D.C., March 1975.

34. House Judiciary Committee, *Report*, December 17, 1974, p. 44.

35. *Time*, January 20, 1975.

36. Ibid., p. 24.

37. *Newsweek*, June 16, 1975.

38. Ibid.

39. Ibid.

40. *New York Times*, June 21, 1975.

41. Mary McGrory, "Rocky on Vietnam," *New York Post*, February 8, 1975.

42. *Washington Post*, April 20, 1975.

43. Peter Lisagor, "The Rockefeller Nod," *New York Post*, June 17, 1975.

44. Charles McCarry, "Win with Rockefeller," *Saturday Evening Post*, February 24, 1968, p. 80.

45. *New York Times*, August 29, 1975.

46. William Rusher, *The Making of the New Majority Party* (New York: Sheed and Ward, 1975), p. 91.

47. *Time*, November 17, 1975.

48. Mary McGrory, "Walking Tall Again," *New York Post*, November 7, 1975.

49. Tom Braden, "Enough Is Enough," *Washington Post*, November 8, 1975.

50. William Kennedy, "Rocky Is 64, Going on 35," *New York Times Magazine*, April 29, 1973, pp. 16ff.

51. Frank Gervasi, *The Real Rockefeller* (New York: Atheneum, 1964), p. 19.

52. Thomas Carlyle, *The Hero*, reprinted in *An Anthology of English Literature*, ed. R. P. McCutcheon and W. H. Vann (New York: Holt, 1931), p. 850.

53. *Press Questions of Governor Nelson A. Rockefeller Following Announcement of Resignation*, Red Room, State Capitol, Albany, N.Y., December 11, 1973, 11:30 A.M., p. 22.

54. *Washington Post*, June 14, 1967.

INDEX

Academy of Political Science, 176, 177
Action Committee for the Liberal Party, 114–115
Adams, Sherman, 194
Adirondacks Park Agency, 11, 80
Advisory Committee on Government Organization, 63
AFL–CIO, 348
Agnew, Spiro, 185–186, 331, 346, 365
Albano, Vincent F., Jr., 46, 67, 131–132, 254, 285, 289–290
Albany (New York): Capitol in, 81–82; Executive Mansion in, 30
Albany Mall, 10, 155 159
Albright, Harry W., Jr., 138
Alcorn, Meade, 277
Aldrich, Alexander, 100
Aldrich, Nelson W., 33, 65
Aldrich, Richard, 185, 289, 290
Allen, James, 101, 248–249, 371
Allende, Salvador, 373–374
Alsop, Joseph, 225
Alsop, Stewart, 204, 220, 270, 284
Aluminum Company of America, 21
American Broadcasting Company, 21
American International Association for Economic and Social Development, 55
American Legion, 172
American Telephone and Telegraph, 21
Amper, Richard, 163
Anderson, Robert B., 56–58
Anderson, Warren, 139
Apple, R. W., Jr., 330
Archdiocese of New York, 26
Argentina, 53

Art collection of Nelson Rockefeller, 47–49
Ashbrook, John, 375
Attica prison riot, 6, 71, 354–363
Aurelio, Richard, 128
Austin, Warren, 60, 61
Automatic Toll Systems, 131
Axenfeld, Gary, 96

Badillo, Herman, 357
Ballard, William, 14
Bank of New York, 140–141
Bankers Trust Company of New York, 140, 141
Banks, 135–141, 146–147; see also specific banks
Barberia, Archie, 251
Bassine, Charles, 344
Bastille Day declaration, 273–274, 276
Bates, Herman, 184
Beame, Abraham, 106, 303
Bearup, Albert J., 163
Belica, Paul, 148–149
Bergman, Bernard, 11
Berle, Adolf, Jr., 203
Berlinger, George, 143–144
Binghamton Sun, 199
Bixby, R. Burdell, 102, 343–344
Black, Eugene, 137
Blaine Amendment, 345
Bligh, Walter, 256–259, 264
Blum, John R. H., 131
Bond issues, 12–13, 146–148, 316
Boyer, Louise, 132, 174–175
Braden, Tom, 283–284, 376
Brasco, Frank, 121

Brennan, Peter, 311, 347, 348
Brock, William, 371
Broder, David, 286, 327
Bronston, Jack, 90
Brooks, Jack, 370
Brown, James, 310
Brownell, Herbert, 231–232
Brydges, Earl, 87
BT Mortgage Investors, 140
Buckley, Charles F., 88–89
Buckley, James, 345–346
Buckley, William F., Jr., 6, 272–273, 279–280, 331
Buildings, construction of, 145–146, 148, 347
Burden, William, 188
Burdick, Eugene, 8
Burnett, Frances Hodgson, 332
Burns, Arthur, 372
Butler, William, 137
Byrnes, James F., 53

Campaign financing, 181–191
Cannon, Howard, 367
Cannon, James, 94, 96, 327, 372
Carey, Hugh, 13, 94–96, 117, 118, 145, 155, 164, 354, 361
Carlino, Joseph, 84, 197, 198, 254, 258
Carlyle, Thomas, 377
Caro, Robert, 110, 114, 200
Caso, Ralph, 30
Celler, Emanuel, 95
Central Intelligence Agency (CIA), 373–374
Chalmers, Arvis, 218
Chapman, Alger, 263, 264
Charter New York Corporation, 137
Chase Manhattan Bank, 20–22, 28, 29, 56, 133–139, 142, 144, 257
Chase National Bank, 45–46
Chemical Bank, 136, 189
Chisholm, Shirley, 370
Church, Frank, 374
Citibank, 141
City Planning Commission, 14
City Title Insurance Company, 131
Civil rights, 234

Civil Service Employees Association, 173
Clancy, John T., 107
Clark, G. Russell, 137
Clark, George L., Jr., 15, 94
Clark, Ramsey, 186
Cohen, William, 186
Colby, William E., 373, 374
Colonial Williamsburg, 21, 25
Colorado Fuel and Iron Company, 34
Columbia Broadcasting System (CBS), 21
Commission on the Constitutional Convention, 195, 197
Commissions, state, 102–104
Committee on Program and Progress, 230
Communism, 11–12
Communist Party, U.S., 12
Congress, U.S., 93
Congressional Reference Service, 335
Connery, Robert H., 176–177
Conservative Party (New York), 94, 118, 238–240
Conservatives (conservatism), 238–241, 244, 245, 272, 273, 276, 286, 375; see also Radical or extreme right
Constella, 211
Construction unions, 347, 348
Cooper, John Sherman, 231
Corbett, Raymond, 80, 348, 349
Corning, Erastus, II, 156, 157
Cotton, Norris, 279
Couri, Aleer J., 256–259, 263, 265
Court of Appeals, New York State, 104
Court of Claims, New York State, 104, 108
Creole Petroleum, 49
Crews, John, 87, 100, 255
Critical Choices Commission, 191, 196, 362, 373
Cuba, 268
Cudmore, Dr. John, 360
Cunningham, Patrick, 117
Curtis, Carl, 276

Dales, Douglas, 171
Darcy, Tom, 375

Dartmouth, Nelson Rockefeller at, 40–41, 71, 72
Davidoff, Sid, 296
De Antonio, Emile, 186
Deardourff, John, 315
Defense policy, 233, 234
Delli Bovi, Alfred, 116
De Luca, Paul, 262
DeLury, John, 296, 298
Dentzer, William, 137–138
De Sapio, Carmine, 121, 205, 206, 208
Desmond, James, 176, 212–213, 235
Detroit News, 327
Dewey, Thomas E., 10, 105, 192–194, 200, 239–240, 259
Diamond, Henry L., 129
DiCarlo (Republican legislator), 96
Dillon, C. Douglas, 23, 189
Dilworth, J. Richardson, 22, 24, 25, 174, 222
Dirksen, Everett, 239
Domestic Council, 372
Donovan, James, 52
Donovan, William J., 51–52
Douglass, Robert R., 69, 80, 86, 120, 128–130, 263, 264, 287, 320, 356, 367
Downtown Lower Manhattan Association, 153
Driman, Robert, 24–25
Drug laws (1973), 352–354
Dulles, John Foster, 206
Dunne, John, 139
DuPont Glore Forgan brokerage house, 143
Duryea, Perry B., Jr., 80, 91, 95, 96, 110, 119, 138; election law violations and, 114–117

Eastern Airlines, 20
Eastman Kodak, 21
Ehrlichman, John, 185–186
Eisenhower, Dwight D., 57, 63, 196, 207–209, 214, 220, 243, 281, 282, 324; criticized by Nelson Rockefeller, 226–228; 1960 Republican Convention and, 230, 231, 233–234
Eisenhower, Milton, 282

Elections, see Gubernatorial campaigns and elections; Presidential campaigns and elections
Electoral campaigns, financing of, 181–191
Electronic Data Systems, Inc. (EDS), 142–144
Elliott, Donald, 14
Elson, Robert, 226, 228
Empire Trust Company, 140
Energy Independence Authority (EIA) (proposed), 372
Epstein, Martin, 87, 100, 255, 256, 259
Equitable Life Assurance Society, 134
Esposito, Meade, 14–15, 79, 95, 118–121, 131
Ethical Culture Society headquarters, 14
Extreme or radical right, 273–277; See also Conservatives
Exxon, 8, 21, 22

Fallout shelters, 219–220
Fifth Avenue Compact, 233
Finger Lakes racetrack, scandal involving, 249–252
Finkelstein, Jerry, 95, 130–131
Finletter, Thomas, 205, 208
First National City Bank, 141
Fiscal policy, 146, 334
Fishbein, Peter, 350
Fisher, Harold, 45, 116
Flatbush Boys' Club, 26
Flynn, F. M., 168
Ford, Gerald, 5–7, 20, 363, 365, 371, 372, 375, 376
Ford Foundation, 23–24
Foreign policy, 233, 266
"Forgotten American" manifesto, Goldwater's, 243
Fortune (magazine), 155–156, 327
Fosdick, Harry Emerson, 365
Free, Lloyd, 344
French, John, Jr., 40–41
Friends of the Rockefeller Team, 189
Fromkes, Otto, 131
Fromkes, Saul, 131
Frost, David, 165

Gallman, Norman, 141
Gangemi, John, 94
Garbage strike in New York City (1968), 296–301
Gardner, Warren, 199
Garrett, Thaddeus, 370
Garrison, John, 108
Garth, David, 202
Gates, Thomas, 188
Gellinoff, Abraham, 259, 260, 263
General Education Board, 34
General Electric Company, 21
Geophysics Corporation, 253
Gerlach, Herb, 198
Gervasi, Frank, 193–194
Giacchio, William, 107
Gilhooley, John J., 185, 290
Gillies, Archibald, 188–189
Gold, Morris, 249–252
Goldberg, Arthur, 133–134, 164–166, 202, 303; 1970 campaign biography of, 70, 174–176, 367; in 1970 campaign for governor, 340–345, 347–349
Goldstein, David, 251, 396n
Goldwater, Barry, 5, 211–212, 233, 234, 245, 299, 323–324, 351, 352, 375; 1964 presidential nomination drive and, 243, 268–269, 276–285; rapprochement between Nelson Rockefeller and (1962–1963), 266, 267
Goodell, Charles, 184, 302–303, 345–346
Gordon, Albert, 189
Gordon, Dr. Harry, 262, 264
Gotbaum, Victor, 133, 143, 298–299, 349
Gottlieb, Stephen, 93
Gould, Samuel, 127
Government Affairs Foundation, 132
Government for Sale report, 236
Governor of New York, Nelson Rockefeller as: election of, see Gubernatorial campaigns and elections; political style of, 81–85; see also specific topics
Governor's Club, 218
Graham, Rev. Billy, 221
Greenspan, Alan, 372
Gubernatorial campaigns and elections: 1958, 64, 193–210; 1962, 202, 237–240, 268; 1966, 202, 287–288, 307–319; 1970, 202, 339–350

Hall, Leonard, 194, 209, 224, 277, 279
Hammer, Frederic, 108
Hampton, Lionel, 310
Hanna, Mark, 182
Harriman, John, 203
Harriman, W. Averell, 62–64, 163, 183; Nelson Rockefeller's first term as governor and, 215–217; in 1958 campaign and election, 194, 196–197, 200, 202–203, 205–208
Harris, Lou, 238, 280
Harrison, Wallace, 13, 36, 37, 49, 53, 58, 59, 132, 155, 157, 158
Hausbeck, Albert J., 90–92
Health, Education, and Welfare, U.S. Department of, 63
Hearst, William Randolph, 206
Heck, Oswald, 194, 198
Heckscher, August, 46
Hein, Sidney, 107
Hellmuth, James G., 140–141, 188
Helms, Jesse, 249
Hentoff, Nat, 289, 298, 302
High schools, course on communism in, 11–12
Hill, William, 199
Hilton, Conrad, 133
Hinman, George L., 72–73, 126–127, 138, 185, 195, 199, 221, 225, 231, 245, 248, 263–264, 269, 274, 311
Hirohito (Emperor of Japan), 29
Hobby, Oveta Culp, 63
Hoffman, John T., 101
Hogan, Frank, 115, 205, 252, 256, 258, 259
Holtzman, Elizabeth, 358, 369, 374
Hopkins, Harry, 50
Housing, 85, 150–152
Housing Finance Agency, 147, 148
Hudson River Presbytery, 270
Hughes, Emmet John, 193, 214, 225–228, 231–233, 292, 325
Hughes, John H., 90, 292, 308
Hughes, Rowland, 63

Humphrey, George, 63
Humphrey, Hubert H., 63, 195
Humphreys, George, 189, 190
Hurd, T. Norman, 127, 143, 215, 217, 267–268

IBM (International Business Machines), 21, 22
Income taxes paid by Nelson Rockefeller, 26–27
Ingraham, Hollis, 109
Inter-American Affairs, Office of, 51, 52
Inter-American Development Corporation, 52
Interamerican Finance and Investment Corp., 56
Interfaith Hospital (Queens, N.Y.), 108–109
International Advisory Board, 62
International Basic Economy Corp. (IBEC), 55, 58
International Union of Dolls, Toys, Playthings, Novelties, and Allied Products, 350
Interstate United, 121, 122
Irwin, Don, 195
Israel, 207
Itek Corporation, 21
Ives, Irving, 196

Jackson, C. D., 214
Jacobs, Jane, 158
Jamieson, Francis, 52, 58–60, 163, 195
Jaquith, David H., 239
Javits, Jacob, 8, 184, 186, 236–237, 239, 243, 259, 277, 308, 321; 1965 mayoralty race and, 290–293
Jews, 41, 344
Johnson, Lyndon B., 63, 88, 129, 224, 278, 281, 327–329
Jones, Franklin, 94
Judgeships, patronage and, 104–108

Kaufman, George, 29
Keating, Kenneth, 200, 277
Kelly, Robert F., 139–140

Kempton, Murray, 283, 311, 322
Kenna, Frank, 101
Kennan, George, 223
Kennedy, John F., 160–161, 238, 244, 245, 268, 278, 338
Kennedy, Robert F., 90, 166, 235, 301, 309
Kennedy, William, 12
Keogh, Eugene, 120
Kheel, Theodore, 130
Khrushchev, Nikita S., 12
King, Larry, 173, 205, 325
King, Rev. Martin Luther, Jr., 86, 329, 331
Kings Lafayette Bank, 131
Kingston, John, 115, 116
Kissinger, Henry, 30, 207, 325
Kissinger, Nancy, 30
Klein, Herbert, 232
Kleindienst, Richard, 282
Knight, Goodwin, 269
Kuchel, Thomas (California Senator), 277
Kunzman, Joseph, 108

Labor unions, 346–350
Laird, Melvin, 284
Langer, William, 66–67
Lanigan, Charles, 102, 103
Lankler, Alexander, 286
Lapham, Lewis, 70, 368
Lasker, Bernard, 189
Lasky, Victor, 174, 175
Latin America (South America), 51, 52, 55; 1937 tour of, 49–50; 1969 trip to, 26, 337–338
Laurino, Louis, 107
Lavine, Abe, 142, 143
Law Enforcement Task Force, 354
Lawrence, David, 227
Leasco Data Processing, 136
Lefkowitz, Louis, 115–117, 124, 185, 204–205, 237, 258, 288, 289, 310
Lefkowitz, Steven, 85
Legislature, New York State, 7–8, 83–97, 215; see also specific topics
Lehman, Herbert, 205
Lenin, Vladimir I., 48

Lerner, Alfred, 107–108
Leviss, Sidney, 107
Levitt, Arthur, 101, 102, 121, 146–147; 149, 174; Albany Mall and, 156; 157; in first term as controller, 216–217; World Trade Center and, 154–155
Levitt, William J., 189
Levy, Gustave, 189
Lewisohn, Richard, 289, 290
Liberal Party (New York), 114, 203, 237, 303, 317–319
"Liberty Amendment," 273
Life (magazine), 226
Lincoln, Abraham, 35–36
Lincoln Center (New York City), 13–14
Lincoln First Banks, 138
Lincoln School, 39, 40
Lindsay, John V., 13, 14, 85, 117, 164, 184, 237, 288–306, 341; garbage strike and (1968), 296–301; 1965 mayoral campaign and, 288, 290–294; 1969 reelection of, 303; Senate seat vacancy and, 301–302; tensions and disputes between Rockefeller and, 295–306
Lockwood, John, 58, 132, 174–175
Lodge, Henry Cabot, 279–281
Loeb, William, 279
Logan, Arthur, 133
Logue, Edward J., 148, 150–151
Lomenzo, John, 94, 101–102
Long Island Railroad, 141
Losee, Tom, 311
Luce, Claire Booth, 270
Luce, Henry, 168, 206, 226, 228
Ludlow (Colorado), massacre of strikers in (1913), 34
Lundy, James, 101

McCaffrey, Neil, 175–176
McCloy, John J., 24
McCrary, Tex, 197
McDonald, Myron, 314
McDonald, Walter, 171
McGrory, Mary, 376
McKay, Robert, 355
McKay Commission, 355–357, 359, 360

McKee, Jean, 276
Mackell, Thomas, 109
McManus, Robert, 163, 171, 231
Macmillan Company, 176
Madigan-Hyland, 154
Maguire, John P., Jr., 249, 250
Mahoney, Walter, 89, 106, 194, 195, 258
Maiorana, Ronald, 66, 163–164, 169–171
Malik, Jacob, 23
Manchester, William, 66
Mandell, Dr. Stanley, 262–264
Manufacturers Hanover Trust, 189
Marchi, John, 303
Marks Oxygen Company, 253
Marshall, Alton, 65–66, 83, 86, 87, 92, 102–104, 108, 119, 127–128, 131, 149, 345
Mass transit, 153
Masserman, Jules, 158
Massolo, Art, 171
Mathias, Charles, 185
Matthew, Dr. Thomas, 108, 109
Mcany, George, 240, 348
Medicaid, 142, 143
Mellon, James R., 47
Mellon family, 186
Merck Corporation, 21
Messersmith, George, 52
Metropolitan Museum of Art, 44
Metropolitan Political Club, 197
Metropolitan Transportation Authority (MTA), 113, 141–142
Milhouse—A White Comedy (film), 186
Miller, J. Irwin, 188
Miller, William, 235, 267
Mills, Wilbur D., 95–96
Minnesota Mining and Manufacturing, 21
Mintz, Hyman (Bucky), 249–252
Mitchell, John, 120–121, 143, 146
Mobil Oil Corp., 8, 21, 22
Monsanto, 21
Moore, Frank C., 132
Moreland Commission, 146
Morgan, Thomas B., 160–161, 205
Morgenthau, Robert, 202, 238
Morhouse, L. Judson, 64, 87–88, 196–

197, 216, 221, 227, 231, 240, 243 246; pardon of, 260–265; scandals involving, 247–259
Morhouse, Sanford, 263
Morning, Emma, 37
Morrow, Hugh, 40, 164, 167, 169, 273, 294, 295, 343
Morton, Thruston, 284
Moscow, Warren, 203–204
Moses, Robert, 110–114
Mott, Stewart R., 189
Moyers, Bill, 7
Murphy, Charles F., 206
Murphy, Margaretta Fitler, see Rockefeller, Margaretta Fitler (Happy)
Murrow, Edward R., 238
Museum of Modern Art, 75
Museum of Primitive Art, 26
Muskie, Edmund, 186
Mutual Security Agency, 62

Nadjari, Maurice, 117–118, 304
Nast, Thomas, 101
National Bank and Trust Co. of Norwich, 28
National Bank of Northern New York, 138
National Commission on Critical Choices, 191, 196, 362, 373
National Guard, 297
National Review, 272
National Savings and Trust Co. of Washington, 28–29
Natural Heritage Trust, 129
Nazis (Nazi sympathizers), 51, 52
Nehru, Jawaharlal, 219
Nevins, Allan, 193
New York City, 13; corruption in, 1960 study, 236; garbage strike in (1968), 296–301; 1961 mayoralty race in, 236–237, 288–289; 1965 mayoralty race in, 288, 290–294; 1969 mayoralty race in, 303
New York City bar association, 353–354
New York Civil Liberties Union, 92
New York Daily News, 206, 211–213, 298, 311, 347

New York Herald Tribune, 236, 268 269, 281
New York Post, 207, 311, 317
New York State, 26, 30; legislature of, 7–8, 83–97, 215; see also Albany (New York); Governor of New York, Nelson Rockefeller as; entries starting with State; and specific topics
New York State Federation of Labor, 348
New York State Racing Commission, 250
New York Times, 21, 168, 169, 206, 268, 281, 299–301, 325, 354
Newsday (newspaper), 115
Newsweek (magazine), 366
Niebuhr, Reinhold, 270
Nietzsche, Friedrich, 201
Nilon, James, 250, 251
Nilon, John, 250, 251
Nixon, Richard M., 108, 184, 186, 200, 243, 267, 299, 328–337, 346; 1958 gubernatorial campaign and, 208–209, 211; 1960 meeting of Nelson Rockefeller and, 231–233; 1960 Republican Convention and, 231–235; 1964 presidential nomination and, 280, 282, 285; 1966 relationship between Rockefeller and, 320–324; 1968 presidential nomination and, 328–332; presidential aspirations of Rockefeller and, 221–226, 228, 229; Vietnam policy of, 5–6; Watergate and, 6
Nixon, Tricia, 165

O'Connell, Daniel P., 99, 105
O'Connor, Frank, 202, 309, 310, 315–317
O'Donnell, Harry J., 164
O'Dwyer, William, 258–259
Office for Coordination of Commercial and Cultural Relations Between the American Republics, 50–51
Office of Inter-American Affairs, 51, 52
O'Neill, Edward, 299

Osterman, Melvin, 256
Oswald, Russell, 71, 355–357, 361, 362
Ottinger, Richard, 202, 340
Oyster Bay Bridge (proposed), 80

Palisades Interstate Park Commission, 99
Panels, 102–103
Parker, Theodore, 359
Parochial schools, public assistance to, 344–345
Partners in Progress report, 62
Patman, Wright, 132
Patronage, 98–109; commissions and panels and, 102–104; judgeships and, 104–108
Peirce, Neal, 10
Pell, Clayton, 368
Penn Central, 141
Percy, Charles, 230–232, 277, 296
Perot, H. Ross, 142–144
Perry, James, 311, 312, 339
Peterson, Russell, 373
Pew, Joseph, 250–251
Peyser, Peter, 184
Pfeiffer, William L., 130, 140, 231, 313, 321
Phelps, Robert, 379n
Phillips Academy, 26
Picasso lithograph, 14–15
Planning Commission, New York City, 14
Playboy (magazine), 72
Playboy Club (New York City), 88, 255–259
Pocantico Hills (Westchester, New York), 8–9, 29, 59
Podell, Bertram, 121
Point Four program, 62
Political Surveys and Analyses of Princeton, 161
Port Authority of New York and New Jersey, 124–125, 153
Powers, Francis Gary, 226
Prendergast, Michael, 119–120
President of the United States, Nelson Rockefeller's aspiration to be, 3–4, 74, 192–193, 211–214, 221–229, 268, 287

Presidential campaigns and elections: 1968, 324; 1972, 336–337
Presidential nomination: 1964 drive for, 268–285; 1968 drive for, 328–332
Press, the, Rockefeller's relationship with, 160–171, 301
Pressman, Gabe, 165
Price, Robert, 280, 291
Procaccino, Mario, 166, 303
Proskin, Arnold, 115
Prospect for America—The Rockefeller Panel Reports, 196
Public authorities, New York State, 146–150
Public Service Commission, 342

Quayle, Oliver, 341–342
Quinn, Arthur, 131

Radical or extreme right, 273–277
Raichle, Frank, 263
Rauh, Joseph, Jr., 20, 23, 175
Ravitch, Richard, 152
Rayburn, Sam, 224
Reader's Digest, 168
Reagan, Ronald, 15, 324
Reapportionment plan, 93–94
Reeves, Richard, 5, 214, 342
Regan, Edward, 102
Republican Convention: 1960, 225, 226, 228, 230, 231, 233; 1964, 5
Republican National Committee, 226
Republican Party (GOP): national, 5, 184, 226, 227, 286; New York State, 7, 82, 183–184, 187, 240; see also specific topics
Reston, James, 169
Revenue-sharing legislation, 93–96, 130
Rhodes, James, 326
Rhodes, John, 8
Riesel, Victor, 346
Rivera, Diego, 47–48
Roberts, Burton, 261, 354
Rockefeller, Abby (David Rockefeller's daughter), 186
Rockefeller, Abby (Nelson Rockefeller's sister), 271, 337, 340

Rockefeller, Abby Aldrich (mother), 33, 39, 41, 49, 187

Rockefeller, David (brother), 8, 20, 22–23, 36, 45, 59–60, 64–65, 142, 158, 187, 257, 269, 271, 303, 337, 340, 367

Rockefeller, John D. (grandfather), 9, 25, 32, 33, 193, 214; early life of Nelson and, 36–39

Rockefeller, John D., Jr. (father), 25–26, 33, 34, 39, 42, 47, 188; United Nations site and, 59–61

Rockefeller, John D., III (brother), 59–60, 187, 337, 341

Rockefeller, John D. (Jay), IV (nephew), 32–33, 64, 67–68

Rockefeller, Laura (Laurance Rockefeller's daughter), 186

Rockefeller, Laurance (brother), 4, 20, 56, 59–60, 65, 99, 129, 168, 186, 187, 190 191, 207, 253, 267, 337, 340, 365, 367; early life of, 35, 40–41, 45, 72; Goldberg biography and (1970), 174, 175, 341

Rockefeller, Margaretta Fitler (Happy) (wife), 22, 26, 71–72, 118–119, 167, 171, 238; effects of Nelson's marriage to, 269–271, 279, 282, 307

Rockefeller, Mark (son), 167

Rockefeller, Martha Baird (stepmother), 187

Rockefeller, Mary (daughter), 39

Rockefeller, Mary Todhunter (first wife), 44, 71, 230

Rockefeller, Michael (son), 26

Rockefeller, Nelson A.: Albany Capitol and, 81–82; Albany Mall and, 10, 155–159; art collection of, 47–49; Attica prison riot and, 6, 71, 354–363; banking policies and relationship with banks of, 135–141, 146–147, see also specific banks; Bastille Day declaration of, 273–274, 276; campaign financing and, 181–191; commissions and panels appointed by, 102–104; Conservative Party and, 94, 118, 238–240; conservatives and, 238–241, 244, 245, 272, 273, 276, 286, 375; construction of buildings by, 145–146, 148, 347; Critical Choices Commission and, 191, 196, 361, 373; at Dartmouth, 40–41, 71, 72; defense policy of, 233, 234; early life of, 32–45, 72; fallout shelters and, 219–220; Fifth Avenue Compact and, 233; garbage strike in New York City and (1968), 296–301; housing policies of, 85, 150–152; income taxes paid by, 26–27; International Basic Economy Corporation (IBEC) and, 55–58; judgeships and, 104–108; labor unions and, 346–350; Latin America and, see Latin America; legislature of New York State and, 7–8, 83–97, 215, see also specific legislation; in 1958 gubernatorial campaign, 64, 193–210; 1960 Republican Convention and, 225, 226, 228, 230, 231, 233; 1961 mayoralty race in New York City and, 236–237, 288–289; in 1962 gubernatorial campaign, 202, 237–240, 268; 1964 presidential nomination drive and, 260–265, 1965 mayoralty race in New York City and, 280, 290–294; in 1966 gubernatorial campaign, 202, 287–288, 307–309; 1968 presidential nomination and, 328–332; 1969 mayoralty race in New York City and, 303; in 1970 gubernatorial campaign, 202, 339–350; patronage and, 98–109; Playboy Club liquor license and, 88, 255–259; political style of, as governor, 81–85; presidential aspirations of, 3–4, 74, 192–193, 211–214, 221–229, 268, 287; public authorities established by, 146–150; radical or extreme right of Republican Party and, 273–277; revenue-sharing legislation and, 93–96, 130; Senate seat vacancy and, 301–302; tax programs and policies of, 215–217, 238, 267–268, 335–336; television commercials for campaigns of, 312–315, 331, 340, 345; United Nations site and, 58–61; Urban Development Corporation and, 13, 85–87, 146, 150–152, 325, 352; vice-presidential confirmation hearings and (1974), 65, 70, 74, 176, 366–370; Vietnam war and, 5–6, 324–

Rockefeller, Nelson A. *(continued)*
327, 375; welfare programs in New
York State and, 142, 143, 334, 351–
352; *see also specific topics*
Rockefeller, Nelson A., Jr. (son), 73,
167, 282
Rockefeller, Peggy (David Rocke-
feller's daughter), 186
Rockefeller, Peggy (David Rocke-
feller's wife), 45
Rockefeller, Rodman (son), 39, 186
Rockefeller, Steve (son), 204
Rockefeller, Winthrop (brother), 35,
184, 187, 340
Rockefeller, Winthrop Aldrich (un-
cle), 46
Rockefeller Brothers Fund, 19, 21–22,
26, 133
Rockefeller Brothers Special Studies,
195–196
Rockefeller Center, 46–47, 58–59
Rockefeller Foundation, 22, 23, 34, 49
Rockefeller Institute, 35
Rockefeller University, 21
Rockland State Hospital, 85
Rodino, Peter, 20, 264, 367
Romney, George, 184, 242, 267, 282,
285, 296, 308, 323, 325–328
Ronan, William J., 51, 67, 89, 105,
113, 122, 124–127, 131, 141, 148, 149,
190, 195, 259–260, 282, 312, 321, 366
Roosevelt, Mrs. Eleanor, 205
Roosevelt, Franklin D., 50–53
Roosevelt, Franklin D., Jr., 168, 207,
316–319
Roosevelt, John, 197
Roosevelt, Theodore, 34, 223, 377
Root, Oren, 135–137, 182–183
Rose, Alex, 317–319
Rosenbaum, Richard, 103, 124
Rosenberg, Anna, 52, 58
Rosenthal, A. M., 169
Rosenthal, Benjamin, 143
Rossetti, Frank, Jr., 120
Ruebhausen, Mrs., 130
Ruebhausen, Oscar, 129–130
Ruggieri, Bernard, 89
Rumsfeld, Donald, 372
Rusher, William, 5, 194, 239, 287, 375

Safire, William, 6, 320–322, 324, 332,
362
Schiff, Dorothy, 168, 174, 207–208,
290, 309
Schoeneck, Charles, 86, 139
Scolaro, Dick, 96
Scott, Hugh, 185, 283
Scotti, Alfred J., 115–116, 260
Scranton, William, 242, 277, 282, 283
Seal Harbor (Maine), Rockefeller
house in, 29, 49
Security National Bank, 131
Sedita, Frank, 120, 309–310
Segarra, Arnaldo, 173
Seidman, William, 372
Senate Rules Committee, 261, 366–368
Seymour, Whitney North, Jr., 120,
217–218, 236
Shapiro, Howard, 261
Shapiro, Sid, 111
Sharkey, William A., 149
Shea, William, 131, 141
Shelters, fallout, 219–220
Simon, Caroline, 72
Simon, William, 372
Sinatra, Frank, 189
Skeffington, Frank (fictional charac-
ter), 12
Slote, Leslie, 163, 170, 171, 322
Smith, Al, 206
Smith, Frank, 361
Smith, Rev. Marshall L., 270
Snyder, Marty, 393n
Social Security, 279
Society of Newspaper Editors, 162
South America, *see* Latin America
Soviet Union, 12, 219, 220
Special Work, Inc., 46
Standard Oil, 45, 49, 50, 69–70, 182
Standard Oil of California, 8, 21, 22
Stans, Maurice, 336
Stassen, Harold, 53, 63, 213
State Commission of Investigation, 100
State Commission on a Constitutional
Convention, 64
State commissions, 102–104
State Council for the Arts, 11, 105
State Council of Economic Advisors,
137

State Council of Parks, 111
State Department, U.S., 52–53
State Liquor Authority (SLA), 87–88, 100
State Thruway Authority, New York, 102
Steffens, Lincoln, 4
Stein, Andrew, 130
Steinberg, Saul P., 136
Steingut, Irwin, 79
Steingut, Stanley, 79–81, 85, 90, 95, 119, 131, 309
Stephens, Willis, 131
Stevenson, Adlai, 208
Stockmeister, Charles F., 90, 91
Stratton, Samuel, 94
Sulzberger, Arthur Ochs, 168
Supreme Court, New York State, 104, 106–108
Sutton, Willie, 135
Sweet, Robert, 14

Tammany Hall, 101, 205, 206
Tax programs and policies, 215–217, 238, 267–268, 335–336
Taylor, George, 167
Teague, Bert, 178
Television (television commercials), 312–315, 331, 340, 345
Teller, Edward, 220, 372, 373
Temporary State Commission on Living Costs and the Economy, 130
Texas Instruments Corporation, 21
Thaler, Seymour, 107
Thayer, Walter, 281
Time (magazine), 206–207, 225–228, 327, 342, 366, 376
Tinker, Jack, 312, 340
Tinker and Partners, 312–315, 331, 340
Tobin, Austin, 114
Trans World Airlines (TWA), 133–134
Travia, Anthony J., 79, 90
Triborough Bridge and Tunnel Authority, 113, 114, 131, 142
Troy, Matthew, Jr., 106–108
Truman, Harry S, 53, 62, 73–74

Udall, Stewart, 88
United Nations, 25, 53; site of, 58–61
United States Steel, 21
Urban Affairs, Department of, 244, 245
Urban Development Corporation (UDC), 13, 85–87, 146, 150–152, 325, 352
Urdstadt, Charles J., 149

Van Arsdale, Harry, 311, 346–348
Venezuela, 27, 29, 50, 55–56, 58
Vice-president, confirmation of Nelson Rockefeller as (1974), 65, 70, 74, 176, 366–370
Vietnam war, 5–6, 324–327, 375
Von Hoffman, Nicholas, 366

Wagner, Robert F., 15, 89, 90, 105–106, 218, 236–238, 291
Waldie, Jerome, 22–23, 369–370
Wall Street Journal, 56, 266
Wallace, George, 6
Walls, Dr. Walter, 261–262, 264
Walsh, Annmarie, 150–152
Ward, William, 44
Washington, George, 36
Washington Evening Star, 268
Watergate scandal, 6, 117
Watson, Arthur, 188
Weaver, Robert, 244
Webb, Charles, 96
Wechsler, Jimmy, 208
Weisman, Steven, 151
Welfare Department, New York State, 142
Welfare programs, New York State, 142, 143, 334, 351–352
Wells, John A. (Jack), 174, 175, 277, 321
Wells, Mary, 312
Wells, William, 94
Westchester County Board of Health, 44–45

White, E. B., 48
White, F. Clifton, 239–240, 281
White, Stanford, 155
White, Theodore, 5, 9, 229, 234, 280, 286, 324, 365
Whitney, John Hay, 188
Wicker, Tom, 287, 356–357, 360–361
Wille, Frank, 137
Williams, Paul, 194
Willkie, Wendell, 50, 182, 192
Willowbrook Children's Center, 161
Wills, Garry, 45, 339
Wilson, Charles, 63
Wilson, Joseph C., 189
Wilson, Malcolm, 114–116, 184, 189, 198, 231, 258, 301–303
Wilson, Woodrow, 4, 338
Woodward, Peggy, 197

World Trade Center, 153–155
Wright, David, 261
Wynne, Toddy Lee, 57–58

YMCA headquarters (New York City), 14
Young, Fred A., 108
Young Republicans, 240, 273–276

Zanuck, Darryl, 189
Zaretzki, Joseph, 81, 85, 87, 90, 92–93
Zeckendorf, William, 58–61, 189, 197, 257
Zeifman, Jerome, 264